BIENNALE ARCHITETTURA 2021

How will we live together?

EXHIBITION

La Biennale di Venezia

PRESIDENT
Roberto Cicutto

BOARD
Luigi Brugnaro
Vice President

Luca Zaia
Claudia Ferrazzi

AUDITOR'S COMMITTEE
Jair Lorenco
President

Stefania Bortoletti
Anna Maria Como

DIRECTOR GENERAL
Andrea Del Mercato

ARTISTIC DIRECTOR
OF THE ARCHITECTURE DEPARTMENT
Hashim Sarkis

LA BIENNALE DI VENEZIA

17TH INTERNATIONAL ARCHITECTURE EXHIBITION

Curator of the 17th International Architecture Exhibition
Hashim Sarkis

Principal Assistants to the Curator
Roi Salguerio Barrio
Gabriel Kozlowski

Managing Editor
Ala Tannir

Research and Development Associate
Xhulio Binjaku

Graphic Identity
Omnivore Inc.

Copy Editors
Patricia Baudoin
Rachel Valinsky

Editorial Assistance
Kathleen Pongrace

MIT Venice Lab
Carolyn Tam
April Gao
Emma Pfeiffer
Arditha Auriyane
Nynika Jhaveri
Jitske Swagemakers
Daisy Ziyan Zhang
Wuyahuang Li
Sam May
Hugh Ebdy
Jinyoung Sim
María Esteban Casañas
Han Ning Tsai
Alice Jia Li Song
Gabrielle Heffernan
Anna Vasileiou
Natasha Hirt
Chantal El Hayek
Pat Pataranutaporn

Director General
Andrea Del Mercato

ORGANISATIONAL STRUCTURE

CENTRAL SERVICES

LEGAL AND INSTITUTIONAL AFFAIRS, HUMAN RESOURCES AND DEPUTY

Director
Debora Rossi

Legal and Institutional Affairs
Martina Ballarin
Lucrezia Stocco

Human Resources
Graziano Carrer
Claudia Capodiferro
Luca Carta
Giovanni Drudi
Antonella Sfriso
Alessia Viviani
Rossella Zulian

ADMINISTRATION, FINANCE, MANAGEMENT SUPERVISION AND SPONSORSHIP, PROMOTION

Director
Valentina Borsato

Administration, Finance, Management Supervision
Bruna Gabbiato
Elia Canal
Marco Caruso
Martina Fiori
Gregorio Granati
Elisa Meggiato
Emanuela Pellicciolli
Cristina Sartorel
Sara Vianello

Sponsorship
Paola Pavan

Promotion
Caterina Castellani
Lucia De Manincor
Elisabetta Fiorese
Stefania Guglielmo
Emanuela Padoan
Marta Plevani

Secretariats

General Secretariat
Caterina Boniollo
Maria Cristina Cinti
Elisabetta Mistri
Chiara Rossi

Protocol Office
Francesca Boglietti
Lara De Bellis

Biennale College Secretariat
Giacinta Maria Dalla Pietà

PURCHASING, PROCUREMENT AND ASSETS

Director
Fabio Pacifico

Purchasing and Procurement
Silvia Gatto
Silvia Bruni
Annamaria Colonna
Cristiana Scavone

Hospitality
Linda Baldan
Jasna Zoranovic
Donato Zotta

Assets
Maurizio Celoni
Antonio Fantinelli

INSTITUTIONAL AND CINEMA PRESS OFFICE

Head
Paolo Lughi

Francesca Buccaro
Michela Lazzarin
Fiorella Tagliapietra

EDITORIAL ACTIVITIES AND WEB

Head
Flavia Fossa Margutti

Giovanni Alberti
Roberta Fontanin
Giuliana Fusco
Nicola Monaco
Maddalena Pietragnoli

TECHNICAL AND LOGISTICAL SERVICES

Director
Cristiano Frizzele

Exhibition Design, Events and Live Performance
Massimiliano Bigarello
Cinzia Bernardi
Alessandra Durand
  de la Penne
Jessica Giassi
Valentina Malossi
Sandra Montagner

Facility Management
Giulio Cantagalli
Piero Novello
Maurizio Urso

Information Technology
Andrea Bonaldo
Michele Schiavon
Leonardo Viale
Jacopo Zanchi

SPECIAL PROJECTS, PROMOTION OF VENUES

Director
Arianna Laurenzi

Special Projects
Davide Ferrante
Valentina Baldessari
Elisabetta Parmesan

Promotion of Venues
Nicola Bon
Cristina Graziussi
Alessia Rosada

VISUAL ARTS - ARCHITECTURE DEPARTMENT

Executive / Head of Organization
Until November 2019
Manuela Luca' Dazio
Since December 2019
Joern Rudolf Brandmeyer

Marina Bertaggia
Emilia Bonomi
Stefania Fabris
Stefania Guerra
Francesca Aloisia Montorio
Luigi Ricciari
Micol Saleri
Paolo Scibelli

VISUAL ARTS - ARCHITECTURE PRESS OFFICE

Head
Maria Cristiana Costanzo

Claudia Gioia

COLLABORATORS FOR 17ᵀᴴ INTERNATIONAL ARCHITECTURE EXHIBITION
Valentina Apollonio
Andrea Avezzù
Valentina Campana
Elena Rosalinda Cattaneo
Riccardo Cavallaro
Gerardo Ernesto Cejas
Marzia Cervellin
Francesco Di Cesare
Francesca Dolzani
Lia Durante
Andrea Ferialdi
Fabrizia Ferragina
Giulia Gasparato
Matteo Giannasi
Susanna Legrenzi
Anna Mason
Daniele Paolo Mulas
Luca Racchini
Elisa Santoro
Marco Tosato
Lucia Toso
Francesco Zanon

CINEMA DEPARTMENT

Director General
Andrea Del Mercato
Secretariat
Mariachiara Manci
Alessandro Mezzalira
Venice International Film Festival Programming Office
Giulia Carbone
Silvia Menegazzi
Daniela Persi
Industry/Cinema Accreditation
Flavia Lo Mastro
Biennale College Cinema
Valentina Bellomo

DANCE, THEATRE, MUSIC DEPARTMENT

Executive / Head of Organization
Francesca Benvenuti
Secretariat
Veronica Mozzetti Monterumici
Programming and Production
Michela Mason
Federica Colella
Maya Romanelli

DANCE, THEATRE, MUSIC PRESS OFFICE

Head
Emanuela Caldirola

HISTORICAL ARCHIVES OF CONTEMPORARY ARTS

Executive / Head of Organization
Debora Rossi
Historical Archives
Maria Elena Cazzaro
Giovanna Bottaro
Michela Campagnolo
Marica Gallina
Michele Mangione
Adriana Rosaria Scalise
Alice Scandiuzzi
Library
Valentina Da Tos
Erica De Luigi
Valentina Greggio
Manuela Momentè
Elena Oselladore

As part of its long-standing contribution to society and culture, Rolex is proud to support the International Architecture Exhibition, La Biennale di Venezia, for the fourth time since 2014 as Exclusive Partner and Official Timepiece.

Media Partner

Thanks to:
Cleary Gottlieb Steen & Hamilton LLP

outset.

swiss arts council
pro helvetia

**WE WOULD LIKE TO THANK THE FOLLOWING DONORS
FOR THEIR GENEROSITY IN SUPPORTING OUR EXHIBITION**

Major Donor
Qatar Museums

Main Donor
LUMA Foundation

Holcim Foundation for Sustainable Construction

Michelangelo Foundation for Creativity and Craftsmanship

Sandra and Tony Tamer

Drees & Sommer

Elise Jaffe + Jeffrey Brown

Rafael Moneo

GOLDEN LION FOR LIFETIME ACHIEVEMENT

Rafael Moneo is one of the most transformative architects of his generation. As a practitioner, and through his broad array of buildings, such as the Kursaal Auditorium, the Prado Museum, the Atocha Train Station, and the Los Angeles Cathedral, he has highlighted the ability of every architectural project to respond to contingencies of site and programme while transcending them. Persistently, he has also accentuated the collective spaces of his projects. As an educator, he has rigorously guided several generations of architects towards architecture as a vocation. As a scholar, he has combined his visual prowess and analytic rigors to help reinterpret some of the most canonical historic buildings with fresh eyes. As a critic of the contemporary scene, he has written on emerging phenomena and key projects and has established some of the most discerning dialogues on architecture with colleagues from around the world.

Throughout his long career, Moneo has maintained a poetic mastery, reminding us of the powers of architectural form to express and to shape, but also to endure. He has also been tenaciously committed to architecture as an act of building.

Moneo has been recognised internationally with the Pritzker Prize (1996), the RIBA Royal Gold Medal (2003), the Prince of Asturias Award (2012), and the Praemium Imperiale (2017), among other awards. The Golden Lion befits the architect who took part in the Giudecca housing project of 1983, who won the Lido competition in 1991, and who has drawn many a lesson for architecture from Venice.

This well-deserved Golden Lion of the 17th International Architecture Exhibition offers a welcome opportunity to consider Rafael Moneo's six decades of professional activity. Displayed, in the Book Pavilion, as a small selection of models and a frieze of single, representative images, the buildings can be seen to respond to Hashim Sarkis' question *How will we live together?*, with an unrelenting faith in the transformative capacity of architecture, its material integrity, its visual complexity, and its profoundly public character. From the Diestre factory to the Palacios winery, Moneo's work both adapts to and reshapes its setting, inviting us to see in a way we hadn't before, and teaching us to appreciate the possibilities that surround us.
—HAYDEN SALTER
—MARÍA FRAILE

Lina Bo Bardi

SPECIAL GOLDEN LION
FOR LIFETIME ACHIEVEMENT
IN MEMORIAM

If there is one architect who embodies most fittingly the theme of the Biennale Architettura 2021, it is Lina Bo Bardi. Her career as a designer, editor, curator, and activist reminds us of the role of the architect as convener and importantly, as the builder of collective visions. Lina Bo Bardi also exemplifies the perseverance of the architect in difficult times whether wars, political strife, or immigration, and her ability to remain creative, generous, and optimistic throughout.

Above all, it is her powerful buildings that stand out in their design and in the way that they bring architecture, nature, living, and community together. In her hands, architecture becomes truly a convening social art.

Just as one example, the design of the São Paulo Museum is exemplary in its ability to create a public space for the whole city, to create spaces inside that are flexible and to be open to experimental and more inclusive exhibitions such as Bo Bardi's own exhibitions. The titles of these exhibitions alone, *The House as Soul, The Dignity of Architecture*, and *The Hand of the Brazilian People*, illustrate very strongly the power of architecture to bring people together.

The Special Golden Lion for Lifetime Achievement *in memoriam* is a long overdue recognition for an illustrious career straddling between Italy and Brazil, for re-enlivening the role of the architect as an enabler of society, and for a woman who simply represents the architect at her best

Achillina Bo, known as Lina, was born in Rome in 1914. Graduated in architecture in 1939, she moved to Milan where she met Gio Ponti. In 1944 she co-directed *Domus* with Carlo Pagani and with the support of Bruno Zevi she created the weekly magazine *A-Attualità, Architettura, Abitazione, Arte*. In 1947 Lina moved to Brazil with her husband Pietro Maria Bardi. Between 1957 and 1969 she built the Museu de Arte de São Paulo (MASP): a large concrete and glass parallelepiped that would become one of the most iconic buildings of Brazilian Paulista architecture. One of her most famous projects is her home in São Paulo, the Casa de Vidro, a Modernist glass box built on a hill immersed in the tropical forest. Between 1977 and 1986 she designed the SESC–Fábrica da Pompéia, a giant community, recreational, cultural and sports centre. Between 1980 and 1994, she worked on the Teatro Oficina, which upended the spatial hierarchies of bourgeois theatre. Lina Bo Bardi's was the architecture of civil commitment, architecture understood as a collective service, free of the constraints of any school of thought; an architecture that was modern and ancient at the same time, popular, vernacular and cultured, artisanal and not industrial, respectful of tradition but innovative as well. Since her death in 1992, the memory and recognition of her work has been advanced by the Instituto Bardi.

Vittorio Gregotti, To Be Continued

SPECIAL GOLDEN LION FOR LIFETIME ACHIEVEMENT

Vittorio Gregotti died too soon for some of his radical ideas to be fleshed out in form, and too soon for the 17th International Architecture Biennale, which has been postponed by the very pandemic that took his life, to say thank you.

Architecture owes a great deal to Gregotti, and La Biennale di Venezia elected to honour his memory by awarding him the Special Golden Lion in 2020, also for his contribution to culture, which is presented and documented in the exhibition *Le muse inquiete (The Disquieted Muses). When La Biennale di Venezia Meets History.* The exhibition, created with materials from the Historical Archives of La Biennale, was curated by all six Artistic Directors.

The fact that there is Biennale Architettura at all is because Gregotti, as director of the Visual Arts Section in 1975, carved out a space for Architecture within La Biennale di Venezia, to present itself as a necessary dimension of Art, with a capital A for both. Through architecture, he further expanded the scope of the Biennale to include the city and the environment. The postmodernism of Paolo Portoghesi's Strada Novissima and Aldo Rossi's iconic Teatro del Mondo may have marked the official beginning of Biennale Architettura in 1980, and they may have outshone Gregotti's forerunner show, but they did not eclipse his generative ideas.

Another of Gregotti's highly recognised contributions to architecture is the commitment he showed, through his leadership of the Italian journal *Casabella*, to create platforms for debate and discussion that explored built form with rigor and as an expression and instrument of social change. This has clearly become a distinguishing disposition of the more recent editions, which the current Exhibition extends and expands: a commitment to building is constitutive of a commitment to a social project.

Yet perhaps the richest dimension of Gregotti's multidimensional oeuvre that remains underdeveloped is his work on geography and architecture. Like many architects of his generation, Gregotti read closely the work of French human geographers like Paul Vidal de la Blache, Jean Brunhes, and Maximilien Sorre, who were interpreted for Italian audiences by geographer Lucio Gambi. Gregotti also assimilated the work of nineteenth- and early-twentieth-century German physical geographers. Specifically, he homed in on the connection between architecture and territory, a concept that has recently gained significant importance but was virtually unexplored at the time. Like many post-war urbanists, Gregotti was invested in addressing the chaotic spread of cities over broad areas. He proposed to recast this terrain positively, not as exurban but as *territory*. In his seminal essay *The Form of Territory,* he first proposed that architecture had a role to play on this territory. Folding the historical and geographical into the concept of phylogeny, Gregotti applied the architect's tools at a territorial scale and connected architecture to larger infrastructural and natural networks.

Territory provided architecture with a fluid and connective context. Gregotti empowered architecture to be transformative of a far vaster context than the city. Gregotti brought architecture of the urban confines and cast it onto the surface of territory. Here lies one of Gregotti's most potent yet least explored ideas. He proposed new tools to assimilate geography, or the exurban, into the architect's repertoire. He also transcended the concept of typology that many of his contemporaries understood to embody the human geographer's idea of form of life. The field and the 'ensemble' emerge as tools that architecture could use to organise the territory across scales. For example, in the University of Calabria project of 1973, on which he collaborated with Lucio Gambi, he proposed an ensemble of large horizontal slabs. Applied in a sequence, these recurring slabs contrasted with the local variations of the topography of the valley while suggesting a continuum from Calabria across the world. Beautifully, his forms never became landscape or camouflaged themselves into geography. They worked to 'modify' the context and improve its conditions while remaining distinctly architectural.

Many architects of Gregotti's generation, including Aldo Rossi, shared his fascination with human geography and abstracted geo-historical forms, but Gregotti was more committed to giving architecture a larger role in this world. He introduced the territory as a positive form and charged architecture to hold together and give sense to the fragments in the extra-urban setting. Rossi historicised and aestheticised the fragmentation and, for some reason, redacted the ecumene into the city. Instead of the inhabited world, he settled for its microcosmic representation in the city. What is perplexing about Rossi is that he, along with architects like Silvano Tintori, were originally critical of Le Corbusier's excursion into territorial thinking in *The Three Human Establishment* because it was, according to them, inattentive to the historical, cultural, and cadastral dimensions of territory. At their intellectual beginnings, both Rossi and Gregotti were immersed in expanding the terrain and impact of architecture, but they each read the terrain differently. For some reason, Rossi's reading and the reading of Rossi prevailed.

Gregotti's readings are yet to be fully fleshed out and his ambitious project for architecture is yet to be continued. The 17th International Architecture Biennale aims to continue from where he stopped all too soon and to explore, guided by his foresight, what architecture can do to the world and in the world.
—HASHIM SARKIS

SPECIAL GOLDEN LION FOR LIFETIME ACHIEVEMENT—*Vittorio Gregotti*

Contents

BIENNALE ARCHITETTURA 2021 EXHIBITION

INTRODUCTIONS
20 Roberto Cicutto
22 Paolo Baratta

HOW WILL WE LIVE TOGETHER?
24 Hashim Sarkis

36 **AMONG DIVERSE BEINGS**
39 Designing for New Bodies
59 Living with Other Beings

76 **AS NEW HOUSEHOLDS**
79 Catering to New Demographics
105 Inhabiting New Tectonics
113 Living Apart Together

142 **AS EMERGING COMMUNITIES**
145 Appealing to Civicness
167 Re-equipping Society
197 Coming Together in Venice
205 Co-Habitats: How we do live together in…
226 **EXTERIOR INTERVENTIONS**

254 **ACROSS BORDERS**
257 Protecting Global Commons
287 Transcending the Urban-Rural Divide
303 Linking the Levant

313 Seeking Refuge
325 Re-sourcing Resources

330 **AS ONE PLANET**
335 Making Worlds
355 Designing for Climate Change
367 Networking Space
378 **EXTERIOR INTERVENTIONS**

382 **MARGHERA – HOW WILL WE PLAY TOGETHER?**

396 **EMBODIED ACTION**
Three Collaborations between Biennale Danza and Biennale Architettura

CREDITS
405 Credits
411 Production Credits
424 Biographies
447 Image Credits
451 Acknowledgments

Introduction

ROBERTO CICUTTO
President of
La Biennale di Venezia

In 2020 we were forced to postpone the 17th International Architecture Exhibition until this year, but we nonetheless managed to stage the 77th Venice International Film Festival, the Dance, Music, and Theatre Festivals, as well as organise *The Disquieted Muses. When La Biennale di Venezia Meets History* exhibition, curated for the first time by the directors of the six arts of La Biennale.

As it was for everyone, 2020 was also the year of Covid-19 for La Biennale di Venezia. But we like to remember the great show of strength the Institution managed to muster by turning to its own resources and putting into play its extraordinary ability to react to the unforeseen and the unthinkable, also thanks to a fundamental collaboration with national and local Authorities.

The Biennale Architettura 2021 also found itself in the same uncertainty this year, but the situation was handled with a great sense of determination, courage, and responsibility by the curator Hashim Sarkis and our invited professionals, along with those representing the more than 60 national participations.

We open the Giardini and Arsenale with an even greatrer awareness of just how much the work of the Biennale mirrors the contemporary world, which is here interpreted and sometimes foreshadowed by the poroposals put forward by the curators and those who participate with their own work.

The query in the title *How will we live together?* has largely been seen as prophetic, and came well before the pandemic.

A hundred and twenty-six years of La Biennale di Venezia history demonstrates how its contemporaneity goes well beyond the forms of art it represents, welcoming the teaching, thought, and provocation of artists from every corner of the world.

If there is one thing in this first year of my presidency that has powerfully touched me it is realising the incredible observational vantage point the Biennale affords us: the Biennale represents a geopolitical map of the world that brings together the most diverse realities from the point of view of politics, economics, and the human condition of those artists who coalesce in Venice from so many radically different places.

And Architecture is undoubtedly the discipline that is most directly able to make headway into that map, revealing its criticality and grasping its positve aspects.

There are those who do not consider Architecture an art, or who at most define it an 'applied art'.

Architecture, however, just like other artistic expressions, finds its *raison d'être* in the profound ties it shares with life and society, when, through creative synthesis, it is able to represent all aspects of human living.

Paolo Baratta, whom I thank for having accepted to accompany this edition after having entrusted it to the curator Hashim Sarkis, says in his presentation: 'We have confirmed that one of the aims of an international exhibition was also that of increasing a desire for Architecture'.

And I would like to add that we have never before had such a need for Architecture.

I wish, first of all, to thank the Ministero della Cultura, the local institutions that support La Biennale di Venezia in various ways, the City of Venice, the Veneto Region, the Soprintendenza Archeologia, belle arti e paesaggio per il Comune di Venezia e Laguna, and the Italian Navy.

Our thanks go to Rolex, our Exclusive Partner and Official Timekeeper for the Exhibition.

We thank the Sponsors who have supported and helped us, and the Donors, who have been essential to the realisation of the 17th International Architecture Exhibition.

In particular, our thanks go to Hashim Sarkis and to his entire team. A heartfelt thank you, finally, to the extraordinary professionalism of my colleagues at La Biennale, who have all worked with great dedication for the realisation and management of the Exhibition for its six-month duration.

PAOLO BARATTA
about the 17th International Architecture Exhibition

After years of constant growth, the Biennale Architettura has finally become an adult.

In the various exhibitions over recent years, the eye of the curator has tended to concentrate on the themes of the discipline, recognising its vitality in periods in which, as we used to say, there seemed to be many creative architects but less and less Architecture. What has also been examined are the new terms within which technologies on the one hand and the demand for well-being and security on the other condition the discipline's horizons. In other moments (and, I would venture, more often), our gaze has moved towards the relationships between Architecture and civil society, assuming a broader idea of the field encompassing the discipline, which has been called upon to offer solutions to diverse individual and common needs.

Hence we have lingered on the theme of the ability of civil society to formulate demands and express these needs, on the hurdles that hold back a greater presence of Architecture, and on the ways these hurdles can be overcome. We have confirmed that one of the aims of an international exhibition was also that of expanding a desire for Architecture, disseminating an awareness of the social advantages that derive from its presence. We have, in other words, observed on quite a few occasions how Architecture can transform us, as individuals, into more aware citizens and not just consumers, and stimulate us to consider the indirect effects of our actions, helping us to better understand the importance of public commodities and free commodities as well as developing a more organic view of *welfare*. Of all the past editions, one I would like to mention here is the edition curated by Kazuyo Sejima, which had a rather momentous title – *People meet in Architecture* (Biennale Architettura 2010). Finally, Architecture helps us not to waste resources and to afford ourselves a modicum of happiness.

These reflections now have to come to terms with the fact that every area of the world is invested by phenomena of intense change. These phenomena are each very different from the others but share a need to impose 'adjustments' to our living conditions.

This was our consideration when we chose Hashim Sarkis to offer an even broader curatorial gaze. Here, architecture becomes the reference point for a vast interdisciplinary commitment as well as a vast cultural and political commitment. It is a sort of call to arms for Architecture, a call that is extended to other disciplines. In fact, we are *obliged* to transmit a state of emergency, in both the developed and the developing world. The changes we are witnessing require new visions and projects (for individual housing, cities, countrysides, nature, and entire territories). These are adjustments that ask us to consider the human and social being as an existence 'in relation to…'; and what is confirmed is that this is our ultimate starting point if we want to deal appropriately with these changes.

In an era where there is a generalised feeling of no longer being in control of a progress that is continually being propagated but of being prey to changes imposed by this progress and where many take advantage of people's ensuing fears, worries, and frustrations to advance campaigns based on an ultra-defensive sense of victimisation, we feel that a Biennale that reminds everyone that the identity of a society or community lies in the quality of the projects it is able to formulate for its own future – to correct mistakes and enhance resources. And, as has been demonstrated by the dramatic portents that have invested the world these past few months, these projects cannot but ensue from a widespread awareness and common collaboration.

And then we once again ask ourselves what the aims of an exhibition such as the Biennale are. Who is it for?

We have often said that the Exhibition wishes to be an instrument for knowledge and dialogue for those who are privy to the world of architecture. But an exhibition is also a 'call' to the general public, a call to become a visitor, a watchful and vigilant visitor, and then to become a first-hand witness, an eyewitness. An exhibition asks visitors to be willing to open their gaze while it also asks curators to be at once scientists and playwrights. To disseminate knowledge is not enough; we have to contribute to awareness. To expose problems is not enough; we have to exploit examples, proposals, projects, and creation to promote a desire for Architecture.

My heartfelt thanks go to the new President Roberto Cicutto, to Hashim Sarkis, to the structure of La Biennale, and to all of those who have contributed to the realisation of this Exhibition in these most complex times.

How will we live together?

HASHIM SARKIS
Curator of the
17th International Architecture Exhibition

We need a new spatial contract

In the context of widening political divides and growing economic inequalities, we call on architects to imagine spaces in which we can generously live *together*:
– *together* as human beings who, despite increasing individuality, yearn to connect with one another and with other species across digital and real space;
– *together* as new households looking for more diverse and dignified spaces for inhabitation;
– *together* as emerging communities that demand equity, inclusion, and spatial identity;
– *together* across political borders to imagine new geographies of association;
– and *together* as a planet facing crises that require global action for all of us to continue living at all.
The participants in the Biennale Architettura 2021 are collaborating with other professions and constituencies – artists, builders, engineers, and craftspeople, but also politicians, journalists, social scientists, and everyday citizens. In effect, the Biennale Architettura 2021 asserts the vital role of the architect as both cordial convener and custodian of the spatial contract.
In parallel, this Exhibition also maintains that it is in its material, spatial, and cultural specificity that architecture inspires the ways we live together. In that respect, we ask the

participants to highlight those aspects of the main theme that are uniquely architectural.

Unpacking the Question

The theme of this Biennale Architettura is its title. The title is a question: How will we live together? The question is open.

How: Speaks to practical approaches and concrete solutions, highlighting the primacy of problem-solving in architectural thinking.

Will: Signals looking toward the future but also seeking vision and determination, drawing from the power of the architectural imaginary.

We: Is the first person plural and thus inclusive of other peoples, of other species, appealing to a more empathetic understanding of architecture.

Live: Means not simply to exist but to thrive, to flourish, to inhabit, and to express life, tapping into architecture's inherent optimism.

Together: Implies collectives, commons, universal values, highlighting architecture as a collective form and a form of collective expression.

?: Indicates an open question, not a rhetorical one, looking for (many) answers, celebrating the plurality of values in and through architecture.

The question, 'How will we live together?' is at once ancient and urgent. The Babylonians asked it as they were building their tower. Aristotle asked it when he was writing about politics. His answer was 'the city'. The French and American Revolutions asked it. Against the tumultuous backdrop of the early 1970s, Timmy Thomas passionately pleaded it in his song 'Why Can't We Live Together?'

It is indeed as much a social and political question as a spatial one. More recently, rapidly changing social norms, the political polarisation between left and right, climate change, and the growing gap between labour and capital are making this question more urgently relevant and at different scales than before. In parallel, the weakness of the political models being proposed today compels us to put space first and, perhaps like Aristotle, look at the way architecture shapes inhabitation in order to imagine potential models for how we could live together.

Every generation feels compelled to ask this question and answer it in its own, unique way. Today, unlike with previous ideologically driven generations, there seems to be a consensus that there is no single source from which such an answer can come. The plurality of sources and diversity of answers will only enrich our living together, not impede it.

We are asking architects this question because we are not happy with the answers that are coming out of politics today. In the context of the Biennale Architettura we are asking architects this question because we believe they have the ability to present more inspiring answers than politics has been thus far offering in much of the world. We are asking architects because architects are good conveners of different actors and experts in the design and construction process. We are asking architects because we, as architects, are preoccupied with shaping the spaces in which people live together and because we frequently imagine these settings differently than do the social norms that dictate them.

In that sense, every space we design simultaneously embraces the social contract that willed the space and proposes an alternative to it. We aspire to enable the best of the social contract and to propose alternatives where we can improve on it. A single-family home may ultimately replicate the explicit values and implicit oppressions of the post-World War II nuclear family model, but we have also seen powerful experiments from architects who have challenged the detached house's familial hierarchies and gender segregations by proposing alternative layouts and degrees of openness.

Hopefully, the question continues to propel us expectantly ahead and, in doing so, to build on the optimism that drives architecture and architects. Our profession is tasked with designing better spaces for better living. Our challenge is not whether to be optimistic or not. There we have no choice. It is rather how successful we are at transposing the inhabitants to better lives through the 'wish images' that we produce with architecture.

The current global pandemic has no doubt made the question that this Biennale Architettura is asking all the more relevant and timelier, even if somehow ironic, given the imposed isolation. It may indeed be a coincidence that the theme was proposed a few months before the pandemic. However, many of the reasons that initially led us to ask this question – the intensifying climate crisis, massive population displacements, political instabilities around the world, and growing racial, social, and economic inequalities, among others – have led us to this pandemic and have become all the more relevant.

A New Spatial Contract

Five people walk into a room that has only four chairs. Who sits where? They can play musical chairs. That's one spatial contract. They can also line up the chairs to form of a bench where they all fit together. That's another. A city decides to build a new subway system. Which parts does it connect, and which does it leave out? There may be economic issues, political rivalries, and technological drivers that guide these decisions, but somehow the layout of the subway system supersedes and becomes a way in which a larger portion of the population connects with each other above and beyond the politics that bind or divide them.

Politics and policies lay out the terms and processes for collective living, but people convene in space, and the space helps shape and transform the social contract they lay out. When Aristotle, for example, wanted to describe the ideal democracy, he could not do so without the city. It was very difficult to imagine a society without the spaces that it occupied. Since then, political theorists have often relied on space to explain but also to enable the society they are imagining. From Rousseau to Rawls, the deliberation of people forming society takes place in a space that helps shape the social contract. If a social contract determines the freedoms lost and gained in order for people to enter society, a spatial contract, determines the methods by which people negotiate these freedoms through their spatial interactions.

We continue to inhabit houses and cities built on outmoded ideas of a good life. The architectural resilience of these spaces may have adjusted to our changing needs over time, but by now they have reached the limits of their elasticity.

Our bodies have acquired new prosthetics and, increasingly, the nascent freedom to express fluid genders. They are being diversified and liberated from uniformity, but the architectural criteria of their comfort are still based on standardised approaches that confine the body and detach it from its environment. Our family lives have evolved and diversified, but we continue to replicate *ad nauseam* the model of the nuclear family house along with its embedded biases of hierarchy and privacy. Our social associations have become more diffused and diverse and yet the space of the community is still centred around values of association that tend to be more inward-looking and claustrophobic. Our cities have long expanded beyond the centralised model of separated land-uses and income groups, but we often continue to think of the good city as one with a centre, spatially organised societal hierarchies, and with its back turned to the rural and nature. Above all, we have become increasingly aware of the global dangers of our spatial practices, including transportation and environmental controls, but we continue to live as if alone on a passive planet of endless resources. To paraphrase the singer Prince, we continue to *party like it was 1999*.

We can no longer wait for politicians to propose a path towards a better future. As politics continue to divide and isolate, we can offer alternative ways of living together through architecture. After all, space often precedes, projects, and survives the human conditions that shape it. A spatial contract could constitute a social contract. We are looking for a spatial contract that is at once universal and inclusive, an expanded contract for peoples and species to coexist and thrive in their plurality.

Towards a Renewed Agency for Architecture

The Biennale Architettura 2021 is motivated by new kinds of problems that the world is putting in front of architecture, but it is also inspired by the emerging activism of young architects and the radical revisions being proposed by the profession of architecture to take on these challenges.

Architects are inherently conveners. They synthesise among different fields and coordinate among different professionals and represent them in front of the client. They are the custodians of the contract. But beyond that, architects suggest possible social organisations through the way they arrange, sequester, and connect spaces. They also shape the monuments, the memories, and the expressions of societies and groups, creating a common language that enables the public to debate and communicate its experiences and cultures.

Architects today are rethinking their tools to address the complex problems at hand. They are also enlarging their table to include other professionals and citizens. To effectively take on the responsibilities being presented to them, architects are extending one of their most important roles, as generous synthesisers of different forms of expertise and expression.

But more than ever, architects are called upon to propose alternatives. As citizens, we mobilise our synthetic skills to bring people together to solve complex problems. As artists, we defy the inaction that comes from uncertainty to ask, 'What if?' And, as builders, we draw from our bottomless well of optimism to do what we do best. The confluence of roles in these nebulous times can only make our agency stronger and, we hope, our buildings more beautiful.

Five Scales

The main exhibition of the Biennale Architettura 2021 comprises works by 112 participants from 46 countries with increased representation from Africa, Latin America, and Asia and with comparable representation of men and women. This Exhibition also includes a series of 24 research *stations* that complement the projects on display with in-depth analysis of related topics. These stations were developed by researchers from universities around the world.

They include the Architectural Association, the American University of Beirut, The Bartlett, Columbia University, Cooper Union, ETH Zurich, Ethiopian Institute of Architecture, Building Construction and City Development (EiABC), ETSAM, Harvard University, Hong Kong University, Iuav University of Venice, KIT Karlsruhe, KU Leuven, Rice University, and the Venice Lab, a consortium of research groups at MIT.

The Biennale Architettura 2021 is organised into five scales: three are exhibited in the Arsenale and two in the Central Pavilion. Projects range from the analytic to the conceptual, the experimental, the tested, and proven to the widely deployed. Each of these is in turn addressed through a series of themes and each one is housed in individual rooms of the Biennale buildings and grounds.

The five scales are Among Diverse Beings, As New Households, As Emerging Communities, Across Borders, As One Planet.

Among Diverse Beings (Arsenale)
– *Designing for New Bodies*: addressing changes in the perception and conception of the human body
– *Living with Other Beings*: foregrounding empathetic behaviour and engagement with other beings

As New Households (Arsenale)
– *Catering to New Demographics*: responding to changing compositions and densities of households
– *Inhabiting New Tectonics*: exploring technologies that enable innovative housing construction
– *Living Apart Together*: expanding the possibilities of the apartment building as a collective housing typology

As Emerging Communities (Arsenale)
– *Appealing to Civicness*: investigating novel ways for communities to organise themselves spatially
– *Re-equipping Society*: proposing new forms of social equipment (parks, schools, hospitals, and so on)
– *Coming Together in Venice*: imagining the future of Venice in light of the challenges of sea-level rise, the pandemic, and changing demographics
– *Co-Habitats*: Showing how we do live together in Addis Ababa, the Azraq Refugee Camp, Beirut, Hong Kong, the India-Pakistan corridors, a Lagos squatter settlement compared to one in Cairo and another in Guadalajara, New York, Pristina, Rio de Janeiro, and the São Paulo area

Across Borders (Giardini, Central Pavilion)
– *Transcending the Urban–Rural Divide*: mitigating the growing social and economic differences between global cities and the global hinterland
– *Linking the Levant*: negotiating sharp political divisions in the Levant region
– *Seeking Refuge*: examining the spatial challenges of forced displacement
– *Re-sourcing Resources*: proposing better distribution of our common resources
– *Protecting Global Commons*: bringing

the architectural imaginary to engage with endangered treasures such as the Poles, the Amazon, the Oceans, the Indo-Pacific Region, and the Air

As One Planet (Giardini, Central Pavilion)
　– *Future Assembly*: proposing a speculative more-than-human future for the United Nations
　– *Making Worlds*: anticipating and calibrating the future of the planet
　– *Designing for Climate Change*: presenting solutions in the face of the global degradation of the environment
　– *Networking Space*: connecting between Earth and outer space.

　In addition to the exhibitions housed in the Central Pavilion and the Arsenale, the grounds of the Central Pavilion's Giardini and the Arsenale feature several installations that relate to one of the five scales. In addition, the Park of Forte Marghera on the mainland also features five related installations: *How will we play together?*

1	Han Tumertekin 227
2	ELEMENTAL (Alejandro Aravena; Victor Oddó; Gonzalo Arteaga; Diego Torres; Juan Cerda) 229
3	Vogt Landscape Architects (Günther Vogt) 231
4	WOJR (William O'Brien Jr.) 233
5	Studio Ossidiana (Giovanni Bellotti; Alessandra Covini) 63
6	Igneous Tectonics (Cristina Parreño; Sergio Araya) 235
7	NADAAA (Nader Tehrani; Arthur Chang) 237
8	Sahel Alhiyari Architects 239
SI1	**SPECIAL EVENT**: (Vuslat Foundation, Giuseppe Penone) 241
	EXTERIOR PERFORMANCE: Adam Kaasa), Thandi Loewenson and David Burns (Fiction Feeling Frame) 247

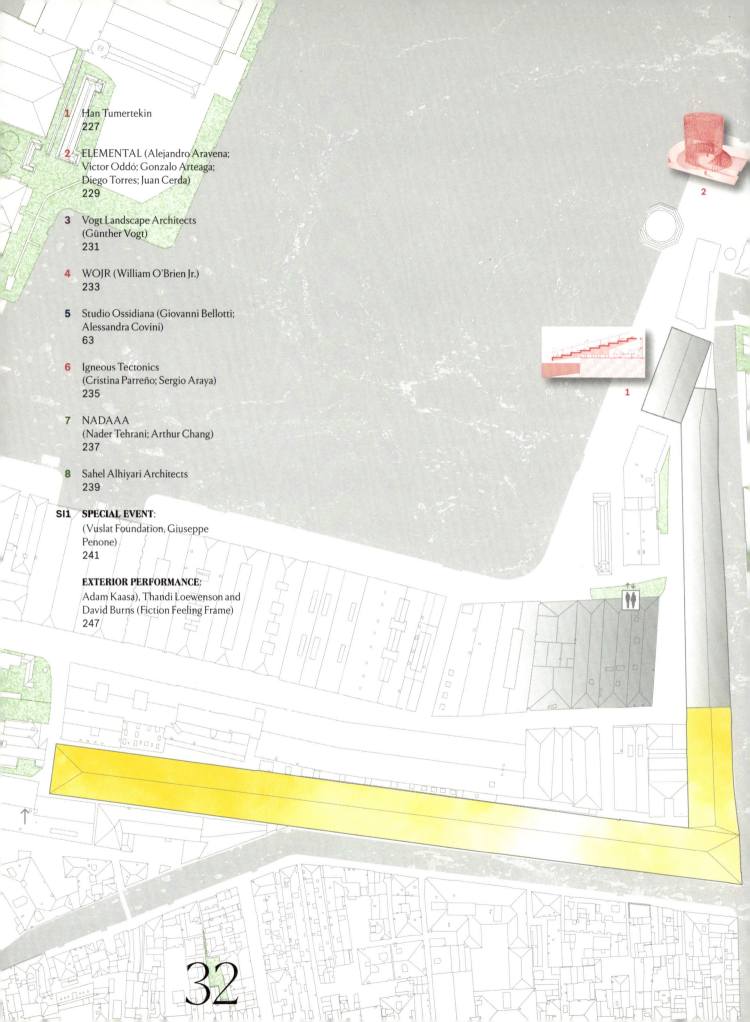

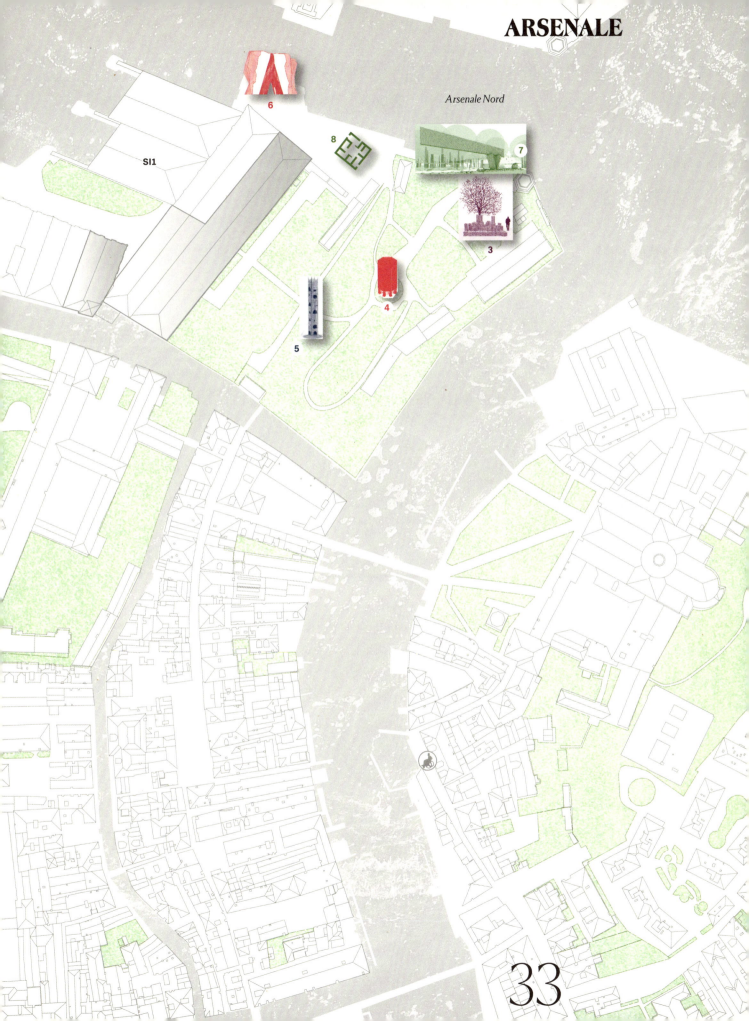

AMONG DIVERSE BEINGS

AS NEW HOUSEHOLDS

DESIGNING FOR NEW BODIES
1. Peju Alatise
2. Ani Liu
3. Azra Akšamija
4. modem (Nicholas de Monchaux; Kathryn Moll)
5. Allan Wexler Studio

LIVING WITH OTHER BEINGS
6. Refik Anadol Studio and Gökhan S. Hotamışlıgil
7. Studio Ossidiana (Giovanni Bellotti; Alessandra Covini)
8. Lucy McRae
9. Parsons & Charlesworth (Tim Parsons; Jessica Charlesworth)
10. MAEID [Büro für Architektur und transmediale Kunst] (Daniela Mitterberger; Tiziano Derme)
11. The Living (David Benjamin)
12. Studio Libertiny (Tomáš Libertíny)
13. Philip Beesley & Living Architecture Systems Group / University of Waterloo School of Architecture

S1 STATION: Matilde Cassani, Architectural Association; Ignacio G. Galán, Barnard College, Columbia University; Ivan L. Munuera, Princeton University; Joel Sanders, Yale University

S2 STATION: David Gissen, Parsons School of Design/The New School University; Jennifer Stager, Johns Hopkins University; and Mantha Zarmakoupi, University of Pennsylvania

CATERING TO NEW DEMOGRAPHICS
14. OPAFORM architects (Marina Bauer; Espen Folgerø)
15. Leopold Banchini Architects (with Lukas Feireiss and Dylan Perrenoud)
16. K63.STUDIO (Osborne Macharia)
17. Superflux (Anab Jain; Jon Ardern)
18. AW-ARCH (Alex Anmahian, Nick Winton)
19. line+ studio (Fanhao Meng)
20. leonmarcial arquitectos (Alexia Leon; Lucho Marcial)
21. ecoLogicStudio (Claudia Pasquero; Marco Poletto)
22. Atelier RITA (Valentine Guichardaz-Versini)
23. ROJO / FERNÁNDEZ-SHAW, arquitectos (Begoña Fernández-Shaw; Luis Rojo)
24. THE OPEN WORKSHOP (Neeraj Bhatia; Antje Steinmuller)

INHABITING NEW TECTONICS
25. NADAAA (Nader Tehrani; Arthur Chang)
26. Achim Menges / ICD University of Stuttgart and Jan Knippers / ITKE University of Stuttgart (Achim Menges; Jan Knippers)
27. Gramazio Kohler Architects / NCCR DFAB (Fabio Gramazio; Matthias Kohler)

LIVING APART TOGETHER
28. Fernanda Canales
29. Aires Mateus (Francisco Aires Mateus; Manuel Aires Mateus)
30. Alison Brooks Architects
31. LIN Architects Urbanists (Finn Geipel)
32. BAAG Buenos Aires Arquitectura Grupal (Griselda Balian; Gastón Noriega; Gabriel Monteleone)
33. Farshid Moussavi Architecture
34. nicolas laisné architectes
35. Lina Ghotmeh — Architecture
36. SsD (Jinhee Park)

S3 STATION: Mark Jarzombek and Vikramaditya Prakash, The Global Architectural History Teaching Collaborative (GAHTC) at MIT with Vikramaditya Prakash, Architecture Uncertainty Lab (A(U)L) at MIT; The University of Washington; and Eliana Abu-Hamdi, GAHTC

S4 STATION: Abalos+Sentkiewicz AS+; Iñaki Ábalos; Renata Sentkiewicz, Harvard University and Escuela Técnica Superior de Arquitectura de Madrid

STATION: Anne Kockelkorn and Susanne Schindler, Master of Advanced Studies (MAS) in History and Theory of Architecture at ETH Zurich

STATION: Daisy Ames, Bernadette Baird-Zars, Adam Frampton, Columbia GSAPP Housing Lab

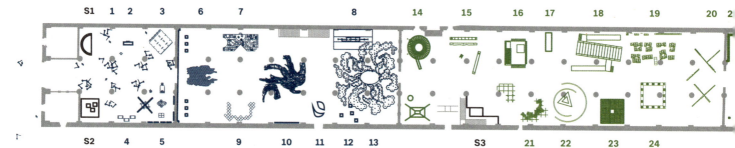

AS EMERGING COMMUNITIES

CORDERIE–ARTIGLIERIE

APPEALING TO CIVICNESS

- **37** Cohabitation Strategies (Lucia Babina; Emiliano Gandol, Gabriela Rendón, Miguel Robles-Durán)
- **38** Fieldoffice Architects (Huang Sheng-Yuan)
- **39** Storia Na Lugar (Patti Anahory; César Schofield Cardoso)
- **40** Arquitectura Expandida (Ana López Ortego; Harold Guyaux; Felipe González González; Viviana Parada Camargo)
- **41** Lacol (Ari Artigas; Mirko Gegundez; Lali Daví; Pol Massoni; Anna Clemente; Cristina Gamboa; Núria Vila; Jordi Miró; Ernest Garriga; Eliseu Arrufat; Laura Lluch; Lluc Hernandez; Arnau Andrés; Carles Baiges)
- **42** Enlace Arquitectura (Elisa Silva)
- **43** raumlaborberlin (Andrea Hofmann; Axel Timm; Benjamin Foerster-Baldenius; Christof Mayer; Florian Stirnemann; Francesco Apuzzo; Frauke Gerstenberg; Jan Liesegang; Markus Bader)
- **44** PRÁCTICA (Jaime Daroca Guerrero; José Mayoral Moratilla; José Ramón Sierra Gómez de León)

RE-EQUIPPING SOCIETY

- **45** Aristide Antonas with Elina Axioti; Mona Mahall and Asli Serbest
- **46** EFFEKT (Sinus Lynge; Tue Foged)
- **47** atelier masōmī (Mariam Kamara)
- **48** Manuel Herz Architects and Iwan Baan
- **49** MDP Michel Desvigne Paysagiste
- **50** TUMO Center for Creative Technologies (Marie Lou Papazian; Pegor Papazian)
- **51** Miralles Tagliabue EMBT (Benedetta Tagliabue; Elena Nedelcu; Joan Callís)
- **52** Ronan & Erwan Bouroullec
- **53** Skidmore, Owings & Merrill (Colin Koop)
- **54** Michael Maltzan Architecture
- **55** Sean Lally
- **56** BASE studio (Barbara Barreda; Felipe Sepulveda)
- **57** OMA (Reinier de Graaf)
- **58** doxiadis+ (Thomas Doxiadis)

COMING TOGETHER IN VENICE

- **59** studio L A (Lorien Beijaert; Arna Mačkić in collaboration with Baukje Trenning)
- **C1** Nicholas de Monchaux; Kathryn Moll; Sandro Bisà; modem; Bisà Associati with catalogtree and University of Virginia Venice Program
- **C2** Laura Fregolent, Università Iuav di Venezia; Paola Malanotte-Rizzoli, MIT
- **S5** **STATION**: Rafi Segal, MIT Future Urban Collective Lab; Sarah Williams, MIT Civic Data Design Lab at MIT Venice LAB; with Greg Lindsay, Marisa Morán Jahn, Studio REV

CO-HABITATS: HOW WE DO LIVE TOGETHER IN…

- **C3** **NIGERIA/EGYPT/MEXICO**: Kent Larson; Gabriela Bila Advincula et al.; MIT
- **C4** **ADDIS ABABA**: Marc Angélil; ETH Zurich; Dirk Hebel; KIT Karlsruhe; Bisrat Kifle Woldeyessus; EiABC et al.
- **C5** **SÃO PAULO**: Daniel Talesnik; Andres Lepik; Architekturmuseum der TUM et al.
- **C6** **AL AZRAQ CAMP**: Azra Aksamija; Melina Philippou; MIT et al.
- **C7** **INDIA**: Rahul Mehrotra; Sourav Kumar Biswas; GSD, Harvard University
- **C8** **BEIRUT**: Sandra Frem, American University of Beirut; Boulos Douaihy et al.
- **C9** **RIO DE JANEIRO**: Farès el-Dahdah; Alida Metcalf; Rice University; David Heyman; Axis Maps; Sergio Burgi; Instituto Moreira Salles et al.
- **C10** **PRISHTINA**: Bekim Ramku; Kosovo Architecture Foundation / OUD+Architects et al.
- **C11** **HONG KONG**: Merve Bedir; Hong Kong University; Sampson Wong
- **C12** **NEW YORK**: Nora Akaw et al.; The Cooper Union

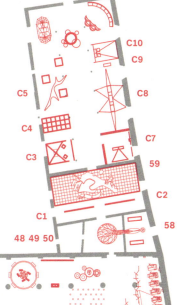

35

Among Diverse Beings

EXHIBITION ARSENALE

Humans, the story goes, gathered together in cities for security, but then they stayed for community. This sense of community is eroding in face of growing individualism, resulting in further isolation. But new forms of interaction among individuals and between individuals and other species are making up for some of this isolation. The internet, artificial intelligence, robots, and alternative realities further complicate this picture by turning communication tools into conversing beings.

    We continue to invent different ways of connecting to one another, but the more technologies and media we introduce, the more we yearn for the interpersonal personal spaces of architecture. Yet these two kinds of spatiality are not mutually exclusive. The digital and the physical are increasingly interwoven, and this section of the exhibition highlights the potential of such hybridity.

    Here, installations feature prosthetics of empathy like clothing, biochemical enhancements, apps, embedded media, communications, and the internet of things. They also imagine the spatial impact of their new communication tools. This section's research stations complement this spectrum by looking at the histories and politics of personal hygiene and accessibility.

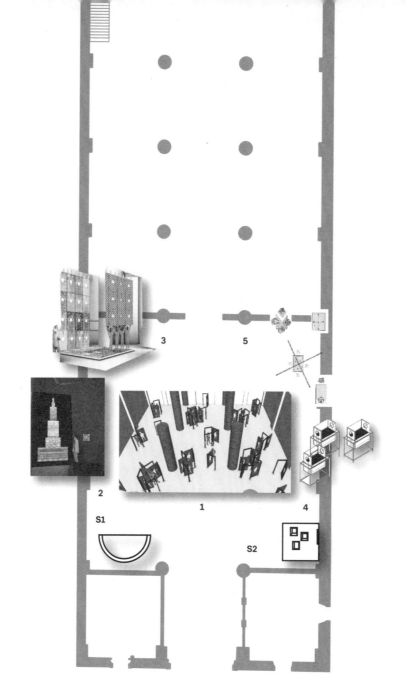

DESIGNING FOR NEW BODIES

AMONG DIVERSE BEINGS

1   Peju Alatise
41

2   Ani Liu
43

3   Azra Akšamija
45

4   modem
(Nicholas de Monchaux;
Kathryn Moll)
47

5   Allan Wexler Studio
49

S1   **STATION**: Matilde Cassani, Architectural Association; Ignacio G. Galán, Barnard College, Columbia University; Ivan L. Munuera, Princeton University; Joel Sanders, Yale University
50

S2   **STATION**: David Gissen, Parsons School of Design/ The New School University; Jennifer Stager, Johns Hopkins University; and Mantha Zarmakoupi, University of Pennsylvania
54

We have all become cyborgs. New technologies have entered our bodies to enhance our performance and augment our awareness. We have also uncovered and embraced the diversity of our genders and ethnicities, and we have become more engaged in our own body politics and those of others.

    This room proposes ways for design and architecture to mediate between our bodies and for the body to mitigate extreme environments through prosthetic extensions that amplify and project our bodily presence across space. The projects explore these mediations between body and space in different settings, ranging from the biological and domestic, the geopolitical, and to extraterrestrial spheres.

Peju Alatise, *Alasiri*, 2020. Sculptural installation

Peju Alatise, *Alasiri*, 2020. Sculptural installation

Alasiri: Doors for Concealment or Revelation, 2020

Eniyan ni ilekun; ti oba gba e laye ki owole, odi alasiri (a person is like a door: to open it is to become part of its secret).

How will we live together? The answer begs for moral inclusion that perhaps architecture alone cannot provide.

A world teeming with nationalist chauvinism that wants to limit human movement has been met with a virus that granted its wish yet paid no heed to national borders. A world so large in contrived differences, yet so small in epidemiological vulnerability, is in constant tension. Cyclic forces vacillate between the common humanity that brings us together in organisational convergence and contrived cultural, racial, and economic differences that push us apart in a metaphorical space into which *Alasiri* thrusts you, the observer.

The 'we' – that is, the human element that must be addressed in order to live together – in this question is worth exploring. This question is especially important in a world where uncontrolled population expansion coupled with environmentally damaging, capitalist consumerism will eventually come to a head with the unavoidable reality of limited space and resources. One certainty is that one must overcome the fear of those who are different from oneself by culture, creed, and colour.

The Yoruba have a saying, '*Oni yara rebete gba ogun omo okurin ti wan ba fera denu*' (The tiniest room can accommodate twenty men if they have a deep understanding of one another). The Yoruba also believe a person is like a door: to open it is to become part of its secret.

Alasiri is a sculptural installation of doors and figures that allows both one's vulnerability and those behind the doors to step through and gives visitors an avenue to explore mutual understanding or misunderstanding. *Alasiri* is the keeper of secrets that one can experience simultaneously as an outsider and insider.

Peju Alatise (Nigerian, b.1975) of Art Accent Studio (Nigeria, est.2006) in collaboration with Adeyemo Shokunbi (Nigerian, b.1966), Fidelis Odogwu (Nigerian, b.1970), and Yinka Akingbade (Nigerian, b.1980)

Doors: mild steel; Human sculptures (1:1): granite dust, resin, fiberglass, textile; dimensions variable

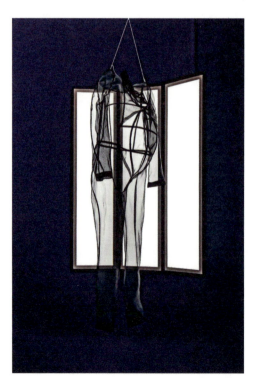

Ani Liu, *Shapes and Ladders*, 2020. Diagram of every level from 0–5

Ani Liu, *Maternity Menswear*, 2020

Ani Liu, *A.I. Toys*, 2020. Image of a current prototype of the project with the digitally generated toys 3D-printed

A.I. Toys Shapes and Ladders: Battles of Bias and Bureaucracy Maternity Menswear, 2020

How does technology shape societal constructs of gender norms? Can design break with problematic histories and reshape cultural norms? This series of works contains a maternity garment, a set of toys, and a video game.

Maternity Menswear is a garment that explores non-female and transgender pregnancy through suiting, blurring boundaries between gender, sex, fertility, and vulnerability. Designed to appear as a sketch of an idea, it is created in silk and rigid boning.

A.I. Toys is a series created with a machine-learning model fed with real toy data marketed as 'boys' and 'girls' toys. These algorithmically generated toys reflect the gendered societal values often placed on children through objects of play.

Shapes and Ladders is a video game that shows how systemic sexism and racism can exist in the workplace. Set in the metaphor of a career ladder, players attempt to navigate through an office building rife with challenges. Players can play as a circle, square, or triangle, for which game mechanics have been designed to reflect real life inequalities different populations face. For example, a circle is more likely to encounter workplace sexual assault, has access to fewer coins, and performs a second shift in childcare. The video game is designed to allow players to cultivate empathy through a first-person simulation of structural inequality. With these insights, the project aspires to inspire players to spark change in real life.

Ani Liu
(American, b.1986)

A.I. Toys: full colour 3D-printed sandstone, acrylic, various dimensions
Shapes and Ladders: Battles of Bias and Bureaucracy: video game, projection
Maternity Menswear: silk organza, 58 × 32 × 202 cm

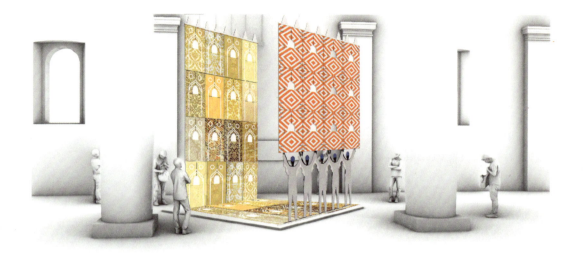

Azra Akšamija, photomontage of the *Silk Road Works* construction site for an inclusive society. In the form of a wearable mosque inspired by Venetian architecture

Azra Akšamija, tessellation of the unfolded safety vests, together with the arrangement of coveralls, references the Islamic architectural features of the Palazzo Ducale in Venice

Silk Road Works, 2020

In a world traversed by zones of contact in which lifestyle choices have become targets for reactionary forms of identity paranoia, wearing a headscarf or a beard in public can be perceived as a threat. *Silk Road Works* engages with subject positions defined by 'otherness' and marginality linked to Islamic identity, aiming to counter cultural biases and propose a vision for architecture of coexistence. Inspired by Venice's historical role as a cultural and commercial hub of Europe's exchange with the East, the installation takes the form of a body-scale construction site for building an inclusive, pluralist society. Informed by the social and cultural history of Venice, architecture becomes a medium to visually deconstruct an essentialist idea of a homogenous, static identity, and to embody the leitmotif of cultural mobility.

This proposition is translated into the design of three architectural wearables: construction workers' safety vests, coveralls, and hardhats. The external tessellation of the safety vests references façade elements of Palazzo Ducale in Venice as well as Mamluk architecture. The vest's interior silk lining, made of damasks and brocade fabrics, alludes to the prayer carpet-like façade elements of the famous Venetian palazzo Ca' d'Oro. Unfolded flat, these vests constitute a wearable, portable mosque. The second type of wearables translates palatial colonnades into construction workers' coveralls featuring Venetian Gothic arches. These 'armpit arches' only become visible once individuals connect their hands. The third set of wearables are construction helmets made of glass. These draw attention to the pressing social, political, humanitarian, and environmental crises along the Silk Road today. The brittleness of the material points at the fragility of the natural and cultural heritage, linking the agency of construction and preservation with the urgencies of architectural destruction and labour exploitation in and through architecture.

Azra Akšamija (Austrian, b.1976) of MIT Future Heritage Lab (USA, est.2016) in collaboration with Lillian Kology (American, b.1985) and Kailin Jones (American/Hongkonger, b.1994) of MIT Future Heritage Lab, and Adriano Berengo (Italy, b.1947) of Berengo Studio (Italy, est.1989)

Vests (33): silk fabrics from various regions of the Silk Road, reflective fabric, reflective and golden piping, clasps and zippers, 130 × 65 cm each; Coveralls (5), Barbarigo silk by Rubelli Venezia, 60 × 175 cm each; Helmets (5), Murano glass, 15 × 22 × 28 cm each

modem, *Space Suit*, 2021. Space Suit study 2, suit

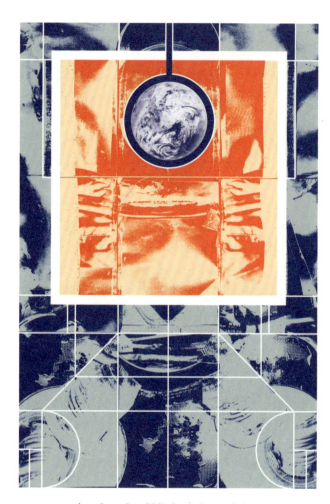

modem, *Space Suit*, 2021. Space Suit study 1, space

Space Suit, 2021

Nicholas de Monchaux (American, b.1973) and Kathryn Moll (American, b.1978) of modem (USA, est.2017)

Spacesuit Glove Prototypes in vitrines (3), gloves (6), dimensions variable

This 17th International Architecture Exhibition asks how we will live together at a range of scales – from the body to the planet. A spacesuit bridges these most extreme scales, revealing the intimacy and fragility of human life that connects them. A spacesuit enables humans to reach a vantage point from which we can understand the subtle truth of Earth's geometry. We live *on* Earth, sustained by a thin atmosphere that rests as lightly upon the globe as fabric might.

    Within this tissue-thin membrane, humans' carbon emissions have caused a climate crisis. And aerosols and global airflows have brought us, this past year, into contagious contact around the world (a 'pandemic', from *pan-demos*, or 'all people'). This installation displays fragments of spacesuit history within objects that are also environments. Cross-hatching the language of reliquary and care, they are an apparatus of protection as much as of display.

    The essential truth within is one of pragmatism and not of perfection. Human bodies are profoundly unsuited for Space, and our flexible hands – so unlike pressure-equalising spheres – create the unique challenge of pressure-glove design. In the long development of spacesuit gloves, ideals of engineering and utopian design principles are discarded almost immediately for an endless chain of measurements, experiments, and prototypes, of which those in this installation are an essential set of links. What is most sacred here is the careful, adaptive, and practical role that architecture must perform, intimately and effectively, across every scale of our human ecology.

Allan Wexler, *Table for the Typical House*, 2010–2020

Allan Wexler, *One Table Worn by Four People*, 1991

Allan Wexler, *Table Worn by One Person*, 2020

Allan Wexler, *Transparent Conversation*, 2015–2020

Social Contracts: Choreographing Interactions, 2020

Allan Wexler (American, b.1949) in collaboration with Ellen Wexler (American, b.1949)

Installation includes eleven different works by the artist: *Table for the Typical House*, 2010 / 2020; *Engagement*, 2012 / 2020; *Sheathing the Rift*, 2014 / 2020; *Eye Level*, 2015 / 2020; *Transparent Conversation*, 2015 / 2020; *One Table Worn by One Person*, 2020; *One Table Worn by Four People*, 1991; *Plein Air Studio*, 2018; *Four Shirt Collars Sewn into a Tablecloth*, 1991; *Four White Shirts Sewn into a Tablecloth*, 1991; *Coffee Seeks its Own Level*, 1990; materials and dimensions variable

I make theatre out of everyday life. I investigate how daily habits and deep-seated rituals inform the spaces we inhabit. I am more concerned with the human spirit within the spaces where we dwell.

The works gathered here for *Social Contracts* illuminate how our environment shapes us, how spaces we inhabit choreograph relationships between and among strangers, couples and the family, with the hope that we can find new ways to live together, better. Some works make visible our current isolation in what should be shared space. Some stage unexpected interactions and fragile social contracts. Some create a delicacy that forces us to navigate together.

Among these:

Plein Air Studio – A portable design studio inspired by John Ruskin. 'I built myself a studio with which to go forth. I inhabit my studio like a garment.'

Coffee Seeks its Own Level – Four people gather for coffee, but when one cup is lifted, coffee flows into the lower cups. To avoid spillage, the group must drink simultaneously, requiring concentration and collaboration.

Table for Typical House – Dissects the dining table into four isolated sections with each family member dining alone. Condiments on each section require the isolated diners to interact. A portrait of an American family.

One Table Worn by Four People – Guests wear one quarter of a table cut with a handheld jigsaw. The uneven edges fit together only one way, forcing participants to search out the other three to complete their table.

Four Shirts Sewn into a Tablecloth – Four pre-owned shirts are joined to form the table's cloth, making visual the physical connection between individuals seated for a meal together.

Your Restroom is a Battleground, 2021

Restrooms are often described as neutral facilities or mere utilitarian infrastructures catering to the universal needs of individuals, when in fact they are contested spaces that are shaped by and in turn shape the ways bodies and communities come together. Restrooms are architectures where gender, religion, race, ability, hygiene, health, environmental concerns, and the economy are defined culturally and articulated materially. In the last few years, the climate crisis, the Covid-19 pandemic, and growing tensions derived from population displacements have made these entanglements more evident. Restrooms are not an isolated design problem but rather symptoms of larger disputes that can be mediated through architectural tools. Restrooms are political architectures; they are battlegrounds.

Your Restroom is a Battleground presents a selection of seven case studies as an installation at the Arsenale. The case studies are presented through dioramas that represent a variety of restroom battles around the world and illustrate how these debates take shape and reflect local and global social concerns and agendas:

Guangzhou, China: Female activist Li Maizi led the famous Occupy Men's Room movement in which some 20 women took over male public restrooms in Guangzhou and Beijing to fight for 'potty parity'. They demanded changing public design standards for restrooms to a ratio of 1.5 women's restrooms for every men's restroom to prevent longer wait times.

Starbucks, Philadelphia, USA: In the wake of the controversial arrest of two black customers who were at the coffee shop for a business meeting (and the community protests that followed this case of racial profiling), Starbucks pledged to open its restrooms to all. However, the coffee giant later restricted public access to another constituency by adding blue lights to some restrooms to thwart the use of intravenous drugs, since blue lights prevent veins from being visible.

Matilde Cassani (Italian, b.1980) of the Architectural Association (United Kingdom, est.1847), Ignacio G. Galán (Spanish, b.1982) of Barnard College, Columbia University (USA, est.1889), Iván L. Munuera (Spanish, b.1980) of Princeton University (USA, est.1746), and Joel Sanders (American, b.1956) of JSA / MIXdesign and Yale University (USA, est.1701) in collaboration with Leonardo Gatti (Italian, b.1991), Maria Chiara Pastore (Italian, b.1980), Pablo Saiz del Rio (Spanish, b.1993), Paula Vilaplana de Miguel (Spanish, b.1985), Seb Choe (American, b.1994), Vanessa Gonzalez (American, b.1997) and Marco Li (Hongkonger, b.1984) of JSA/MIXdesign (USA, 1992)

Physical model and audio, 400 × 200 × 100 cm

Your Restroom is a Battleground installation view, 17th International Architecture Exhibition 2021

STATION

AMONG DIVERSE BEINGS—*Station*

51

Geoff Livingston, *Gavin Grimm Speaks at Title IX Protest*, Washington DC, USA, 2017

Ashraf Hendricks, *Overflowing Toilets in RR Section of Khayelitsha*, Cape Town, South Africa, 2016

Giacomo Pirozzi, *Girls walking towards newly constructed latrines at Shirichena Primary School, Mhondoro district about 60 km south of Harare*, Mhondoro, Zimbabwe, 2011

Shane Burcaw and Hannah Elizabeth, frame from the video *Man With Disability Falls Into 'Accessible' Toilet*, Minneapolis, USA, 2018

STATION

Housing, Colombia: A disabled individual, his mother, and attendant have been struggling with the use of restrooms in hotels in a country with a large number of disabled individuals due to its prolonged war. The generic technical and spatial solutions of these facilities contrast with the personalised retrofits they have implemented in their own domestic bathroom to accommodate their specific needs.

Gloucester High School, Virginia, USA: Transgender high school student Gavin Grimm filed a lawsuit against the school board's discriminatory transgender policy that forced him to use an isolated restroom in a retrofitted janitor's closet rather than share the communal facility with his male classmates.

Khayelitsha, South Africa: Black residents in Khayelitsha, one of Cape Town's poor settlements staged protests after being denied access to waterborne sanitation and flush restrooms that are provided in predominantly white neighbourhoods. This situation reinforces the legacy of apartheid and has caused a public health crisis that has been exacerbated by droughts.

Canterbury Prison, United Kingdom: The installation of footbaths and squat latrines was denounced by different groups who opposed the use of government funds to accommodate the religious and cultural practices of Muslim inmates.

Port-au-Prince, Haiti: After the devastating earthquake of 2010, poor wastewater management at a United Nations Peacekeeping camp spewed raw sewage into local waterways and sparked a cholera outbreak that infected thousands. This outbreak put a glaring spotlight on Haiti's sewage system, locating the infrastructure of a geopolitical map with an uneven balance of powers.

The sequence of models situates each case study within a wider network of socio-technical spatial entanglements and illuminates both the issues at stake and the multiple actors that participate in each battleground.

The case studies presented in the Arsenale contextualise interventions at the Giardini restrooms (page 381). The two components of the exhibition relate to each other through the logic of medical research: 'from bench to bedside' – from abstractions in the laboratory to the specificities of lived experience. The case studies presented in the sequence of models at the Arsenale allow the audience to understand and locate the restroom within a wider set of polemics around the world in which different communities are testing new forms of coexistence. Restrooms are spaces of segregation, yet they can also become spaces of freedom.

An Archaeology of Disability, 2021

The accessibility of historic architecture not only determines who can experience the past, but also informs how one thinks about disabled people in history.

This installation presents an experiment in historically reconstructing the Acropolis in Athens. A classical archaeologist and architecture historian, a historian of classical art, and a physically disabled historian and theorist of architecture thus recover ideas about bodies and impairment at one of the most canonical, influential, and notoriously *inaccessible* historic architectural sites.

The project explores what it means to reconstruct lost elements of the Acropolis through the lens of human impairment. Such an approach is in contrast to the pursuit of 'accessible heritage'; it balances the historic authenticity of architecture and the technical modifications made for contemporary accessibility. This alternative to accessible heritage is what the authors of this project call 'an archaeology of disability'. This not only recovers artefacts relevant to contemporary disabled people, but it involves reconstructing the past in languages and forms relevant to disability and its experience.

The reconstructed elements include an enormous and virtually unknown 5th-century BCE ramp that once connected the Acropolis to the Agora below; a gallery of paintings in the Acropolis, at the top of the ramp that offered respite from the climb; a small stone seat, described by a visitor to the gallery over 2000 years ago; and a fragment of a low stone wall that might also be used as a place for a weary traveller to rest.

The ramp's form is reconstructed as a tactile, touch-based model that transmits a sense of the vibrations caused by the crowds, animals, and carriages that once climbed it 2500 years ago. The gallery, whose paintings are known only through textual description, is reconstructed in sign language. The seat is reconstructed to suit

David Gissen (American, b.1969), of Parsons School of Design/The New School University (USA), Jennifer Stager (American, b.1970) of Johns Hopkins University (USA) and Mantha Zarmakoupi (Greek, b.1975) of University of Pennsylvania (USA)

Embodied Translations, ASL reconstruction of Acropolis and Agora Murals, c. 500 BCE, video, 5'; reconstructed stone seat, c. 500 BCE, 50 × 40 × 40 cm; reconstructed weathered stone, c. 500 BCE, 50 × 30 × 50 cm; reconstruction of Acropolis ramp, wood and foam model, speaker, 75 × 10 × 30 cm, printed photographs of the Acropolis (1850–present), dimensions variable

Photographer unknown, entry to the Acropolis in 1850 and before its restoration. Collection of the Library of Congress.

STATION

AMONG DIVERSE BEINGS—*Station*

Mantha Zarmakoupi, entry to the Acropolis in 2020 and showing fragments of monumental ramp in foreground

An Archaeology of Disability, 2021. Tactile pattern on stone seat reconstruction

any number of people's physical capacities. And the stone wall fragment is reconstructed with a braille-like weathered pattern and communicates the optical effect of weathering in a more tactile form.

Collectively, these reconstructions reconsider disability and the historic past, moving beyond technological fixes to predetermined physical objects. Rather, disability emerges as a form of historical inquiry, archaeology, and reconstruction, informed by the experience of collective human difference across space and time.

LIVING WITH OTHER BEINGS

AMONG DIVERSE BEINGS

6 Refik Anadol Studio and Gökhan S. Hotamışlıgil
61

7 Studio Ossidiana (Giovanni Bellotti; Alessandra Covini)
63

8 Lucy McRae
65

9 Parsons & Charlesworth (Tim Parsons; Jessica Charlesworth)
67

10 MAEID [Büro für Architektur und transmediale Kunst] (Daniela Mitterberger; Tiziano Derme)
69

11 The Living (David Benjamin)
71

12 Studio Libertiny (Tomáš Libertíny)
73

13 Philip Beesley & Living Architecture Systems Group / University of Waterloo School of Architecture
75

Our bodies are ecologies. They also belong to different ecosystems in which we are not alone. This room is dedicated to rethinking these ecologies more inclusively and symbiotically and to designing spaces in which these ecologies could thrive. How does architecture recognise, represent, and help us live with other beings? How does it include the microbiomes of the body or the birds, bees, luffas, soils, and fungi as partners in building and inhabiting these ecosystems?

Refik Anadol Studio, *Sense of Space Diagram A*, 2021

Refik Anadol Studio, *Sense of Space AI Data Sculpture B*, 2021

Sense of Space, 2021

Refik Anadol (Turkish, b.1985) of Refik Anadol Studio (USA, est.2015) and Gökhan S. Hotamışlıgil (Turkish/American b.1962) of Harvard University

3D AI Data Sculpture, projection, custom software, archival digital material, robotic large-scale 3D printing, 4-channel sound, dimensions variable

A pioneer of modern neuroscience in the late nineteenth century, Spanish scientist Santiago Ramon y Cajal once said, 'as long as our brain is a mystery, the universe, the reflection of the structure of the brain will also be a mystery'. His statement not only suggests a two-fold complexity about the simultaneous materiality and the abstractness of perception, but also implies a close affinity between human imagination and advancements of neuroscience. No wonder that Cajal's legacy was founded in his artistic approach to studying the *architecture* of the human brain, developing numerous drawings that facilitated his discoveries.

Sense of Space follows Cajal's vision and focuses on various meanings of perception at the intersection of architecture, neuroscience, visual arts, and machine learning. Whether it is about a creative mind and its artificial counterpart co-creating architectural spaces or about understanding how our minds architect connections among memories, artificial intelligence plays a crucial role in the development of the symbiotic relationship between these disciplines.

The installation represents this symbiosis by showcasing a fully immersive, audio-visual, and 3D-printed architectural structure created by plotting data points reflecting how our brains learn, remember, and experience discrete emotions. The collaboration with the Human Connectome Project (HCP) lies at the heart of the project, as the dataset is based on HCP outputs collected from approximately 4,500 people from different age groups scanned by Siemens MRI Scanners. By training a machine-learning algorithm using this data, this project generates a machine that artificially imagines human neural networks. At Harvard's Sabri Ülker Center, infinitely dynamic and molecularly defined biological forms are produced with nanometric details never before achieved. The data represents FIB-SEM imaging, annotation, and segmentation of 22,035 liver sections. Machine learning, AI, and 3D modelling and printing reveal the real and spectacular resolution of the inner molecular architecture of a hepatocyte. These displayed novel perspectives define how form relates to function in life, and how molecular architecture determines health or disease.

Studio Ossidiana, *Variations on a Bird Cage*, 2019-2021

Studio Ossidiana, *Variations on a Bird Cage*, 2019-2021. Overall view

Variations on a Bird Cage, 2019–2021

Developing the theme of living together, Studio Ossidiana presents an ongoing research into the objects, spaces, and materials that mediate the encounter between people and other animals.

Variations on a Bird Cage is an exploration of the objects through which humans formalise their encounters with birds – animals which, along with people, have most contributed to the globalisation of nature, inhabiting in every culture a place both physical and metaphorical. Combining historical research and new architectural types, working prototypes and new materials, the installation spatialises the relation between bodies/species through a series of intermediary objects, translating the actions of retreating, advancing, abandoning, transforming, domesticating, feeding, and playing into a performative object-space.

The installation aims to rethink the archetype of the cage as a physical language rather than an enclosure, addressing the physical, corporeal nature of the cage as well as its metaphorical power, its capacity to abstract, to represent ideas of 'nature', and inform relations between species. While the 'cage' expands from the tender to the coercive, the ironic to the dramatic, the metaphorical to the caloric, we see the actions embedded in 'living together' becoming the ingredients for a project of mutual transformation, of exchange between humans and other animals, as the 'cage' shifts from a form of seclusion to a mediative object.

Giovanni Bellotti (Italian, b.1987) and Alessandra Covini (Italian, b.1988) of Studio Ossidiana (The Netherlands, est.2016) with Sze Wing Chan (Hongkonger, b.1990), Marie Saladin (French, b.1988), Ebru Guner (Dutch, b.1996), Daniele Ceragno (Italian, b.1996), Lyubov Viller (Russian, b.1991), Jackie van Dijk (Dutch, b.1999), Riccardo de Vecchi (Italian, b.1993), Mariagiulia Pistonese (Italian, b.1992), in collaboration with Baukje Trenning (Dutch, b.1969), Tomaello Bv (Dutch, b.1924), Luigi D'Oro Studio (Italian, b.2004)

Platform for Humans and Birds: expanded clay, concrete, cork, seeds, hempcrete, rammed earth, 700 × 315 × 35 cm; Dovecote towers (3): expanded clay, rammed earth, hemp, cement, 40 × 40 × 180 cm; Field of Models (33): gypsum, copper, balsa wood, steel, limestone, various dimensions; Perches for birds (9): Pinewood, 30 × 30 × 270 cm; Outdoor installation: Dovecote tower: Metal structure and shingles, 50 × 50 × 500 cm

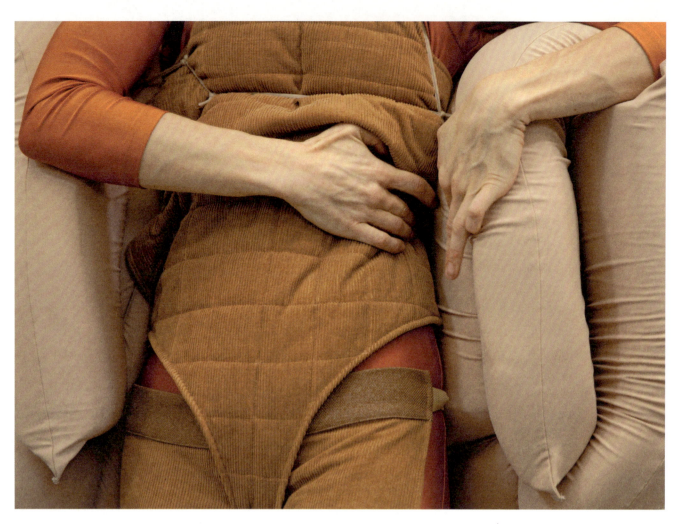

Lucy McRae, *Future Survival Kit*, 2020. Material study

Lucy McRae, *Future Survival Kit*, 2020.
Material study

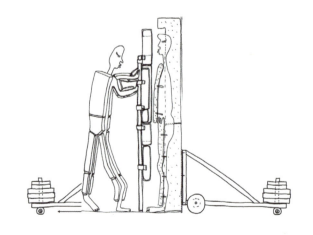

Lucy McRae, *Future Survival Kit*, 2020. Sketch

Heavy Duty Love, 2021

Lucy McRae (Australian, b.1979) of Lucy McRae Studio (USA, est.2009)

Scientists are accelerating ways to direct our evolutionary path – powerful genetic engineering tools, such as CRISPR, can fundamentally redesign our species. Be it gene-edited babies or children grown in artificial wombs, playing with the very building blocks of life creates terror and inspiration in equal measure.

Tarpaulin, carpet underlay, memory foam, textile, timber, steel, castors, weight plates, dimensions variable

Heavy Duty Love is a mental health prop from a future that has yet to happen; a domestic, sporty device sandwiching the body between layers of squishy stuff, normally used in camping or construction. If we do head towards a future where life is designed from scratch, would we seek new types of intimacy? *Heavy Duty Love* would be found in domestic spaces, compensating for a lack of human touch in early life. Could spongelike machines build trust and connection, reinforcing the protective embrace of a now-lost parent by virtue of such lab grown origins?

Inspired by bleeding edge technology, this cautionary narrative wants to engage with science at street level, merging complexity with the familiar. In Lucy's world, art is no longer the vessel but connects to the bulk of science and tech – debating the uncomfortable and complex, jointly forging new types of future through science and story.

Catalog for the Post-Human products, clockwise from top left: *Best Selfer, Clickbaitwear, AI Bias Kit, Morning Ritual, Mycopops,* and *NootDial*

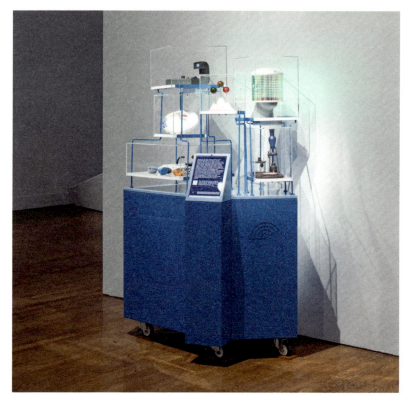

Catalog for the Post-Human Vending Machine, installation view, in the exhibition *Designs for Different Futures* at the Philadelphia Museum of Art

Catalog for the Post-Human, 2020

Jessica Charlesworth (British/Canadian, b.1979) and Tim Parsons (British, b.1974) of Parsons & Charlesworth (USA, est.2014)

Mixed media installation, Abstracta display system, LCD TV monitors, acrylic surfaces, physical models, c. 600 × 900 cm

Catalog for the Post-Human is a satirical installation that draws upon research into the future of work and human enhancement to highlight the nature of our post-human condition. Building on the theme of the Biennale, the project asks 'How will we live together if we are forced to augment ourselves to stay competitive?' The Venice iteration of this multipart project manifests as the trade fair stand of a fictional, near-future organisation, *Catalog for the Post-Human*, showing a range of body-related objects for gig-economy workers.

Imagining a future where success depends on our ability to be permanently cognitively sharp, quantifying ourselves with data, and able to work the long and irregular hours assigned by algorithm-run corporations, *Catalog for the Post-Human* provides tools to help workers cope with circumstances in which their bodies may be pushed to the limit. Adjust your circadian rhythms to your work schedule. Dial up the right cognitive state for your next gig using smart drugs. Safeguard your microbiome with soil-based probiotic lollypops or absorb vitamins intravenously while you work. Using the fictional, commercial environment as a method of engagement, the project intends to provoke conversations about the ethical and social dimensions of our technologically mediated futures.

What are the logical conclusions of the work/life changes we're already seeing? How will AI, brain-computer interfaces, and constant corporate surveillance affect our behaviours? What are the physical and psychological consequences of giving over body and mind to the unrelenting productivity of data-driven capitalism?

All images: MAEID, *Magic Queen*, 2020

Magic Queen [from the Artificial Ecologies series], 2020

Daniela Mitterberger (Austrian, b.1988) and Tiziano Derme (Italian/Austrian, b.1987) of MAEID [Büro für Architektur & Transmediale Kunst] (Austria, est.2015)

Soil, robotic arm, 1100 × 650 cm; Video projection

Magic Queen is a hybrid environment incorporating and fusing biological systems with organic materials and machines, creating an ecosystem of empathy and coexistence. It explores the relationship between natural elements, technology, and living systems favouring the creation of an ecology of non-human subjects. It is a built habitat that can restore and nurture itself, redefining the role of living systems in architecture. It is a performative 3D-printed soil robotic garden. Sensors respond and machine learning creates continuous feedback among sensing, virtualising, and induced change. Its inhabitable space combines visual, auditory, olfactory, and haptic features to capture the sensual experience of this new, mediated form of nature. Nothing in it could exist without the presence of the other: interconnectivity in biological entities. Fungal flora and soil structure depend on the robot to nurture them; the robot relies on their existence to move. The interconnectivity and performativity of all elements generates ambient sound, and a visual interface uncovers the otherwise invisible stream of impact and growth.

The installation is left to its own devices to continuously recreate and regenerate. The robotic gardener hangs upside down, scans, and nurtures the underlying, techno-organic soil landscape. This robot is equipped with a watering system to garden the seeds of the mushrooms in the soil and a machine vision system to detect and register changes in the surface texture and bio-growth on the structure. The ambient sound comprises artificially produced sounds as well as natural ones, continuously influenced and manipulated by the movements of the hanging robot and changes in the structure. The entirely biodegradable soil is fabricated using a new, robotic, binder-jetting process for granular bio-composites and non-toxic, organic binding agents. The 3D-printed terrain shows the potential of a fully reversible construction process for architectural and landscape components.

Magic Queen is a performative architecture. It gathers human and non-human subjects and technologies to create an environment where manufacturing, machine vision, sensor systems, visual, auditory, and olfactory interfaces are part of the built environment.

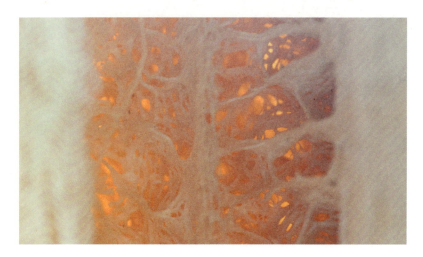
Bioreceptive material prototypes

Bioreceptive material prototypes

The Living, multispecies architecture, 2020

Alive: A New Spatial Contract for Multispecies Architecture, 2020

David Benjamin (American, b.1974) of The Living (USA, est.2008)

Luffa, plywood, microbes, humans, 360 × 260 × 410 cm

Microbes are invisible to the human eye, but they are everywhere in our buildings and cities. They are in the air, on the walls, and embedded in even the cleanest surfaces. At the same time, each individual human hosts trillions of microbes, which help keep us alive. And the ecosystem of each individual is intertwined with the ecosystems of everything we touch. We have always lived together with microbes, and microbes have always connected us to each other and to architecture.

Today it has become clear that public health depends on a vibrant microbiome. According to the latest science, the emotional, social, and physical well-being of humans is interconnected with the well-being of microbes. With this in mind, buildings might be designed to include symbiotic environments for humans and microbes. Buildings might be reconceptualised as microbial reservoirs. More specifically, studies suggest that *diverse* microbial communities within architecture are the best ones for human health.

Alive: A New Spatial Contract for Multispecies Architecture explores architecture for promoting diverse microbial communities through the calibration of texture, light, and air flow. It imagines a new direction for 'probiotic buildings' and multispecies architecture. As a prototype for twenty-first-century 'living architecture', it involves a room made of textured, porous, organic material that provides abundant surface area and many different microclimates for many types of microbes. This architecture includes both macro-spaces for humans and micro-spaces for microbes as well as material interfaces for exchanges among these different species.

In a broader sense, the project is a prototype for a new spatial contract. It also connects the idea of *living together* to concepts about diverse microbial communities – as well as concepts about diverse, human communities; sharing tactile experiences; and Venice as a historical site of exchange.

Tomáš Libertíny, *The Gate, Beehive Architecture*, 2012–2021

Tomáš Libertíny, *The Gate* – in progress, *Beehive Architecture*, 2012–2021

Beehive Architecture, 2021

Tomáš Libertíny (Slovak, b.1979) of Studio Libertiny (The Netherlands, est.2007)

This installation consists of several 1:10 pavilion models that were generated and produced by honeybees in natural beeswax. The project gently harnesses the power and intelligence of nature to propose new modes of architectural experience as well as the economy of use of structural material.

The concept started in 2006 with experiments collaborating with honeybees by introducing a sophisticated artificial scaffolding in their beehive. The bees act together as a swarm and perform multiple and very complex architectural computations including measuring temperature, tensions, and structural load and size, given the constraints of local weather, the size of the beehive, and overall richness of the surrounding flora. The structure's informality and what might be called its imperfections bestow an inherent beauty. The process of building the hive can take from several weeks to a couple of years.

This project proposes that honeybees might also be of help in designing particular architectural structures for large-scale applications. Bees are cloud engineers: they can analyse and design lightweight, architectural skins. They marry the accuracy of technology with the organic characteristics of nature to create an architectural experience that is both aesthetic and functional. The final objects/pavilions from the beehives will be scanned using Computer Tomography and fabricated and assembled in segments at a different scale and with different material.

The beeswax pavilions are as much a beautiful testimony to the power of nature as they are a poetic translation of what the future of architecture could be. Only in using this back-and-forth process between nature and technology informing each other can humans remain in balance with their surrounding environment. In this, perhaps, lies an answer to how we might live together.

The Gate, beeswax sculpture, 30 × 30 × 60 cm;
The Chapel, beeswax sculpture, 40 × 40 × 70 cm;
The Junction, beeswax sculpture, 40 × 40 × 20 cm;
Passage, installation, white marble, 200 × 150 × 200 cm; video projection, 5', 500 × 250 cm

Philip Beesley, concept sketch of *Grove* cosmology, 2020

Philip Beesley Studio Inc., *Grove*, 2021.
Rendering of entrance to installation

Grove, 2021

Grove is a gathering space that offers a vision for inclusive open building. A soaring canopy of luminous, shimmering lacework clouds hovers above a central projection pool enclosed by a forest of delicate basket-like columns. An array of custom speakers embedded within the columns form a 3D soundscape by Amsterdam-based collaborators 4DSOUND and Salvador Breed. Visitors are immersed in forest-like shadow plays and fields of voices that range from gentle whispers to intense crescendos.

The concave, circular pool-like screen at the centre reveals a film by London filmmakers Warren du Preez and Nick Thornton Jones exploring intricate geometries that move from inert crystalline minerals into surging life forms. *Grove* is twinned with another interactive environment entitled *Meander*, located in Cambridge, Canada. The film expands the space of *Grove* with a virtual exploration of *Meander*'s interwoven layers and its constantly transforming immersive architecture. The fundamental journey in *Grove* is from stasis into movement, from death into life.

Free citizenship was long defined by protective city walls, yet those same walls have also fuelled catastrophic changes that befall us now. New scientific paradigms can offer a renewal for architecture. Entropy has long seemed the opposite of order, but emerging science suggests it can be redefined as a positive and creative force that seeks maximum freedom and potential. Like dissipative natural forms, such as clouds, waves and dunes, this new kind of architecture can maintain coherence while generating entropy in precarious restorative and healing qualities. *Grove* offers a vision where people can mesh their bodies with their surroundings, creating renewed and shared worlds grounded in empathy. The Vitruvian figure of classical times was framed by hardened crusts and pure shells. *Grove* reveals how a new fertile figure within open boundaries might replace that past creature.

Philip Beesley (Canadian, b.1956) of the University of Waterloo School of Architecture (Canada, est.1967) and Philip Beesley Studio Inc. (Canada, est. 1973), the Living Architecture Systems Group (Canada, est.2016)

Mixed physical and virtual media with software behaviour programming, 890 × 910 × 550 cm

As New Households

EXHIBITION ARSENALE

Much of the thinking about the dwelling unit has been based on the ideal and idea of a nuclear family. Suburban houses and the modern apartment units, both ubiquitous around the world, exalt the values and organisation of the single family with its deeply engrained notions of public and private: reception areas, dining rooms, kitchens, family rooms (dens), single bedrooms for the children, and carefully sequestered guest spaces. The values extend beyond the household; they touch on the organisation of society and the institutions that support it. The convergence of economic and ideological factors that may have led to the prevalence of this model are slowly giving in to many other values challenging the ideals of the nuclear family as the only model for living together at the household scale. Fewer than one third of households today around the world consist of nuclear families. The nuclear family is no longer as prevalent a model. Other models such as single dwellings, extended or multigenerational households, and other forms of cohabitation are growing around the world.

In this section architects present a breadth of responses to these ongoing social transformations from around the world. They include transformations from within the model of the nuclear family itself and from without. They also investigate the methods of production involved in housing construction, and they propose new technologies and typologies for new, often collaborative, models of household. The stations, in turn, focus on the histories and technologies of housing.

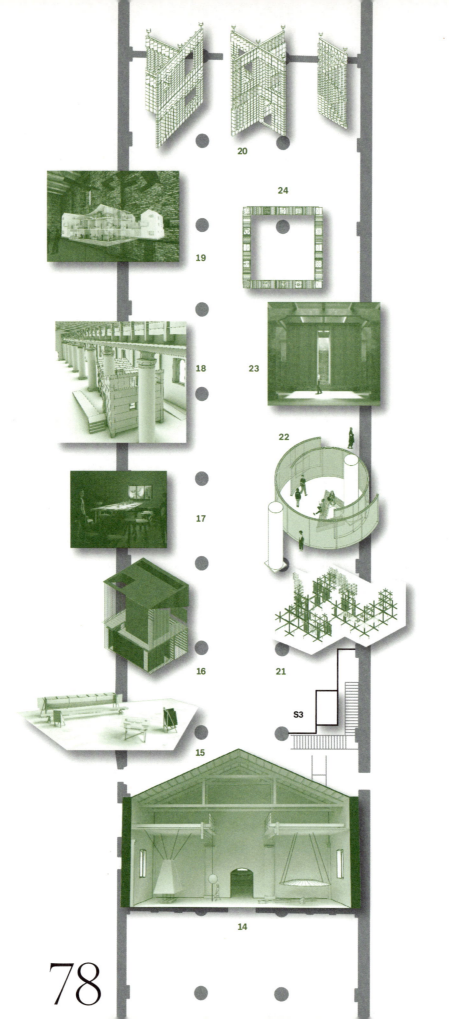

CATERING TO NEW DEMOGRAPHICS

AS NEW HOUSEHOLDS

14 OPAFORM architects
(Marina Bauer;
Espen Folgerø)
81

15 Leopold Banchini Architects
(with Lukas Feireiss and
Dylan Perrenoud)
83

16 K63.Studio
(Osborne Macharia)
85

17 Superflux
(Anab Jain; Jon Ardern)
87

18 AW-ARCH
(Alex Anmahian,
Nick Winton)
89

19 line+ studio
(Fanhao Meng)
91

20 leonmarcial arquitectos
(Alexia León; Lucho Marcial)
93

21 ecoLogicStudio
(Claudia Pasquero;
Marco Poletto)
95

22 Atelier RITA
(Valentine Guichardaz-Versini)
97

23 ROJO/FERNÁNDEZ-SHAW, ARQUITECTOS
(Begoña Fernández-Shaw;
Luis Rojo)
99

24 THE OPEN WORKSHOP
(Neeraj Bhatia; Antje Steinmuller)
101

S3 **STATION**: Mark Jarzombek and Vikramaditya Prakash et al.
102

Our demographics are changing. Our households are, too. In this room, the participants reflect on how changes in the shape and composition of the family, regarding who lives together under the same roof, will affect the architecture of the dwelling. Thus, these projects also respond to the housing necessities of refugees, migrants, aging populations as well as to communities who are economically and climatically vulnerable. They address these changes by exploring technologies of self-construction, ideas of densification, and the incorporation of spaces of work and production into the household. They also revisit typologies that are more adaptable to changing demographics and to a variety of gradients between individual and communal spaces.

OPAFORM, a module that provides comfort is added and the agricultural building is reprogrammed for tourism, *A Barn*, developed and built by OPAFORM, 2016

OPAFORM, strategies for abandoned farm buildings on the Norwegian west coast. By adding architectural modules in wool and wood, historic barns are infused with new life, *The Barns They Are A-Changin'*, 2015

Make a Space for My Body, 2019–2020

In exploring soft transformation of existing structures, OPAFORM adds independent modules to old buildings, providing them with new typologies embodying high spatial qualities.

This installation presents three anthropometrically scaled spaces. Through materiality, spatial properties, and formal expression, the modules engage in a direct dialogue with the historic exhibition space of the Biennale, incorporating the surrounding building envelope into the displayed project. The installation aims to enrich the architectural experience without diminishing the essence of the valuable existing space.

With the human body as a guideline, the modules are given shape according to programmatic needs of solitude or community. Their clear geometry promotes the subtle nuances of the surrounding space. An accentuated materiality is driven by the specific properties of wool and wood, with the two materials paired and refined into climatised forms to make spaces for bodies. In each module the materials are manipulated slightly differently, with techniques derived from vernacular traditions. Visitors can fully engage with the items by entering them, resting body and mind in a safe space within the busy atmosphere of the Biennale.

The city of tomorrow is largely already built. An important challenge for architects is to develop intelligent ways of utilising built environments without tearing parts of it down, acknowledging the limits of our planet's resources. The exhibited pieces are reversible additions that elaborate on scarcity and abundance by creating flexible spaces for living with soft footprints.

Marina Bauer (Finnish, b.1977) and Espen Folgerø (Norwegian, b.1980) with Nikolina Søgnen (Norwegian, b.1989), Turid Skåden (Norwegian, b.1992), Ziqian Zhang (Chinese, b.1991), Tord Øyen (Norwegian, b.1993) of OPAFORM (Norway, est.2011)

Structure: wood, prints on wood, woven and brushed cheviot wool suspended with spruce wood frames, dimensions variable; Suspended ball: Steam-bent laminated oak wood covered in nunofelted silk chiffon and merino tops, d. 120 cm; Platform: wood, 44 × 240 × 300 cm; Bowl: pine barrel construction with laminated oak tension band and steel base, covered in felt of mixed sheep wool, d. 500 × 50 cm

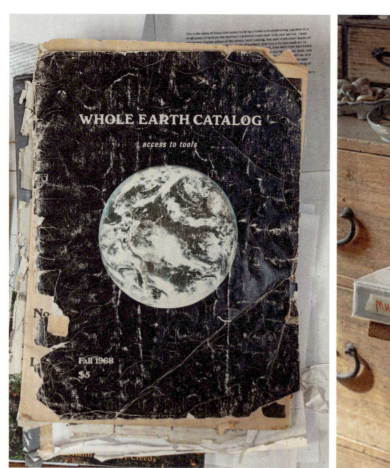

House of Lloyd Kahn, Bolinas, California, 2020

There Are Walls that Want to Prawl, 2020

There Are Walls that Want to Prawl shares, analyses, and speculates upon the content of three iconic counterculture publications on organic architecture published half a century ago by now 85-year-old publisher and builder Lloyd Kahn: *Domebook One* (1970), *Domebook 2* (1971), and *Shelter* (1973). The various 'de-growth' models presented in these books are discussed again as serious alternatives to conventional forms of building and living together.

Thanks to the paths opened by other sourcebooks such as *The Whole Earth Catalog* (1968), these publications gave agency to individuals and rapidly became highly successful how-to bibles of own-build construction. They provided access to the tools of the counterculture movements that praised ecology, self-sufficiency, and DIY methods of action. In the pre-internet age, these publications became major players as alternative educational tools and bestselling compendiums.

More than just manuals, these books also tell beautiful tales of the people who decided to create different households, reimagining a way of life in a more conscious relation with the environment, liberated from capital and its alienating methods of production. The critical reflection of the success and failure of these radically poetic and equally utopian constructions of the past provide an opportunity for insights for both present and future.

Mixing historical documents, contemporary interviews, natural experiments, and speculative architecture, *There Are Walls that Want to Prawl* acts as an imaginary landscape and discursive platform that juxtaposes the naturally grown with the artificially constructed. Here, structural models made from the wood of various homes and domes featured in Kahn's *Shelter* publication are presented alongside the more recent architectural models of architect Leopold Banchini, in combination with *in situ* mycological experimentations on mushroom growth, thus offering an alternative vision on how to live together in the future.

Leopold Banchini (Swiss, b.1981), with Lukas Feireiss (German, b.1977), Dylan Perrenoud (Swiss, b.1980), in collaboration with Lloyd Kahn (American, b.1935)

Audio recording, archival material, architectural models, mycological experimentations, glass vitrines, dimensions variable

Osborne Macharia, *KEJA 1.0*, 2021. Eastern view

Osborne Macharia, *KEJA 1.0*, 2021. Front view

KEJA, 2019

Osborne Macharia (Kenyan, b.1986) of K63.Studio (Kenya / Canada, est.2013), in collaboration with Cave Bureau (Kenya, b.2014)

Reclaimed shipping pallets, GI pipes, corrugated iron sheets, printed canvas, 628 × 458 × 516 cm

The technological and social awareness of African millennials has given rise to a new breed of young creatives in the slums of Nairobi. These creatives, thinkers, and makers are into different artistic expressions, but one thing is certain – they want to make a change in their surrounding and built environment to express who they are.

A majority of these millennials either do not have the financial capacity to move to more affluent urban dwellings or have family members who depend on them for financial support. The result is people customising their individual living spaces (most ranging between 15 m^2 to 20 m^2) into inspiring places where they can work, rest, and host/entertain. This space is what people call *KEJA* – Nairobi slang meaning home.

As empty land within informal settlements becomes scarce, will it challenge the creative individual to build above the pre-existing family unit? What will this look like? The solution has to be one of a utopian African future. A pragmatic solution is a functional, modern, culturally-aware and -situated, personal yet inclusive space. It fits a communal ecosystem that interacts more broadly with its environment and enhances community engagement.

Superflux, *Refuge for Resurgence*, 2020. Cutlery

Superflux, *Refuge for Resurgence*, 2020. Table

Superflux, *Refuge for Resurgence*, 2020. Window view

Refuge for Resurgence, 2020

Having survived Earth's abrupt shift to an era of precarious climate, a multispecies community gather in the blasted ruins of modernity to find new ways of living together.

Working together to carve out a new world from the smouldering remains of the old. Working together to forge enduring forms of sharing and survival. Working together to revive this land, once a place of order and control. A place where all species, all forms of life, were once forced to submit to an alien law. A law that dictated what could live and where. A law that labelled anything that did not obey its monolithic order: 'weed', 'pest', or 'vermin'. A law that for a time felt relentless, unending, unstoppable; until the planet rebelled and threw this house of cards to the wind. Now, in the ruins of that old world, those weeds, pests, and vermin have risen and reclaimed their rightful place at the table of planetary ecology.

Their rightful place in a new home. A home built on humility, resourcefulness, and imagination. A home strong enough to weather the storm, to rise from the flood, to endure the heat.

Humans, animals, birds, plants, moss, and fungi gathering around a shared hope. A hope in the life that remains. A hope in the resurgence of life stretched thin around this rock, painting its surface blue and green as it spins wildly in the vast blackness.

Superflux's installation, *Refuge for Resurgence*, is a multi-species banquet set after the end of the world. Centred around a majestic oak table, the scene lays bare a conversation between the paralysis of fear and the audacity of hope.

Anab Jain (Indian/British, b.1976) and Jon Ardern (UK, b.1978) of Superflux, London, (UK, est.2009) in collaboration with Sebastian Tiew (Malaysian, b.1994)

Table: wood, 70 × 450 × 140 cm; Table settings, dimensions variable; Stools: wood, 50 × 50 cm, heights variable; Tools: natural and reclaimed waste such as discarded plastic, circuit board, salvaged metal, dimensions variable; Display screen, 146 × 251 × 6 cm; Ceramic plates, dimensions variable.

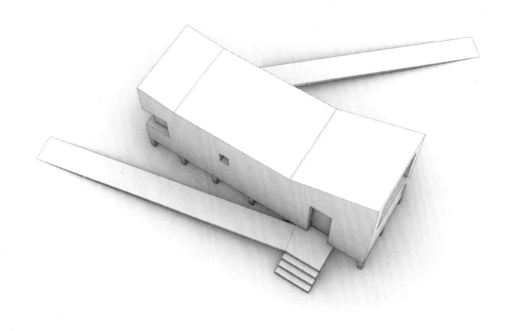

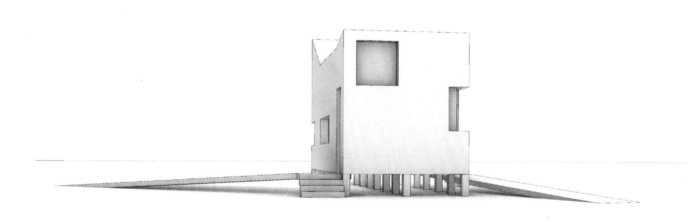

All images: AW-ARCH, *House+Plus*, 2021

House+Plus, 2021

Alex Anmahian (American, b.1959) and Nick Winton (American, b.1961) of AW-ARCH (USA, est.1992) in collaboration with Chris Corson (American, b.1972) of Ecocor (USA, est.2009)

1:1 outdoor installation, 420 × 1260 × 36 cm; Indoor installation: scaled models, modular composite wood panels, modular plywood furniture, digitally printed drawings, dimensions variable

The notion of the accessory dwelling unit (ADU) in the United States has evolved over the recent past, from meaning an in-law accommodation – in support of multi-generational living in cities with minimal housing options – to being understood as a sustainable form of intensifying demographic diversity by attracting a rich cross-section of the socio-economic spectrum. By strategically locating ADUs within underutilised urban lots and suburban backyards, inevitable densification is achieved through an infusion of tiny housing among existing units, rather than through the introduction of large-scale apartment blocks. As it addresses housing needs, the ADU can be environmentally beneficial to its community and has the potential to enrich existing neighbourhoods by providing economical housing for a variety of lifestyle choices.

House+Plus is an approach to the ADU project with the following preconditions: mass customisation; limited set of modular components; passive-house standards; and reconfigurable interior space. In essence, it is a case study of a house enclosure within which modular furniture defines space and life. Here, modularity encourages spatial configurations and compositional fenestration that freely responds to the specific needs of private life, just as it actively participates in forming and informing collective space.

The modularity of the building panels is systematic in nature, allowing customisation of building form, quality of light, and spatial arrangement. The modular furniture is designed for ease of transport, configuration, and reconfiguration, as needs or lifestyles change. The furniture is further intended to inspire invention and imagination in practical use as well as spatial organisation. The furniture modules have no intended top or bottom, leaving each inhabitant free to choose, organise, and enhance the system.

All images: line+ studio, *Dongziguan Affordable Housing*, 2016

Rural Nostalgia | Urban Dream, 2018

Meng Fanhao (Chinese, b.1979) of line+ studio (China, est.2018)

Physical model of Dongziguan (1:30), resin and plaster, 1050 × 500 cm; physical model of *Stray Bird Art Hotel* (1:25), 100 × 35 cm; physical model of teahouse in Jiuxing village (1:40), 60 × 60 cm

The three projects, *Dongziguan Affordable Housing*, *Stray Bird Art Hotel • Songyang*, and *Teahouse in Jiuxing Village*, represented in this installation are not only about the design of spaces, but also the design of rural communal experiences guided by architectural design.

The urban and rural realms have increasingly become an inseparable social ecosystem. To be responsive to these conditions, architectural design should consider the experience of its end users and be reflective of the local lifestyles where it is situated. Offering high-quality local experience and engaging a unique natural environment should be considered together for architecture to seamlessly integrate traditional regional contexts and contemporary lifestyles. Through such design, one can build rural experiences for urban people and build urban dreams for rural villagers in seeking to understand how we will live together.

Rural Nostalgia | Urban Dream is an installation that mainly consists of a large 1:30 street space model of the Dongziguan village. The streets and lanes are empty and the buildings are solid. At its entrance are eight typical family houses and a village activity center, which aim to represent programmatic uses and life scenes from the village. Visitors can walk into the streets and alleys to experience a representation of the daily life of villagers from the perspective of human beings, forming an interactive relationship between street space, rural life, and exhibition experience.

leonmarcial arquitectos, *Interwoven*, 2021. West view

Interwoven, 2021

Alexia León (Peruvian, b.1970) and Lucho Marcial (Peruvian, b.1962) of leonmarcial arquitectos (Peru, est.2012)

Screen walls (2), each 345 × 613 × 30 cm; Panguana wood blocks (over 1800), metal 700 × 1250 × 700 cm

Households interact with their environments. They form networks that spatially modify, manage, and control their territories. Not only do they allow one to gain environmental awareness at a territorial scale, but households might also transform crucial relationships for cohabitating at the most immediate levels. Such a dynamic of social exchange would allow a culture of living that plays a critical role in how we will live in the future, as a response to conditions of local and global change. When understood as an environmental pattern, within the process of urbanisation, the act of sharing and exchange among households allows the latter to regain a decisive political role on a planetary scale.

This installation celebrates the interweaving of households and their environments using architectural means. Reinterpreting the lines of domestic private property which often restrict one's notion of households leads to a transformation at the broader, public level, one which allows for the construction of open structures that provide more equitable and dynamic opportunities for change. *Interwoven* presents a spatial fragment focused on transitions and interactions between households that dissolve outside–inside and public–private boundaries, thus reshaping the way people interact and coexist.

The intent to reshape communal relationships should transform architecture at all of its scales: this includes rethinking basic building blocks. Architecture should be able to respond directly to rapid changes in temperature, cross ventilation, light, programmes, and visual needs. This installation presents one such dynamic system and uses a tropical fast-growth reforested wood of the Peruvian Amazonia. Panguana (*Brosimum utile ssp. ovatifolium*) is generally discarded in construction practices but commonly used by native artisans who, with the usual generosity of ancestral cultures, share the secret of its use.

ecoLogicStudio, *PhotoSynthetica Tower*, 2019. Interior court of the *PhotoSynthetica Tower* with view towards the Bio.Tech.Comb labs

ecoLogicStudio, *HORTUS XL Astaxanthin.g*, Centre Pompidou, Paris, 2019. Front view of the 1:1 scale living prototype sculpture and cyber-gardeners at work

ecoLogicStudio, *BioBombola*, London, 2020. Domestic Algae Garden in a London warehouse

BIT.BIO.BOT.
A Collective Experiment in Biotechnological Architecture, 2021

Claudia Pasquero (Italian, b.1974) and Marco Poletto (Italian, b.1975) of ecoLogicStudio (UK, est.2005), with the Synthetic Landscape Lab at Innsbruck University (Austria, est.2017) and the Urban Morphogenesis Lab at the Bartlett UCL (UK, est.2012)

Lab grade borosilicate glass, 3D-printed PLA bioplastic, living cultures of Spirulina platensis in liquid and jellified medium, stainless steel, dimensions variable

BIT.BIO.BOT. installation is a 1:1 scale experiment in the cultivation of the urban microbiome. It is designed to test a model of permanent co-existence between human and non-human organisms in the post-pandemic *urbansphere*. The installation's biotechnological architecture acts as a medium to tackle several urban vulnerabilities. Its core biological mechanism is photosynthesis, powered by the sun and the metabolism of living cultures of *Spirulina platensis*. One of Earth's oldest organisms, *Spirulina* is an edible cyanobacterium capable of re-metabolising pollutants in the air to transform them into one of the world's most nutritious foods.

This is a real urban laboratory. It combines advanced architecture with microbiology to build an artificial habitat, a dwelling where urban algae can be grown collectively. Every phase of the project's conception, fabrication, cultivation, and post-Biennale repurposing contributes to the experiment of coexistence.

The advanced architectural system is the result of ten years of bio-digital design research and combines computational design strategies (BIT) with proprietary digital fabrication techniques (BOT) to implement a collective microbiological cultivation protocol (BIO). Each unit is modular and independent. After the 17th International Architecture Exhibition, each cultivation unit will become an educational algae garden and find its permanent location at the participating schools and research institutions. The microbiological gardens will be part of biology labs and educational programmes on urban air quality and future food. Pupils will be able to use them regularly to develop novel urban practices of planetary cultivation.

The post-Biennale collective experiment will inform the future of the *BIT.BIO.BOT* project into a distributed synthetic urban organism in which bacteria, autonomous electronic devices, digital algorithms, and other forms of non-human intelligence coexist.

Atelier RITA, *Emergency Shelter for Refugees and Roma Community*, 2017

Listen Up, 2017

The *Emergency Shelter for Refugees and Roma Community* is a project commissioned by the non-profit organisation Emmaüs Solidarité as part of a solution to the continuous influx of refugees into Paris. It is located in a disused water treatment plant in the suburban city of Ivry-sur-Seine. This large disused industrial site (90,000 m²) awaits a new urban project. The *Emergency Shelter* was built to house 400 people for a period of six months.

This humanitarian programme raises questions about the current state of the world and appears to challenge architects. The *Emergency Shelter* looks into architecture for basic needs while also engaging questions on how to design spaces for dignified living and with functional qualities to vulnerable populations who come from different cultures. The project is thought of as a town, a common habitat regardless of the geographic and national origins of its inhabitants. From its most public to its most intimate spaces, the shelter is designed for an easy transition into community life.

The *Emergency Shelter* needed to be built very quickly – it took four months and one week between November 2016 and March 2017 – which naturally led to resorting to a prefabrication system. This presented another opportunity – reuse – which makes sense in terms of resilient architecture. In the logic of a circular economic model, a second life can be imagined for the prefabricated wood modules. They could even be reused on another site, especially since the *Emergency Shelter* is planned to remain on this site for five years only.

The installation gives voice to people living in the shelter through interviews and conversations initiated around the concept of the household and guided by the thematic question *How will we live together?* Shelter residents share their stories and memories about their lives here and elsewhere. What emerged was that living together is, undeniably, sharing together and listening to each other.

Valentine Guichardaz-Versini (French, b.1985), with Emilie Bonnaire (French, b.1992) and Gaspard Brousse (French, b.1993) of Atelier RITA (France, est.2016), in collaboration with David Bourreau (Franco-Dutch, b.1971) of DB Film (France, est.1995)

Fabric curtains, recycled plastic, stand steel structure with rails, projection video, audio, dimensions variable

Rojo/Fernández-Shaw, *Imagined Households / Intensified References*, 2019–2020. General view

Rojo/Fernández-Shaw, *Imagined Households / Intensified References*, 2019–2020. Close-up view

Imagined Households / Intensified References, 2019–2020

Luis Rojo (Spanish, b.1962) and Begoña Fernández-Shaw (Spanish, b.1962) of Rojo/Fernández-Shaw, arquitectos (Spain, est.1994), in collaboration with Franco Gilardi (Argentine, b.1992) & Luis Moreda (Spanish, b.1994)

Metal frame, ceramic tubes, honeycomb wood composite panels, digital images, mirror panels, 500 × 500 × 490 cm

Economic flows, informational networks, transnational organisations, logistical management, transportation infrastructures, capital logic, and consumer culture are predicated on permanent states of continuity. A flowing reality that engulfs not just objects but also humans in two simultaneous processes: the movement of migrants and the movement of tourists.

Both rely on the continuous movement of bodies and the factual collapse of physical boundaries. The first is a forced displacement, the second an intensified experience. One is driven by necessity, the other indulges on entertainment. For opposed reasons and through inverse channels, migrants and tourists override national borders, occupy transient spaces, re-enact imaginary identities and pursue a simulated sense of permanence. And though they share these mechanisms inadvertently, together they have come to define persistent patterns of displacement and relationship with places, cities, landscapes, histories, and memories.

The transient body of the tourist and the displaced identity of the migrant undermine the conventions of space conceived through limits, domesticity founded on stability, or identities built on actual memories. They occupy a new social and physical environment characterised by the collapse of space, the extension of the generic, and the agency of intensified referential images.

Imagined Households / Intensified References displays four digitally made images and their reflection within four virtual rooms. The images contain coded references through which identities are constructed and displacements are channelled. The delocalised referential clichés of comfort and consumption that instigate the desire – or the need – to displace are confined as images within other images inside the impersonal architectures of migration and tourism. Four images that represent four different configurations of an imaginary space of displacement, digitally constructed to reproduce the hyper-reality of intensified references for migrants and tourists. Four reflections; the constructed visions and imaginary references are enhanced by the virtuality of the mirror image and its specular intensification. Four interior spaces that, though configured as rooms, are visible yet inaccessible.

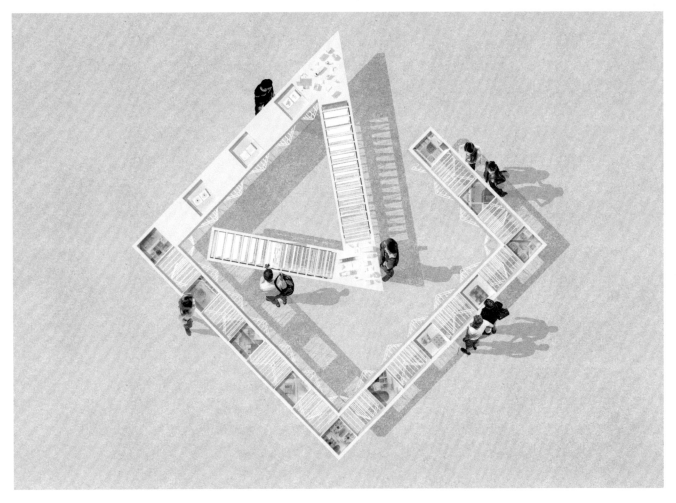

All images: The Open Workshop, *Commoning Domestic Space*, 2018-2020. Commune Prototype

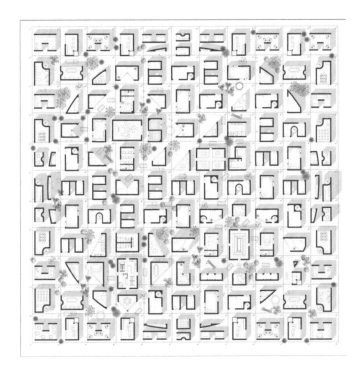

Commoning Domestic Space, 2018–2020

How and where to locate collective values are at the core of reconciling what it means to live in a pluralistic society. If pluralism is to be understood as the dialectic of individual distinction and collective equality, the public realm becomes the arena for political negotiation. How individuals and collectives are mediated through architecture is most clearly manifested in co-living housing typologies, where a renegotiation between public and private realms offers new social and spatial arrangements. *Commoning Domestic Space* unpacks precisely that by looking closely at hardware, software, and *orgware* – a set of organisational and governance structures that rule a space – as a way of providing more agency to residents with respect to how they can live together.

Today, urban dwellers are often starving for more affordable housing to allow them to create meaningful social units and embrace contemporary ways of living while still reflecting alternative family forms. *Commoning Domestic Space* is a design and research project that uses 35 case studies – built, speculative, designed, and informal – and five speculative designs to better understand the role of: (i) *hardware* of spatial arrangements, their frameworks, and the physical interfaces between the public and private; (ii) *software* or the social types that inhabit these spaces, their family units, communal endeavours, forms of reappropriation, and scales of sharing; and (iii) *orgware*, which includes governance structures, distribution of domestic labour, and the organisation of economics, resources, and power.

Living together is difficult – it requires sacrifice, patience, and flexibility. Moreover, sharing space with others is predicated on an ability to assert identity and lay claim over private territory. Creating a closer fit between the physical form of domestic space and its social and governance structures requires an in-depth examination of spatial strategies and of the process through which they are produced. Most importantly, the projects in *Commoning Domestic Space* centre on the building, maintenance, and governance of a domestic commons, which has offered meaningful social units around shared activities, institutions of culture, community, and empowerment.

Neeraj Bhatia (Canadian, b.1980) of The Open Workshop (Canada/ USA, est.2013), supported by research by Neeraj Bhatia and Antje Steinmuller (German, b.1971) of CCA Urban Works Agency (USA, est.2013)

Physical Models (10), wood, card, concrete, 48 × 48 × 10 cm; Computer Monitors (4), 3D prints (35), plastic, resin, 7.5 × 7.5 × 7 cm; overall installation, wood, steel, 554 × 554 × 103 cm

Many Houses/ Many Worlds, 2021

Many Houses/Many Worlds is a collaboration between O(U)R, the Office of Uncertainty Research, and MIT GAHTC, the Global Architectural Teaching Collaborative.

O(U)R is a design research practice dedicated to rethinking architecture in terms of the emergent scientific, social, and political parameters of the twenty-first century. O(U)R projects explore the entanglement between the planet and the cosmos. *A House Deconstructed*, showcased in this 17th International Architecture Exhibition, looks at a recently constructed house in Seattle, Washington, and analyses it according to four vectors, each of which we interpret as a type of consciousness that is silenced once the owners get the keys to the front door: 1) Atomic consciousness; 2) Production Consciousness; 3) Labour Consciousness; and 4) Source Consciousness. The study showed not just the astonishing globality that is at play in making even a small house, but also the high degree of uncertainty in how to describe the backstory of the building, even though that backstory is foundational to the project of modernity.

GAHTC's mission is to provide cross-disciplinary, teacher-to-teacher exchanges of ideas and material in order to energise and promote the teaching of all periods of global architectural history, especially at the survey level. Importantly, it aims to support teachers in the classroom as an integral part of education.

The GAHTC portion of the installation features an interactive screen that allows viewers to navigate the Earth to highlight houses from around the world. These structures will range from the humble to the grand, even including some unexpected 'houses' such as tea and coffee houses, ice houses, school houses, and the like. All houses shown in the exhibit are part of the ongoing research by members of GAHTC.

Mark Jarzombek (American, b.1954) and Vikramaditya 'Vikram' Prakash (American, b.1963) of The Global Architectural History Teaching Collaborative, GAHTC (USA, est.2013) at MIT (USA, est.1861) in collaboration with Vikramaditya 'Vikram' Prakash of Architecture Uncertainty Lab, A(U)L (USA, est.2020) at MIT, The University of Washington (USA, est.1861), and Eliana Abu-Hamdi (American, b.1979) of GAHTC

Materials and dimensions variable

UNA CASA DECOSTRUITA
A HOUSE DECONSTRUCTED

STATION

Paul Montie Design, *Many Houses/Many Worlds*, 2021. AUL / GAHTC installation

100DANISH, *Many Houses/Many Worlds*, 2021. GAHTC, interactive experience

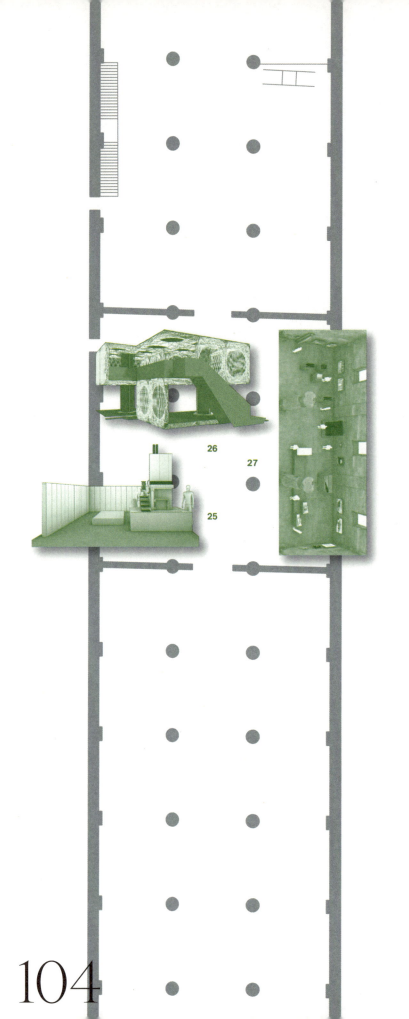

INHABITING NEW TECTONICS

AS NEW HOUSEHOLDS

25 NADAAA
(Nader Tehrani;
Arthur Chang)
107

26 Achim Menges / ICD
University of Stuttgart
and Jan Knippers / ITKE
University of Stuttgart
(Achim Menges;
Jan Knippers)
109

27
27 Gramazio Kohler
Architects / NCCR DFAB
(Fabio Gramazio;
Matthias Kohler)
111

A century ago, when cement and the concrete frame were introduced into housing construction, they led to the open plan layout of the house and in turn to changing conceptions of privacy within the household. Slowly, walls between the public and private areas of the house started coming down.

This room explores how new materials and technologies are prompting architects to reimagine dwellings. The projects also present more efficient and creative ways of using natural resources. They also connect between the practices of building a house and the practices of inhabiting it. Ultimately, they elevate new materials and methods of construction into new poetics of inhabitation.

NADAAA, *Rural Apartment Cabin, CLT Panel Assembly*, 2020

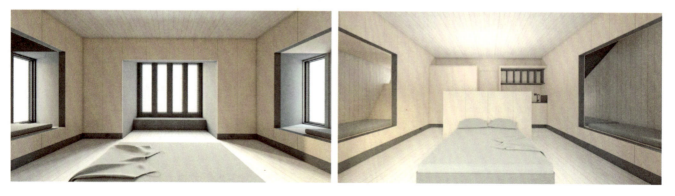

NADAAA, *Rural Apartment Cabin, Inner Sanctum*, 2020

Other Ways of Living Together, 2021

Nader Tehrani (Iranian-American, b.1963) and Arthur Chang (American, b.1977) of NADAAA (USA, est.2010)

Physical model, digital printing, dimensions variable

This project inspects the country house in the rural landscape, which is often conventionally thought of as a luxury; and yet, one is reminded about how the social landscape of rural areas has changed in recent times. The necessity of social distancing brought forth by Covid-19, the possibilities of working productively online, and the dynamic nature of the family unit all point to the need for new forms of flexibility to live together. As such, this work offers varied configurations of programmatic adaptability that allow for total cohesion or relative autonomy for the various segments of the building. In this respect, the country house could serve as a *Rural Apartment Cabin* depending on how it is used.

The *Rural Apartment Cabin* also revolves around material research, whose efficiencies allow for strategic uses of building technologies. The organisation involves a staircase that winds around the periphery of a stacked, one-room structure linking two wall systems, one solid, cross-laminated timber (CLT) and the other hollow-balloon framed. If conventional construction revolves around 4' by 8' sheet panels, or masonry blocks at 8" by 16", or other such diminutive modules, CLT radicalises the possibility of gargantuan dimensions whose width and height for this structure average 8' by 24'.

The CLT is especially advantageous with its large panel sizes, off-site construction, low tolerances, and thermal mass, and the stick frame within relies on its hollow core to thread its mechanical, electrical, and plumbing systems strategically to the stacked rooms without any added horizontal ducting. The two wall systems need each other, while the double layer offers the inner core of the rooms added environmental insulation. Equally importantly, this unique stair allows for access to rooms without ancillary corridors, minimising net to gross waste; in turn, the liminal spaces above and below the stairs allow for additive programs such as sleeping bunks, toilets, showers and storage areas within the depth of this thickened mass, in effect, redefining a new approach to *Existenzminimum*.

University of Stuttgart, Institute for Computational Design and Construction
(ICD, Achim Menges et al.) and ITKE Institute of Building Structures and Structural Design
(Jan Knippers et al.), M*aterial Culture*, 2021. Perspective view

University of Stuttgart, Institute for Computational Design and Construction
(ICD, Achim Menges et al.) and ITKE Institute of Building Structures and Structural Design
(Jan Knippers et al.), *Material Culture*, 2021. Photo of slab-component mock-up (1:5)

Material Culture: Rethinking the Physical Substrate for Living Together, 2021

Construction ranks among the human activities that consume materials the most and is significantly detrimental to the environment. Explorations into a new material culture in architecture are, therefore, necessary. Nature provides just such a paradigmatic alternative: almost all biological, load-bearing structures are made from fibre composites. Fibrous construction offers a profoundly different material approach for building human habitats in the future.

Maison Fibre – the central component of this installation – is a radical model of a material future for architecture. Developed for the 17th International Architecture Exhibition, it is the first inhabitable, multistorey, fibrous structure of its kind, made entirely from glass and carbon fibre composites. Each building element is individually tailored using a robotic fabrication process, resulting in a distinctive expression while using a minimal amount of material. A change in material culture entails larger ecological (material and energy), economic (value chains and knowledge production), technical (digital technologies and robotics), and sociocultural matters – all notions that are embodied in *Maison Fibre*. The latter showcases an architecture of minimal impact and allows visitors to explore a novel material articulation, one which reduces fiftyfold the weight footprint of buildings compared to Le Corbusier's model for the twentieth century.

The two complementary elements of the installation, entitled *Materialisation* and *Materiality Perspectives*, display the multiyear research on robotic materialisation strategies. They also indicate the manifold materiality of a fibrous architecture, ranging from mineral fibres capable of withstanding extreme conditions to natural fibres that can grow in annual crop cycles.

Achim Menges (German, b.1975) with Niccolò Dambrosio (Italian, b.1988), Rebeca Duque Estrada (Brazilian, b.1989), Fabian Kannenberg (German, b.1991), Katja Rinderspacher (German, b.1978), Christoph Schlopschnat (German, b.1988), and Christoph Zechmeister (Austrian, b.1985) of ICD Institute for Computational Design and Construction (Germany, est.2008), Cluster of Excellence IntCDC at the University of Stuttgart, and Jan Knippers (German, b.1962) with Nikolas Früh (German, b.1987), Marta Gil Pérez (Spanish, b.1986), Riccardo La Magna (Italian, b.1982) at ITKE Institute of Building Structures and Structural Design (Germany, est.1950), Cluster of Excellence IntCDC, University of Stuttgart

1:1 material prototype, glass fibre and carbon fibre composites, 1000 × 1000 × 577 cm

Gramazio Kohler Architects, *NEST*, 2016.
NEST – original state

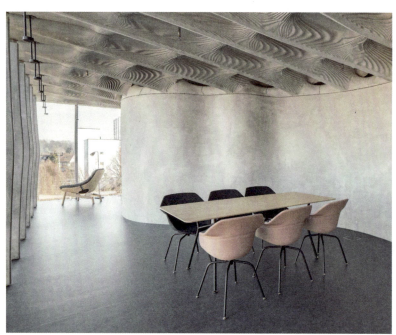

NCCR DFAB, *DFAB HOUSE*, 2019. Communal Area

Gramazio Kohler Architects, *NEST*, 2016. Atrium

Research as Architecture: A Laboratory for Houses, Homes, and Robots, 2019

Research as Architecture presents a design attitude that proactively curates spatial, temporal, and technological processes that reach beyond form and create novel identities responding to the complexity and unpredictability of our planet.

The installation is a visual journey through two exemplary and radical projects. It presents the design of *NEST*, a dynamic plug-in platform for architectural research and innovative building technologies, and *DFAB HOUSE*, an experimental building that demonstrates research in computational design and digital fabrication. As *DFAB HOUSE* literally plugs into *NEST*, the visitor is confronted with hitherto unseen entanglements of architectural scales, temporalities, and authorships.

Used as an academic guesthouse and experimental office space, *NEST* serves as a living lab for sustainable construction. It consists of a central structure, media backbone, and flexible platforms that allow for the exchange of complete living and working units in a plug-and-play mode.

DFAB HOUSE is a collaborative design and research demonstrator on the *NEST* building. As part of the full-featured building project, researchers from seven chairs of ETH Zurich have joined industry experts and planning professionals to explore and test how digital fabrication can change the way we design and build.

The installation presents a sequence that invites the visitor to discover the conceptual relationship between the two projects. On the one hand, *NEST* addresses the central question of how to design an architectural structure that is open-ended by definition and introduces the context set for the *DFAB HOUSE*. On the other hand, *DFAB HOUSE*, as one example of many possible plug-in buildings, embraces *NEST*'s invitation as incubator to spark a worldwide, unique, interdisciplinary collaboration of architects and scientists.

Fabio Gramazio (Swiss, b.1970) and Matthias Kohler (Swiss, b.1968) of Gramazio Kohler Architects (Switzerland, est.2000) + Gramazio Kohler Research ETH Zurich (Switzerland, est.2005) in collaboration with Benjamin Dillenburger (German, b.1977), Jonas Buchli (Swiss, b.1977), Robert Flatt (Swiss, b.1969), Joseph Schwartz (Swiss, b.1957), Walter Kaufmann (Swiss, b.1967), Guillaume Habert (French, b.1977) and Konrad Graser (German, b.1977) of ETH Zurich (Switzerland, est.1855) + NCCR Digital Fabrication (Switzerland, est.2014)

Architectural models (1:50 and 1:10), digital prints on aluminium, videos, 1:1 prototypes, dimensions variable

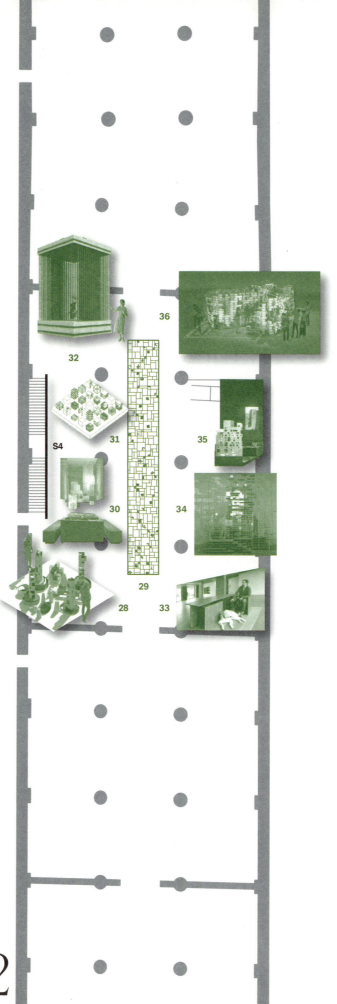

LIVING APART TOGETHER

AS NEW HOUSEHOLDS

28	Fernanda Canales 115
29	Aires Mateus (Francisco Aires Mateus; Manuel Aires Mateus) 117
30	Alison Brooks Architects 119
31	LIN Architects Urbanists (Finn Geipel) 121
32	BAAG Buenos Aires Arquitectura Grupal (Griselda Balian; Gastón Noriega; Gabriel Monteleone) 123
33	Farshid Moussavi Architecture 125
34	nicolas laisné architectes 127
35	Lina Ghotmeh— Architecture 129
36	SsD (Jinhee Park) 131
S4	**STATION**: Abalos+Sentkiewicz AS+; Iñaki Ábalos 132
	STATION: Anne Kockelkorn and Susanne Schindler et al. 136
	STATION: Daisy Ames, Bernadette Baird-Zars, Adam Frampton et al. 140

A city is born when two houses share a wall. The apartment building represents the archetype of urban life and of living together. This room is dedicated to the apartment building, in different permutations brought together from across the world to celebrate; it explores new cohabitation variables: degrees of compactness, kinds of sharing, and different conceptions of privacy and collectivity. Its broad range of scales and designs attests to architecture's role in experimenting and imagining communal life. It also suggests a wealth of possibilities waiting to be explored.

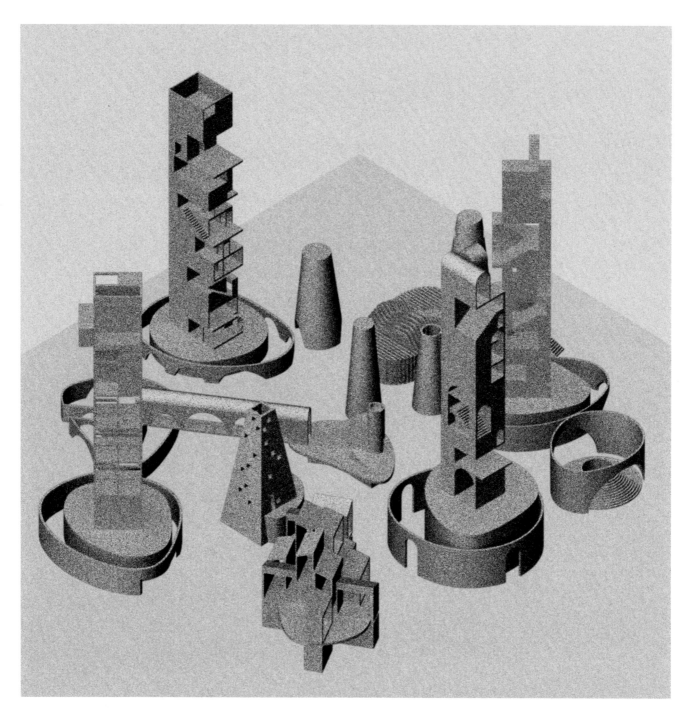

Fernanda Canales, *After the House*, 2021. Vertical *vecindades* and collective spaces with no divisions between living/working, private/public, owners/dispossessed

After the House: Privacy in a Shared World, 2021

Fernanda Canales (Mexican, b.1974)

Physical models (16), acrylic, PVC, dimensions variable

How will we live together? In houses that redefine ownership, the relation between private and public space, and collectivity.

This project revokes the oppositions between public and private, owners and dispossessed, and living and working. The focus lies on the space that exists between the private realm of a bed and the collective sphere of a sidewalk.

After the House consists of four models showing housing projects designed as a reinterpretation of *vecindades*, urban multifamily tenements with mixed-use housing arranged around courtyards with shared services. These were a main typology in Mexico in the past three centuries and essentially forgotten after the 1950s. This project redefines the historical *vecindades* typology in order to portray flexible design and a shared sense of belonging. It is a project that seeks more diverse ways of living, by acknowledging the fact that citizens share space, air, water, and cities.

The models in the installation are an abstract reinterpretation of a housing project, Viviendas Monte Albán, recently completed by the architect in Mexico in 2020. Four vertical models allow visitors to understand the private spaces and the spatial configuration of the interiors, as well as how the different apartments relate to each other across collective spaces. It is a project that reflects the idea of building a versatile system based on the coexistence of individual needs and collective desires.

Aires Mateus, *Ground*, 2021. View 01

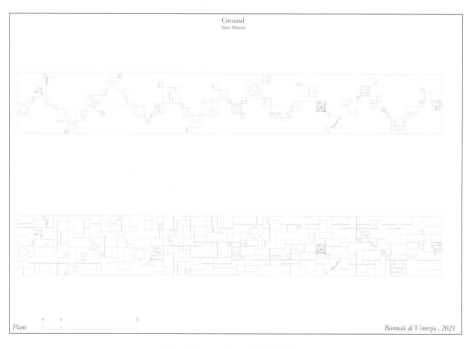

Aires Mateus, *Ground*, 2021. Plans

Ground, 2021

Francisco Aires Mateus (Portuguese, b.1964) and Manuel Aires Mateus (Portuguese, b.1963) of Aires Mateus (Portugal, est.1988)

Hand made concrete slabs, gold finishing, 2210 × 300 × 8 cm

Architecture answers to its time. Some things, however, never change: we live together under the same sky; we live together on the same ground. The sky above our head, the ground under our feet: a natural metaphor of community. To recover this evidence, this installation emphasises the relation between what is above and below us: by taking root in the earth, *Ground* allows us to apprehend the immense ceiling.

Confined and still open, this piece consists of 345 square and rectangular concrete elements distributed along 22 metres in length and 3 metres in width. The central backbone of this work is formed by 60 of these elements which show, dug in their thickness, a possible spatiality.

Ground establishes a deep bond with the place in which it is inserted, evoking its nature: the alternation of intact and excavated surfaces gives life to a micro-landscape in continuity with the floor of the Corderie where it is exhibited; the horizontal unfolding along the ground opposes the vertical development of the columns of the building; the concrete carpet emphasises the longitudinal attribute of the nave.

Simultaneously, other meanings that transcend time and place are disclosed: the excavated concrete blocks evoke the primitive act of digging, adding a further, autonomous level of interpretation.

In the overlap between the correspondence to a specific space and the independence from it lies the deepest meaning of *Ground*: it belongs to one place and at the same time it is able to recall others.

Such is the ambition of architecture: to reveal what is already there, to disclose a new awareness, to draw the void in between, to affirm our human condition.

To do so, one ground is enough.

Alison Brooks Architects, *Home Ground*, 2020–2021. Axonometric drawing

Home Ground, 2020–2021

Alison Brooks (Canadian, b.1962) of Alison Brooks Architects (UK, est.1996)

Housing defines the way we live together in cities – as households and by shaping collective ground. Each of Alison Brooks Architects' housing projects consciously frames urban space at street level. They are also often enlivened with sheltered and internal spaces where diverse communities can congregate in new kinds of 'home ground'. By bringing disparate projects together, this installation aims not for the 'ideal city' but, rather, one that reflects the contingencies and complexities that shaped each of them.

Physical models, table, screen, 475 × 314 × 333 cm

City neighbourhoods are largely formed by housing at a typological level: block arrangements, plan organisation, density, service, and communal spaces. Architecture shapes them at a closer level – through its forms, proportions, materials, and detail. Twenty-first-century housing is also where people work, create, and communicate in the infinite space of a digital universe. There is now, therefore, a need to rethink the architecture of housing as civic infrastructure that enables human potential. It must nurture day-to-day personal experience and creative work and also support collective public life. It must be generous enough to enable multiple uses over time. It must offer a form of cultural identity that enables communities to feel at home. It must help make daily life beautiful.

Home Ground represents housing projects as ephemeral veils that hover above a table. In contrast, earth-bound arcades, halls, commons, forums, and workspaces ground each building. These shared spaces suggest a condition of reciprocity between the private realms of housing and their public context. Casting them into the surface of a table invites the Biennale's global audience to coalesce momentarily and begin new conversations. Is it possible to reconceive housing as civic buildings that offer a more generous, complex, and poetic framework for living together?

LIN Architects Urbanists, *Bremer Punkt I*, 2011–Ongoing

Bremer Punkt, 2011—ONGOING

Finn Geipel (German, b.1958), with Giulia Andi (Italian, b.1972), John Klepel (German, b.1982) of LIN Architects Urbanists (Germany, est.2001)

Physical models (25), wood, acrylic glass, gypsum, cardboard, paper, rigid foam, c. 30 × 30 × 30 cm each

Rising housing market pressures call for novel solutions. How can one meet the urgent need for affordable housing, despite constantly rising construction costs? Urban extensions notwithstanding, inward development is conceived as the most sustainable approach for urban growth. The focus is shifting towards raising density in centres and peripheries. Building cities within cities provides opportunities to vary the urban fabric and to enhance the social, typological, and programmatic mix.

In 2011, the adaptable *Bremer Punkt* building type was developed for the *Ungewöhnlich Wohnen* (Unusual Living) competition, offering opportunities to prototype infill buildings with a variety of contemporary, affordable, and flexible housing in modernist, post-war housing schemes. On a footprint of about 14 × 14 metres, the four-storey timber cube flexibly plugs in to the urban fabric, sensitively responding to the existing structure. It is surgically inserted in order to activate niches in the urban fabric, while retaining the neighbourhood character, defined by its green spaces.

The new buildings' modular hybrid construction allows for a wide range of designs able to respond to individual demands and offer site-specific solutions. Access, housing mix, and façade can be tailored to the site. New buildings can provide between 4 and 11 flats. In total 22 flat types can be configured in various layouts and stacked on 4 floors almost at will. Thanks to its modular system, the *Bremer Punkt* offers solutions for diverse and socially mixed populations in both subsidised and free-market housing.

The installation in Venice is a field of 25 models at a scale of 1:50, addressing an array of topics ranging from inhabitants' needs to various forms of collective living and various configurations at an urban scale.

All images: BAAG, *Architecture of Transitions*, 2021. Perspective views

Architecture of Transitions, 2021

The world population is constantly growing, and people may have to get used to living increasingly close to each other in the near future. At the same time, the current pandemic has made many of us wonder what our connections to others will look like from here on.

The distances between people are characterised by spaces, which, depending on their qualities, can either bring them closer together or drive them apart. When these mediating places are shaped as meeting spaces, their capacity to propose new spatial and social agreements becomes evident.

Building envelopes are a ripe field of exploration for such spaces of transition and encounter. Their spatial qualities can greatly affect the types of social relations and interaction they ultimately generate. Building envelopes often delimit and calibrate the degrees of closeness and remoteness between people, spaces, and other actors.

Architecture of Transitions looks into how architecture can promote better relations between people, ones that ensure an equitable and respectful use of space. At the same time, the project asks how boundaries can be designed to encourage new bonds with non-human agents.

From the perspective of a local South American context, the project also investigates the ways in which these types of envelopes are constructed. What materials are they made of? Where do these materials come from? Why is it that similar materials are often used across different buildings? How does the use of such common and readily available materials then affect their spatial identity?

This project argues for envelopes as spaces that relate individuals to otherness, and seeks to further explore this threshold space and its different materialisation.

Griselda Balian (Argentine, b.1982), Gastón Noriega (Argentine, b.1982), Gabriel Monteleone (Argentine, b.1982) with Victoria Cuadrado (Argentine, b.1991), Bruno Marcolini (Argentine, b.1988), Matilde Dalmaso (Italian, b.1998), Leticia Virguez Lalli (Argentine, b.1992), Máximo Bertoia (Argentine, b.1993), Sofía Preliasco (b.1999) and Gabriel Reiners (b.1997) of BAAG Buenos Aires Arquitectura Grupal (Argentina, est.2008)

Wood, steel, single models (5), 182 × 182 × 300 cm

Farshid Moussavi Architecture, *The Multistory Residential Block as a Social Platform*, 2020.
Interview with Florence, resident

Farshid Moussavi Architecture, *The Multistory Residential Block as a Social Platform*, 2020.
Exterior view at night

The Multistory Residential Block as a Social Platform, 2021

Farshid Moussavi (British, 1965) of Farshid Moussavi Architecture (UK, est.2011)

Film projections, dimensions variable

In a series of lectures at the Collège de France in 1977 titled *How to Live Together*, Roland Barthes questioned the concept of living collectively: what distance from others must one keep to both develop sociability while maintaining individual freedom? This question remains relevant for designers of any multistorey residential block.

    The Îlot 19 residential block project at La Défense–Nanterre – the subject of this installation – is one exemplary response to the above enquiry. The project is characterised by a sense of scalelessness of the external envelope to create a sense of unity among inhabitants. Its internal arrangement contradicts the convention of housing people in apartments purposely built for their demographic in different parts of the block. The different homes are stacked to eliminate any features that distinguish one from the other. Given the likelihood of a diverse group of residents, the building is designed around the premise that living together should not preclude individual freedom. This framework thus allows for both connectivity and isolation, enabling inhabitants to coexist in harmony, while also retaining their privacy.

    The block's common areas and their elements with the building's envelope act as a non-deterministic framework or social infrastructure through which the inhabitants can interact with one another. This social infrastructure comes with limits and thresholds: between the public realm and the building interior, and between the shared spaces and each private apartment. Each of the elements in those spaces is, therefore, thought of as a social prompt; does one keep the door open for one's neighbours, for example, or does one wait for them to go in first? Through the practice of sharing these common elements, the project encourages inhabitants to test and develop their interpersonal relationships and learn how to live together.

Nicolas Laisné, *One Open Tower*, 2020

One Open Tower, 2020

A generous, open-ended building to unlock innovative uses of space and shape new ways of being together.

A Mixed-use Future

As architects, our mission is to create new kinds of buildings that make more room in cities while putting joy back into sharing space. Such is the *One Open Tower*, represented at the 17th International Architecture Exhibition as a five-meter-high model. As a tall building, it vertically increases inhabitable space. Inside, several programmes are integrated so as to mix functions and populations. This project stems from the belief that mixed-use buildings are the key to strong urban communities: they open up space, favour interaction, and create unexpected synergy. People can meet even when they are not heading the same way.

A Diversity-Fostering Architecture

Inside the building as well as on its rooftop and numerous terraces, residents live, work, dine, play sports, or garden. Their neighbours are welcome to join them: the *One Open Tower* is designed to benefit a larger portion of the population than its own permanent residents, with its public spaces comprising restaurants and other communal spaces. The tower is fully integrated in the urban fabric and promotes a new lifestyle based on exchange and diversity. As visitors to the exhibition walk up the stairs around the model, they discover the variety and coalescence of the building's different purposes. Videos encourage visitors to dive into the multiple experiences characteristic of this type of architecture of the future. An essential component of the installation, Guy Limone's artwork, materialises the presence of people and their unpredictable use of this hybrid and open space.

Nicolas Laisné (French, b.1977), with Edouard Bettencourt (French, b.1989), Marie Blin (French, b.1992), Thibaut Blondet (French b.1994), Edoardo Caizzi (Italian, b.1995), Philipp Fritsch (German, b.1995), Mirella Verdes Montenegro Gosa (Spanish, b.1986), Franck Handgraaf (French, b.1989), Thomas Jochem (French, b.1998), Louis Julien-Laferrière (French, b.1988), Tristan Ponsot (French, b.1984) Cinzia Scandurra (Italian, b.1989), e Edwin Toledo (Mexican b.1984) of nicolas laisné architectes (France, est.2005) in collaboration with Guy Limone (French, b.1958), Volume Agencement (France, est.1972), C²CI Ingénierie (France, est.2010), Thomas de La Taille (Belgium, est.2021), Le Sommer Environnement (France, est.2002), Habx (France, est.2016), Colonies (France, est.2016)

Lacquered steel tubes and wood panels, screens, and physical models, 440 × 370 × 510 cm

Lina Ghotmeh—Architecture, *Stone Garden*, Beirut, 2020

Stone Garden. Resilient Living: an Archaeology of the Future, 2021

Lina Ghotmeh (French Lebanese, b.1980) of Lina Ghotmeh—Architecture (France, est.2016)

1:30 physical model of the building containing photographic prints and LED screens with video montage, 205 × 95 × 300 cm; Material samples: clay, cement, pigments, metal, dimensions variable

Putting on display the recently completed *Stone Garden* tower in Beirut, this installation portrays the capacity of architecture to act as a healing tool and be an active player in building resilience at times of crisis. Located near the city's industrial port, a mile away from the epicentre of the explosion that ripped through half of the Lebanese capital in August 2020, the project takes its roots from its context: a war-torn cityscape lingering in constant upheaval. The installation counts a scaled model of the building containing photographs and videos and narrating the story of Beirut and that of the making of the project.

    The architecture of the building showcases alternative ways of living while dealing with questions of space restriction, memory, nature, living, and urban density. Echoing Beirut's ruins invaded by nature, the tower manifests a persistent and optimistic emergence of life with large openings housing lush gardens, inviting nature at the heart of the dwellings and the city. With its earth-covered, custom-made, combed skin, the tower bears traces of the hands of workers, many of whom were forced to flee to the city because of neighbouring wars and unfavourable living conditions. This process invites artisans to participate in the emotional realm of architecture, transforming it into a meditative tool for bringing people together. The project also challenges the typical apartment plan replicating an identical social construct and sprawling across the glazed towers of the city. The asymmetric openings of the façade frame the sea, like photographs, and personalise the apartments at each level. These large windows generate new forms of communal spaces.

    Today, the tower – housing apartments as well as an art platform dedicated to image, photography, debate, and reflections from and about the Middle East – has withstood the explosion. Its envelope, with its measured windows, allowed it to act much like a bunker facing the event. The building shielded both its inhabitants and the neighbouring buildings. It rises as living archaeology, a host of life, memory, and nature.

SsD Architecture and Urbanism, *Songpa Micro Housing*, Seoul, South Korea, 2014

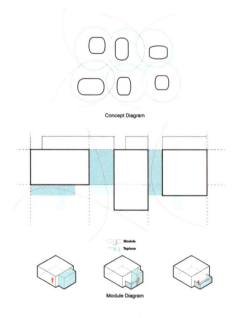

Diagrams illustrating the concept of *tapioca spaces* as semi-public spaces introduced between modular units to general porosity in the building

Micro-Urbanism, 2018

Jinhee Park (South Korean, b.1972) of SsD Architecture and Urbanism (South Korea/USA)

Acrylic and steel, 750 × 400 × 160 cm

By focusing on the smallest common denominator, *Micro-Urbanism* proposes solutions that mediate the small details and the big picture. Architecture, which is static in nature, is being challenged to accommodate rising urban density, housing cost, and environmentally extortive development. These challenges are made especially evident as household types and sizes fluctuate due to changing definitions of family and gender roles and life events such as marriage, divorce, childbirth, death, and longevity. SsD Architecture and Urbanism proposes a new housing prototype in which self-sufficient micro units are combined into *tapioca spaces*: shared, ambiguous spaces that provide opportunities for extending the perceptual and behavioural boundaries of individual units. Like the gel around tapioca pearl, soft intersections between public/private and interior/exterior allow flexible and diverse unit combinations, encouraging longer occupancy cycles and generating a robust, social fabric for sustainable community growth.

Songpa Micro Housing – represented in this installation and consisting of eight base units that are 12 m^2 each – in South Korea achieved this flexibility by mining the discrepancy between maximum floor area ratios and zoning envelopes. Utilising tapioca spaces such as semi-public circulation spaces, balconies, and the thickness of walls, a single floor plan serves various occupancy scenarios: from isolated studios to shared housing and large single-family residence.

Another example from this installation, *Oasis Place* – made up of 1,700 housing units in Kuala Lumpur, Malaysia – tests the same principles on a larger scale. The project presents over twenty distinct unit types in a wide range of scale from a studio to a signature mansion by shifting and combining two basic housing modules. The 'micro' view allows the system to address environmental issues such as solar radiation, shading, and ventilation, and curate urban experiences and public landscapes.

This installation aims to demonstrate architecture's ability to influence economy, politics, culture, and environmental sustainability at the scale of an object, of architecture, a city, or a territory, through such case studies.

Communal Atemporal Palaces, 2016–2020

Iñaki Ábalos (Spanish, b.1956) in collaboration with Sofía Blanco Santos (Spanish, b.1990), Armida Fernández (Mexican, b.1988) and José de Andrés Moncayo (Spanish, b.1991) of the Graduate School of Design at Harvard University (USA, est.1936) and ETSAM / UPM (Spain, est.1844)

Research dossier and digitally printed poster, 84 × 59.4 cm

Attempts to define a timeless dimension for architecture are especially recurrent among modern architects, such as, for example, in architect Bruno Taut's *The City Crown* (1919), which included 72 exemplary architectural illustrations from multiple locations and times. Sigfried Giedion tried with *The Eternal Present: The Beginnings of Architecture* (1964) to mount an almost universal compendium of architectural and artistic phenomena capable of persisting through time and very different civilisations. Christopher Alexander's *The Timeless Way of Building* (1979) introduced the concept of 'quality without a name' to develop an almost esoteric argument that somehow escapes the narratives and argumentations of architectural treatises, although it does not renounce illustrations and drawings of examples. These examples cross time and different locations as evidence of the plot thesis common to these essays and the idea of timelessness. Not without fear of falling into an interpretive excess, one who enters into research on palatial structures with a more or less communal character enters into this temporal space with relative ease. One sees the spatial structure of the Walpi in First Mesa (Arizona, USA) crowning an entropic territory without being able to avoid the image of the clay model made by Mies van der Rohe for the Weissenhof colony, also a 'city crown'. The performance of the architect Mies van der Rohe is modest yet dominated by his prolific volume, in which the elevation is drawn perfectly so as to demonstrate his organising intention of the whole.

There is also the well-known episode of the Italian charterhouse that inspired Le Corbusier in his *Journey to the East* (1911) and gave rise to his first project of a large residential – almost communal – palace that is at the same time modern and timeless, the *Immeubles-villas* (1922). This project was concieved with the youthful intention to solve the housing problems of the modern city, but it allowed him to build his first installation in Paris: the 1924 pavilion of L'Esprit Nouveau. This pavilion replicates one of the residential modules of the complex, and contained a large advertising display of Le Corbusier's *Ville Contemporaine* (The Contemporary City), and its associated dioramas exposed inside.

STATION

Alex McLean, *First Mesa*, Arizona, USA, 900 CE. Aerial view

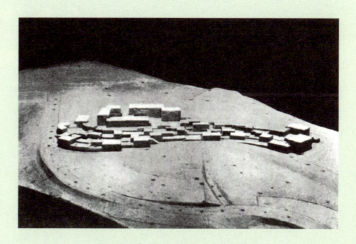

Mies van der Rohe, *Weissenhofsiedlung*,
Stuttgart, Germany, 1926. Clay model

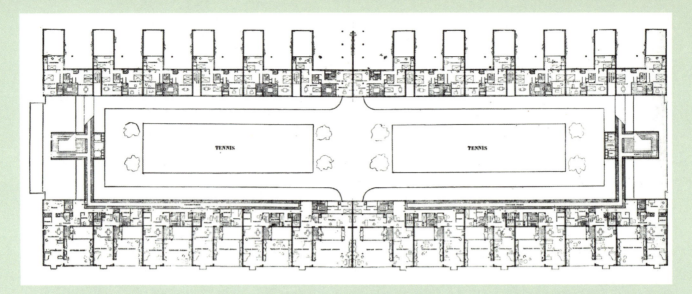

Le Corbusier, *Immeubles-Villa*, 1922. Plan

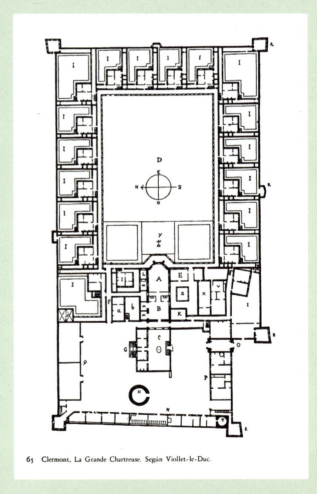

Eugène Viollet-le-Duc, *Clermont Charterhouse*, France, 1858.
Drawing of a typical Carthusian plan

STATION

If one can immediately recognise the youthful projects of Mies van der Rohe and Le Corbusier, will it not be a sign that, despite the reluctance that one can have about the timelessness of architecture, one could at least harbour the reasonable doubt that there is something at the core of the discipline that makes the Nietzschean idea of Eternal Recurrence something more than a poetical–philosophical resource?

When looking at architectural experiences that, in the most ambitious cases, are 'outside the time or they transcend it', it becomes observable that across cultures and motivations there stems an impulse to build outside the existential and economic unit of the family. It is this accrual of a timeless dimension that we consider latent while simultaneously in a continuous state of excitement in this collective investigation. And this, perhaps, is one of architecture's most attractive sediments.

Cooperative Conditions: A Primer on Architecture, Finance, and Regulation in Zurich, 2021

Non-speculative Households at the Heart of Global Finance

Zurich is a centre of global finance and exemplifies the associated pressure of a financialised real estate market. At the same time, Switzerland's largest and historically most industrialised city has a century-old tradition of non-profit housing. Since the 1990s, the city's cooperative movement – activists, city officials, architects – has re-appropriated this form of permanently de-commodified development. Today, approximately 20 percent of the city's housing stock is cooperatively owned and permanently withdrawn from the for-profit sector. In the process, cooperatives have realised new and highly experimental architectural forms of living together that challenge the established understanding of the household and the dwelling unit. New typologies include cluster housing, or groups of micro-units assembled into a larger whole, and apartments for large households, sometimes with access to a serviced kitchen. These projects have also reframed the dimension and role of shared spaces, whether on the interior or exterior of the buildings. Zurich's cooperatives thus demonstrate that non-profit housing can respond to very specific housing needs whose high material and socio-spatial quality remains exempt from commodification.

What Makes Them Possible?

The generous and complex floor plans, sectional arrangements, and shared spaces serve as the project's point of departure to ask: What makes these forms of living together possible? What enables a commitment to non-speculation within a for-profit real estate market? Who possesses what kind of land on which terms? Which criteria determine the rent? How much equity is required to take out a mortgage? It is these hard-to-grasp abstractions of loans and leases, taxes and deeds, by-laws and policy measures that have immediate impact on building programs and built form. Conversely, specific socio-spatial imaginaries and their corresponding architectural propositions are

Anne Kockelkorn (German, b.1975) and Susanne Schindler (Swiss/American, b.1970) of the gta Institute, Department of Architecture at ETH Zurich (Switzerland, est.1854) in collaboration with Dorothée Billard (French, b.1975) of Monobloque (Germany, est.2004), Rebekka Hirschberg (German, b.1990), and the students of the MAS in History and Theory of Architecture at ETH Zurich

Projection, digital printing, 550 × 550 cm

Müller Sigrist Architekten, *Kalkbreite*, 2012–2014. Roof terrace and courtyard

STATION

AS NEW HOUSEHOLDS—*Station*

137

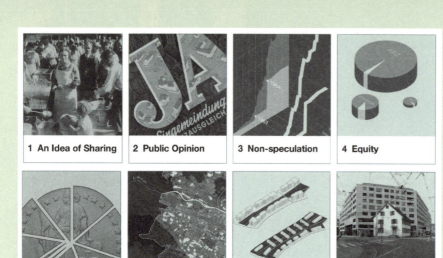

Overview of eight dossiers

Otto Streicher, *Siedlung Ottostrasse*, 1925–1927. Courtyard with dining place

Duplex Architekten, *mehr als wohnen*, 2009–2015. Atrium

Schneider Studer Primas Architekten, *Zwicky-Süd*, 2009–2016. Access galleries

STATION

often what drives the search for new financial or regulatory constructs – such as the garden city in the 1920s or shared living environments in the 2000s.

Thinking in terms of Conditions, Instruments, Origin Stories, and Intersections

To understand the conditions that make cooperative housing desirable and feasible in Zurich today, one needs to understand not only their present mode of functioning, but also how the social agreement to implement its corresponding laws and regulations emerged over the last 100 years. Toward this end, this research station identifies eight basic conditions of cooperative housing: An Idea of Sharing; Public Opinion; Non-Speculation; Equity; Debt; Land; Zoning; and The Competition. The project explains the workings of each condition in light of two or three specific instruments. It then highlights the historic constellation that made the emergence of these instruments possible at a particular moment in time. Finally, it shows their implications for social space and intersections with built form through contemporary and historic examples.

Specificity and Transferability

Thinking in terms of these conditions and instruments and their long-standing historic continuity allows one to articulate the socio-political specificity that underlies Zurich's cooperative housing, while at the same time making an argument for their transferability. Switzerland has enjoyed a remarkable continuity and longevity in its institutions, a political system organised from the local to the national, with a long-standing history of sharing natural resources – all of which are aspects that are hardly replicable. What *can* be transferred to other places, however, are the ways in which activists, city officials, cooperative organisations, and architects have used legal, financial, and regulatory instruments, as well as the architectural imagination, to realise new ideas of living together. The instruments this station describes can be negotiated within specific political struggles elsewhere and will play out when deployed over time. Articulating the conditions and the specific instruments for architecturally experimental *and* permanently de-commodified forms of living together is thus essential if one is to realise and maintain such housing in the future, not only in Zurich, but in other, and very different settings.

Housing the Future: A New 'New Law' For New York City, 2021

Daisy Ames (American, b.1984), Bernadette Baird-Zars (American, b.1983), and Adam Frampton (American, b.1980) of the Housing Lab (USA, est.2019) at the Graduate School of Architecture, Planning, and Preservation (USA, est.1881) at Columbia University (USA, est.1754) in collaboration with Ericka Mina Song (Canadian, b.1991), Erin Purcell (American, b.1990), Juan Sebastián Moreno (Colombian, b.1991)

LCD screen projections (2), dimensions variable

New York City contains a multitude of housing typologies throughout its five boroughs, most of which have been understood as a generic backdrop to the tall, slender buildings that define the city's skyline. The multidisciplinary Housing Lab at Columbia University's Graduate School of Architecture, Planning, and Preservation argues that these overlooked buildings embody complex legacies that remain critical for the future of living together. The goals of this installation are twofold: to extract elements from overlooked housing projects that have unique assemblies of materials, design, code, and urban morphology; and to recast selected elements into climate-adaptive and future-oriented outputs that hold a promise for new models of living for inclusion, resilience, and access.

In 1901, a broad-reaching Tenement House Law, often called the 'New Law', shaped a citywide boom in construction of small and medium buildings of four to six storeys that embodied early twentieth-century ideas about improved light and air. Through their abundance, the New Law Tenements and other overlooked typologies represent a unique socio-historical inheritance – with real currency and value within society – that provided much of New York City's housing stock. By extracting elements and assembling a new kit of parts from this overlooked housing stock, the aim of this project is to develop creative approaches to recast models for future housing and cities, at the intersection of climate resiliency, inclusivity, and access in 2050, and produce potentially a New 'New Law'.

STATION

How can historical, regional networks of material sourcing in New York State's Hudson Valley lay the groundwork for material processes in future, low carbon models of construction?

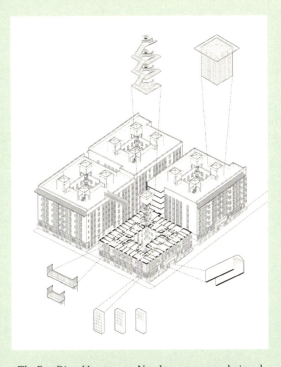

The East River Homes were New Law tenements designed to maximise light and air for tuberculosis patients and their families. The unique spatial innovations created healthy, dignified homes and still remain a case of exemplary architecture in New York City.

As Emerging Communities

EXHIBITION ARSENALE

Class and ethnicity cleave the lives of cities and communities, but less harsh realities are emerging. They may be altering the rigidly bound land-uses and communities of the past, but architects and planners have yet to imagine future human cohabitation more holistically. The new open-sourced downtowns of millennials, the sharing of economies and spaces, but also the new forms of experimental settlement around urban edges, are creating new forms of social collectivity. These new, architecturally driven communities offer viable forms for emerging communities. If there is no single answer to the question of how to live together, architecture certainly plays an important role in shaping each answer.

The impact of digitisation on the economy and on the future of work has led to new distribution of land-use at the scales of regions, cities and neighborhoods. New industries, and alternative agricultures are entering the city.

This part of the 17th International Architecture Exhibition includes examples of emerging social infrastructures from across the world (schools, community centres, public spaces) that enhance these new collectivities. It offers new ways of thinking about how people can participate in creating space(s) – often combining digital and interpersonal approaches. Importantly, it also shows how some of these collectives express themselves in new forms of communal living and public spaces. This selection of compelling communal and housing experiments expresses new forms of collective living.

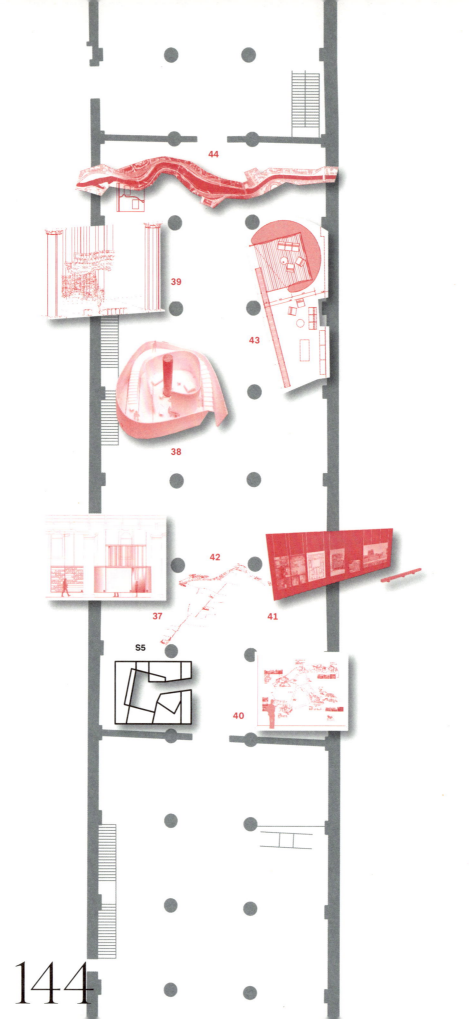

APPEALING TO CIVICNESS

AS EMERGING COMMUNITIES

37 Cohabitation Strategies (Lucia Babina, Emiliano Gandolfi, Gabriela Rendón, Miguel Robles-Durán)
147

38 Fieldoffice Architects (Huang Sheng-Yuan)
149

39 Storia Na Lugar (Patti Anahory; César Schofield Cardoso)
151

40 Arquitectura Expandida (Ana López Ortego; Harold Guyaux; Felipe Gonzalez Gonzalez; Viviana Parada Camargo)
153

41 Lacol (Ari Artigas; Mirko Gegundez; Lali Daví; Pol Massoni; Anna Clemente; Cristina Gamboa; Núria Vila; Jordi Miró; Ernest Garriga; Eliseu Arrufat; Laura Lluch; Lluc Hernandez; Arnau Andrés; Carles Baiges)
155

42 Enlace Arquitectura (Elisa Silva)
157

43 raumlaborberlin (Andrea Hofmann; Axel Timm; Benjamin Foerster-Baldenius; Christof Mayer; Florian Stirnemann; Francesco Apuzzo; Frauke Gerstenberg; Jan Liesegang; Markus Bader)
159

44 PRÁCTICA (Jaime Daroca Guerrero; José Mayoral Moratilla; José Ramón Sierra Gómez de León)
161

S5 **STATION**: Rafi Segal, MIT Future Urban Collective Lab; Sarah Williams et al.
162

During the Renaissance, the very administration of the construction of many new cities turned into the administration of political life in these cities after they were built and inhabited. The spatial contract preceded and then shaped the social contract. The participants in this room imagine how emerging social groups seek to shape their social relationships and their civicness through the processes of building and how the inclusions, transparencies, and participatory practices shape their commons, whether collective housing, new institutions, or shared amenities.

The projects and research station in this room offer architectural approaches to providing inhabitants with their rightful, democratic access to basic necessities such as housing and education. By designing apartment buildings, parks, or whole neighbourhoods, they retool architecture to negotiate and reconceive the commons in communities.

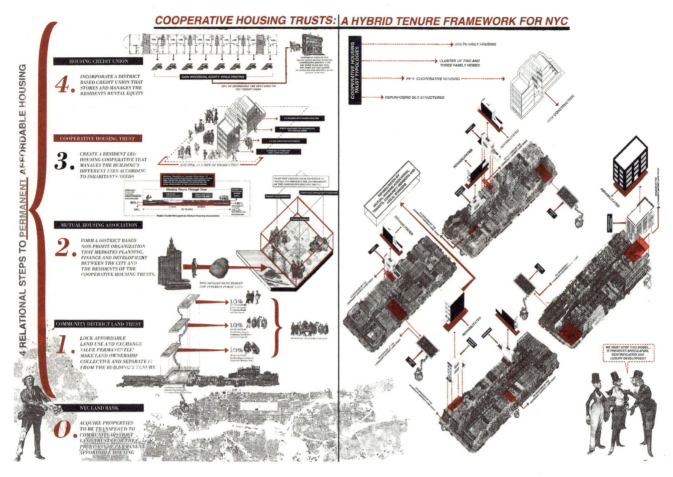

Cohabitation Strategies, *Uneven Growth*, 2014. Diagram for a *Cooperative Housing Trust*, The Museum of Modern Art, NY

Cohabitation Strategies, *Playground for Useful Knowledge*, 2015. Action 3: preparing Mifflin Square Alliance Festival

How to Begin Again: An Initiation Towards Unitary Urbanism, 2021

Lucia Babina (Italian, b.1970), Emiliano Gandolfi (Italian, b.1975), Gabriela Rendón (Mexican, b.1976) and Miguel Robles-Durán (Mexican, b.1975) of Cohabitation Strategies (The Netherlands, est.2008)

Site specific installation, mixed media, 550 × 1160 × 600 cm

The constant exploitation of urban communities and the planet enables the current state of urbanisation. It is capitalism's tendency to pursue what Marx called 'the enforced destruction of a mass of productive forces' via the contemporary processes of urbanisation and its devastating consequences to communities, cultures, and the environment. Yet there are forces that contrast this tendency and are building daily an alternative that has an impact at a local scale. *How to Begin Again* is an initiation to a new awareness of the possibilities of building sustainable, equitable, and inclusive cities.

This is the course of action to this initiation. First and foremost, it is important to decondition oneself from thinking that cities can only thrive through maximising capital accumulation. People need to practise to better connect with others, learn to cooperate instead of competing, build shared visions, and establish dialogues with the environment. The next step is to acknowledge and experiment with the radical forms of knowledge that have been sustaining productive cohabitation and building critical communities. Local forms of expertise and popular knowledge ought to be given prominence and more serious consideration. These critical forms of urban consciousness need to be integrated into radical forms of scientific knowledge that defy the relations of oppression towards the production of just cities.

New knowledge must be adapted to local circumstances, and while new relations and understandings are tested, original methodologies arise that expand the limits of singular disciplines and coalesce diverse forms of conceiving and acting on cities. This leads inevitably towards Unitary Urbanism, or the recognition that the urban does not belong to a singular discipline, to a distinctive vision, but that it is a coalition of diverse forces that together blossom. Ultimately each one of us is responsible for participating in this paradigm change. *How to Begin: An Initiation Towards Unitary Urbanism* empowers its visitors with a socially responsible perspective on cities. Are we ready to act?

Fieldoffice Architects, *First Vascular Bundle*, Jin-Mei Pedestrian Bridge across Yilan River, 2005–2008

Living in Place, Enabling the Coming-Together, 1995–2008

An Experience to Engage with Space, Participate in Shaping a Culture, and Create Communities

Sheng-Yuan Huang (Taiwanese, b.1963) of Fieldoffice Architects (Taiwan, est.1994) in collaboration with Sheng-Feng Lin (Taiwanese, b.1970) of Atelier Or (Taiwan, est.2011) and Tsai Ming-Liang (Malaysian, b.1957)

This installation enables people to come together and simultaneously experience space, time, and culture. It is not the architecture, landscape architecture, nor the space that is important when formatting this togetherness. What is critical, independent from the structures themselves, are the mechanisms created via the works of the architects that ultimately enable and facilitate people to gather and engage in common activities. As a result, the collective experience and memories of the people form the basis of community, shape culture, and define 'the place'.

Iron, stainless steel plate, 1135 × 1145 × 480 cm; Physical models (8); Materials and dimensions variable, projections (3), 10'; Monitors, tablets

Living in Place is a spatial framework that invites visitors to enter, participate, and engage with the physical structures. Whether to see the installation, walk through the space, interact with each other, or see the other installations – the variety of individual motivations, the interpersonal exchange, the communal interactions bring out the essence of what community embodies in place. The installation consists of four components:

The Stairs: the element that leads visitors to enter and acts as the demarcation of the 'transient' zone.

The Door: the interface between the transient zone and the inner void.

The Void: the inner space, which becomes a 'place' when people are present.

The Media: includes film, models, and stools that communicate ideas.

Creating a void that invites people and activities to flow in, thereby occupying and shaping it, is central to the design. Film and documentary help to communicate what Huang sees and senses from the environment he operates in; the evolving live models that are continuously being reshaped convey his design ideas; and stools represent the autonomy of users and also document how visitors form communities as they are rearranged and occupied.

Textures of drought, Cabo Verde

Waiting for water rituals of everyday life, Cabo Verde

Hacking the Resort Territorialities + Imaginaries, 2021

Patti Anahory (Cape Verdean, b.1969) and César Schofield Cardoso (Cape Verdean, b.1973) of Storia Na Lugar (Cabo Verde, est.2016)

Site-specific installation, mixed media, 300 × 300 × 600 cm

Hacking the Resort explores the typology of the all-inclusive resort in designated Special Tourist Zones in Boa Vista Island, Cabo Verde, as microcosms of disparities but also of possibilities. While they are a testament to the consumption patterns and labour politics of the global economic system, this work looks for slippages and gaps in these staged spaces of leisure and abundance for some. As spaces of confluence, where tourists and the local labour force meet in a choreographed dance of labour and leisure, water in its imaginary and real forms becomes a protagonist presenting an opportunity to fabulate ruptures that will dream more equitable ways of living and being together.

This proposal builds on the imaginary of a maritime country, surrounded by the immensity of Blue Ocean, where massive resorts roll out monumental pools that extend horizons of blue. Yet, ironically, Cabo Verde is a country that suffers from extreme scarcity of potable water, where precipitation is sparse, and very irregular; sometimes several years pass without rain, as is true of the last three years (2017–2019). Water management is a major concern in the country. With the massive increase in tourism, the pressure on water resources is even greater, particularly for islands such as Boa Vista, with almost nonexistent natural water reserves. Despite investments in water production and treatment units, the situation for the population has remained unchanged. Water is summoned as witness and protagonist in search for breaches in the tourism narrative.

Arquitectura Expandida – AXP, *La Casa de la Lluvia de Ideas* (*The House of the Rain of Ideas*), 2012–present. A cultural and environmental community space. Self-building process. La Cecilia neighbourhood, San Cristóbal District, Bogotá D.C. (CO)

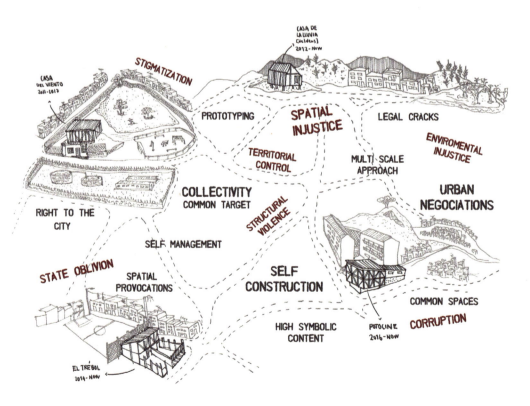

Arquitectura Expandida – AXP, *Peripheral and Tactical Architecture*. Drawing. Self-built and self-managed spaces in the peripheries of Bogotá: a city crossed by structural violence, yet with multiple initiatives of citizen action.

Tactical and Peripheral Architecture, 2021

Arquitectura Expandida's work is characterised by the development of urban negotiations in contexts of geographic, social, economic, and decisional urban peripheries. Such strategies allow for the exploration of alternative forms of community organisation, citizen participation in public policy, and self-management of common spaces. Ultimately, these are processes in which to explore how to live together, while doing, researching, learning, and building together.

In these processes there are constant parameters that define the playing field: a strong asymmetry of power relations within the city; a critical approach to human/urban rights; an inter-scale approach that stems from the study and documentation of controversies at the regional level, or even the planetary scale with a local impact (such as migration or climate change); the demand for policies that mitigate spatial injustices in the city; up to 'the poetics of the screw', which is exercised when direct action within communities happens.

This action is materialised in complex and long processes of self-construction and collective self-management of common spaces, architecture(s), and landscapes. There is no single recipe for these urban negotiations, since they are based on open organisational models; nevertheless, the practice has developed a series of crosscutting tactics applicable to most of their projects.

These spaces are used for everyday community meetings but are also a vindication in the cultural and ecological dimensions for the popular peripheries of Bogotá: *The House of the Rain of Ideas* (*Casa de La Lluvia de Ideas*) (2012–present) is a symbol of the struggle for environmental rights; *The Potocinema* (*La Potocine*) (2016–present) denounces, through cinema, the deficit of community cultural spaces. On the other hand, *The House of the Wind* (*La Casa del Viento*) (2011–2017) and *The Clover Community House* (*El Trébol*) (2014–present) advocate for culture, literature, and urban/street art as cultural integration strategies for the young and the excluded.

Ana María López Ortego (Spanish, b.1981), Harold Guyaux (Belgian, b.1981), Felipe Gonzalez González (Colombian, b.1983), Viviana Parada Camargo (Colombian, b.1986) of Arquitectura Expandida (Colombia, est.2010)

Physical models, drawing with archival material on PVC film, 400 × 180 × 20 cm

All images: Lacol, *La Borda Cooperative Housing*, 2018

Cooperative Housing That Builds Community, 2020

In architectural design, cooperative housing projects can be used as a framework for experimenting in the production of collective housing. This makes it possible to overcome some of the limitations of conventional developments of public and private housing. With public developments, there is often a fear of the inhabitant, who is a complete stranger. This makes it impossible to introduce changes that may affect residents' established way of life and future management. As for private developments, the logic and standards of the market impose themselves and make it easier to render housing an object of consumption, which many times leads to mediocre solutions.

The particularities of the cooperative model offer the possibility of questioning pre-established values and practices. And architecture must respond. The main conditioning characteristics of these projects have been self-promotion, collective ownership, community life, and reducing environmental footprints linked to notions of climate comfort.

To rethink the relationship of the surroundings to community life, it is necessary to redefine the transition between public and private, blurring the limits of domestic space. It is also important to rethink new collective programmes adapted to a model of coexistence for each community. Spatially, circulation plays a central role together with the cooperative's communal spaces. It, indeed, can help generate encounters and instances for socialisation among the members of the cooperative as well as with the neighbourhood at large. This is especially true in the case of the project represented in this installation, where the building extends inwards the concept of public space and the multiple functionalities of the city.

This project, realised with La Borda cooperative in Barcelona, has been both a learning process as well as an experiment in rethinking and creating new forms of contemporary dwelling in the city.

Ari Artigas (Spanish, b.1985), Mirko Gegundez (Spanish, b.1985), Lali Daví (Spanish, b.1985), Pol Massoni (Spanish, b.1985), Anna Clemente (Spanish, b.1985), Cristina Gamboa (Spanish, b.1985), Núria Vila (Spanish, b.1985), Jordi Miró (Spanish, b.1985), Ernest Garriga (Spanish, b.1985), Eliseu Arrufat (Spanish, b.1985), Laura Lluch (Spanish, b.1985), Lluc Hernandez (Spanish, b.1985), Arnau Andrés (Spanish, b.1985), and Carles Baiges (Spanish, b.1985) of Lacol (Spain, est.2009)

Physical model, wood, 90 × 40 × 125 cm; Curtain, 1110 × 600 cm; Photographs 250 × 166 cm; Projection, 500 × 281 cm; video projection, 380 × 213 cm; 4 tables, wood, each 239 × 80 × 85 cm

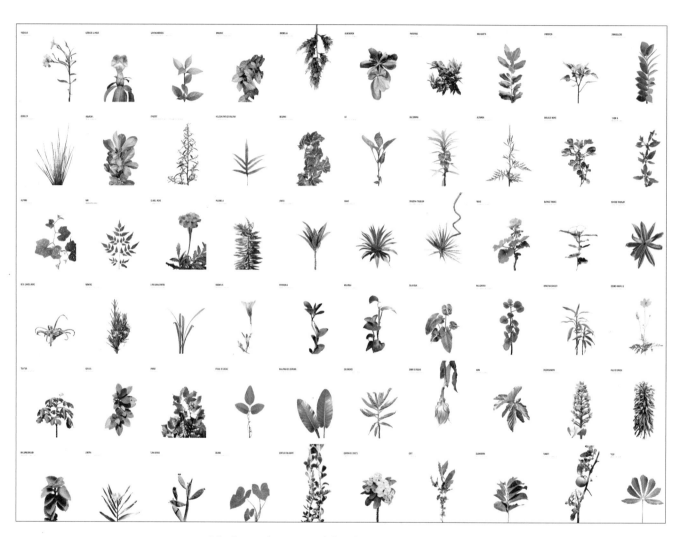

Ethnobotanical Dictionary of Plants from Gardens in La Palomera, produced as part of the program *Integration Process Caracas*, Compendium of 60 / 260 species exhibited, 2018-2020

The Complete City: La Palomera, Acknowledgement and Celebration, 2018-2020

Even though *barrios* are the home of half of Caracas's population, they are not acknowledged as part of the city. The programme *Integration Process Caracas*, addresses this lack of recognition, not by 'improving' the *barrio*, but rather by showcasing rich spatial and cultural dynamics that already exist. For example, the *barrio* La Palomera has a network of open green spaces defined by 1.75 hectares of walkways, staircases, and squares riddled with lichens, shrubs, and ivy growing spontaneously in the cracks of pavements and walls. The presence of greenery is further complemented by at least two dozen vegetable and flower gardens with plants cultivated for cooking, curing illnesses, and keeping insects away. The gardens embed a knowledge that ancestors, who once migrated from rural areas, have passed down. The *Ethnobotanical Dictionary of Plants from the Gardens of La Palomera* and a model and large-format book of the gardens and public walkways record their stories and understanding of nature of the *barrios*' open spaces and acknowledge what a *barrio* already is.

Similarly, *barrio* residents still practise traditional dances and music, performed in cultural traditions such as the *Cruz de Mayo* and the *Paradura del Niño*, which were once part of harvesting rituals. *Barrio* residents have kept them alive; they represent an opportunity for non-*barrio* neighbours to celebrate the city's cultural wealth. Integrating a fragmented city is as much a symbolic process as it is a spatial one. Recognising the livelihood inherent in gardens or dancing in the *barrio*'s public spaces represents a fundamental premise in any urban process of integration.

Elisa Silva (American and Venezuelan, b.1975) of Enlace Arquitectura (Venezuela, est.2007), in collaboration with Sergio Dos Santos, María Virginia Millán, Sofía Paz, Verónica González, Carol Arellano, Jaeson Montilla, Gabriela Álvarez, Emily Yánez and Valeria De Jongh

Black and white images printed on 8 sheets of vynil paper, 90 × 250 cm each; plywood model, scale 1:30; Books

raumlaborberlin, *Floating University*, 2019. Opening night

raumlaborberlin, *Haus der Statistik*, 2015–2020. Concept drawing

Instances of Urban Practice, 2020

Floating University and *Haus der Statistik* are both located in Berlin, adjacent to outstanding places: *Floating University* neighbours Tempelhof (air)field, and *Haus der Statistik* is just off Alexanderplatz.

Floating University is a carefully designed place, where human-made architectures intertwine with the habitat of a multitude of other organisms. In a water basin consisting of polluted, urban, surface water, it presents a paradoxical paradise for parallel and common actions – a place of ongoing surprises and encounters. The openness of the structures motivates the permeation of ideas and relationships among the different university groups, initiatives, neighbours, and other Berlin inhabitants.

Haus der Statistik is a German Democratic Republic office complex from the 1960s, now being transformed into a space for art, culture, and social and educational programming, run by a coalition of people from civic society. It was the site for 'making futures school', the prototype for a school for spatial practice that acts as an engaged form within an evolving situation. Looking deeper into collaborative modes of knowledge production and exchange, the architects focused on questions about architecture as a resource and architecture as a collective form. The school itself is conceived as a collaborative testbed with more than 150 participants and 500 visitors.

Both projects offer complex forms for supporting emerging communities to co-create future cities.

The installation in Venice brings real-scale architectural elements from *Floating University* into an exhibition context. These are combined with large-scale image prints, drawing the audience into the atmosphere of the place. The structure operates as both exhibit and usable elements inviting people to spend some time, relax, and potentially delve deeper into the offered information. This is an opportunity to inhabit space and potentially engage in conversation in a potential space of encounter.

Andrea Hofmann (German, b.1969), Axel Timm (German, b.1973), Benjamin Foerster-Baldenius (German, b.1968), Christof Mayer (German, b.1967), Florian Stirnemann (Swiss, b.1976), Francesco Apuzzo (Italian, b.1972), Frauke Gerstenberg (German, b.1968), Jan Liesegang (German, b.1968) and Markus Bader (German, b.1968) of raumlaborberlin (Germany, est.1999)

Bubble: plastic sheets, shuttering board, timber beams; table, billboard, plywood chairs, scaffold, neon light, materials and dimensions variable.

PRÁCTICA, *River Someș*, 2017–ongoing. Urban Beach

PRÁCTICA, *River Someș*, 2017–ongoing. Zone 1 Plan

River Someș: Across Communities and Ecosystems, 2017–ONGOING

Jaime Daroca (Spanish, b.1986), José Mayoral (Spanish, b.1985), and José Ramón Sierra (Spanish, b.1989) of PRÁCTICA (Spain, est.2016)

Physical model, CNC milled EPS, 2019 × 479 × 40 cm; Digital projection, 2.019 × 479 cm; Digital printing on polycanvas, (2) 550 × 270 cm

The *River Someș* project is a contemporary example of river regeneration and re-naturation efforts. It aims to connect the diverse communities of the city of Cluj-Napoca in Romania, as well as to reconnect them to the local fauna and flora species that have been forced out of their natural habitat on the riverbanks. Such a challenging process comprises a wide range of agents and complex interventions aimed at revitalising the natural biodiversity and collective consciousness of River Someș.

The project imagines the river as a new, active, social space for interrelating that operates across scales and programmes. It defines how inhabitants of Cluj-Napoca interact among themselves and with their surrounding ecosystem. On a community scale, it becomes a space for its dwellers – Romanian and Hungarian, Christian and Jewish, local and foreign, old and young – to gather and exchange ideas. On a territorial scale, it connects the city of Cluj-Napoca with every other territory watered by the stream as it flows to the Black Sea, such as the Someș River in Transylvania, the Tisza in Hungary and Serbia, and the Danube across Romania, Bulgaria, Moldova, and Ukraine. This waterway makes the inhabitants of Cluj conscious of their role within a much larger community across their entire continent; it calls for global understanding and comradeship.

This ambitious project, though finite in time and space, has multiple ramifications that affect entire communities across social orders and physical boundaries. It acts as a new piece of participative infrastructure that addresses both local and global conditions. It promotes a new frame for dialogue and interaction by means of architecture, and it unites the efforts of a wide multidisciplinary team of architects, landscape designers, engineers, urban planners, government agencies, and everyday users – all looking for answers to the question of how we will live together.

Open Collectives: Architecture for an Equitable Digital Economy, 2020

Rafi Segal (Israeli/American, b.1967) of Future Urban Collective Lab (USA, est.2019) at MIT (USA, est.1861) and Sarah Williams (American, b.1974) of Civic Data Design Lab (USA, est.2012) at MIT, in collaboration with Greg Lindsay (American, b.1977), Marisa Morán Jahn (American, b.1977) of Studio REV- (USA, est.2000)

Plywood and wooden frame structure, digital screen, projection, video, interactive website, 560 × 600 cm

Other publics are possible.

The public we know emerged in the West from the labour movements and trade unions of the late nineteenth century, fusing the cooperative spirit of beneficial societies with the class solidarity of workers striving for political power. From these strands also emerged modern collectives, which, supported by the contributions of their members, broke from the totalising project of the state. Even the most political examples – such as Zionist *kibbutzim* – were ultimately more concerned with bolstering their social and economic rights and resilience.

The ascent of neoliberalism hollowed out both publics – the state and the collective – to profit the market and the individual. The results have been dire, to say the least: rising inequality, and greater poverty, the privatisation of the public realm, and the criminalisation of public space.

The advent of the Internet added a third pillar, the network, which sought to replace collectives through the so-called sharing economy – in reality, immense digital platforms such as Uber and Airbnb, which transformed once-private possessions (a car, a home, one's time) into financialised assets.

The collapse of the public(s) and repeated failures of the market created a void being filled by something new. The binary divide between increasingly weak publics and a greater momentum towards privatisation has invited a multitude of Open Collectives bound by a common cause but boundless in their ability to change and grow.

Central to these efforts are digital networks, which once promised to rewire communities before being hijacked by the markets and platforms they spawned. But there remains a path not taken, harnessing digital tools and networks to organise intentionally across space and time. By marrying the scope and scale of now-ubiquitous personal technologies with the shared goals, pressing needs, and strong ties of collectives, could one produce a network greater than the sum of its nodes?

Open Collectives are voluntary and dynamic groups of people sharing common goals and values combining the scale and connectivity

Axonometric view of Quipu Collective Market designed to support the Quipu Digital Marketplace, Villas de San Pablo, Barranquilla, Colombia. Quipu empowers local economies and enables low-income people to exchange goods and services

STATION

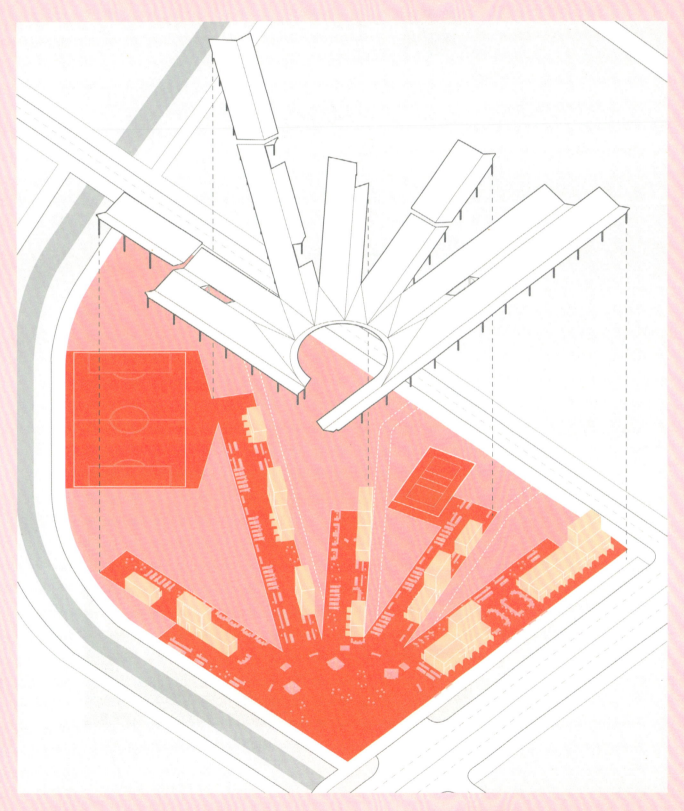

AS EMERGING COMMUNITIES—*Station*

163

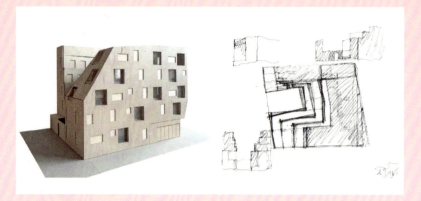

Carehaus is the US's first intergenerational care-based cohousing project; a five-storey *Carehaus* will be built in Baltimore, MD, US. Architect: Rafi Segal A+U with collaborating artist Marisa Morán Jahn

Designed by MIT Future Urban Collectives Lab and Civic Data Design Lab, *Open Collectives Digital Platform* collects perspectives on sharing and mutualism, and engages a worldwide audience with historic and present examples of collectives

CareForce, a project by Marisa Morán Jahn with the National Domestic Workers Alliance that amplifies the voices of caregivers, fostering new models for care-based cohousing

of digital platforms with the kinship of physical space and face-to-face interaction. Their permeable, hybrid physical/digital networks are designed so membership and functions can expand and contract economically, environmentally, and/or socially and encourage new forms of sharing. They promise to bridge public and private and create new conditions with further room for growth.

Open Collectives are intentional but open-ended, asynchronous but real-time, and distributed but local. They operate simultaneously at multiple scales in multiple locations, ranging from total commitment to thriving on slivers of members' attention, reorienting themselves around singular goals or functions, while leveraging new forms of engagement and collaboration. Achieving their full potential means coupling digital and physical platforms to support and reinforce each other.

What's missing is a new type of architecture of urban fabric and social networks to strengthen solidarity across the physical and digital realms. It must enable them as it simultaneously defines their ability to function as an institution capable of reshaping society.

Some began life as online-only networks that later realised their aims required a physical form. *Quipu*, for instance, is a Colombian micro-currency platform for informal merchants that has begun designing actual marketplaces for those thwarted by regulation. Another example, *Mosaic*, is a housing construction start-up in Arizona harnessing machine learning to create the networked equivalent of a barn-raising. It, too, realized it needs local depots where members can meet to share advice and recruit builders.

Others only later leveraged networks to expand their scope and scale. In downtown Haifa, Israel, *Communit* seeks a new scale of co-living to allow residents to take stewardship of an entire neighbourhood, rather than a single floor or building. And *Carehaus* offers a vision of cooperative care and homeownership for elderly caregivers in New York City to alleviate the isolation endemic to caregivers and care receivers alike.

How will these open collectives change the city over time? It is already evident, for example, how cohousing prototypes such as Berlin's *baugruppen* point to entirely new models of financing, design, and decision-making. If the state shaped the public architecture of the twentieth century, perhaps *Open Collectives* will define this one's.

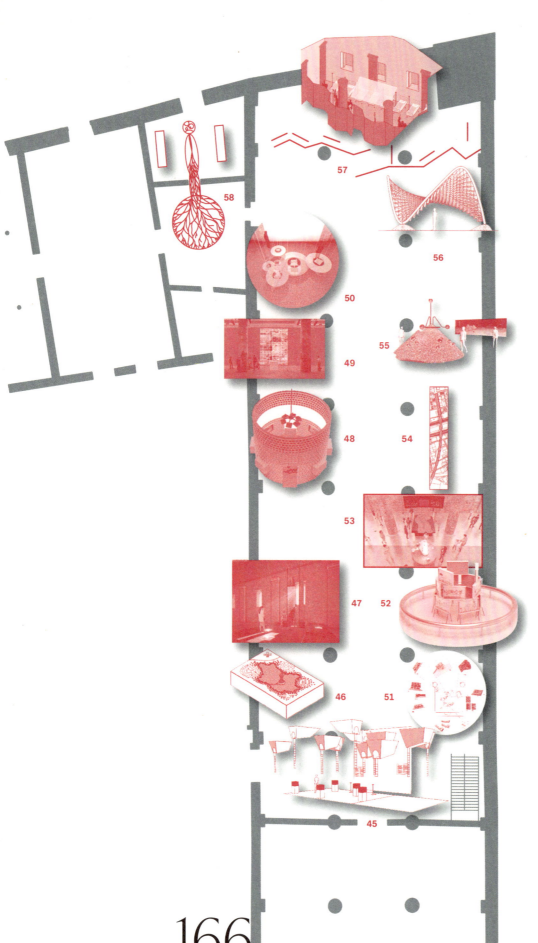

RE-EQUIPPING SOCIETY

AS EMERGING COMMUNITIES

45 Aristide Antonas with Elina Axioti; Mona Mahall and Asli Serbest
169

46 EFFEKT (Sinus Lynge; Tue Foged)
171

47 atelier masōmī (Mariam Kamara)
173

48 Manuel Herz Architects and Iwan Baan
175

49 MDP Michel Desvigne Paysagiste
177

50 TUMO Center for Creative Technologies (Marie Lou Papazian; Pegor Papazian)
179

51 Miralles Tagliabue EMBT (Benedetta Tagliabue; Elena Nedelcu; Joan Callís)
181

52 Ronan & Erwan Bouroullec
183

53 Skidmore, Owings & Merrill (Colin Koop)
185

54 Michael Maltzan Architecture
187

55 Sean Lally
189

56 BASE studio (Barbara Barreda; Felipe Sepulveda)
191

57 OMA (Reinier de Graaf)
193

58 doxiadis+ (Thomas Doxiadis)
195

Our social equipment no longer caters to our needs. Schools, hospitals, and parks have been privatised and lost their function as public spaces and as expressions of their community's common good.

The projects in this room reimagine social equipment to address new forms of public life such as extended educational programmes, interactive parks, and collective meditation spaces. They highlight the potential of new social equipment to express the values of emerging or disenfranchised communities, to reconcile the divide between private and public institutions, or to embrace the environmental consciousness of the new generation.

Antonas Office, *Theatre of Normality, The Lounge of the Vending Machines*,
2021. Print on Tyvek, 90 × 40 cm

Antonas Office, *State of Inverted Tents*, 2021.
Print on Tyvek, 42 × 22 cm

Antonas Office, *Theater of Normality, The Hall of Hammocks*, 2021.
Print on Tyvek, 90 × 40 cm

The Hall of Protocols, 2021

Aristide Antonas (Greek, b.1963) of Antonas Office (Greece, est.2006), in collaboration with Elina Axioti (Greek, b.1981), Mona Mahall (German, b.1976), and Asli Serbest (Turkish, b.1977)

Physical constructions, video projections, monitor, audio, archival material, digital prints, hand drawings, 1600 × 650 × 640 cm

The Hall of Protocols is an installation of a non-accessible system of inverted tents hanging from the ceiling and including a number of looping texts, short films, images, archival, and hand-drawn material.

It presents three post-urban protocols as wall projections, while additional screenings provide visual documentation and perform three short dialogues referring to the history of withdrawal in Western philosophy (with texts by Plato, Avicenna, and Descartes, elaborated as theatre scripts and directed as conversations between humans and robots). The protocols forming the main part of the installation are meant as pseudo-legislative texts; they propose strategies for occupying the post-network urban territory and a theatrical understanding of urban time in the frame of the digital web.

The current pandemic is treated as a new unpredictable condition of the city one must consider when attempting to answer the question *How will we live together*, today, with the apparatus of architecture. The inverted tents and the set of video loops put into question this condition of post-urbanity; three of them show the scrolling protocols, three show the performed theatrical dialogues, while others give additional visual information.

Two protocols refer to a constitution of two hypothetical *internet states* – the state of the inverted tents and the state of mobile rooms – both giving form to current changes of everyday life, and both facing the movement of humans across abandoned cities and the countryside. Human mobility is thereby approached as a necessarily stable element for the years to come. A third protocol refers to a transformed social sphere hypothetically projected to a new social space named *theatre of normality*. This takes the viewer into a different common sphere of the post-urban condition conceived as a public performance.

EFFEKT, *Urban Village Project*, 2019

EFFEKT, *Ørsted Home*, 2018

Ego to Eco: Learning from Nature, 2020

Sinus Lynge (Danish, b.1977) and Tue Hesselberg Foged (Danish, b.1977) of EFFEKT (Denmark, est.2007)

Physical models, birch wood, grow table, and tree seedlings, 260 × 400 × 80 cm

Humanity is facing one of the most significant design challenges: climate change. Unless we collectively rethink the way many of us live, build, consume, and produce energy, water, and food, humans will not be able to sustain current living standards on Earth. At the same time, this challenge presents a far-reaching opportunity to reconnect our civilisation with the ecosystems that sustain us and the natural environment from which we evolved.

For billions of years nature designed a diverse web of interdependent ecosystems supporting millions of species that coexist within the boundaries of our planet. As humans continue to build habitats, one must eliminate waste by establishing circular resource loops. To better face this new ecological era requires a paradigm that no longer distinguishes between existing human systems and the natural ecosystems we depend on as a species. From this perspective, technology and design are no longer seen as separate from the natural world.

To change the path of our civilisation, one needs to acknowledge that human evolution is social – driven by collective desires and aspirations. Design can give shape to these aspirations and propose new ways of living that seriously consider the needs of both people and the planet. By applying natural principles in design, humans can strive to close the gap that currently exists between the built and natural environments, for the mutual benefit of both human and nonhuman life.

Ego to Eco is an installation that seeks to explore how to design human communities based on the principles of nature.

atelier masōmī, *Making of an Artisans' Valley*, 2020

atelier masōmī, *Artisans' Valley*, 2020–ongoing. Exhibition perspective view

Making of an Artisans' Valley, 2020

Mariam Kamara (Nigerien, b.1979) of atelier masōmī (Niger, est.2014), in collaboration with the Tuareg Sculptors Collective (Niger)

Wood platform, hand-carved wood panels, physical wood model, LED screens, 700 × 600 × 45 cm

The Gounti Yenna Valley has long divided Niger's capital city of Niamey into two. In the 1800s, this division was established between the French colonisers and local citizens. Today, the valley divides the city across a wealth and education gap.

With a walking tour, both physically and metaphorically, through the work of Niger's Tuareg artisans, this installation proposes a new social contract for how Niamey's citizens might experience the valley as a place of unity.

The journey through *Making of an Artisans' Valley* comprises a whimsical promenade peppered with semicircular, perforated shells inspired by Niger's rural cylindrical clay granary clusters. Visitors can take a seat on the wooden benches set against panels clad with embossed leather tiles as they watch the stories of the artisans who made them in the video documentaries that appear on the screens. The sensitivity of the craftsmanship is evident in the hand-carved brass floor panels, a piece of Niger's heritage, reminiscent of a sacred ground paved with the earth's riches.

In the afterlife of the 17th International Architecture Exhibition, the artisans, who live 6,000 km away, will get the panels back after the exhibition closes and their work will have reached a much wider world beyond the artificial geopolitical borders that exist between visitors to this exhibition and the crafters in Niger.

As the panels find new life in the hands and workshops of the Tuareg artisans, the aspiration is to begin another investigation into ways we can all live and indeed walk together towards a better tomorrow.

Construction of Pediatric and Maternity Hospital in Tambacounda, Senegal

Brick production for the Pediatric and Maternity Hospital

The Many Lives of Tambacounda Hospital, 2018–2020

Manuel Herz (Swedish, b.1969) of Manuel Herz Architects (Switzerland, est.1999), Iwan Baan (Netherlands, b.1975), Josef and Anni Albers Foundation and Le Korsa (USA, est.1971), and Magueye Ba (Senegalese, b.1977) and Therese Aida Ndiaye (Senegalese, b.1968) of Tambacounda Hospital (Senegal)

Site-specific installation, mixed media

The Tambacounda Maternity and Pediatric Hospital, established by the Josef and Anni Albers Foundation and its NGO Le Korsa and designed by Manuel Herz, is currently being constructed in the city of Tambacounda, in eastern Senegal. Offering approximately 150 hospital beds, it represents a major contribution to the health system of Senegal's eastern region.

The Many Lives of Tambacounda Hospital shows the multiple dimensions, economies, materialities, and narratives in which the Tambacounda Hospital is embedded. It aims to uncover and illuminate the many processes and lives a building embodies, precipitates, and connects to. The installation asks questions such as: Who are the stakeholders in the design process? Who are the contractors and construction workers? Who are the users? Where does the money come from and where does it go? How is the project used over its lifetime? What impact does it have on the community? What other projects does the hospital trigger? What does the planning application process reveal about the culture of administration? How can the production of architecture be a form of research and inquiry?

Beyond the architectural design of the hospital, the installation gives voice to central figures, such as Magueye Ba, the general contractor who also practices medicine in the afternoons and, additionally, documents projects such as a village school that required a test-façade.

As it presents the many lives of the hospital, this project emphasises that the time has come to understand architectural projects such as the Tambacounda Hospital as central to architecture's mission. This hospital project should not be seen as architecturally marginal but, instead, as demonstrating and uncovering processes that are fundamental to our discipline as a whole.

MDP, Qatari landscape, Doha coastline, 2008–2016

Qatar Transforming Landscapes

Michel Desvigne (French, b.1958) di Michel Desvigne Paysagiste, MDP (France)

Over the years, MDP has designed a series of very large urban interventions in Doha, Qatar – on sites spread over such a large area that one can almost speak of a territorial project.

Panels, materials and dimensions variable

For the first project, the team meticulously studied the Qatari landscape, seeking out elements that might nourish landscape projects located in the city. As always, natural geography yields particular forms and situations, which include agricultural and urban practices. The dry river valleys – the famous *wadis* – sometimes carry runoff water and concentrate a little moisture the rest of the time. Sparse but specific vegetation develops in this environment, producing shapes that flow and meander. Agriculture has created dykes, reservoirs, and canals, whose logic and geometries are superimposed on natural geography and topography. Many of the mangroves growing on the coast, where they form a precious ecosystem, have been destroyed in the Gulf by port, industrial, or tourist developments – although some have been conserved. There are also dunes, the places where they touch the water, lagoons, and so on. In reading and rereading the landscape, its history and practices, and transposing it, it became possible to establish a vocabulary for the differently scaled projects that followed.

Such projects have the dimensions of the public spaces that should have potentially been built in French suburbs, where it has never been possible to project continuously over a distance of 10 or 15 kilometres.

TUMO Center for Creative Technologies, *TUMO Paris*, 2018

Learning (to Live) Together, 2020

Learning (to Live) Together.
The future of Schools and the Architecture of Walk-Away Pedagogy

For young people around the world, learning is non-consensual: students go to school because they have to. Yet the most effective learning environments are ones from which students can walk away but don't. How would pedagogy and learning spaces change if education were consensual? The social dynamic resulting from such changes would be one that can build the educational foundations of a less segregated, less coercive, and more purposeful society.

 The TUMO Center for Creative Technologies addresses the architecture of 'walk-away pedagogy' and the future of learning. It explores physical environments where teenagers belong to a highly inclusive, evolving community of peers learning together while learning to learn, live, and work together. It features spaces that reflect a radical, new approach to education and its spatial expression across scales – from urban contexts and buildings to interiors and furniture, devices and software.

 The TUMO Center showcases learning environments in the densest of urban areas as well as remote villages and open fields, through various architectures: The Convergence Center in Yerevan and the Pyramid of Tirana by MVRDV; the TUMO Paris at the Forum des Halles; TUMO centres in Berlin, Beirut, and beyond; and the foundational learning environments designed by Bernard Khoury / DW5. The integrated interior and furniture designs include mobile and floating workstations, plug-and-play 'umbilical cords', and freeform bleacher spaces and learning boxes – physical reflections of the pedagogical platform.

 Embedded in the TUMO project is a live demonstration of technologies and digital interfaces generating hyper-personalised, dynamically updated learning paths, self-learning content, and hands-on learning labs.

Marie Lou Papazian (American/Armenian, b.1964) and Pegor Papazian (American and Armenian, b.1963) of the TUMO Center for Creative Technologies (Armenia, est.2011) in collaboration with Bernard Khoury (Lebanese, b.1968) and Winy Maas (Dutch, b.1959)

Materials and dimensions variable

Miralles Tagliabue EMBT, *Collective Housing and Market at Plateau Central*, 2017.
Conceptual collage: Living within a Market – Another kind of housing

Miralles Tagliabue EMBT, *Collective Housing and Market at Plateau Central*, 2017.
View: outdoor market and public space

Living Within a Market: Plateau Central Collective Housing and Market, 2017–2024

Benedetta Tagliabue (Italian, b.1963), Elena Nedelcu and Joan Callís of Miralles Tagliabue EMBT (Spain, est.1994) in collaboration with Ilimelgo (France, est.2006)

This project consists of a journey through a series of models to showcase the design process of the *Plateau Central* project in Clichy-Sous-Bois in the metropolis of Paris.

Central to the installation is a 1:50 model section of the building as an analogy of Georges Perec's novel *Life: A User's Manual* to represent the lifestyle of the inhabitants of *Plateau Central*. A way to enhance the project's strong public character – the terraces, the urban gardens, the common areas, the market, and its relation to the plaza – by showing its significance within the building and enhancing the powerful impact it contributes to the district.

The growth of the population and the economic situation both lead to a scenario where the house unit is becoming smaller and smaller; while the current pandemic is forcing us to reflect on how important it is to have an outdoor space where one can expand the limits of each home and enjoy the open air. Thus, the time we are experiencing places urgency on the need for spaces that are linked to collective housing and that allow conviviality and the feeling of being part of a community.

The *Plateau Central* building is constructed in a neighbourhood mainly consisting of an immigrant population and is closely related to a marketplace. In the project, the apartments are in the centre of a system that includes urban agriculture on the roofs, terraces as common spaces for the neighbours, and the presence of a food market inside the volume of the same building – conceived not only as a commercial space but also as a community space and a tool for greater social integration.

The experience of this outer area of Paris points out the fact that activities linked to food are some of the most efficient ways to achieve active participation from the collective. A market, therefore, seems to be a perfectly adequate scenario for this purpose.

Scaled model of a section of the *Plateau Central Collective Housing and Market* building (1:50); Scaled models of site, volume, façade, and details: wood, paper, acrylic, scales and dimensions variable

Ronan and Erwan Bouroullec, *Lianas, Urban Reveries*, 2016

Ronan and Erwan Bouroullec, *Nuages Promenade, Urban Reveries*, 2016

Ronan and Erwan Bouroullec, *Ring Bench, Urban Reveries*, 2016

Urban Reveries, 2016

Ronan Bouroullec (French, b.1971) and Erwan Bouroullec (French, b.1976)

The *Urban Reveries* installation is a wide-ranging research project of possible development solutions for cities, a repertoire of new principles that may be imagined in very different urban settings.

Ring bench, galvanised steel, screen projection, d. 500 cm

    Like a large open sketchbook, the solutions are proposed while wandering through models, photographs, and animations presented on screen. The installation is designed to be immersive and to transport the visitor into different scenarios, with each model presented as an exercise in an urban fiction. A large number of ideas were produced over the course of a year, some of which are presented here as pilot models. This intense research resulted in thirteen proposals, which were turned into models that were given special treatment.

    This research demonstrates the need to bring new, natural forms back into the city: plants, animals, water, and fire. Most of these proposals are based on the way in which nature comes into contact with the city. They take urban functions into consideration and offer new perspectives on the relationship between buildings, the quality of paving, the positioning of a fountain or the planting of a jungle: all those human attentions that would turn the city into a place of enchantment.

Skidmore, Owings & Merrill with European Space Agency,
Moon Village Earth Rise, 2020

Life Beyond Earth, 2020

Skidmore, Owings & Merrill (USA, est.1936), in collaboration with European Space Agency (Paris, est.1975)

CNC and 3D-printed physical models; LCD display with animated film; Digital prints, dimensions variable

A new, global initiative to return to the Moon is underway, with the goal to create a permanent base for research and exploration. What does this mean for the future? Will our generation be the first to establish a home on another celestial body? How could this redefine our notions of community?

Space exploration has the potential to increase scientific knowledge and innovation; it may also transform our understanding of life on Earth. Along with recent advancements in technology, the entry of private companies into the field opens up possibilities for partnerships between governments and industry – new alliances that can elevate the capacity to pursue bold visions of the future.

Life Beyond Earth results from an international, multidisciplinary initiative launched by the European Space Agency (ESA) to explore the potential for inhabited environments on the Moon. Expanding the territory of architecture, the project inspires visitors to envision future societies in new environments and to confront the challenges for sustaining human life in the extreme conditions of outer space.

The proposed Moon Village draws on the creative and scientific expertise of both the architecture and space industries. SOM and ESA established a cross-functional design and engineering methodology, bringing a range of experts together to develop near-term and long-range strategies – from the design of the first habitation units to a master plan for lunar infrastructure. Science, industry, and the human experience are all essential to the outcome. Eventually, the Moon Village may grow into a thriving international community: a hub for research, space exploration, and even tourism.

Two models bring the concept to life: a 1:500 scale site model shows the Moon Village in its context, on the ridge of a lunar crater, while a 1:15 scale model of a single habitation unit allows visitors to imagine life inside. Display boards and an animation visualise the journey to the Moon and the construction of the settlement. Seeking to define what humans need not just to survive in space, but to truly thrive there, the installation presents an altogether new approach: integrating space architecture, engineering, urban design, and resource management to support a sustainable way of life beyond Earth.

All images: Michael Maltzan Architecture, *Sixth Street Viaduct and Park*, 2020

The Sixth Street Viaduct Replacement Project, 2020

Michael T. Maltzan, FAIA (American, b.1959) of Michael Maltzan Architecture (USA, est.1995)

Suspended 3D-printed model, 400 × 20 × 190 cm; Video

The new Los Angeles *Sixth Street Viaduct* is a transformative infrastructure project for the City of Los Angeles and the single largest bridge project in its history. The Viaduct and other ambitious infrastructural projects are collectively challenging the history of infrastructure as a divisive element and instead evolving the idea of infrastructure to become one of *civicstructure*, moving from a monoculture of singular use to a *multiculture* of connection and urban vibrancy.

The new *Sixth Street Viaduct* will replace the original 1932 bridge and unite the historic Boyle Heights community to the east and the expanding Arts District to the west. The Viaduct is more than a simple replacement thoroughfare crossing the Los Angeles River. Instead, it foresees a multimodal future for the city, one that accommodates cars, incorporates significant new bicycle connections, and increases connectivity for pedestrians, not only at the bridge's endpoints but along the entirety of the span, linking the bridge, the river, and urban landscapes below. Challenging the long-held notion that infrastructural elements in cities are single-purpose, divisive elements, the Viaduct instead reimagines the city's infrastructural network as vital physical, social, and cultural catalysts that can unite, rather than divide, our cities.

The installation introduces the project at three scales: (1) the physical reality of the Viaduct itself as an armature of connective components that facilitate a multimodal experience of the structure; (2) the social, cultural, and economic impact the project will have on the City of Los Angeles, most directly on the regions that have influenced the viaduct's design (the historic neighbourhood of Boyle Heights, the transforming river-adjacent industrial landscape, and the re-emerging Arts District); (3) the conceptual ideation of the bridge as it illustrates a new approach to infrastructural responsibility and connectivity, the new *civicstructure*.

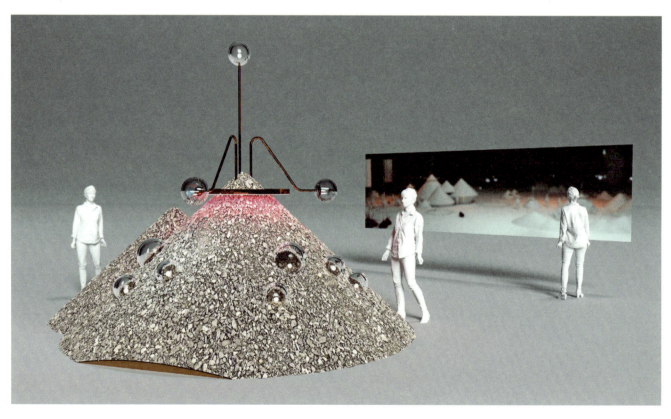

All images: Sean Lally, *Shaped Touches*, 2020

Shaped Touches, 2021

*Sean Lally (American, b.1974)
of Sean Lally Architecture
(Switzerland)*

Multiplayer video projection;
Prototype, stone, steel,
550 × 550 × 360 cm

Architecture's shape is a negotiation between the control of the environment and the body's ability to perceive that information. As the human body increases its range of sensorial abilities through advancements in healthcare and access to wearable technologies, climate change is simultaneously redefining one's expectations for future environments. Architects are in a position to foreshadow the opportunities and implications these pressures will have on shared public spaces. *Shaped Touches* offers a proposition for how architecture will define its shape and the relationships of people and communities touching that space.

Through the use of a multi-player video game platform, the project illustrates the opportunities and implications for the public spaces of cities. The game installation is on a three-minute cycle, restarting each time for a player to explore the design space. As each game begins, that player is randomly provided three changes to their existing sensory perception. This could include the ability to see within the near infrared spectrum of light, hear low frequency sound, or even lose access to an existing sensory perception. As these new senses are provided, so are the correlating environments: designed lighting in infrared, the ability to hear plants communicate in low frequency, and an inability to hear common sound frequencies. As each game resets, the base architecture takes on additional material variables and design. Other players in the game from around the world cross the visitors' paths, experiencing different sensory abilities and architectural spaces than them. The visitors and other players share the same space, while each experiencing unique architectures, evoking the ways in which shared public space has fragmented. A built prototype within the installation demonstrates the materiality of the design simulated in the video.

Architecture is a shaped touch between the body and the array of information the body interfaces with. Architecture's shape is less of an objective form shared by those with physical access and more of a spectrum of sensorial shapes for those with varying access to these increasingly available materials, shaped by architects.

BASE studio, *Flocking Tejas*, 2021. Exterior view of the pavilion

BASE studio, *Flocking Tejas*, 2021. Interior view of the pavilion

Flocking Tejas, 2021

Bárbara Barreda (Chilean, b.1982) and Felipe Sepúlveda (Chilean, b.1985) of BASE studio (Chile, est.2016), in collaboration with Arup engineering (UK, est.1946)

Model scale: 1:3,
207 × 404 × 155 cm
and digital projection

How can systemic thinking and generative design methods contribute to new ways of living together? Can they become a tool for bringing tradition and identity together in a contemporary way? Can they help design global customisable architectural strategies, adaptable to diverse local sustainable solutions? Can they contribute to the creation of accessible and dignified spatial experiences for the many?

Architecture seeks to understand people's needs and desires, their demands for architecture to better deal with the complexity of individuals and communities, and their histories, traditions, aspirations, and prospects. Through systems that bring together past and future, techniques and technology, analogue and digital, one can begin to shape a more inclusive architecture. One that establishes a technological middle ground to reconcile tradition and design advancements.

Flocking Tejas is an emergent and adaptable architectural system that arises from questioning the architectural and construction qualities of clay tiles. It examines how, over time and across various cultures, their use has often been limited to construction systems with seemingly static, predictable, and flat organisational principles. Utilising contemporary design techniques, this project instead seeks to explore new spatial and formal repertoires that reimagine and enhance the usage and possibilities of traditional materials.

This system's design grants dynamic variations and architectural applications for clay tiles. Its intrinsic ability to create semi-open common spaces makes it essentially a social enabler that allows for inclusiveness and spatial generosity.

In the context of the Biennale, *Flocking Tejas* aims to expose visitors to a physical, architectural experience that strives to trigger questions and evoke images and speculation about the spatial, social, and identitarian potential of architecture.

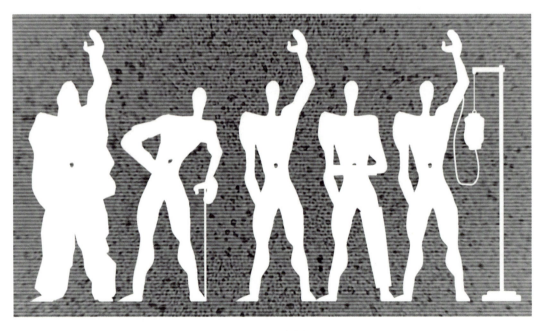

All images: OMA, *Hospital of the Future*, 2020

Hospital of the Future, 2019–2021

We could claim to live longer than any previous generation in human history, with average life expectancy doubling in the last century. Thanks to improvements in sanitation, nutrition, and medicine, most humans may live to the age of 73. Illness was once less something to die from and more something to live with. Then came the new coronavirus, seemingly upending all previous assumptions. In 2021, the chronic conditions related to aging and lifestyle have suddenly become an acute problem. Pundits, observing the impact of the virus, muse about 'the new normal', but how *new* is new, and how *normal* was normal?

Can technology save humans? Will gene therapy and 3D-printed organs become widespread? Will 5G networks revolutionise healthcare and unleash promising leaps in effectiveness? What about hospitals? Can they keep abreast of these technological advances? With increasing evidence that Western models of healthcare may have reached their limits, what are the alternatives?

If living a long life no longer means living a life in good health, this installation asks: What is the role of the healthcare institutions humans have put in place to promote healthy lives, and what will they look like in the future?

Reinier de Graaf (Dutch, b.1964), with Hans Larsson (Swedish, b.1983), Alex Retegan (Romanian, b.1982), Sofia Hosszufalussy (Italian, b.1995), Elisa Versari (Italian, b.1990), Matthew Bovingdon-Downe (British, b.1988), Benedetta Gatti (Italian, b.1994) of the Office for Metropolitan Architecture (The Netherlands, est.1975).

Medical curtains in steel frame 300 × 100 cm; Field hospital beds, mobile sink; MDF 'Modulor' figures, LED spotlights; Screen 500 × 288 cm

doxiadis+, *Entangled Kingdoms*, 2019–2020.
Collecting live fungi from the Arsenale

doxiadis+, *Entangled Kingdoms*, 2019–2020. The magic fungi garden

Entangled Kingdoms, 2019–2020

How will we live together on this multispecies planet? By understanding, respecting, and connecting to the web of entanglement that is life on Earth.

The twentieth century was imbued by Darwinism with a conflictual framework. As we witness the Anthropocene's mass extinction in the twenty-first century, we are obliged to achieve a new balance that stems from understanding nature as a web of dependencies among all kingdoms of life. In such a model, ecosystems and the surface of the Earth itself are superorganisms with multiple subjects acting in close collaboration as well as competing with one another. Humans only exist thanks to this web of life and to the subtle and constant exchanges among all living organisms.

An unsung hero of this web is the kingdom between plants and animals, that of the fungi. Creators and facilitators of life, fungi are as resilient as rock and can turn rock into soil through pedogenesis. They form mycelium networks making extraordinary sentient connections among trees. They are recyclers, metabolising decomposing organic matter, returning it to the biological circle. Without them life on Earth could not exist.

Entangled Kingdoms has been developed with experts, where design consists of minutely observing and understanding an environment and ecosystem before developing a creative concept to enable a thriving, multispecies solution. This project presents fungi spores collected from the two rooms of the Arsenale in which the installation is located and then cultivated in the mycology department at the University of Athens. At the Biennale, these return as a 'fungi garden' in a two-part installation. Having first placed humanity in the wider context of the plant, animal, and fungi kingdoms, this project invites reverent reflection on the complexity, beauty, and also invisibility and ubiquity of fungi in the world around us.

Thomas Doxiadis (Greek, b.1970), Marina Antsakli (Greek, b.1980), Despoina Gkirti (Greek, b.1979), Dionysia Liveri (Greek, b.1976), Angeliki Mathioudaki (Greek, b.1978), Ioanna Potiriadi (Greek, b.1986), Alexandra Souvatzi (Greek, b.1993), and Evanthia Beristianou (Greek, b.1992) of doxiadis+ (Greece, est.1999) in collaboration with Zacharoula Gonou-Zagou (Greek, b.1958), Julia Pitts (British, b.1967), Alkestie Skarlatou (Greek, b.1978), Peter Aslanidis (Greek/American, b.1974), Helliniki Meletitiki (Greece, est.1985), and Cathy Cunliffe (British, b.1972)

Installation including a hanging metal frame with tropical plants, d. 450 cm; Lightweight structure, 1200 × 50 × 380 cm; Giant petri dish with fungi collected from the Biennale, d. 100 cm; Dried mushrooms, lichens, mushroom substrate; Magnifying glasses; Hanging leaves 550 × 160 cm and 640 × 225 cm; Downlights, spotlights; multichannel audio, speakers

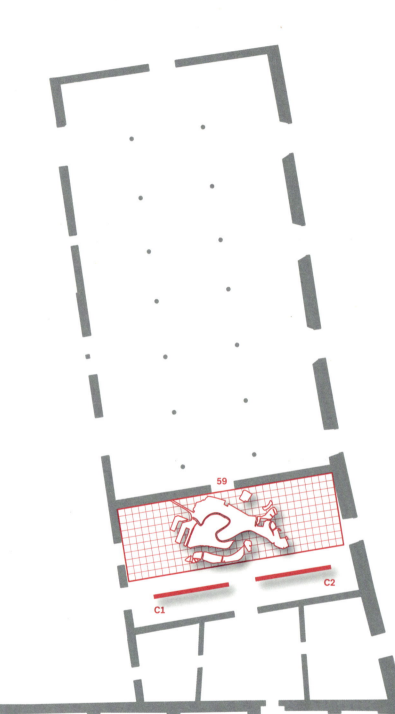

COMING TOGETHER IN VENICE

AS EMERGING COMMUNITIES

59 studio L A (Lorien Beijaert; Arna Mačkić in collaboration with Baukje Trenning)
199

C1 Nicholas de Monchaux; Kathryn Moll; Sandro Bisà; modem; Bisà Associati with catalogtree and University of Virginia Venice Program
201

C2 Laura Fregolent, Università Iuav di Venezia; Paola Malanotte-Rizzoli, MIT
203

Venice has suffered a lot lately – floods, the pressures of mass tourism, the coronavirus. It has suffered with and for the rest of the world.

This room celebrates the perseverance of our host city, the rich historical examples it has set as a space for cohabitation between land and sea, between East and West, among different ethnicities, and between tourists and citizens. These projects venerate Venice's beautiful fragility, especially in face of climate change, by foregrounding its co-dependency on its broader contexts, with its archipelago, lagoon, and its experiments with old and new technologies.

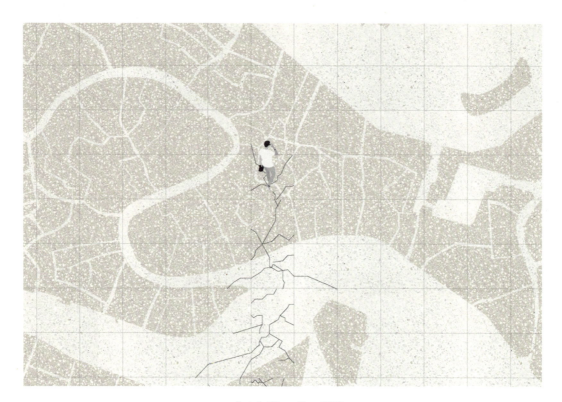

studio L A, *City to Dust*, 2019

studio L A, *City to Dust*, 2019. Marco Cappelletti, photograph of Venice during the Covid-19 pandemic, 2020

City to Dust, 2020–2021

Lorien Beijaert (Dutch, b.1986) and Arna Mačkić (Dutch, b.1988) of studio L A (the Netherlands, est.2016), in collaboration with Baukje Trenning (Dutch, b.1969)

Terrazzo Tiles,
1866 × 602 × 2 cm,
printed photographs (12),
59,4 × 42 cm

Venice is an empty city where beauty became visible again. But behind this beauty lies the world of the Covid-19 pandemic: a world of disease, despair, and loss. A catastrophe for Venetians as well as many other communities around the world.

This pandemic largely travelled with the large-scale movement of people around the globe. Being one of the most visited cities in the world, it is not a coincidence that the pandemic hit Venice hard.

Venice is a city in which the theme 'communities' has a charged connotation. In recent years, its inhabitants have been crowded out by tourism. The city's beauty, which attracts attention and visitors, simultaneously represents its biggest threat. The large numbers of tourists are bringing the city closer to its demise. As visitors and participants of the Biennale, we inevitably take part in this dynamic. This project allows visitors to experience this duality and to form a new perspective on the city, the human community, and themselves.

The installation brings forward the contentious effects of tourism on the city, by making visitors a part of the work and assigning them the agency of impacting it. It is an installation that changes continuously. It is a representation of the city of Venice made in *terrazzo* tiles and placed on the floor of a space in the Arsenale grounds.

Conceived as a threshold, visitors must cross and walk over the *terrazzo* floor installation in order to enter the next room. However, if one is not careful enough, each step might slowly cause a part of the city to break. Each step, then, causes one to confront one's own footprint in the deterioration of Venice.

Bisà and modem, *Amended Service Study*, 2021

Servizio Modificato (Amended Service), 2021

For all the continuities represented by Venice, the city–lagoon system is deeply threatened. Once a metropolis, Venice now hosts less than 51,000 permanent residents, who in recent years serve an annual tourist population of 12 to 20 million. The lagoon, for thousands of years a cultivated balance between sea and silt, has in the past 40 years undergone ecological shifts – of level, composition, ecology, and salinity – that threaten its very existence.

Historically, Venice was not confined to the dense network of *isole* shaped from sandbars in the early Middle Ages and cleaved by the Grand Canal. Rather, it was an interlinked archipelago stretching the length and breadth of the lagoon, in which a variety of innovative, incompatible, or inconvenient functions were diffused. Today, communities in the lagoon and its margins – tourists, residents, and commuters alike – move separately along highly prescribed routes, yet rarely across the surface of the water that connects them.

Taking very literally the challenge of this 17th International Architecture Exhibition to 'work together […] to imagine new geographies and associations', this project is a catalyst for new journeys and trajectories. Its framework, extending from a point of departure in the space of the Arsenale with a development indipendent from the Exhibition, will expand to encompass the mediated journeys of students, critics, ecologists, and architects in the fall of 2021; a symposium at the Biennale's conclusion; and ongoing research by the University of Virginia Venice Program and other partners.

It is in the nature of Venice that one encounters debates about the future not in the linear language of policy documents, but rather through labyrinthine arguments on causes and effects. This quality of conversation reasserts the essential complexity and interconnectedness of any city and its ecology. Here, particularly, Venice remains essential.

Sandro Bisà (Italian, b.1973) of Bisà Associati (Italy, est.2012), Nicholas de Monchaux (American, b.1973), and Kathryn Moll (American, b.1978) of modem (USA, est.2017), in collaboration with catalogtree (Netherlands, est.2001) and William Sherman (American, b.1955) of the University of Virginia Venice Program (est.1979)

Site-specific installation, mixed media

Venice: the past and the present, *Resilience of Venice*, 2020

Resilience of Venice, 2020

Laura Fregolent (Italian, b.1966) at University Iuav of Venice (Italy) and Paola Malanotte-Rizzoli (Italian, b.1946) at MIT (USA, est.1861)

Plasterboard, digital printing, video projection, 750 × 300 cm

The overall theme of this project is Venice's resilience addressed in two different and complementary ways.

The first focus is on the physical and morphological components of the city's resilience. Over more than a thousand years, the lagoon has changed from a state of sedimentation brought into the lagoon by the rivers to a present state of erosion. Human interventions in the twentieth century made the city and the lagoon resilient for survival in an industrialised world. The challenge for the future is to ensure resilience to global warming and the danger of an unprecedented rise in sea levels. The completion of the four barriers known as MOSE and their successful testing are a major step in the attempt to protect the city and the lagoon from flooding as sea levels rise in the foreseeable future.

The second focus is on the urban aspects of resilience through the 'walkability' and accessibility of the city's historical centre, and the functions on the ground of the historic centre. The different types and activities are analysed and drawn, underlining the residential and commercial spaces that will not be accessible in 2050 for about 81 days a year with floods as high as 105 and 110 cm or more. The analysis of these functions and the distress caused by floods help to define the quality of life.

This installation presents a map that underlines the projects carried out in the lagoon after the 1966 flood by the different institutions involved (state, region, and municipality). The idea is to highlight a perspective of the physical and social fragility of the city, of the continuous interventions it witnesses at different scales, and of the enormous economic investment. The resilient capacity of Venice, if properly managed, can reverse the trend that the city bears.

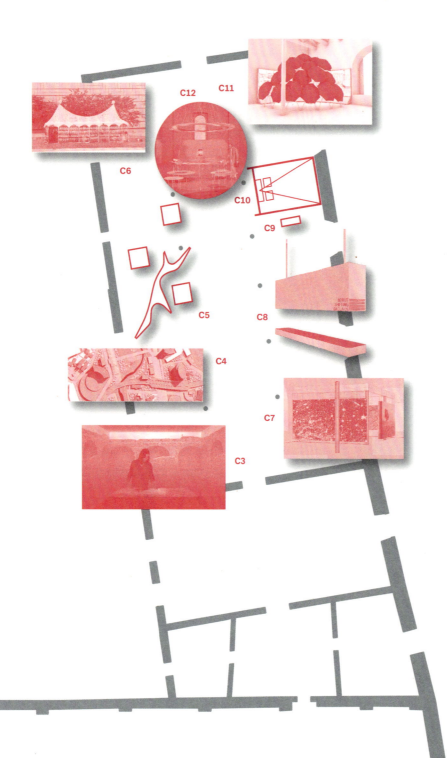

CO-HABITATS: HOW WE DO LIVE TOGETHER IN...

AS EMERGING COMMUNITIES

C3 **NIGERIA/EGYPT/MEXICO**: Kent Larson; Gabriela Bila Advincula; MIT Media Lab City Science Group
207

C4 **ADDIS ABABA**: Marc Angélil; ETH Zürich; Dirk Hebel; KIT Karlsruhe; Bisrat Kifle Woldeyessus; EiABC et al.
209

C5 **SÃO PAULO**: Daniel Talesnik; Andres Lepik; Architekturmuseum der TUM et al.
211

C6 **AL AZRAQ CAMP**: Azra Aksamija; Melina Philippou; MIT Future Heritage Lab et al.
213

C7 **INDIA**: Rahul Mehrotra; Sourav Kumar Biswas; GSD, Harvard University
215

C8 **BEIRUT**: Sandra Frem, American University of Beirut; Boulos Douaihy, PLATAU PLATFORM For Architecture and urbanism et al.
217

C9 **RIO DE JANEIRO**: Farès el-Dahdah; Alida Metcalf; Rice University; David Heyman; Axis Maps; Sergio Burgi; Instituto Moreira Salles et al.
219

C10 **PRISHTINA**: Bekim Ramku; Kosovo Architecture Foundation/ OUD+Architects et al.
221

C11 **HONG KONG**: Merve Bedir; Hong Kong University; Sampson Wong
223

C12 **NEW YORK**: Nora Akaw et al.; The Cooper Union
225

Architects often draw on precedents from their contexts. How we will live together will no doubt be inspired by tested models of cohabitation from our surroundings. In this room, architecture students and professors from universities across the world describe their own environments and how citizens and architects cumulatively created viable forms of cohabitation over the years.

Whether as protesters creatively appropriating and reshaping urban spaces, as commuters from different ethnic communities encountering each other on their way to work, or as refugees from various locations redefining a collective home out of borrowed architectures, our cumulative human ingenuity has shaped our environments over centuries.

MIT City Science group, *With(in)*, 2020. Maitane interacts with the urbanscape. Photograph of the installation

MIT City Science group, With(in), Fufu, tamales, and peas, 2020. Image collage

With(in), 2021

This is a story about connection. The MIT Media Lab City Science group presents an immersive window into the worlds of three women in three settlements: Eva in Guadalajara, Mexico; Gihan in Cairo, Egypt; and MamaG in Port Harcourt, Nigeria. The installation takes visitors to the fringe neighbourhoods and community centres in Guadalajara, the vertical slums and bustling restaurants of Cairo, and the tiny homes and crowded markets of Port Harcourt. In the lives of each individual, we examine the micro and the macro, from the gentle care of fixing one's hair each morning to the cultural swells of holidays, religious ceremonies, and funerals. In these places, far from our own, we learn and inquire, we gather and we listen, in the hope of better understanding the complexity of the world and possibilities for how we will live together in the future.

As extreme urbanisation unfolds at an astounding pace, all three locations reflect the chaos and the importance of community. One woman's journey can be both individual and global when viewed in the context of the others. How does rapid urbanisation impact the community we seek, and how do intimate domestic activities such as food preparation and celebration reflect a larger cultural context?

Kent Larson (American, b.1953), Gabriela Bílá Advincula (Brazilian, b.1990) and the City Science group at the Media Lab (USA, est.1985) at Massachusetts Institute of Technology (USA, est.1861) in collaboration with the With(in) protagonists: Eva (Mexico), Gihan (Egypt) and MamaG (Nigeria)

Immersive projection, 3D models, wood, 440 × 620 cm

Marc Angelil et. al, *Quo Addis? – Conflicts of Coexistence*, 2020. Anticipated hybridisation of Addis's territory, based on the juxtaposition of spatial interventions, superimposed onto the residue of past layers of nation-building processes, digital model

Quo Addis? Conflicts of Coexistence, 2020

In Addis Ababa, the hybridisation of territory comes in the form of shiny ensembles overshadowing indigenous settlements, traffic arteries disrupting the labyrinth of pedestrian paths, and agro-industries springing up next to what is left of subsistence farms, to mention just a few of the more striking spatial juxtapositions – and all of this superimposed on what is left of layers of past nation-building processes.

Woven into this already complicated spatial hybrid are mixed modes of social organisation (ethnic affiliations, religious groups, agricultural cooperatives, neighbourhood associations, trade unions), along with various modes of production (agricultural, industrial, microentrepreneurial, service-oriented), all coexisting in multiple forms to produce a composite economy, including practices that are considered informal.

This is the terrain on which coming iterations of Ethiopia will have to be shaped, rather than being wished away in some blank-slate development venture or beautification scheme.

Quo Addis? – Conflicts of Coexistence includes a speculative model of the city of Addis Ababa. The model is made of multiple layers, each representing a particular political regime whose traces remain in Addis Ababa's urban socio-spatial fabric: (1) the Age of Empire, 1889–1936; (2) the Italian occupation, 1936–1941; (3) US- and European-sponsored modernisation under Haile Selassie, 1941–1974; (4) the USSR-backed socialist regime, 1974–1991; (5) European Development Assistance, 1991–2005; (6) Meles Zenawi's *grands projets*, 2005–2012; and (7) contemporary mega-development ventures sponsored by foreign actors – the UAE, Saudi Arabia, China, and so on (2012–today).

To this amalgam, add one more layer – one foregrounding alternative ways Addis Ababa might live together.

Marc Angélil (Swiss/American, b.1954) at ETH Zurich (Switzerland, est.1854), Katharina Blümke (German, b.1992) and Dirk Hebel (German, b.1971) at KIT Karlsruhe (Germany, est.2009), Jenny Rodenhouse (American, b.1984), and Bisrat Kifle Woldeyessus (Ethiopian, b.1979) at the Ethiopian Institute for Architecture, Building, Construction and City Development, EiABC (Ethiopia, est.1954)

Model of Addis Ababa (1:75), wood, metal, concrete, Plexiglas, 200 × 560 × 210 cm, screen-projected video, dimensions variable

Paulo Mendes da Rocha and MMBB Arquitetos (Fernando Mello Franco, Marta Moreira, Milton Braga), the thirteenth-floor rooftop pool, Serviço Social do Comércio (SESC) 24 de Maio, 2001–2017

Access for All: São Paulo's Architectural Infrastructures, 2019

Daniel Talesnik (Chilean, b.1979) and Andres Lepik (German, b.1961) of the Architekturmuseum der TUM (Munich, Germany, est.2002) in collaboration with Mariana Vilela (Brazilian, b.1981), Kathryn Gillmore (Chilean, b.1978), Ciro Miguel (Brazilian, b.1980), Pedro Kok (Brazilian, b.1984), Danilo Zamboni (Brazilian, b.1986), Guilherme Pianca (Brazilian, b.1987), and Gabriel Sepe (Brazilian, b.1986)

For decades, São Paulo has seen investments in architectural infrastructures that help alleviate the lack of public space in the megacity. Many of these projects also provide São Paulo's 12 million inhabitants with access to recreational, cultural, and athletic programmes, much-needed in this dense metropolis of tremendous inequality, high crime rates, severe traffic issues, and serious public health problems. *Access for All: São Paulo's Architectural Infrastructures* presents a selection of these public-, public-private-, and privately-owned buildings, public spaces, and infrastructure projects at different scales that attempt to create inclusive places for urban society to thrive.

The featured projects are presented with a focus on their programmatic characteristics rather than their formal qualities, which are usually the emphasis in scholarship on Brazilian architecture. Regardless of when they were constructed, the projects are analysed as they stand today, through newly commissioned photographs, films, architectural drawings, illustrations, models, and interviews.

Access for All looks partly at how the city is designed incrementally by architects at the building scale. Conversely, it shows how the accumulated built logic of the city has an impact on its architecture and public spaces. The installation emphasises how architecture weaves in and out of the city, blurring the boundaries between buildings and the public realm. Sidewalks merge into ramps, stairs, and escalators, and at times reappear in the cityscape as elevated or sunken squares, rooftop terraces, and gardens.

While many cities around the world are still chasing the Bilbao effect – the creation of a monofunctional, signature architectural work by a famous architect to attract tourism – *Access for All* advocates for architecture that serves diverse cultural, social, and recreational functions, all aimed at sustaining the needs of São Paulo's residents.

Aluminium cubic frames with textiles (4), 160 × 160 × 160 cm; digital printing and projection, dimensions variable; wood and steel bench, 600 × 60 × 50 cm

MIT Future Heritage Lab, *Displaced Empire*, 2017. Adobe structure referencing monuments from Palmyra and Aleppo in front of Al Azraq Camp's T-Shelters

MIT Future Heritage Lab, *Displaced Empire*, 2019. The T-Serai portable palace made of humanitarian textiles and discarded clothes

Displaced Empire: Al Azraq Refugee Camp, Jordan, 2016–2019

Azra Aksamija (Austrian, b.1976) and Melina Philippou (Cypriot, b.1988) of MIT Future Heritage Lab (USA, est.2016) in collaboration with Natalie Bellefleur (Canadian, b.1992), Stratton Coffman (American, b.1992), Jaya A. Eyzaguirre (Chilean/American, b.1992), Lillian P. H. Kology (American, b.1985), Catherine Lie (Indonesian, b.1992), Calvin Zhong (American, b.1996) of MIT Future Heritage Lab, Zeid Madi (Jordanian, b.1991) of Cluster Labs (Jordan, est.2016), Raafat Majzoub (Lebanese, b.1986) of The Khan (Lebanon, est.2016), Mary Mavrohanna (Cypriot, b.1994) of the University of Cyprus (Cyprus, est.1989), Dietmar Offenhuber (Austrian, b.1973) of Northeastern University (USA, est.1898)

The traditional ideal of living in a single-family home on privately-owned land is no longer tenable. Conflicts, climate change, and inequality are key factors shaping this new reality of scarcity and displacement.

Focused on Al Azraq Refugee Camp in Jordan, one of the region's largest camps established in 2014 to shelter more than 35,000 displaced Syrians, *Displaced Empire* speculates about a near-future world in which the majority of people have been forcibly displaced. Al Azraq Camp has become the capital of the global 'displaced empire'.

In this story, Wael, a young man born in Syria and growing up in Al Azraq Refugee Camp in Jordan defies this reality daily. Despite being confined, he weaves his life through new friendships with young people such as Jar and others who come from different parts of Syria. Jar dropped out of school because he does not see how traditional education could better his future, but he can teach how to mitigate the unbearable heat of the standardised T-shelters with DIY air conditioners and shisha fountains. Wael is heading to the 2020 Olympics for a taekwondo match.

The T-Serai is the *Empire*'s HQ, a portable palace reflecting on the surplus and scarcity in the architecture of displacement. The tent and drawings of everyday life in the camp are the result of multiannual collaborations across borders. Imperial almanacs laser-burned on denim banners depict the reverse urbanisation phenomena of the camp through the lens of inventions created by Syrian refugees. The ingenuity and resourcefulness of Al Azraq residents reveal the cultural, emotional, and architectural needs of displaced people within a context of scarcity, trauma, confinement, and struggle for a future. By altering and domesticating the standardised humanitarian T-Shelters, displaced Syrians humanise humanitarian architecture using art and design as a medium of self-determination and world building.

Tent: humanitarian textiles, discarded clothes, military camouflage mesh, and a modified carport, 590 × 286 × 470 cm; Almanac banners (13), 60 × 100 cm; Laser-burned drawing and text on denim, 38 × 58 cm

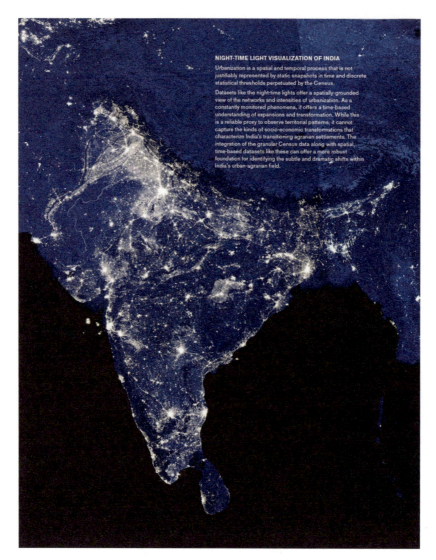

NASA Earth Observatory images by Joshua Stevens, using Suomi NPP VIIRS data from Miguel Román, NASA GSFC

Becoming Urban: Trajectories of Urbanisation in India, 2021

Rahul Mehrotra (American/Indian, b.1959), Sourav Kumar Biswas (Indian, b.1986) at Harvard Graduate School of Design (USA, est.1936) in collaboration with The Lakshmi Mittal and Family South Asia Institute (USA, est.2003) at Harvard University, and Architecture Foundation (India, est.2016)

Projection film, 356 × 200 cm; Digitally printed graphic boards of gatorboard (10), dimensions variable; Voile scrims with aluminium structure, graphic panels (4), dimensions variable

India's urban discourse is dominated by a focus on large cities and the splintering urbanism of informal settlements often housing the majority of the urban city's population. We recognise that settlement typologies considered informal are the result of aspirational migrants facing a dearth of institutional solutions in cities. Without an anticipatory framework to address housing and infrastructure, the self-built housing and settlement typology from the so-called hinterland makes its way into the material economy of the city and creates a range of building forms that are lumped into the universalised rubric of the slum.

Becoming Urban decentres the study of settlements from metropolitan cities to the larger territory in order to understand the dynamics of migration that have shaped India's large cities and the processes of urbanisation that are now transforming the hinterland. By taking a territorial view, this project reinforces the idea these low-rise, self-built typologies will continue to house India's future urban population not just within large metropolitan cities but across tens of thousands of settlements.

By deconstructing dichotomies – formal–informal, urban–rural, ecology–politics – at various scales, the installation offers alternate readings of settlement patterns, migration flows, and shifting livelihoods within India's 'urban–agrarian field'. At the subcontinental scale, it focuses on the dichotomy of political versus ecological imaginaries by using the Indo-Gangetic plain to speculate on a re-conceptualisation of political borders. The Indus and Ganges river basins are home to more than 800 million people who are divided by some of the deepest political borders between India, Pakistan, Bangladesh, Nepal, and Afghanistan. The contested borders dividing various political entities within a landscape unit defined by water is yet another ideological barrier that has to be reimagined to effectively address rapid urbanisation and massive displacements in the era of climate change.

Wissam Chaaya, Beirut Port before (top)
and after (bottom) the August 2020 blast, 2021

Beirut Shifting Grounds, 2021

Beirut Shifting Grounds is a research project that spanned over two years, just as Beirut was going through major changes at an unprecedented rate with the collapse of its economy, the devaluation of the national currency, the viral outbreak of Covid-19, and finally the deadly Beirut Port explosion that ripped the city apart on 4 August, 2020. In the face of the pervading adversity, this period was defined by a wave of activism, collective self-organisation, and bottom-up mobilisation the likes of which had never been seen in the modern history of the country.

Through four parallel narratives of improvisation, reclamation, and production, the installation foregrounds spatial practices at the ground level of Beirut that allow people to adapt through uncertainty and change.

At the human scale, five short films present encounters with the act of being in Beirut's public realm through shifting conditions: privatisation, political control, pandemic, and post-disaster destruction. Each film features installations by groups of architecture students from the American University of Beirut designed to poke their users' awareness to such internalised conditions.

At the urban scale, a video projection showcases the life of seven neighbourhoods in Beirut through transitional moments: pre-revolution (October 2019), pre-lockdown (March 2020), post-blast (September 2020); emphasising their urban transformation, ground occupation, socio-economic drivers, and taxonomy of improvisations at the ground level. This installation also emphasises the agency of urban space to accommodate public expression.

At the architectural scale, the project reflects on the spatial modes of production that shaped Beirut's ground up to the Port blast.

The installation invites an open speculation on the architecture of the ground and its proclivity to support collective appropriation, offering the possibility of a city that still belongs to its inhabitants amid shifting conditions.

Sandra Frem (Lebanese, b.1980) at the American University of Beirut (Lebanon, est.1866) and Boulos Douaihy (Lebanese, b.1979) of plateau | platform for architecture and urbanism (Lebanon, est.2010) in collaboration with Carla Aramouny (Lebanese, b.1980), Rana Haddad (Lebanese, b.1966) and Nicolas Fayad (Lebanese, b.1985), of the American University of Beirut

Suspended MDF box, digital printing on vinyl, videos, 550 × 40 cm

Marc Ferrez (1843–1923), Largo da Carioca Fountain, c. 1890.
Situated Views of Rio de Janeiro, imagineRio/IMS, 2020

Robert Polidori (1951), street scene, Rocinha, 2012.
Situated Views of Rio de Janeiro, imagineRio/IMS, 2020

Situated Views of Rio de Janeiro, 2021

imagineRio charts changes in Rio de Janeiro's landscape and topography over time, as the city has existed and as it has been imagined. A seamless integration of photography and cartography highlights the spaces of gathering, be it where people have historically come together or where they have imagined coming together. Through georeferencing views of the city in the nineteenth and early twentieth centuries, its plazas, parks, squares, streets, waterfronts, and the central urban forest are now seen in remarkable geographic detail. Images from photographers such as Marc Ferrez (1843–1923) and Augusto Malta (1864–1957) stand out regarding the evolution of Rio de Janeiro's social and collective spaces.

Both extremely talented photographers, Ferrez and Malta were fundamental actors in the creation of official images of Rio de Janeiro. Ferrez accompanied Rio's *fin de siècle* urban transformation by photographing its construction projects, and his use of large-format and panoramic devices towards the end of the 1870s made him the only Brazilian photographer to work at the limits of photographic technology. Malta was hired as the official photographer of mayor Pereira Passos, Brazil's version of a Baron Haussmann, and his intense and rigorous photographic work plays a fundamental role in understanding one of the most radical urban interventions in the early twentieth century: the demolition of Morro do Castelo.

Driven by the question posed by this Biennale's title and in contrast with the selected historical images of official narratives, this installation also presents visual narratives focused on the ever growing and self-constructed spaces of the Rocinha and Maré Favelas. Frequently represented as areas of scarcity, favelas are historically strong spaces of gathering, where residents strive to engage in processes of community formation and use of public spaces.

Farès el-Dahdah (Lebanese, b.1964) and Alida Metcalf (American, b.1954) at Rice University, (USA, est.1912), David Heyman (American, b.1980) at Axis Maps (USA, est.2006), and Sergio Burgi (Brazilian, b.1958) at the Instituto Moreira Salles (Brazil, est.1992)

Display 75"; Leap Motion Controller; Mac Mini

Babau Bureau KAF18, Traces of Palladio, Prishtina Centre, 2018

Prishtina Public Archipelago, 2020

Bekim Ramku (Kosovar, b.1979) of Kosovo Architecture Foundation / OUD+Architects (Kosovo, est.2012) in collaboration with Nol Binakaj (Kosovar, b.1981) Kosovo Architecture Foundation (Kosovo, est.2012)

Projection, 400 × 300 cm, digital prints (5), 84 × 119 cm

The *Prishtina Public Archipelago* research looks at the current state of the public 'islands' in the centre of the capital of Kosovo. The research focuses on the structures constructed during socialist Yugoslavia that were originally designed as inclusive public spaces, how they were transformed through political and social changes in the past several decades, the situation those events created, and how they are currently used. The five structures, the subject of this installation, are the square of Brotherhood and Unity, Rilindja print house, the Grand Hotel, Kino ARMATA, and the Boro & Ramiz Centre.

In the last century, Prishtina underwent drastic political and cultural changes that few cities in Europe experienced. Since the 1900s, Kosovo has been ruled by the Ottoman Empire, the Austro-Hungarians, the Bulgarians, Serbia, the Yugoslav kingdom, the Yugoslav Socialist Federation (SFRJ), Serbia and Montenegro, as well as by the UN Mission (UNMIK); each of these has had a great influence on the cultural and architectural kaleidoscope that is Kosovo today.

From the moment the Yugoslav regime decided to establish the first Albanian-speaking university in the country in 1969 up to the beginning of the 1980s when the Kosovar Albanians demanded greater autonomy within Yugoslavia, Prishtina saw a boom in construction of public infrastructure. New neighbourhoods, parks, sport centres and recreational spaces, university buildings, dorms, cinemas, and so on were erected. However, because of the political turmoil that followed the wars of the 1980s and 1990s, the production of public and social spaces was completely halted.

This installation consists of a documentary, spatial analyses, and a set of papers in the form of a book that delves into the issue of publicness in similar contexts to that of Prishtina.

Merve Bedir and Monique Wong, *Unsettled Urbanism, Fluid City*, 2020

Unsettled Urbanism, 2020

Merve Bedir (Turkish, b.1980) at Hong Kong University (Hong Kong, est.1911), Sampson Wong (Hongkonger, b.1985) of Add Oil Collective (Hong Kong, est.2014)

Digitally printed mural drawing, digitally printed panel drawings, video installation, dimensions variable

The city of Hong Kong is a space of extreme interaction and moving together, an open and distributed system that is young, fluid, and formless. The blink-of-the-eye, fast, and effective flow characterises the city's movement. Tactics are organised and experimented bodily and digitally, modified and iterated thanks to self-initiative. Devising ways to avoid surveillance and methods for struggle can be tested and learned on-site in a couple of hours. Technology functions as something that affords users to widen the base of, make, validate, and accelerate the city's movement. In this city, places of institutional power are deserted temples, 'decommissioned fortresses', nothing but stage sets. The city square is not the site of insurrection – the shopping mall is. Nature is a continuation of the movement in representation. Infrastructure is vital and trans-scalar. Home is mobile.

Unsettled Urbanism identifies the three main aspects of the city-in-movement: 'Be Water', the movement and tactics of people defining a fluid public space; 'Transformed typologies', the architectural typologies and spaces that have been completely transformed by people's use; and 'Technology as affordance', the coalescence of physical and digital spheres that enable another experience and production of urban space. The emerging interpretations of this city show how flexibility, fluidity, and openness offer the possibility of another urbanism that is not static and deterministic.

This installation opens up questions about the spatial contract in which spatial design is presumed to be implemented, how collective spatial intelligence is created, how the city is re-lived, and the continuous becoming of the city and the public.

Sally Chen, Nienying Lin, *Microcosms and Schisms, Deep Segregation*, 2020

Microcosms and Schisms, 2021

To address how we will live together, we must recognise that *we* refers to a fictive entity, which nonetheless determines a sense of place-and-kin, and consider the various ways and modes it may mean to live (Katherine McKittrick, 2015). A fundamental property of architecture is to demarcate, delineate, and segregate. Confronting processes of differentiation, architecture also registers ruptures and transgressions and it articulates modes of connection and wilfully denies perceived and established boundaries.

In this sense, the urban becomes a constellation of controlled microcosms, carefully constructed spaces of urban interiority, and containment of climates, ecologies, and bodies. This installation presents critical readings of New York interiorities and the transgressions and breaches that characterise them: the façade and the politics of the envelope, the public park as a space of manufactured wilderness and urban collectivity, spaces of climatic control and environmental inequality, and the city's sites of sanctuary and transnational solidarity.

Nora Akawi (Palestinian, b.1985), Hayley Eber (South African, b.1976); Lydia Kallipoliti (Greek, b.1976), Lauren Kogod (American, b.1961), Ife Vanable (American, b.1981) of The Irwin S. Chanin School of Architecture at the Cooper Union (USA, est.1859)

Metallic rings, stools and steps, steel structure 400 × 450 × 370 cm; Model trains carrying physical models in motion; Screens with archival material, photographs, and drawings

EXTERIOR INTERVENTIONS

View of the *Ferry Market* in Istanbul

View of the *Building Steps* in Istanbul

Side by Side, 2019

Istanbul's unique geography, where the sea and the land meet at the same level, enables a vibrant public life at the waterfronts of the city. It also provides a series of transitional spaces where inhabitants crisscross the Bosphorus as part of their daily routines. This project is inspired by this everyday urban mobility, transitional spaces, and urban travel. It is interested in the ways in which 'mobility makes place' (Jensen, 2009) and explores the possibilities and potentials of bringing people together, side by side in places they have not been before.

Side by Side utilises already existing urban elements in hybrid forms. The *Building Steps* and *Ferry Market* in Istanbul revitalise İstinye, a former shipyard area. The steps have multiple functions, connecting the coastal road to the waterfront, vista area, and socialising space. The *Ferry Market* hosting farmers', book, and crafts markets can all be reached by a Bosphorus ferry in this public space. Both of these designs will bring various groups of people together in novel forms. They enable a new set of unpredictable encounters through hybrid forms, a new spatial contract at water's edge.

By building steps in the Arsenale, *Side by Side* provides a contextual re-interpretation of the Istanbul design. This spatial intervention enables a pause, a stopover in the circulation of Biennale visitors and invites them to stand side by side on the water edge, offering a vista and relaxation area on top and a shaded area underneath where representations of the Istanbul *Building Steps* and *Ferry Market* are displayed on market stands.

This project that enables possibilities for living together at the water's edge is also intended to inspire different cities.

Han Tümertekin (Turkish, b.1958), in collaboration with Ayfer Bartu Candan (Turkish, b.1967), Mert Kaya (Turkish, b.1993), Tuna Ortaylı Kazıcı (Turkish, b.1982), Sena Özfiliz (Turkish, b.1974), Hayriye Sözen (Turkish, b.1971), Hakan Tüzün Şengün (Turkish, b.1971), Ahmet Topbaş (Turkish, b.1973), and Zeynep Tümertekin (Turkish, b.1991)

Installation with models, sketches, drawings, and photographs

EXTERIOR INTERVENTIONS

Malón (plunder raids carried out by Mapuche into Chilean territory during the nineteenth century, *War to Death*) by Claudio Gay, 1854

Parliament of Negrete, March 3, 1793. Illustration of the Parley between Mapuche and Spaniards by Claudio Gay, 1854. Image mediated by Elemental superimposing the *Künü* proposal on it

Chileans and Mapuche, Building places to get to know each other (KÜNÜ), Building places to parley (KOYAÜ-WE)

Alejandro Aravena (Chilean, b.1967), Gonzalo Arteaga (Chilean, b.1977), Víctor Oddó (Chilean, b.1975), Diego Torres (Peruvian, b.1979), Juan Cerda (Chilean, b.1980) of ELEMENTAL (Chile, est.2001)

Wooden tripods, steel ring, d. 1900 cm × 1500 cm

Mapuche comes from *Mapu* (Earth) and *Che* (People).

Mapuche and Chileans have been in conflict since the formation of the Republic, and at its core there has always been the question of land. One potential clue to understanding the complexity of the issue may lie in the fact that in Spanish there are no distinct words for Land and Earth. As such, there is sometimes a tendency to mix the dispute over Land, its ownership, and historical property rights with a deeper notion of Earth as planet, as if they were the same thing.

In recent times, the conflict's violence has escalated. So, how will the Mapuche people and Chileans live together?

This project explores an alternative path to violence. Sitting at this table are some of the incumbents: a Mapuche territorial organisation and a Chilean forestry company. Both live in the same territory; both intend to remain there, and both understand that confrontation has not solved the problem. Any possible rapprochement process is at least two-fold: a condition reflected in this installation organised as *KÜNÜ* and *KOYAÜ-WE*.

First, it is important to make space for and facilitate more symmetrical knowledge of the other between the different parties. As such, the project called *KÜNÜ* uses architecture as a portal to the Mapuche cosmology.

Once the field is levelled, the aim is to reinstall the old tradition of Parleys. To highlight this issue, the installation in Venice comprises a *KOYAÜ-WE*: a place to parley that will then travel back to Chile to fulfil that intended function.

This installation is therefore a documentary chronicling the first two chapters of the eventual rapprochement between the Mapuche and the Chileans.

EXTERIOR INTERVENTIONS

Vogt Landscape, *Migrating Landscapes*, 2021. Model front

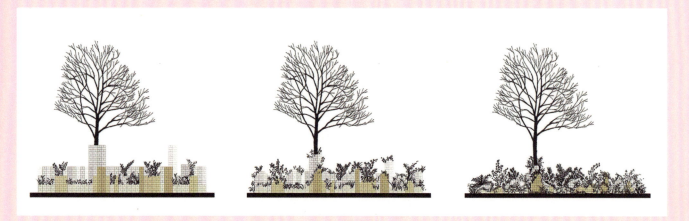

Vogt Landscape, *Migrating Landscapes*, 2021. Process sketches

Migrating Landscapes, 2020

This installation, located outdoors in the gardens of the Arsenale, consists of a megastructure that works as a model of the city on which it stands: a topography made of architecture. The hard-pressed bricks that make up this urban landscape are made of soil from different regions across the country, offering a sort of architectural, material mapping of a region whose flora, like that of the world, is constantly changing. As the vegetation grows between the cracks of this city model, architecture is transformed into landscape.

This landform extends under the silhouette of an old tree, and one of the most important vegetation and landscape elements of public space across the European continent: *Platanus hispanica*. Placed at the centre of the installation, this magnificent deciduous tree signifies the beginning of the garden under Napoleonic rule as well as the introduction of non-native flora into the city's green spaces.

The installation not only maps the territory through a deconstruction of its architecture, but also acts as a timeline of the changes in vegetation undergone by the city of Venice. These are made visible in the form of a faded planting scheme of non-native flora introduced to the city. The project presents a synthetic history of ecological change and the manipulation of land.

The urban landscape gives way to a rugged topography accommodating the seeds of change, giving way to a new type of landscape that reimagines the implicit relationship between landscape and architecture.

Günther Vogt (Lichtensteiner, b.1957) with Violeta Burckhardt (American, b.1987), and Simon Kroll (German, b.1984) of Vogt Landscape Architects (Switzerland, London, Berlin, Paris, est.2000)

Hard-pressed earth blocks, planting earth, gravel, seeds, vegetation, water, 600 × 600 × 170 cm

EXTERIOR INTERVENTIONS

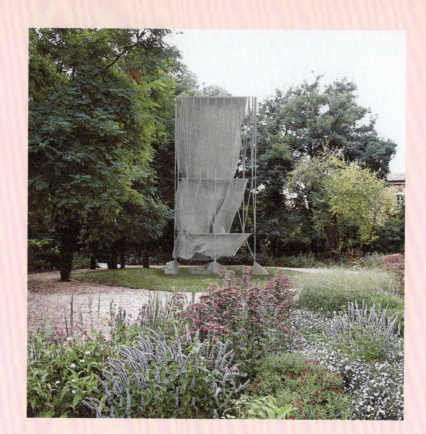

WOJR, *Tower of Winds*, 2020. Collage

WOJR, *Tower of Winds*, 2020. Site plan

Tower of Winds, 2021

William O'Brien Jr.
(American, b.1978)
WOJR (USA, est.2013)

Stone, steel, fabric,
450 × 450 × 900 cm

Tower of Winds is concerned with the cultivation of shared experiences. The project makes visible aspects of the environment that are omnipresent, conditions that we all share in common.

As an object watched from a distance, the fabric in this installation registers the movement of the air; a barometer of local winds informed by global weather patterns. As an environment, it is a vertically oriented room, a tall drum with a frame at the top. The drum is made of three tiers, each with an increasing number of facets. Transitioning from an octagon near the ground to a smoother figure above, the geometry suggests a confluence of individual perspectives into a collective or shared view of the sky. Simultaneously, the sectional condition offers a horizontal gaze, outward from under the drum, of the Giardino delle Vergini gardens beyond on the Biennale grounds.

Tower of Winds is inspired by Ettore Sottsass and Eulàlia Grau's *Vuoi sederti al sole..., o vuoi sederti all'ombra* (from their series *Metaphors*, 1973), which highlights modest means of creating a place of respite, protection, and reflection for an individual – a vertically-oriented shade and a chair. This contribution provides that as well, and at a scale fit for living together.

EXTERIOR INTERVENTIONS

Technologies to turn carbon into rock, 2017

Igneous Tectonics, *Carbon to Rock,* 2020. Section of installation in Venice

Carbon to Rock: Geology and Technology at Work for Design in the Age of Climate Change, 2021

Cristina Parreño Alonso (Spanish, b.1978) and Sergio Araya Goldberg (Chilean, b.1971) of Igneous Tectonics (USA, est.2017), in collaboration with Matěj Pěc (Czech, b.1984) of Pec Lab at MIT (USA, est.2017).

Outdoor installation: volcanic rock, 200 × 200 × 200 cm; World Map: Igneous Dymaxion, wood

When Nobel Prize winner Paul Crutzen postulated that humans have become a geological force, he was pointing at the collapse of the human–nature divide. But perhaps more importantly he was proposing a new point of view of the role of humans in shaping natural systems, a point of view that moves beyond the decline caused by the technological achievements of human civilization and instead points out its potential in enabling the sustainable use of natural resources and, with it, the human potential to stop and reverse climate change.

Carbon to Rock_Patagonia is a small architectural intervention in the Volcanic Basaltic Plateau of the Chilean Patagonia, commissioned by CONAF, Chile's national forest corporation. The project is a carved space that introduces new intelligence in the use of volcanic basaltic rock, which latest research proves can effectively capture CO_2, while serving as a small temporal refuge for the scientific community that comes to study the problem of climate change in Patagonia and its impact on indigenous communities and ecosystems downstream. Volcanic basaltic rock has recently been discovered to enable rapid carbon mineralisation for permanent disposal of anthropogenic carbon dioxide. *CarbonRock_Patagonia* highlights the possibilities the materiality of these volcanic lands offer. It creates a space for researchers with minimal means to reinterpret geological forces and indigenous vernacular systems. It also brings awareness to basaltic rock as a possible, sustainable, contributing solution to climate change, through its potential for carbon capturing, setting up a small pilot infrastructure for CO_2 absorption.

Carbon to Rock_Venice is an immersive architectural installation. It's a volcanic, inhabitable space in the Biennale's Giardini delle Vergini that re-enacts *Carbon to Rock_Patagonia* bringing awareness to the problem of global warming. *Carbon to Rock* is a small-scale project with global-scale impact that imagines new ways in which architecture can integrate space, material, tectonics, and cutting-edge technologies of CO_2 absorption with volcanic rocks as new material strategies for design in the age of climate change.

EXTERIOR INTERVENTIONS

NADAAA, *Veneta Porta Lignea*, 2021. View from vaporetto

Veneta Porta Lignea, 2021

Nader Tehrani (American, b.1963) and Arthur Chang (American, b.1977) of NADAAA (USA, est.2010)

Cross-laminated timber, steel, 1800 × 198 × 435 cm

The Giardino delle Vergini occupies a critical location in Venice, at once a destination at the end of the Arsenale, but also its gateway as one arrives by boat. Metaphorically, the Biennale as a venue rarely offers an opportunity for an extended 'essay'; its budgets and sites are better aligned with something akin to haiku, in brevity, with assembly and disassembly strategically conceived. As such, this has been an opportunity to recall the symbol of Venice, the winged lion of St Mark who holds the welcoming words in an open book to the waters: *Pax Tibi Marce Evangelista Meus*.

    With an eye towards optimisation, this project adopts a panel of cross-laminated timber as a single member which has been carved and stencilled, without waste – articulating a base, a shaft, and a lintel – whose function is to frame the threshold into the Giardino. The base serves as a wood foundation, liberating it from any penetration into the Venetian soil. The piloti is triangulated, a figural 'V', and an allusive registration of the open book containing Venice's welcoming words – all while framing a view of the fortification tower beyond the lagoon. The lintel is displaced asymmetrically, cantilevering over the passage of arrival, pushing the structural capacity of this installation to its limits; a stone of Venice maintains its balance on the opposing end. Set on the stones of the *fondamenta*, this wood construction is a reminder of the very woodpiles that hold up this maritime city.

EXTERIOR INTERVENTIONS

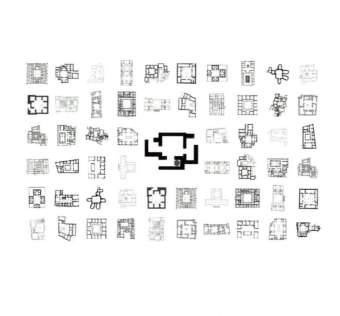

Sahel Alhiyari, *Untitled*, 2021. Floorplan and content

Untitled, 2021

How will we live together?
The nature of this question implicitly points to the critical state of our current global conditions, whose future developments and possibilities cannot be predicted with ease or certitude, and so imagining the space or the physical form of any scenario for future cohabitation can be ambiguous, if not daunting.

Perhaps at such times, with crisis in full view, the focus can shift towards an assessment of what remains viable and valid in terms of architecture; or rather, which ideas or solutions have the power to transcend or outlive such critical conditions.
In short, how may such ideas or solutions endure and regenerate with a profound capacity for adaptation that they transcend any cultural or temporal boundaries.

History has demonstrated how certain paradigms have the ability to continually emerge, through the mediation of our collective memory, into multitudes of formal manifestations and identities. Such continuity is possible by embracing overarching spatial principles that remain essentially fixed and constant.

This archetypal prominence allows for the development of solutions that pervade a vast spectrum of structures regardless of the considerable diversity of their contexts. A particularly powerful example of this is the domestic courtyard typology which, despite the plurality of its formal versions, elicits a primordial sense of familiarity, order, and a memory of what may be imagined as an ancestral home.

This installation depicts the courtyard house through the convention of plan-making as its main compositional conduit. It brings together domestic fragments and spatial sequences that exhibit the immense proliferation and spatial impact of this typology, as well as the potential varieties it can produce.

This is achieved through a random juxtaposition of diverse floor plans belonging to various periods, cultures, and geographic locations. The floor plans line up the space of the installation with a repeated pattern, reminiscent of a cryptic text, or a glyph-like code that describes various incarnations of one idea that continually shifts, adapts, and evolves to express the ever-changing patterns of human habitation.

Sahel Alhiyari (Jordanian, b.1964) of Sahel Alhiyari Architects (Jordan, est.1998) in collaboration with Sissel Tolaas (Norwegian b.1963)

Concrete blocks with plan inscriptions, scent molecule diffusers (soil),
720 × 1080 × 230 cm

Giuseppe Penone, *Idee di Pietra – Olmo* (Ideas of Stone – Elm), 2008.
Bronze, river stone 870 × 280 × 170 cm
Installation view, Château de Versailles, Paris 2013

SPECIAL EVENT

THE LISTENER

*Vuslat Foundation
Chairwoman: Vuslat Doğan
Sabancı; Curator at Large:
Chus Martinez; Artistic
Director: Merve Yeşilada
Çağlar*

*Giuseppe Penone
(Italia, 1947)*

THE LISTENER

Beginnings are magical. They demand a high sense of responsibility that enables us to care about each ensuing step as well as a sense of delicacy to engage meaningfully with others along the way. The work of Italian artist Giuseppe Penone has been imagined by the Vuslat Foundation as the only possible beginning to announce its birth. The mission of this new initiative is to enhance generous listening. Generous listening is engaging the heart as well as the mind. All our cultures share a 'listening lineage' that can be traced from the poets to the rivers and all the conversations in between but that is also present in the history and future of science and, of course, in nature.

Why then a tree? Because a tree reveals to us the fundamental aspects of nature and its consciousness. A tree teaches us the work of imaginative creation, since a tree is *all attention*. Its life depends on listening to all the elements, to taking them in. It is a dynamic of mutuality. Our Foundation needed the touch of that tree to convey our vision. We would like to deepen feelings of care and mutuality through forms of listening that will nourish society and the values of respect and freedom. We would like to work with artists and storytellers, but also educators and designers, to strengthen the many different bonds that will be the foundation of a transformative process towards equality and a nonbinary world. We are under the impression that instead of reaching immodestly for answers to the 'Big Questions' about how the human mind forges meaning, we can engage in an attentiveness with those senses that will help us to identify even more meaningful forms of relating. To create a language that both speaks and cares, to construct an analysis that encompasses all forms of life and a science that is designed to keep the values that matter for a future of true belonging to Earth.

To find your voice, you need to listen.

THE TREE

I asked a neurophysiologist friend how my brain allowed me to understand what it meant for my love to be like a red rose. 'Hmph, I work on a single neuron in the squid.' His answer motivates me to reflect on how, over centuries, we have been structuring the way we look for answers. My friend was right in what he said. It took centuries and an incredible mental effort to isolate that single cell. And that's why it's difficult to remember the significance of working on a single cell while pondering on the nature of love. Probably trees would laugh at the human efforts to divide the world in parts. Is it not obvious the earth is what wood is? Or is not air another name for the leaves? Are not all the winters and summers of the past contained in the trunk? And the storms and the winds? They are remembered in the shape of the tree. And all other trees around that tree share the same experiences, the same forms, the same relationship to the elements and yet they are unique. It is actually absurd – if you think about it – that we are calling them 'trees'. Probably they think of us as having a poor memory, unlike them. We are unable to tell them apart and see and remember and name their uniqueness. With the exception of Giuseppe Penone.

Oh! I know, some may be thinking that these ideas are poetic and bear no reality to the doings of our every day, to the goals of science. However, in the last decades – if not a whole century – we have been experiencing the tension between those that separate between forms and functions and those defending embodied theories, theories that aim to surpass the dualisms that shape our relations with nature, but also with others. In that sense no other artist reflects and cares so deeply about the possibility of becoming one with nature like Giuseppe Penone. The tree that is standing in the water of the Laguna in Venice is a witness and a companion at the same time. A witness of the destruction of those of its own species, of the lack of human respect for remaining in balance with nature, for nurturing the tongues of interspecies communication. But this tree is also a companion that emerges from the water despite the disasters – past ones, but also this current pandemic. It holds a stone, as if in the storm he could still rescue a friend – the mountains. The stone and the tree already address the symbiosis between Earth, and air and wood, but also among all the organs, the brain, the hands, the body, the braces, the roots, the leaves, the light… all those

SPECIAL EVENT

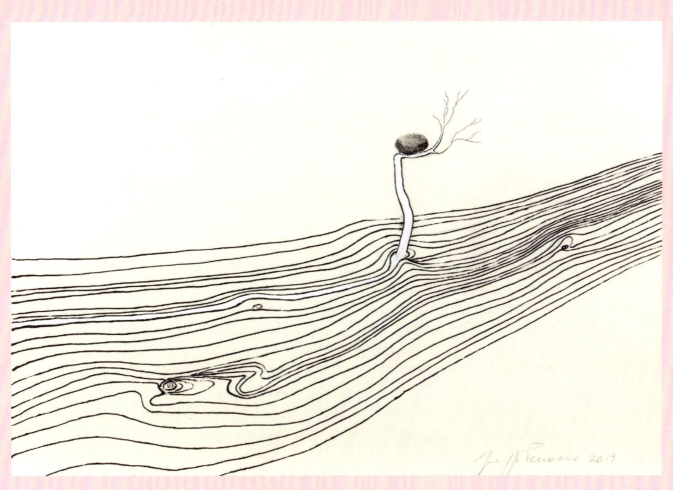

Giuseppe Penone, *Fleuve* (River), 2019.
Pencil and china ink on paper 33 × 48 cm

organs breathing, dreaming, touching, telling... but also listening.

This tree is meant as a gift. A gift to all of us, in a time of sorrow, as a messenger for regeneration.
—Chus Martinez

A TREE IN THE VENETIAN LAGOON

The slow flow of the river of sap inside the trunks of trees. The fast and heavy flow of bronze as it melts into the network of branches and the trunk of a tree, becoming sculpture.

Casting plants in bronze emphasises the perfect mimesis that exists between the two elements and the way their colours are influenced by the climate. The very technique of bronze casting follows the logic of plant growth. The channels that distribute the metal throughout the network are formed like the branches of trees. Due to gravity, metal flows towards the dark centre of the earth, while plants rise up towards the light.

The purpose of painting is to cover a surface, bringing it to life through colour, the purpose of sculpture is to discover, to expose forms, to reveal the life of matter.

Dust settles, covers, creating shade, complying with the force of gravity, a tree feeds on dust.

In the work *Idee di Pietra – Olmo* (Ideas of Stone – Elm), the stone supported by the branches is made up of countless crystals, like the individual thoughts that constitute our memory.

When unexpected feelings disrupt and create ripples through the slow flow of sensations that envelop and impregnate our brain like a fluid, ideas – both similar and opposite – gather around them in order to weigh up their value.

It is the seed around which a thought takes shape, which, like a crystal, develops in a coherent manner, following a defined pattern that grows in the space occupied by our senses, which we then set aside along with the other thoughts contained in our memory.

They form the bulk of our memories, accumulating over the course of our lives like the continuous germination of crystals that incessantly form the earth's crust.

SPECIAL EVENT

The thoughts contained within a human brain are like the countless crystals within a stone, suspended between the branches of a tree.

The veins of water that spring from the ground flow into the bodies of living beings, in the streams that flow into rivers, which then flow into the sea like the branches on the trunk of a tree. In the sea itself, the shapes of veins, streams, rivers, and trees are recreated by the currents.

A tree that rises from the water evokes the fluidity of which we find ourselves a part.
—Giuseppe Penone

ABOUT VUSLAT FOUNDATION

Vuslat Foundation is a global initiative established in 2020 with the intent of creating a movement that will make generous listening to oneself, to others, and to nature the new norm of human connectedness. Founded by Vuslat Doğan Sabancı, the foundation denotes not her name but honours the perennial concept of *vuslat*, which refers to both the journey and the blissful experience of reuniting with ourselves and with others.

Established in Switzerland with offices in Istanbul and London, Vuslat Foundation works with artists, storytellers, changemakers, and thought leaders. By implementing global programmes reaching diverse constituencies, Vuslat Foundation is committed to placing generous listening at the very core of human connection by 2030, in parallel with the UN SDGs. Through partnerships with academia, the Foundation develops knowledge, research, methodologies, and tools on generous listening; cultivates generous listening in the ecosystems of youth and children; partners with civil society to offer the practices of generous listening in their work; and engages with artists and storytellers to inspire and build awareness on generous listening.

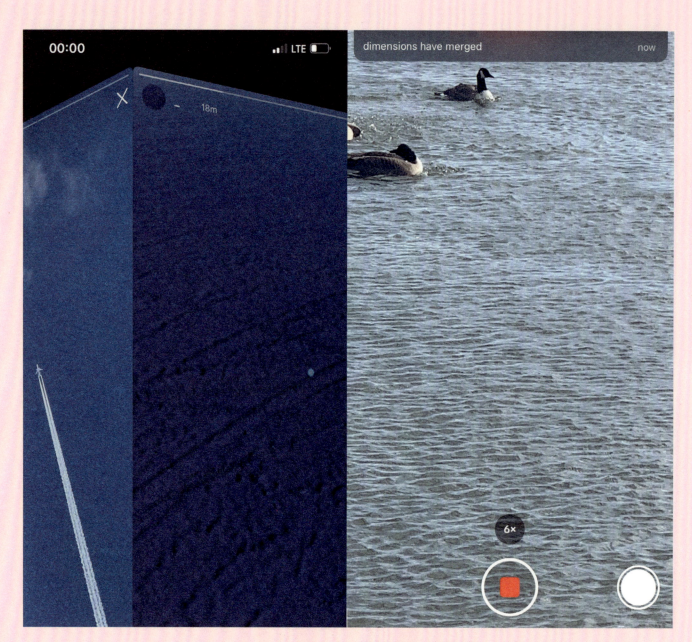

Linn Phyllis Seeger, *ONOE 01*, 2021

RELAY, 2021

PERFORMANCE

Adam Kaasa (Canadian-British, b.1982), Thandi Loewenson (Zimbabwean, b.1989) and David Burns (American, b.1972) of Fiction Feeling Frame (UK, est.2020) at School of Architecture, Royal College of Art (UK, est.1837)

RELAY is a durational conversation, a ritual in circumferential publicness, a performance becoming telegraph, current, message.

RELAY is resonance, synchronicity, amplification, and interference. It is a live act of tuning and retuning, finding meaning as much in static, dead air, and the space held between words, as in the weight, force, and matter of speech.

RELAY is the capacity to negotiate distance and time through a circuitry of interconnected broadcast, rather than the persuasion of instantaneity. It suggests the capacity of language, of energies, of influence to manifest through the technology of the discussion, of two bodies in relation, then two more and two more and bodies and bodies.

RELAY is as if a global circuit of people were sitting in a circle and one by one we turned left and then turned right, an ongoing relayed conversation. Each brings into relief ideas, books, people, histories, disagreements, citations, places, fictions, alt-futures, so that a set of tender circles emanates and expands like a pebble in dark water.

RELAY is the performance of the whisper, of gossip, of chatter. It practices the impossibility of being everywhere, hearing everything. It operates against human time, sleep time, productive time. It is about the impossibility of doing it all, at the same time, and the realisation that *all* depends on *each* in relay with the other.

RELAY invites us to become a submarine telegraph line, electromagnetic current, fibre optic cable, telephone pole, radio wave, sine, cosine, tangent. We are not a message transmitted through a relay. Rather the relay becomes the message as infrastructure.

RELAY broadcasts broadcasts, platforms platforms, and channels channels. It listens in on intimacies sited elsewhere and elsewhen. It collects a process of watching, observing, recording, transcribing. It is a sitting with, a being with, a radical togetherness that is fractured by time and geographical isolation. It invites a coming and goingness, a performance unique to everyplace and everyzone. It is a liveness experienced with multiple beginnings and multiple endings.

RELAY performs itself as loss, leaks, disconnection, glitches, interruption. These are not gaps of meaning, but precisely the meaning of bandwidth.

RELAY is a nonscripted scripting where sound becomes script becomes document becomes trace becomes live becomes comment. Each move is an integrated co-, a co-scripting, of co-sounds, co-documents, co-liveness, the you and me and us and there, and then, and was, and is, and might of co-traces.

RELAY sits within larger histories of communication, transmission, cables, and signs; of the power of connection in histories of war, colonisation, empire, pedagogy, performance, and liberation. It is an experiment in relay as message as wave, wave as wake, wake as sound, and space in time.

RELAY relishes the insurgency of what it is to feel for someone through the limitations and ruptures of the channels we have at hand. It is happening now, now-now, now and again, through multiple forms of feeling through others and others feeling for you, refusing the limitation of the box, screen, container, and cell, and instead revelling in a line of sensing passed on, in the round.

PERFORMANCE

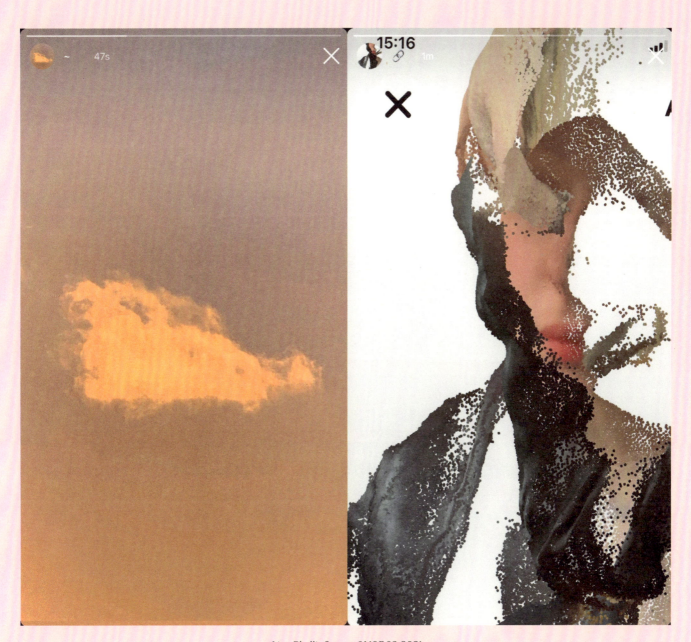

Linn Phyllis Seeger, *ONOE 02*, 2021

1 Le Consortium-Land
(Franck Gautherot; Seungduk Kim;
Catherine Bonnotte; Géraldine Minet
in collaboration with Patrick Berger,
Aristide Antonas, Junya Ishigami)
379

2 Matilde Cassani; Ignacio G. Galán;
Ivan L. Munuera
381

SI3 SPORT PLATFORM
Architekt Christoph Lechner
& Partners
299

Book Pavilion
Golden Lion for Lifetime Achievement
Rafael Moneo

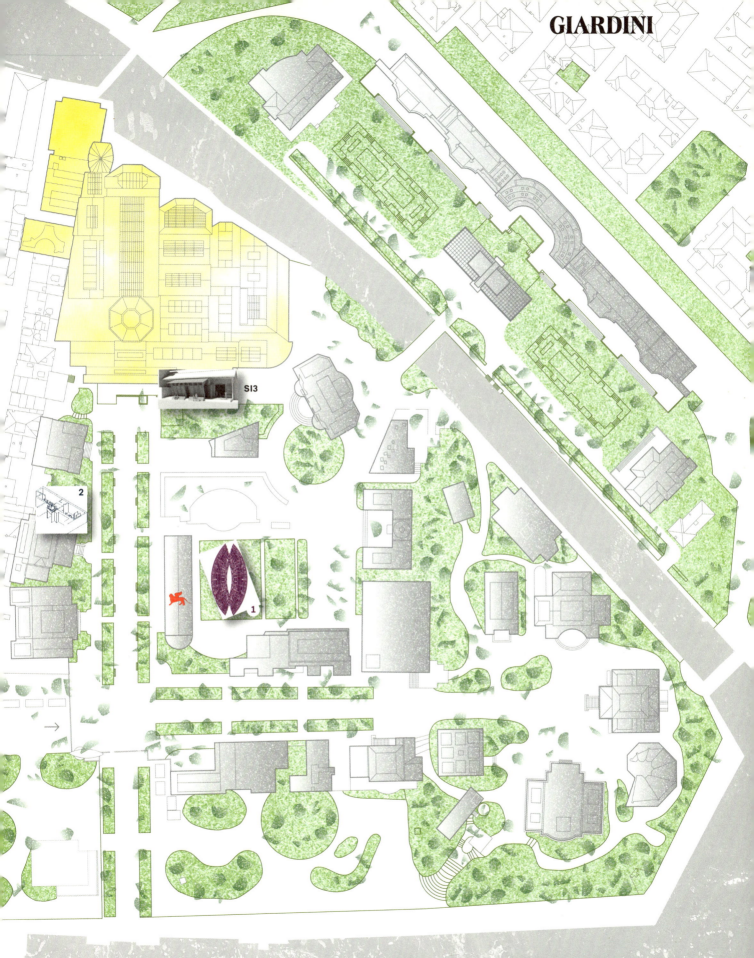
GIARDINI

251

ACROSS BORDERS

PROTECTING GLOBAL COMMONS
1. Dan Majka & Gary Setzer
2. Studio Tomás Saraceno
3. GFA (Guillermo Fernández-Abascal; Urtzi Grau)
4. Monsoon Assemblages and Office of Experiments (Lindsay Bremner; Neal White)
5. John Palmesino; Ann-Sofi Rönnskog; Territorial Agency
6. Pinar Yoldas
7. Giuditta Vendrame
8. Self-Assembly Lab (Skylar Tibbits; Jared Laucks; Schendy Kernizan)
9. Somatic Collaborative (Anthony Acciavatti; Felipe Correa; Devin Dobrowolski)
10. ACASA GRINGO CARDIA DESIGN (Gringo Cardia with AIKAX, Takumã Kuikuro, and People's Palace Projects, Paul Heritage)
11. La Minga (Pablo Escudero)
12. Atelier Marko Brajovic (Marko Brajovic; Bruno Bezerra)
13. UNLESS (Giulia Foscari Widmann Rezzonico)
14. Lateral Office and Arctic Design Group (Mason White; Lola Sheppard; Leena Cho; Matthew Jull)

TRANSCENDING THE URBAN-RURAL DIVIDE
15. Dogma (Martino Tattara; Pier Vittorio Aureli)
16. Rural Urban Framework (Joshua Bolchover; John Lin)
17. Studio Paola Viganò
18. Paula Nascimento
19. Smout Allen (Laura Allen; Mark Smout; Geoff Manaugh)

LINKING THE LEVANT
20. Foundation for Achieving Seamless Territory (FAST); Malkit Shoshan
21. AAU Anastas (Elias Anastas; Yousef Anastas)

SEEKING REFUGE
22. Decolonizing Architecture Art Residency (Alessandro Petti; Sandi Hilal)
23. Wissam Chaaya
24. Forensic Oceanography (Charles Heller; Lorenzo Pezzani)

RE-SOURCING RESOURCES
25. Chair of Günther Vogt ETH Zurich
26. Olalekan Jeyifous and Mpho Matsipa

- **SI3** SPORT PLATFORM: Architekt Christoph Lechner & Partners
- **S1** STATION: Viviana d'Auria, KU LEUVEN
- **S2** STATION: Justinien Tribillon, The Barlett School of Planning

AS ONE PLANET

- **SI2** Collective Exhibition Within Exhibition
Future Assembly (Caroline A. Jones, Hadeel Ibrahim, Kumi Naidoo, Mariana Mazzucato, Mary Robinson, Olafur Eliasson, Paola Antonelli, Sebastian Behmann)

MAKING WORLDS
- **SI1** Frontispiece (Michal Rovner)
27. Cave_bureau (Karanja Kabage; Stella Mutegi)
28. TVK (Pierre Alain Trévelo; Antoine Viger-Kohler)
29. Plan B Architecture & Urbanism (Joyce Hsiang; Bimal Mendis)
30. Christina Agapakis, Alexandra Daisy Ginsberg & Sissel Tolaas
31. Daniel López-Pérez; Reiser + Umemoto; Princeton University School of Architecture
32. S.E.L (Verena Paravel; Lucien Castaing-Taylor)

DESIGNING FOR CLIMATE CHANGE
33. Kei Kaihoh Architects
34. DESIGN EARTH (Rania Ghosn; El Hadi Jazairy)
35. OOZE and Marjetica Potrč; Eva Pfannes; Sylvain Hartenberg; Marjetica Potrč

NETWORKING SPACE
36. Weitzman School of Design (Richard Weller)
37. Urban Theory Lab (UTL) / Department of Architecture, ETH Zurich; Neil Brenner; Christian Schmid
38. spbr arquitetos (Angelo Bucci)
39. Bethany Rigby
40. Mabe Bethônico

- **S3** STATION: Architectural Worlds (Hashim Sarkis; Roi Salgueiro Barrio; Gabriel Kozlowski)
- **S4** STATION: Sheila Kennedy; Janelle K Knox-Hayes; Miho Mazereeuw, MIT Urban Risk Lab; James Wescoat, MIT Aga Khan Program for Islamic Architecture at MIT Venice Lab

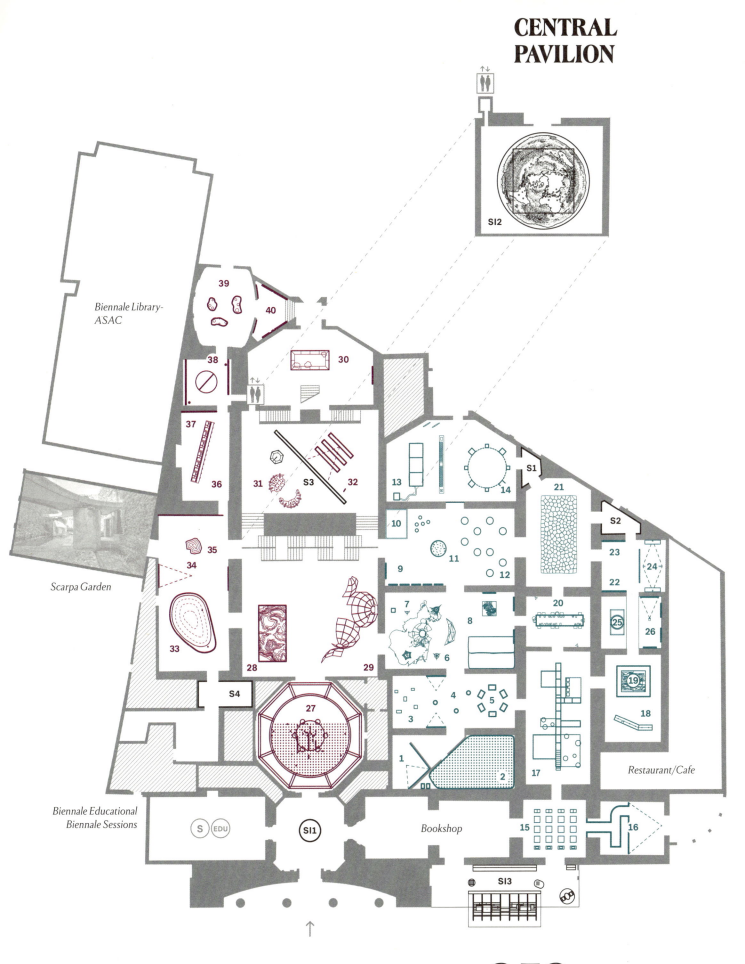

CENTRAL PAVILION

253

Across Borders

EXHIBITION GIARDINI

We have marked the surface of the earth with strong spatial borders which have consequently produced serious inequalities among us – among nations, regions, and cities and among classes and ethnicities. Invariably, these borders impede our connectedness to each other, and our search for shared values and they delay the need to come together in order to address the challenges of globalisation.

The differences, for example, between global cities and their hinterlands have produced sharp economic divides that shape some of today's polarised politics. Can we imagine better forms of living across these cruel borders to emphasise equity over functionality? Can geographic connectedness overpower the politics of exclusion?

Another example. These borders at the urban scale no longer correspond to the existing realities of land use. Modern planning principles drew very strong boundaries between living areas, working areas, and areas of leisure, but the changes in the nature of industry, work, and recreation compel us to connect these functions rather than separate them. Can we imagine cities where functional mixing helps bring back a much-needed vitality to our living and working spaces alike?

This section of the exhibition includes architects who have worked on transcending boundaries by design. They use architecture to cross existing boundaries through international hubs, refugee housing, living on the rural–urban edge, connecting human and nonhuman habitats, inventing new, mixed land uses. This section also includes two stations focusing on the cross-border potential of migrant citizens and natural systems.

In parallel, the curators of the national pavilions have also been invited to work together, to be inclusive of other nations that do not have pavilions, and to imagine, through architecture, new forms of association across nations.

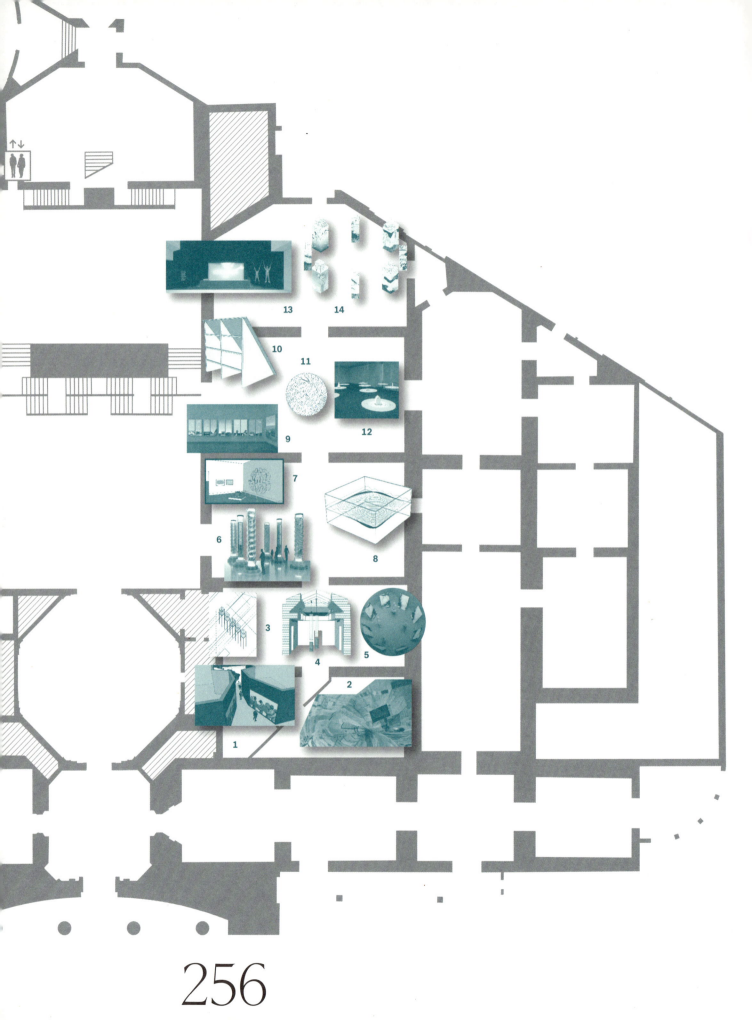

PROTECTING GLOBAL COMMONS

ACROSS BORDERS

1. Dan Majka & Gary Setzer
259

2. Studio Tomás Saraceno
261

3. GFA
(Guillermo Fernández-Abascal; Urtzi Grau)
263

4. Monsoon Assemblages and Office of Experiments
(Lindsay Bremner; Neal White)
265

5. John Palmesino; Ann-Sofi Rönnskog; Territorial Agency
267

6. Pinar Yoldas
269

7. Giuditta Vendrame
271

8. Self-Assembly Lab
(Skylar Tibbits; Jared Laucks; Schendy Kernizan)
273

9. Somatic Collaborative
(Anthony Acciavatti; Felipe Correa; Devin Dobrowolski)
275

10. ACASA GRINGO CARDIA DESIGN
277

11. La Minga (Pablo Escudero)
279

12. Atelier Marko Brajovic
(Marko Brajovic; Bruno Bezerra)
281

13. UNLESS
(Giulia Foscari Widmann Rezzonico)
283

14. Lateral Office and Arctic Design Group
285

Our global commons have been divided, and as a result diminished, by political boundaries. This series of five rooms shows how the architectural imaginary can reintroduce these commons to the world and reconnect them. The planet's poles and oceans, the Amazon basin, and the Earth's atmosphere need reconnecting and resuscitating. Together they highlight what architecture can do to unify our experiences of the planet's common spaces.

As unfathomable as these places may be, architecture can make us aware of their vulnerability. As much as architecture had a hand in damaging them, it must also now play a role in protecting them.

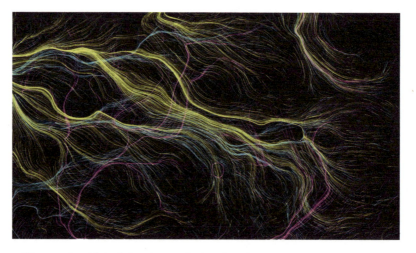

All images: Dan Majka & Gary Setzer, *The Corridor: Climate Change, Border Permeability, and Ecosystem Resilience*, 2021. Video stills

The Corridor: Climate Change, Border Permeability, and Ecosystem Resilience, 2021

As climate change alters habitats and disrupts ecosystems, where will animals move to survive? And will human development prevent them from getting there? *The Corridor* is an installation that uses three-channel video and sound to address the relationship between border permeability and ecosystem resilience in a time of climate change. This project posits that to *thrive together* with nature in a time of intensifying climate change, one must reconsider how to incorporate permeability into borders and the matrix in between natural environments.

The Corridor marries science, geography, video, and sound to challenge how one thinks about the border between humans and nature in the Anthropocene. The floor plan of the project facilitates a symbolic passage for viewers – their movement through the various stations of the installation parallels and the directed movement of animals through a wildlife crossing structure. Crossing structures are one solution ecologists have employed to maintain corridors that connect natural habitats. These corridors provide animals with safe passageways through human-developed borders (such as highways) and are one potential strategy that enables animals and humans to live together more harmoniously.

Flanking video projections – featuring trudging groups of personified animals hauling packed moving boxes – lead the viewer through a central corridor to an immersive map replete with a dynamic visualization of animal migration data developed at the Nature Conservancy. The map uses electrical circuit theory to show the average direction in which over 2,900 animals in North and South America would have to move in order to adapt to climate change-induced habitat shifts.

Under climate change, animals will be required to move and adapt to new habitats at a rate never before seen on Earth. This installation articulates the dramatic urgency of the situation.

Dan Majka (American, b.1980) of The Nature Conservancy (USA, est.1951) and Gary Setzer (American, b.1974)

Three-channel video installation and sound, 967 × 715 × 500 cm

Museu Aero Solar in Milan, with Alberto Pesavento, Bert Theis, and Maurizio Bortolott and the support of Isola Art Center, 2007

Museu Aero Solar in Munich at the Aerocene Festival, Olympiaberg, with Tomás Saraceno, Susanne Witzgall, Beate Engl, Denis Maksimov, Timo Tuominen, Erik Bordeleau, Alice Lamperti, Roxanne Mackie, Erik Vogler, Gwilym Faulkner, Camilla Berggren Lundell, Charles Gonzalez, Rebecca Schedler, Jasper Humpert, Saverio Contini, Dario Lagana, and Andrea Familari, 6–11 September, 2019

Museo Aero Solar For an Aerocene Era,
2007–ONGOING

Aerocene Foundation (International, est. 2015), initiated by Tomás Saraceno (Argentinian, b.1973).

Museo Aero Solar is an open, growing collection of community-built floating museums from around the world. Plastic bags are reused, cut, pasted, and joined to create canvases for drawing and writing personal stories. They invite visitors to reuse and recycle, turning a notorious material of the Anthropocene into a mind-expanding material for an Aerocene era. To date, hundreds of thousands of plastic bags that would otherwise fill landfills or the ocean have been rescued from over 50 communities across more than 30 countries in an act that embodies an ethos of care and responsibility.

This *Museo Aero Solar* was realised in Buenos Aires, Argentina, in 2018 and for two years it has been collecting the stories, relationships, and struggles of incarcerated peoples who chose to participate in the sculpture's construction. In the era of Aerocene there are millions of associations, communities, connections. All together, whether in the construction or the display of this floating museum, we participate in the conversation about terrestrial power structures including borders and punitive control – elements whose barriers discriminate disproportionately but impact us all.

The Aerocene is an era to live and breathe in; a stateless state, both tethered and free-floating; a name for change. Aerocene is an era free of borders and fossil fuels, a common imaginary towards an ethical re-alliance with the environment, the planet, and the cosmic web of life to emerge beyond anthropocentrism. It is an invitation to change our most harmful attitudes to assure an atmosphere of ecological sensitivity and cleaner, brighter futures.

Museo Aero Solar; Collective project initiated by artist Tomás Saraceno through conversations with Alberto Pesavento. Open and growing collection of community-built Floating Museums: sun-powered air balloons, reused plastic bags cut, pasted, and joined together; video *Aerocene Backpack*; Portable flight-starter-kit enclosing an aerosolar sculpture, including: ripstop balloon, canvas backpack, recycled plastic bottle, sensing devices; internal and external air quality, pressure, humidity, and temperature sensors, remotely operated photo and video camera, GPS tracker, portable solar power bank, long range Wi-Fi module, antenna, and computer interface. *Aerocene, launches at White Sands, NM United States*, Single channel video, 8 min *Pacha*; From the series *Fly with Aerocene Pacha*; Single-channel colour video, 34 min 35 sec

Hamish McIntosh, *Indo Pacific Air 1*, 2020

Folk Costumes for Indo Pacific Air, 2021

Guillermo Fernández-Abascal (Spanish, b.1986) and Urtzi Grau (Spanish, b.1976), GFA (Australia, est.2018) Fake Industries (Spain est.2006)

Air and Plexiglas
50 × 50 × 50 cm

In the months that preceded the global spread of Covid-19, a series of events transformed the atmosphere of the Indo-Pacific region: the bushfire smoke along the east coast of Australia, the tear gas used in the Santiago de Chile and Hong Kong protests, the Indian Supreme Court ruling on Delhi's pollution failures, and activists covering iconic statues with respirators across Johannesburg and Pretoria. They all mapped political struggles taking place in the region's air and triggered a proliferation of masked faces before the entire world had to wear one.

Folk Costumes, Indo-Pacific Air constructs the prehistory of the region's current masked state. The installation replicates five atmospheric conditions of the end of 2019 and collects the architectures for the body they produced, providing visitors with a glimpse of the region's highly politicised air. The resulting map of the Indo-Pacific is an installation of five enclosed, sealed environments, each an example of the air people breathe. They show how, before the global pandemic, masks and respirators defined the Indo-Pacific imaginary as the future folk costumes of a region in the making.

Not unlike those invented in the nineteenth century, these folk costumes are also socio-technological constructions. They combine responses to environmental conditions, cultural and political concerns, and available techniques and technologies. Yet they neither illustrate an essential link between national identity and land, nor imply symbolic, structural, or semiotic explanations to validate colonial empires or the existing social orders. Instead, culture here is understood to be processual, and these garments exemplified it. They are created through agency, practice, and performance. They help navigate – and often challenge – the relationships between local conditions and global networks. They are masks, wearable architecture that renders the air of the region visible.

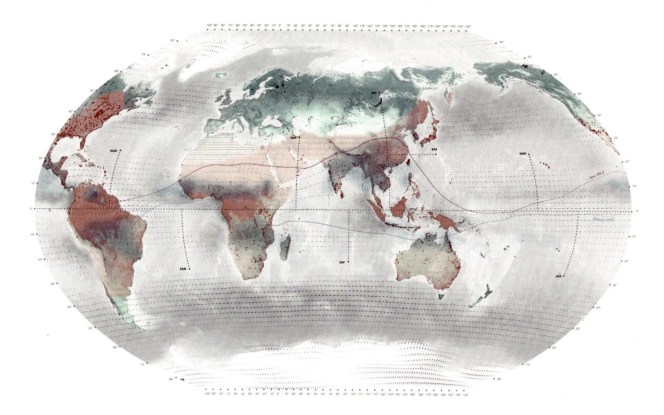

Speculative map showing relations between the dispersal
of *Pantala flavescens* and the global monsoon system

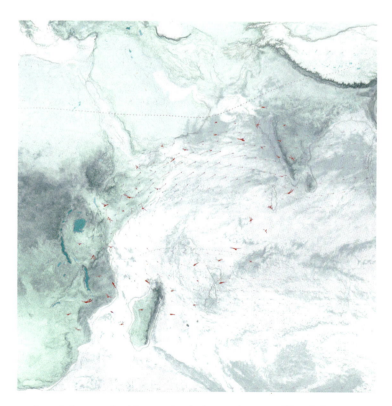

Speculative map of multi-generational migratory journeys of *Pantala flavescens*
from India to Africa using seasonal meteorological systems

Between the Dragonfly and the Barometer: Living Borders in a Changing Monsoon Climate, 2020

This project is an immersive installation that challenges and redefines ideas of border, scale, and agency. It is framed by the monsoon, a global weather system animated by the earth's revolutions around the sun. It draws on climate data, field work, and immersive time-based media to convey how climate change and anthropocentric activity are resulting in increasing monsoon volatility, the shortening of monsoon rain periods, and more frequent and more extreme weather events. These have an impact on human and non-human life in the Indo-Pacific Region.

In the installation this region is defined not by human bordering practices, but by the flight of a species of dragonfly (*Pantala flavescens*) that follows the monsoon from east Africa to south east Asia. Video of the dragonfly recorded and collected during fieldwork is projected into the exhibition space on the floor and visitors' bodies as they walk through the installation. This highlights the vulnerability of the dragonfly to human-induced monsoonal shifts. The installation focuses on three monsoonal cities around the Bay of Bengal: Chennai, Dhaka, and Yangon. They are represented as core samples of meteorological and geological data in the form of freestanding columns programmed to emit light and sound, animated by climate data. A topographic model of each city region is inserted into the columns and can be viewed through small openings. This highlights the scale of the plane of habitation in relation to the volume of the monsoon.

Lindsay Bremner (British, b.1954), John Cook (British, b.1989), Beth Cullen (British, b.1982), and Christina Leigh Geros (American, b.1982) of Monsoon Assemblages (UK, est.2016–2021) and Neal White (British, b.1966), Erik Kearney (Irish, b.1968), and Bill Thompson (American, b.1970) of Office of Experiments (UK, est.2004)

MPEX spinnaker nylon cloth, Jesmonite, aluminium, mixed media and print, dimensions variable

Territorial Agency, multi-temporal transformation analysis of the metropolitan region of Houston, Texas, with projected sea level rise in grey for a global temperature 3° Celsius higher than pre-industrial levels, *Sensible Zone*, 2021

Territorial Agency, multi-temporal transformation analysis of the Nile Delta and the Suez Canal, with projected sea level rise in red for a global temperature 3° Celsius higher than pre-industrial levels, *Sensible Zone*, 2021

Sensible Zone, 2021

Ann-Sofi Rönnskog (Finnish, b.1976) and John Palmesino (Italian, b.1970) of Territorial Agency (UK, est.2007)

7-channel video installation on LED screens with sound, dimensions variable

Sensible Zone is a proposition to engage the most important theme for the future of human cohabitation: sea level rise. We might have just enough time to keep oil in the ground and reduce its dangers of global warming and climate chaos. We have 30 years to change what we have destroyed in the last 30 years of rapid urbanisation; 30 years to become sensible to the multiple transformation processes of the Earth and prepare for a new architecture.

If we were to meet the minimum targets of the Paris Agreement of maintaining global warming within 2° Celsius above pre-industrial levels, there would be energy locked in the Earth System to lead to sea levels' surging towards six metres. This would submerge land currently occupied by around 760 million people globally, and affect the immediate livelihoods of more than 1.5 billion people.

The sensible zone is the most sensitive to this intensification. It is the thin strata between − 200 m where photosynthesis transforms sunlight into life, and + 200 m where urbanisation networks and the extension of logistical systems are enmeshed with the fragile trophic upwelling linking ecologies of the ocean and the vast interconnected habitats on land. It is also the most surveyed, measured, gridded, and extracted zone of our planetary city: it is swathed in remote sensing technologies.

It is the most sensitive component of the Earth System, responsible for climatic homeostasis and susceptible to rapid variations from small perturbations. It is a zone where multiple forms of sensible life cohabit and interact. It is a zone sensed and sensible, a tangential space where images emerge. It is a zone of multiple ways of sensing the planet, of multiple horizons, swelled by sea level rise.

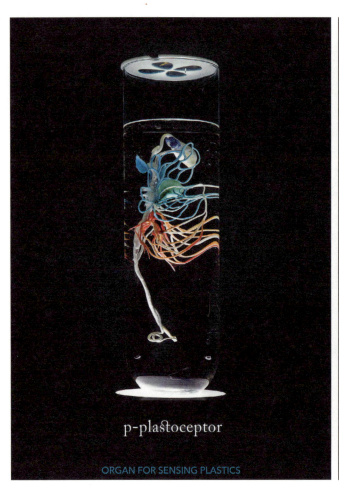

Pinar Yoldaş, *Ecosystem of Excess*, 2014

Hollow Ocean, 2021

Pinar Yoldas (Turkish, b.1979) of Yoldas Lab (USA, est.2018) in collaboration with Merve Akdoğan (Turkish, b.1996), Ege Doğan (Turkish, b.1995), Uzay Doğan (Turkish, b.1995)

Acrylic Cylinders, d. 60 × 1.5 × 300 cm (×4), d. 80 × 1.5 × 300 cm (×1), 3D Printed (SLS, Nylon) Barnacle Ornaments, 60 × 60 × 150 cm, Acrylic Vortex Structure, 110 × 300 cm, 3D Printed (PLA) Sculptures, 50 × 50 × 200 cm (×5), upcycled plastics, PETG, polyclay, 50 × 50 × 20 cm, steel column supports, d. 140 × 160 cm (×5), steel water tank 60 × 50 × 350 cm, floor vinyl print, 1000 × 1700 cm, LED lighting units, d. 50 × 5 cm (×14), coloured filter, 400 × 1200 cm

The ocean, in this project, has six chapters. Each chapter belongs to death. The first chapter is *Plastic Ocean*, which looks at the material invasion of aquatic life with man-made synthetic polymers. Entering the food chain both as prey and predator, plastic simply kills. The second chapter is *Dark Ocean*. At the darkest depths of the ocean floor, humans are drilling for an equally dark substance called petroleum. Their machines are loud and cruel, their methods spread toxicity and chaos. The third chapter is *Phantom Ocean*. As humans devour shrimp stir fry, overfishing has devoured 90% of top predators and continues to kill in a hungry hunt for what our species calls seafood. Consequently, phantom nets (ghost nets) keep hanging in this vast volume of water for eternity, intertwined in decaying bodies of marine turtles, manta rays, hammerheads, angel sharks, dolphins, whales, and orcas. The fourth chapter is *Acid Ocean*. Ocean chemistry is complex and delicately balanced, providing a salty womb that allows myriad creatures to proliferate. A minute change in acidity, however, can and will take billions of lives. Caused by the uptake of the excessive CO_2 in the atmosphere as an outcome of anthropogenic activity of the last 60 years or so, exoskeletons of corals, plankton, squid, mussels, barnacles, and many more erode under high acidity. The fifth chapter is *Stifled Ocean*. As oceans, just like land, are rendered man-made, with a new temperature, new salinity, and new acidity levels dictated by anthropogenic forces, ocean life is stifled. One such example is change in thermohaline circulation, which is known as The Conveyor Belt. These currents deliver oxygen to deep water habitats. When these currents stop, oceans' beating hearts are gone. The last chapter is *Hollow Ocean*. Almost a summary of all chapters above, this chapter is dedicated to global warming. Although as of 2021 we are witnessing some of these effects – such as new types of skin disease that affect dolphins and lobsters or the endangerment of arctic species – a high-resolution picture of what awaits oceans is highly speculative. *Hollow Ocean* is an installation intended to provide a glimpse at potential future changes to maritime environments.

Giuditta Vendrame, *Planisfero politico*, 2017

UNLANDED, 2015–ONGOING

*Giuditta Vendrame
(Italian, b.1985)*

Borders are physical and legal devices to define territories, designed to control and regulate the movement of bodies. They tend to be traced and visible on solid and earthly matters. On restless environments borders make explicit their transitoriness and their paradoxical existence. Water adapts and changes the state of matter; it freezes and evaporates. Giuditta Vendrame draws subtle and imaginative settings where rivers, lakes, seas, and oceans are not topographical dividers but connectors.

Mixed media, paper collages, glass, sea water, tape, pallet, dimensions variable

In *What Is the Purpose of Your Visit? – A Journey Towards the High Seas* (2015), the artist undertakes a 14 hour journey across the Mediterranean Sea towards the high seas, where, the United Nations Convention on the Law of the Sea declares, no state can claim sovereignty. There she collects 50 litres of international water and ships it to different places. She conceives this portable portion of the high seas as a moveable exception zone, as an embassy without nationality in which our political, social, and economic status is suspended. This gesture offers a spatial opportunity, a symbolic zero-degree zone.

In *Planisfero politico* (2017) and in the series of collages (2017, ongoing), fragments of oceans, seas, rivers, and lakes mask the land of different world maps, suggesting alternative images of the world where water becomes an instrument of deterritorialisation and dematerialisation and addressing the notion of citizenship, territory, and sovereignty. This operation allows us to subvert the modern conception of the nation–state, which is linked to roots, soil, and land.

We will live together in a humid world. We are immersed in the sea, in a floating and collective space, where we are able to reimagine a different, less terracentric, less bounded order of the world – a humid world ever in constant motion.

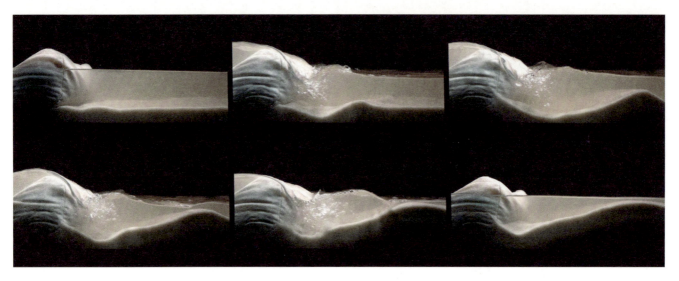

A series of photographs showing the laboratory wave tank experiments where sand accumulation (right) is generated based on the interaction between the ocean and the submerged geometry (left)

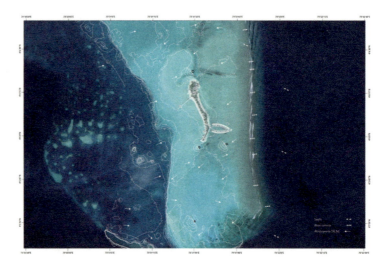

A composite site drawing and satellite image showing ocean forces and bathometry data

An aerial photograph taken during construction of the second field installation in October 2019 showing the barge and a single bladder (10 × 4m) placed underwater

Building with Waves: Growing Islands and Coastlines Through Wave Energy, 2020–ONGOING

As climate change progresses and sea levels continue to rise, island nations and coastal regions face a growing risk of going underwater. With more than 40% of the world's population living near coastlines, it is imperative to find novel approaches to address this mounting threat. Through research on self-assembly and self-organisation, this project proposes to collaborate with the natural forces of ocean waves and the accumulation of sand to be able to grow sandbars, islands, and beaches over time.

Typical attempts to fight coastal erosion rely on static physical barriers or continual coastal dredging, which attempt to resist constantly changing natural forces. Here, the goal is instead to work with the forces of nature, harnessing waves to build rather than destroy. Realised with collaborators in the Maldives, the project presents and deploys submersible devices that utilise wave forces to accelerate and guide the accumulation of sand in strategic locations. By adapting the shape and placement of the devices to seasonal changes and storm directions, the approach aims to grow sand topographies naturally and sustainably.

If this radical approach is successful, it has the potential to change the long-term viability of island nations and coastal regions. This could also ensure the survival of coastal communities that are currently being threatened by flooding as well as create new land, which may have been inhospitable previously, or create entirely new areas to live. Such an approach to climate adaptation and natural construction could be used around the world for maintaining and growing coastlines and island nations in the face of increasing natural disasters and rising sea levels.

Skylar Tibbits (American, b.1985), Schendy Kernizan (American, b.1985), and Jared Laucks (American, b.1985) of MIT Self-Assembly Lab (USA, est.2013) at Massachusetts Institute of Technology (USA, est.1861) with Sarah Dole (Sri Lankan, b.1988) and Hassan Maniku (Maldivian, b.1989) of Invena (Maldives, est.2019), with Tencate (multinational, est.1953)

Glass tank, water, sand, 200 × 200 cm; geotextile bladder, 600 × 400 cm; video screens

Bird's eye view of the Amazon River Basin looking west from the Atlantic.
The view depicts the importance of key architectural projects in choreographing
a new relationship between forest, river, and city in twenty-first-century urban Amazonia

Manaus: A New Contractual Agreement between City and Forest in Urban Amazonia, 2020

Through a specific design project sited at the confluence of three rivers (Black, Amazon, and Mindú), *Manaus* argues for a new contractual agreement between city and territory by looking beyond the traditional definitions of cities and what constitutes the urban in the context of the Amazon Rainforest. The city of Manaus exemplifies the predominant disconnect between city and the soils of urban Amazonia. Since the 1500s, Western models of urbanisation in the region have continuously cleared the forest rather than engage it, conceiving of cities as external to their immediate, botanical environs. This condition has been exacerbated throughout the last seventy years as Manaus's main economy came to rely increasingly on its free trade zone, an island specializing in the assembly and distribution of appliances and motorbikes to global markets.

Today, as the free trade zone is weakening under signs of economic decline, Manaus, like other cities in Amazonia, is looking for new, key economies, focusing on biological research and drawing from the ecologies of the Amazon to develop its new, twenty-first-century economic engine. Building on the legacy of Prussian explorer Alexander Von Humboldt, who in the seventeenth century combined techniques of scientific inquiry and the visual arts to document northern South America from the Amazon River basin to the Andes Mountains, this project spans geographic and architectural scales to imagine new ways of inhabiting the forest.

Situated along the Mindú River, a spine that connects the Black River to the Reserva Florestal Adolpho Ducke, the project proposes a series of urban interventions that forge a new civic infrastructure fostering social and economic cooperation between the cycles of the river, forest, and city. Through the careful examination of five archetypal elements – the tower, the mat, the linear bar, the island, and the bridge – the project proposes an urban imaginary that advocates for the co-existence of ecological conservation and urban development, tempering the harsh divide between city and forest in the Amazonian region.

Anthony Acciavatti (American, b.1981), Felipe Correa (Ecuadorian, b.1976), and Devin Dobrowolski (American, b.1982) of Somatic Collaborative (USA, est.2010) in collaboration with Konstantina Tzemou (Greek, b.1991), Evan Shieh (American, b.1989), Inhwi Hwang (South Korean, b.1997), Chengxin Sha (Chinese, b.1990), and Xingyu Zhang (Chinese, b.1997)

D-bond digital prints (×10), 62 × 153 cm; D-bond print (×1) 153 × 153 cm

Aki

Ipatse Village

OCA RED: Living Beyond the End of the World, 2021

As forests burn, rivers dry up, and the climate shifts, *OCA RED* enables visitors at the Biennale to connect their own past, present and future to the everyday life of indigenous villagers from the Brazilian Amazon.

In the Xingu territory, sixteen indigenous communities maintain the first millennium existence of their ancestors, defending their lands, rivers, forests and culture, while negotiating transitions and exchanges with contemporary life.

OCA RED is an immersive audio-visual installation in which filmmaker Takumã Kuikuro invites the world to connect to the Xingu way of living together, celebrating indigenous, communal ways of living in harmony with the earth, and sharing a vision for all our futures.

OCA RED brings the Ipatse Village of the Upper Xingu to the Central Pavilion, providing an intimate insight into how less than 700 Kuikuro people preserve our planet as they nurture their land and conserve their traditions. Takumã Kuikuro reveals the constant and evolving transition his people maintain between their ancestral past and the future for which they are preparing. As they engage and exchange with what most threatens to destroy them, the Kuikuro invite us to imagine how we might live together beyond the end of the world we have known so far.

Takumã Kuikuro (Brazilian, b.1983) of AIKAX (Brazil, est.2002), Gringo Cardia (Brazilian, b.1957) of ACASAGRINGOCARDIA Design Studio (Brazil, est.1991), and Paul Heritage (British, b.1958) of People's Palace Projects (United Kingdom, est.1997) in collaboration with Thiago Jesus (Brazilian, b.1984), Jackson Tinoco (Brazilian, b.1987), Glauber Vianna (Brazilian, b.1979), Nathaniel Mann (British, b.1982), and Spectaculu School of Art and Technology (Brazil, est.1999)

Amazon Hope: Kuikuro Lives: Wood, projection, 300 × 370 × 140 cm; *OCA*: wood, metal, fabric, wool, 876 × 450 × 317 cm

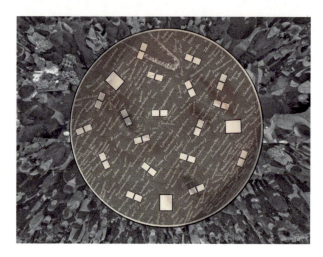

Between Map and Territory.
The cartographic base of the Ecuadorian installation

Shadows of Colonisation. Medicinal plants, waters, territories,
and Indigenous traditions of the Andes Mountains & Amazon Valleys
erased by European colonial science. Detail

The Map that Fooled the World. Alexander von Humboldt & Aimé
Bonpland's 1805 *Géographie des plantes équinoxiales.
Tableau physique des Andes et pays voisins.*
Tableau, 54 × 84 cm

The Quino Treaty, 1532–2029

Renewing Territorial Relations with the Cinchona Plant at the Centre of the World by Decolonising Quinine & the Global Discourse on Conservation

This 497-year project charts the legacy left behind by extractivist forces of colonial powers in the search for the elusive *Quino tree*. Its prize bark has been sought after for more than a millennium by European imperial powers for the medicinal extract that is the only natural cure for malaria on the planet: quinine. Like the Indigenous Peoples who have safeguarded its territories, the Quino tree has resisted all attempts at chemical substitution, biological simulation, or mass synthetisation.

As evidenced by the history of the Quino tree, there is a fundamental territorial conflict at the centre of the transnational world today, resulting in the oppression, exploitation, and elimination of Indigenous Peoples – Kechwa, Saraguro, Wuarani Tsáchila, Chachi, Epera, Awa, Shuar, Achuar, Shiwiar, Cofán, Siona, Secoya, Zápara, Andoa, Waorani, and Afro-Ecuadorian Peoples. Thus, the Quino tree is more than a taxonomical species that Prussian naturalist Alexander von Humboldt mapped in 1805: it is a living world of soils, airs, climates, temperatures, territories, histories, beings, and peoples.

As a declaration of sovereignty and self-determination, this installation proposes a counter-history that transcends the extractive divide between the colonial metropolis and resource hinterlands of this capitalist cosmos. It is a treaty whose history of resistance, subsistence, and resilience led by Indigenous women proposes a way to rebuild relations with the Quino tree, its peoples, and its territories. *The Quino Treaty* acknowledges that, until the systems of dispossession and dehumanisation – including regional conservation measures, national land policies, foreign scientific interventions, international patent laws, and transnational trade agreements – are dismantled, a decolonial future, where we can live together, cannot take place.

The *Quino Treaty* is about building a different world and undoing dangerous imperial and extractivist impulses by mending and rebuilding relations with Indigenous Nations who fight for the self-determenitation of this natural world.

Pablo Escudero (Ecuadorian, b.1984), Ghazal Jafari (Iranian/Azeri, b.1982), Pierre Bélanger (Canadian, b.1971) in collaboration with Alejandra Pinto (Ecuadorian, b.1988), Patricia Yallico (Ecuadorian, n.d.), Alexander Arroyo (American, b.1984), Hernan L. Bianchi Benguria (Chilean, b.1982), Natalia Dueñas (Ecuadorian, b.1988), Tiffany Kaewen Dang (Canadian, b.1989) of La Minga (Ecuador, est.2016) / OPEN SYSTEMS (USA, est.2001)

Quinine Pill: chloroquine phosphate, 7.5 × 2.5 mm, pharmaceutical blister packs, 8 × 6.5 × 0.5 cm; Painted plywood base, ultraviolet and infrared LED lighting, d. 200 × 35 cm; Digitally printed map on Omega-Bond, d. 200 × 0.5 cm; Book: *Quino Treaty, 1532–2029*, 16 × 13 × 2 cm

Atelier Marko Brajovic, *Amphibious: Living Between Water and Land in the Amazon*, 2020

Amphibious: Living Between Water and Land in the Amazon, 2020

Atelier Marko Brajovic (Brazil, est.2006)

The Amazon is a liquid landscape where boundaries between land and water move constantly, dramatically influencing the biotic and abiotic environment. From ancestral times, humans learned to adapt to transforming landscapes by living in highly organised societies. Floating architecture and agroecological practices have proven to be highly efficient systems that work symbiotically with the rainfall season's changing environmental patterns. Similarly, numerous other species organise themselves in cooperative colonies and dynamic relations with different organisms to increase their resilience. In both human and non-human instances, the survival strategy is consistent: cooperation and interdependence.

Amphibious: Living Between Water and Land in the Amazon looks into collaborative strategies of different amphibious organisms and human waterfront settlements at three interconnected levels – real and imagined. First, the biological strategies of the most successful Amazonian organisms that adapt to changing conditions between water and land; second, the ingenious architectural solutions found in human settlements that organise living in the liquid boundary environment; and third, a conceptual project of an amphibious floating village for the Anthropocene, consisting of self-organising and regenerative off-grid units that connect synergistically with the Amazonian metabolism.

The Amazon is a natural, high-tech laboratory of the future, the most advanced and complex ecosystem for both learning and applying functional, behavioural, and structural knowledge to design future villages and cities that exist in harmony with changing environmental conditions. It has the potential of being a model for other regions around the world that will, in the not-so-distant future, inevitably be subjected to floods caused by climate change.

Rounded counter with printed sheet (12): MDF, metal hairpin legs, 90 × 90 × 72 cm; tablets (12); 3D printed models (8): organic resin, 14 × 14 × 20 cm

Resolution. Six months of darkness.
The ultimate metaphor of the collective neglect of Antarctica is embodied by the pixelated and fragmented view offered by Google Earth of the Southernmost continent. Much like the blanks on imperial maps, such 'white-outs' reveal the existence of a coveted web of growing economic and strategic interests, tensions, and international rivalries deliberately enveloped in total darkness, as is the continent for six months per year. Only the interdisciplinary knowledge of scholars and practitioners who devoted their lives to Antarctica and explored its territory through scientific research can enlighten us by producing an uncensored, high-resolution image of the continent

The Antarctic Suit. The First Architectural Envelope. A portable environment that allows humans to survive in the hostile environment of the coldest and driest desert of Planet Earth. Developed by D-Air Lab (an experimental company that has experience in suiting cosmonauts for Space) in collaboration with UNLESS, the human-scale architectural envelopes (equipped with heated filaments that record and broadcasts physiological data) have been tested and deployed at Concordia Station on the Antarctic Plateau in occasion of the 2020 XXXVI Italian expedition

Antarctic Resolution, 2020

Antarctic Resolution advocates to urgently remove the goggles of Heroic Era explorers and reject the pixelated view of Antarctica offered to the world by Big Data companies, to construct a high-resolution image of the continent's geography, governance system, contemporary geopolitical significance, unparalleled scientific potential, and extreme inhabitation model.

Antarctica ejects the structures humans build on its ice. The relentless movement of glaciers towards the oceans, their calving, preludes to a future in which disembodied technologies and forms of surveillance allow for the reduction of anthropic footprint in favour of automated scientific research. A future in which the designer's intelligence shifts scales from polar cities to responsive Antarctic Suits.

The present imbalance between ice melting and iceberg forming via snowfall, which occurs six times faster than forty years ago, provokes an alarming global sea level rise and produces augmented thundering soundscapes. Reproduced in a performative installation informed by scientific data, the so-called 'ice thunders' awake one's conscience and call for action.

Learning from Antarctica's tradition of cooperation and driven by the conviction that the knowledge of Antarctica ought to be shared as a Global Common, *Antarctic Resolution* launches a platform, in which planetary citizens can engage in a coordinated and unanimous effort – independent of nations – to shape the future of Antarctica, and, in turn, of Spaceship Earth.

Giulia Foscari (Italian, b.1980) and UNLESS (Germany, est.2019), in collaboration with Arcangelo Sassolino (Italian, b.1967), D-Air Lab, Dainese (Italy, est.1972), David Vaughan (UK, b.1962) of British Antarctic Survey (UK, est.1962), Lars Müller Publishers (Switzerland, est.1983), Scott Polar Research Institute (UK, est.1920), and The Polar Lab (Argentina, Brazil, Chile, Hong Kong, UK, est.2018)

250 times per second. Installation by artist Arcangelo Sassolino, developed in collaboration UNLESS. Scientific data provided by David Vaughan; Air turbine powered by electrical system, stainless steel, 315 × 530 × 170 cm

Antarctic Resolution. Call for Action; Curated and edited by Giulia Foscari/UNLESS; Produced in collaboration with the Polar Lab and over 200 polar experts; Lahnite plates (1000), 30 × 39 cm, wooden podium, 745 × 69 × 80 cm

Snow Goggles. Tools of resistance; Heroic-Era Goggles used by Captain Robert Falcon Scott; Carved wood, ribbon ties, 1.35 × 4.2 × 4 cm

Antarctic Suit. The first Architectural Envelope; The Antarctic Suit prototypes; developed by D-Air Lab in collaboration with UNLESS; Internal layer: silk, 100% polyester, 150 × 170 cm; External layer: PA / PTFE (wind-stopper); 100% polyester (exterior envelope), 160 × 190 cm, Camelux (thermal exchange optimiser), twins grapheme (thermal distributer); Mid layer (heat containment element) and Nativa silk pad (human-body heat-radiation reflective element)

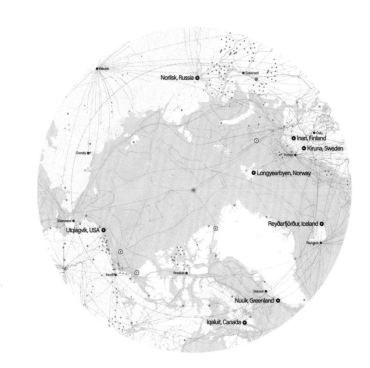

Circumpolar Map

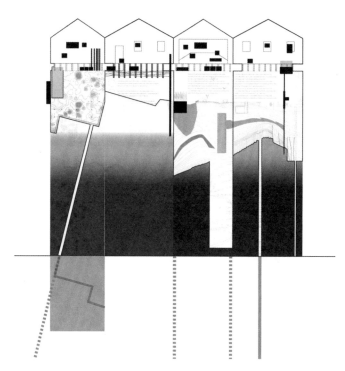

Circumpolar House core sample

Contested Circumpolar: Domestic Territories, 2021

Lola Sheppard (Canadian, b.1972) and Mason White (Canadian, b.1973) of Lateral Office (Canada, est.2004) with Leena Cho (American, b.1982) and Matthew Jull (Canadian, b.1970) of Arctic Design Group (USA, est.2012)

Physical models with embedded drawings and objects, varying from 30 × 30 × 130 cm to 50 × 50 × 130 cm

Claimed by the eight Arctic nations – Canada, Finland, Greenland, Iceland, Norway, Russia, Sweden, and the United States – while also being the native territory to numerous Indigenous peoples, the Arctic is a complex, contested space in the twenty-first century. Territorial claims, resource extraction, climate change, and ongoing colonialism reflect the range of ways in which inhabitation has been imposed and negotiated in the last hundred years. Simultaneously, emplaced stories of daily life of inhabitants who call the Arctic home further reflect a richly heterogeneous, cultural landscape at the forefront of accelerated transformations.

Contested Circumpolar: Domestic Territories represents key narratives of inhabitation from each Arctic nation that reveals deep connections from the domestic interior to the landscape territory. The installation situates domestic life entangled with broader sociocultural, economic, and geopolitical forces, and it is conceived as 'extracted core samples' capturing place-specific, domestic–territorial linkages that are also emblematic of collective matters of concern in the Arctic.

A series of rooms located on top of each vertical core juxtaposes the seemingly banal but distinct artefacts and architectures of domestic life, while the visual narratives on the underlying cores expose interlinked contexts that give shape to these domestic scenes. Material culture, spatial practices, and old and new technologies are depicted, as is evidence of a transforming region. The models further capture the full range of realities and urgencies surrounding the daily life and livelihood of Arctic inhabitants. At a local scale, the uniquely northern municipal infrastructures required to enable modern inhabitation are described. At a regional scale, the relationships between communities and land, such as Indigenous subsistence practices, are highlighted. At the transnational scale, the models document the by-products of globalisation and the dislocation and relocation of communities which they engender.

From mould to mines, from rooms to regions, the circumpolar domestic space embodies the frontline of transnational politics, Indigenous self-determination, and radical socio-environmental adaptation.

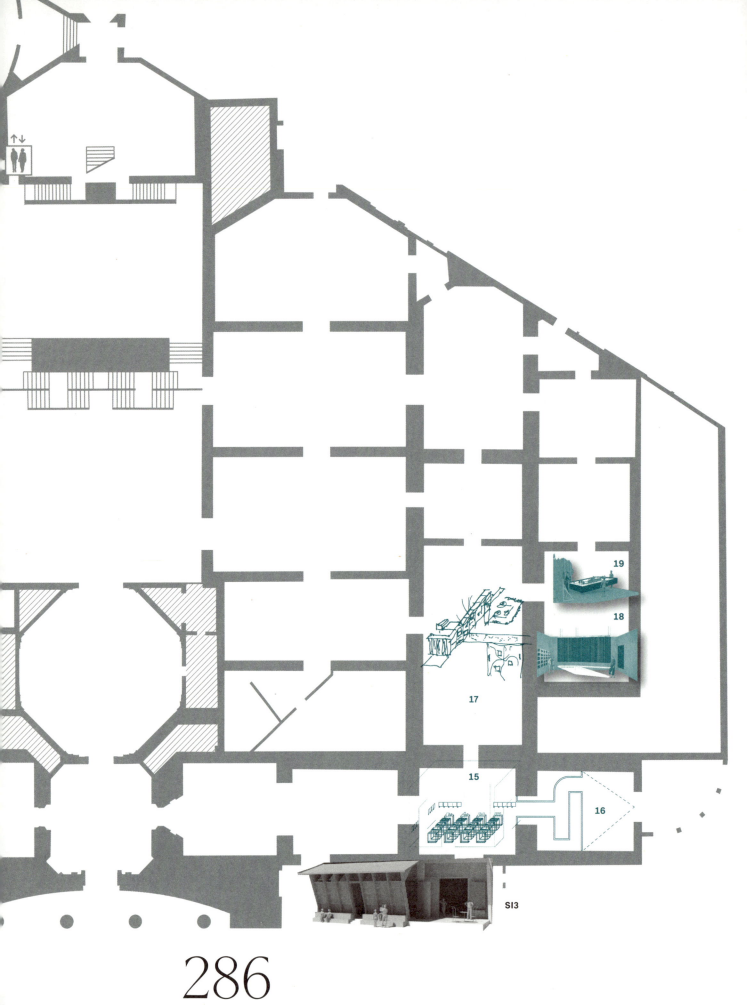

TRANSCENDING THE URBAN–RURAL DIVIDE

ACROSS BORDERS

15 Dogma
(Martino Tattara;
Pier Vittorio Aureli)
289

16 Rural Urban Framework
(Joshua Bolchover; John Lin)
291

17 Studio Paola Viganò
293

18 Paula Nascimento
295

19 Smout Allen
(Laura Allen; Mark Smout;
Geoff Manaugh)
297

S13 SPORT PLATFORM:
Architekt Christoph Lechner
& Partners
299

We live in a world divided into global cities and a global hinterland. This division spatially demarcates the political differences and vast economic inequalities of today.

This room is dedicated to imagining how these spatial boundaries can be straddled through architectural means either by introducing middle grounds, by reimagining more inclusive suburbs, or by addressing the roots of this divide within the economies and spaces of cities.

Dogma, *Grab your mother's keys, we're leaving*

Dogma, *You always seemed so sure that one day we'd be fighting*

The Opposite Shore. The suburban settlement from private property to co-operative living, 2016–2019

The suburb is arguably one of the most controversial legacies of the twentieth century. It embodies a way of life driven by the pastoral dream to live away from the city. Yet, for years, suburbs played into the idea of private property as the fundamental social characterisation of a liberal, democratic ethos. For many governments, promoting the individual ownership of a single, detached home was a way to individuate and establish the family as the cornerstone of society. A strict separation of life and work and the full privatisation of domestic labour defined the suburbs: the house represented the safe haven for family living, preserved from the promiscuity of the workplace and social relationships. Suburbs in Europe today are in steep decline as both social and environmental constructs. Yet the suburbs are still there and will remain for a long time to come.

The Opposite Shore takes this decline as an opportunity to propose a gradual yet radical, structural transformation of suburbs, which involves remaking their form and their social contract. Conducted in collaboration with the planning authorities of Flanders (Departement Omgeving), the project focuses on a series of case studies in Flanders, Limburg, and the valley of the Dender river specifically. It reveals possible design strategies for retrofitting suburban settlements across different scales, by enhancing open space, allowing cooperation among inhabitants, and by supporting the functional mix of traditionally monofunctional settlements.

Pier Vittorio Aureli (Italian, b.1973) and Martino Tattara (Italian, b.1976) of Dogma (Belgium, est.2002) in collaboration with Celeste Tellarini (Italian, b.1994), Anna Panourgia (Greek, b.1994), Antonio Paolillo (Italian, b.1987), Mariapaola Michelotto (Italian, b.1993), Yi Ming Wu (Canadian, b.1998), Theodor Reinhardt (German, b.1998), Perla Gísladóttir (Icelandic, b.1996), and Rachel Rouzaud (French, b.1997)

Physical models, publications, digital printing, 850 × 750 × 180 cm

The Chinese countryside in transformation
(underground house, Shaanxi Province)

Video collage by day: dug-out house on the bottom, Chinese landscape on the top

Split Lives: Stories from the Underground House, 2020

Joshua Bolchover (Birtish, b.1974) and John Lin (Taiwanese/American, b.1975) of Rural Urban Framework (Hong Kong, est.2007)

Immersive installation: screen video projection (4), physical models, 550 × 420 × 500 cm

In the past, many rural communities collectively built houses for their individual members.

The process of house-making directly strengthened the community. The design of vernacular dwellings embodied the ingenuity of everyday housebuilders and explored their ability to respond to a rich diversity of challenging environments with limited resources. Now, processes of urbanisation have transformed how people live together. Driven by demand and economy, new rural housing often feels similar around the globe, built with hired workers following generic construction techniques. The culture and craft of house building is becoming increasingly obsolescent as tradition is eschewed for industrialised materials and means of construction.

The dug-out house from northern China is a unique typology that stems from the material constraints of the site – where there was no available stone or wood – and environmental conditions, making it cool in summer and warm in winter. A large central courtyard is excavated in the earth and contains shared family spaces with living spaces carved outwards along each edge. Farming, the livelihood of these original dwellers, however, remains above ground. Today, at many sites, this farmland has been replaced by housing, factories, or infrastructure. Yet, as urbanisation encroaches and disrupts the surface, the dug-out houses remain. Some stay as they were, some are only used seasonally, others have changed programmatically, and some lie abandoned. These vernacular earth dwellings have born witness to the radical transformation occurring across China's once rural landscape.

Split Lives elucidates the dialectic between the past and the present, the traditional and the generic, and the rural and the urban that shapes and configures China's contemporary condition today. Stories of the split lives of these dwellings and their inhabitants reveal a glimpse into what life is like in China today, oscillating between the scale of the house and that of the territory.

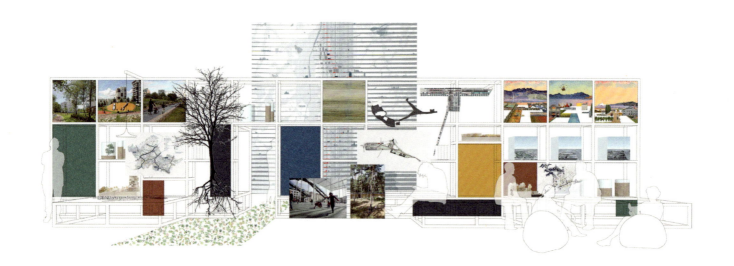

Studio Paola Viganò, *The Biopolitical Garden*, 2021

The Biopolitical Garden, 2021

In this installation, biopolitical space is considered not only as a coercive instrument, a control apparatus exerted over a population, but as a powerful reservoir of possibilities for the subjects to emancipate themselves, among humans and between human and non-human species. The current ecological, social, and economic transition demands the redefinition of the modern biopolitical project by reconsidering the role of space in the betterment of communal life. In such a transition, space, as a collective capital, a support, and an agent, is paramount.

The Biopolitical Garden, heterogeneous and varied as all gardens are, is a space of coexistence and is about spaces of coexistence: objects, lives, desires, and practices shaping and interacting in the same space. *The Biopolitical Garden* exhibits different ideas about the design of the transition as a new biopolitical project. It is a light and permeable shelf, a scaffold in dialogue with the walls, the passages, the floor, and the sky that orients the reading.

This installation is an archive, a laboratory, and an atelier. The archive is always under tension with the arrival of new materials and evolving interpretations. Here, only few fragments of it are visible. The laboratory produces prototypes of living together. The atelier, a special model of knowledge production and coexistence, is full of projects related by affinities and narratives. The three figures of coexistence combine the work of StudioPaolaViganò and Studio Bernardo Secchi & Paola Viganò, including research investigations with Habitat Research Center–EPFL, IUAV, UVA, and other academic institutions.

The four episodes – *Prototypes of the Transition*, *Utopia for Our Time*, *Design a Horizontal Metropolis*, and *Towards an Urbanism of the Living Soil* – delve into some of the extraordinary challenges about the future of cities and territories. They embed a designer's long-term reflection on how we will live together.

Paola Viganò (Italian, b.1961) with Alessio Tamiazzo (Italian, b.1990), Simona Bodria (Italian, b.1976), Qinyi Zhang (Chinese, b.1985), Laura Dalla Pietà, (Italian b.1990), Bertrand Plevinski (Belgian, b.1989), Mathilde Meurice (French, b.1995) of Studio Paola Viganò (Italy, est.2015), in collaboration with Tommaso Pietropolli (Italian, b.1989) of Lab-U (Switzerland, est.2013) and Habitat Research Center (Switzerland, est.2017) at École Polytechnique Fédérale de Lausanne, EPFL (Switzerland, est.1969)

Maps, wooden models, cardboard models, photographic panels, books, soil samples, plants, tree, 1300 × 360 × 300 cm

View from *Prédio do Livro*, modernist building, onto neighbouring informal settlements, Luanda, Angola, 2020

View from Prédio do Livro, modernist building onto Porto de Luanda, Angola, 2020

Prédio do Livro, modernist building, Luanda, Angola, 2020

Unfolding Urban Ambiguities: Prédio do Livro, 2019–2020

Paula Nascimento (Angolan, b.1981) and Jaime Mesquita, (Angolan, b.1979) of Oba Architects (Angola, est.2013), and Iris Buchholz Chocolate (German, b.1974) and Kiluanji Kia Henda (Angolan, b.1979) in collaboration with Ngoi Salucombo (Angolan, b.1981)

Installation, wood, fabric, wind, acrylic
350 × 180 × 342 × 70 cm;
projection 225 × 369 cm

The world today is increasingly interconnected and defined by a convergence of information, media, and cultures that produce new and overlapping relationships of proximity. Ours is a time of deep-seated anxieties: the rise of xenophobia, extreme politics, and the closing of borders call for an architecture or spaces that can respond positively to these events – non-aligned spaces of freedom that entail spontaneous social interaction.

This project continues a long-term reflection and study on the city of Luanda – a city of sharp contrasts whose uncontrolled growth created ambiguous zones where the formal and informal meet in unexpected ways revealing different configurations and potential articulations within urban space.

The site is a modernist tower block transformed over the years by distinct modes of occupancy, located at the intersection between different neighbourhoods – the end of the planned city and the beginning of the self-built neighbourhoods. Its short lifespan allows one to reflect upon and imagine radical futures for the site. What happens after the erasure of this building and the collapse of the border it represents? How does architecture manifest itself in those conditions?

Working within this ambiguous place and navigating its dichotomies, this project considers the interstitial as a crossing space, a potential meeting place, or a space of encounters. It thus explores the possibilities of a common ground that links the two distant neighbourhoods and that is activated through spontaneous and ephemeral activities – a catwalk for life to unfold and a catalyst for human relations to form.

Smout Allen Manaugh, *Rescue Lines* mapping

Smout Allen, *Rescue Lines*. Coniferous landscape

Rescue Lines, 2021

Mark Smout (British, b.1972)
Laura Allen (British, b.1969)
of Smout Allen (UK, est.1997)
in collaboration with Geoff
Manaugh (American, b.1976)

Composite drawing of digital and analogue techniques on acrylic and wood, c. 280 × 320 × 70 cm

Once again I see,
These hedgerows, hardy hedgerows,
Little lines of sportive wood run wild.
William Wordsworth

Orchards, grids, and proving grounds. Hedges, paths, and instruments. Nurseries, zoos, and labs.

Rescue Lines proposes a world in which the forests of the United Kingdom, both ancient and modern, can be expanded, restored, and connected once again. The project takes the form of a series of south-to-north ecological bridges – linear super-landscapes – along which displaced or endangered species can safely travel and threatened human economies can thrive.

At the heart of *Rescue Lines*, elaborate forest proving grounds serve to host new, prototype landscapes. Inside these experimental facilities, species hardened against climate change are both cultivated and preserved, forming tactical landscape 'starter packs' ready for planting elsewhere. Within these proving grounds, resident stewards also monitor speculative plant-measurement labs: whole-tree temperature chambers, soil-acid gauges, canopy-enrichment nets, and deep-ground rhizotrons where members of the public can watch in real time as roots expand through designer soil.

Worms, birds, moulds, and other species also live here, eager to follow the northward expansion of the 'rescue lines', tracking the warming gradients of the planet's collective future. Even the internal sounds of this new, climate-adapted ecology can be checked daily inside recording studios staffed by acousticians trained to hear the subtlest notes of landscape change.

Rescue Lines explores the future of green infrastructure through the lives of those who engage with it. This project connects ecological zones and economic territories at the same time, suggesting that longitudinal lines of connection, bridging forests across the United Kingdom as a model for sites elsewhere, can help us all prepare – hectare by hectare – for a climate-changed world.

Christoph Lechner, Sketch

Joseph Heintz the Younger, *Competition on the Ponte dei Pugni in Venice*, 1673. Oil on canvas

SPORT PLATFORM – 2021

Christoph Lechner (Austrian, b.1966) of Architekt Christoph Lechner & Partners (Austria, est.2012) in collaboration with Georg Wizany (Austrian, b.1980) and Reto Schindler (Austrian, b.1965) of Architekt Christoph Lechner & Partners, curatorial project Kevin Moore (American, b.1964) and Trevor Smith (American), and the Qatar Olympic and Sports Museum (Qatar), the Institute of Sport Sciences at the University of Vienna (Austria, est.1977), and Park Books (Switzerland, est.2012)

Materials and dimensions variable

Sport has long been an intrinsic part of human culture, with myriad formations according to specific societies that populate and have populated our globe. Exercising is a need for every human body. Surely it is social and fun to do this together? Part of living together is playing together and watching play.

One answer to the question 'How will we live together?' might be: Let us play together and if we are tired, we observe – let's watch them play! And while we engage in sport, by playing and watching, we concentrate on the cosmos of sport and forget conflicts. The Greek king Iphitos from Elis (ninth century BCE) sent a messenger to the oracle of Delphi to find out how to help his people deal with the horrors of war and the plague of epidemics. The oracle told him to organise a big party, the Olympic games, and to invite his enemies to play in order to pacify them. This myth is still alive.

Sport is a physical ritual with clear-cut rules. Surely it is about who is faster, stronger, smarter, and so forth? Human ambitions may be lived out in a specific framework. There are winners: the stars of sport, who might be idolised and sometimes worshipped like gods in ancient Greece by their fans. In our societies sport occurs on different levels: children playing and learning from sport, fitness and health, amateur sports to live out ambitions, professional sport to become the best in the nation or even the world – to make ends meet, become rich, become a star, or to become an idol. Competitive sport is not always fair and does not only have winners. Sport brings people together, yet sport and its structures also have the power to separate and divide by age, class, ethnicity, and gender. There is only one gold medal. The rest might be perceived as losers. Stadiums might not only be seen as wonders of architecture and engineering art – they also have to be accounted for as political symbols and economic markers.

Sport has tools and instruments. Sport needs space: a level, a field, a table, streets, sometimes an ocean or a mountain. Sport triggers architecture to house the ritual and the audience. Contemporary global mega-sport events alter cities and their infrastructure – for better or worse – to be hospitable for guests and to move people who might come to visit from all over the globe for big games. Great architects (stars) are commissioned to design buildings in which the stars of sport perform. It is a natural match. The contemporary media has given another layer to the culture of sport. The physical presence of the audience is not a fundamental act of the play anymore. The audience and the fans only need a smart screen to follow their sport. The downside: we don't get together and we can't be social, and the moneymaking spin-offs of sport distract the audience from the actual play.

Sport Platform is an installation that considers the two upcoming sports mega-events: the next Tokyo Olympics and the FIFA World Cup Qatar 2022 and their architectures and urban designs. Two pillars advertise popular sport and culture in Doha and Tokyo. The collage-like ball-wall reflects and illustrates sport in relation to the globe, the idea of nations coming together in the architecture and environment of sport, the real object, memorabilia, the star, the local, and the downsides of sport. A vignette display case shows a football star who, after retiring from his sport, became an architect and designed a stadium. Two seats from that stadium became an installation. The floor of the *Sport Platform* is an artful all-sports field. The people wall towards the Giardini, made out of bright yellow concrete formwork boards, protects the *Sport Platform* and is a grandstand in itself, showcasing people (visitors) on the risers. Steps invite visitors to sit and observe the play. The making of the *Sport Platform* is team play.

SPORT PLATFORM

Khalifa International Stadium in ar-Rayyan, design by Dar Al Handasah. 2014

Arne Müseler, *Tokyo Olympic Stadium*, design by Kengo Kuma. 2015–2019

Ramesh Daha, *Gerhard Hanappi – Soccer Player and Architect*, acrylic on canvas. 2020

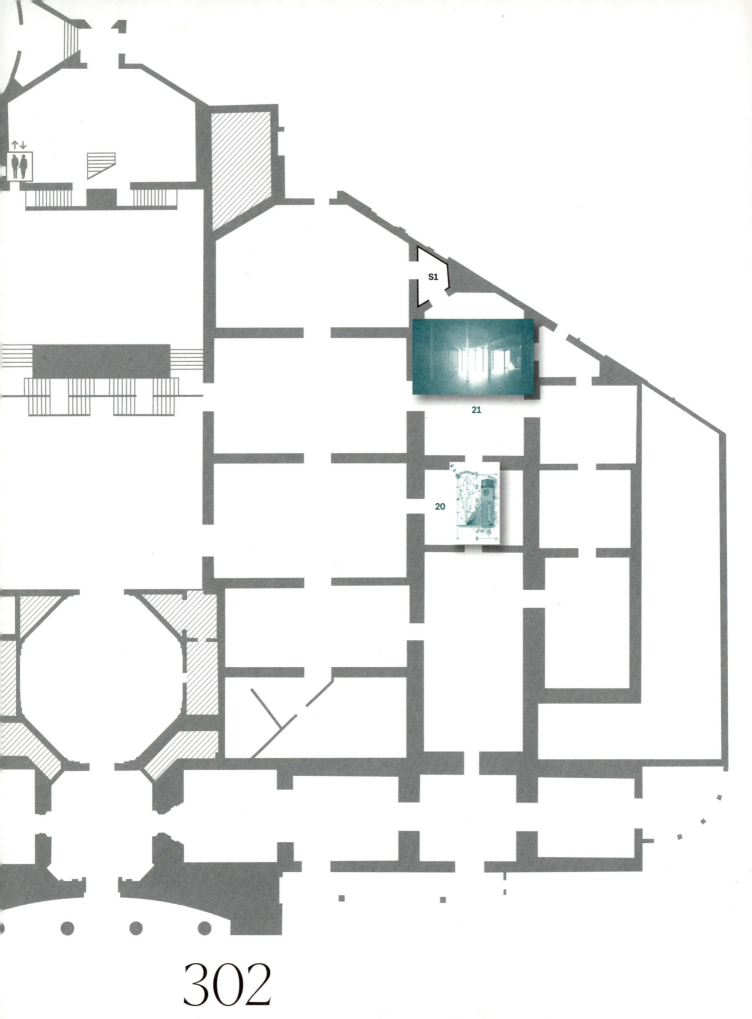

302

LINKING THE LEVANT

ACROSS BORDERS

20 Foundation for Achieving Seamless Territory (FAST); Malkit Shoshan
305

21 AAU Anastas (Elias Anastas; Yousef Anastas)
307

S1 **STATION**: Viviana d'Auria, KU Leuven
308

This room offers examples of architecture mitigating political divides. Focusing on the Levant as an example, the participants propose inclusive communal spaces, architectural structures, and construction systems that transcend political boundaries. Architecture's synthetic, multi-actor approach to creating spaces for convening helps advance the possibility of generously living together across ethnic, religious, and political divides.

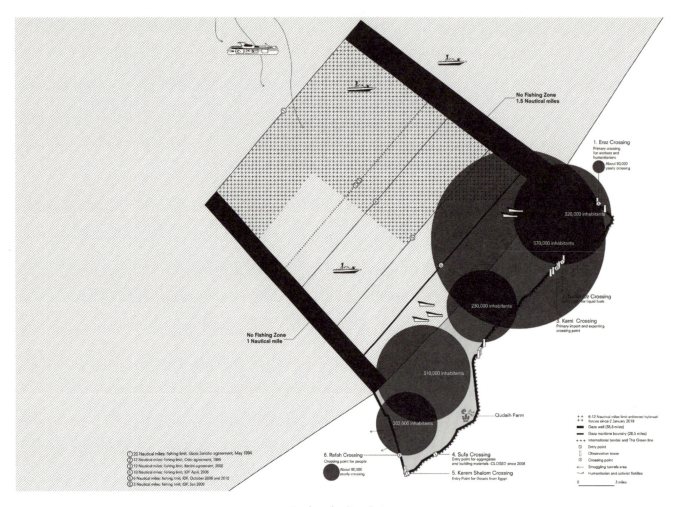

Borders, the Gaza Strip

Qudaih farmer working the land

Tomatoes in the Qudaih greenhouse

Watermelons, Sardines, Crabs, Sands, and Sediments: Border Ecologies and the Gaza Strip, 2010–2020

Foundation for Achieving Seamless Territory (FAST) (The Netherlands/USA, est.2005) with contributions by Amir Qudaih (Palestinian, b.1993) and the Qudaih family (Palestinians), Yael Berda (Israeli, b.1976), Sandra Kassenaar (Dutch, b.1982), and Malkit Shoshan (Israeli/Dutch, b.1976).

For nearly a century, fluctuations in the Israeli–Palestinian borders have affected both humans and nature. They have also led to the formation of spaces of exception, and to environments that, at times, seem paradoxically more resilient and sustainable than others.

Border Ecologies and the Gaza Strip traces the transformation of a small farm in Kutzazh, an agricultural village situated along one of the most militarised borders of Gaza and Israel. The installation tells ten stories that highlight daily life in the farm. It links mundane objects such as watermelons, sardines, sand, and sediments to bureaucratic protocols, Israeli-imposed restrictions, and continued violence, met by collective acts of survival, resistance, mutual aid, and solidarity.

Dinner table installation, mixed media, dimensions variable

One such story is centred around wheat, an indispensable strategic crop and staple diet in Palestine. In late spring, Gaza's wheat crops ripen and are ready for harvesting. The end of the harvest is celebrated with a party and the beginning of a new wedding season. *Wheat and Weddings* illustrates how two small wheat fields are used for collective festivities. Unlike other farmed lands in the area, which are used for crop rotation, these two small fields remain monocrop to allow space for summer communal gatherings.

Seafood, on the other hand, is contingent on Israeli fishing restrictions that dictate the distance a fishing boat can sail from the shore. Each mile farther out to sea means access to different species; sardines and crabs can be captured within the imposed six-mile limit, while mackerel and tuna can only be caught farther out. Israel's control not only affects Gazans' freedom, livelihood, and what they eat, but also influences marine biodiversity.

The project builds on ongoing conversations between Amir Qudaih and Malkit Shoshan over the past year, and on FAST's previous projects, such as *Atlas of the Conflict; Israel–Palestine* and *Zoo, or the letter Z, just after Zionism*.

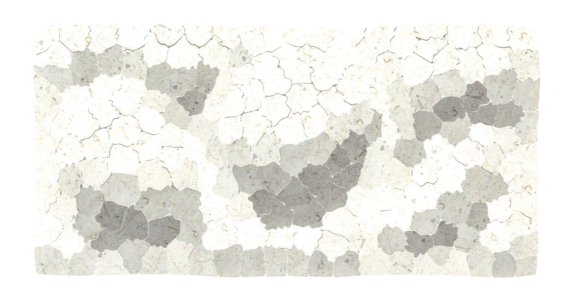

All images: AAU Anastas, *All-purpose*, 2020

All-purpose, 2020

Elias Anastas (Palestinian, b.1984) and Yousef Anastas (Palestinian b.1988) of AAU Anastas (Palestine, est.1979)

Stone, 600 × 400 × 300 cm

All-purpose focuses on differences and similarities, analogies that bring together cultures through architecture and by highlighting their non-hierarchical yet intricate dependencies. It challenges established relations of knowledge supremacies in order to imagine new possible ways of living together.

The installation presents a new form of architecture that stems both from Palestine and from the rest of the world, and investigates material explorations and architectural living spaces. It is an examination of the state of stone in contemporary architecture in Palestine. Although the change in the use of the material over time is largely linked to global transformations in the construction world, the installation is meant to showcase the evolution of the material in relation to contextual political, urban, and cultural conditions. As such, the intersections of global and local events are used as a lens to both better understand the present state of stone in Palestine as well as place its future in a wider global discourse on the use of the material in contemporary architecture. The title of the exhibition, *All-purpose*, refers to a known expression used for versatile construction materials and/or products that can be applied in different situations. It also alludes to the systematic consumption of stone in Palestine as a physical and symbolic matter serving multilayered agendas. This project establishes links between different scales, periods, and locations in Palestine and beyond as a way of blending approaches and place the use of stone in contemporary architecture at the intersection of local and global matters. In the disparate cultural context of Palestine, certain architectural attributes, originally found locally, returned to Palestine as imported elements. The installation challenges the approach of imperial transmissions of knowledge. Instead, it traces the origins of architectural elements and techniques beyond borders and historical periods. *All-purpose* builds up its content on stone matters, a six-year-long, experimentation-based research that formalises into a series of site-specific stone structures in Palestine.

dis B orders: resonating stories of three border topologies, 2019–2021

Viviana d'Auria (Italian, b.1978), Claire Bosmans (Belgian, b.1990), and Khalda Imad Mubarak El Jack (Sudanese, b.1991) at KU Leuven (Belgium, est.1425)

Video projection, digital printing

Borders are commonly set against flows, as unchanging barriers regulating migration – the epitome of movement. More recently, however, their actual immovability has been questioned: borders have been observed as migrating themselves. As such the boundedness of landscapes and identities, challenged by escalating socio-ecological issues, have been fundamentally questioned. They are viewed as a thickness and not as a line that is produced by hindering, suspending, or impeding passage. In such a context, they also become borderlands that consist of liminal spaces that are about limbo and deferral as much as they are about encounter and political potential. This contribution thinks through border topologies by scrutinising three resonating stories. Explored at seemingly different scales, they illustrate the dis-orders generated when borders are posited as part of an impermeable landscape.

The first story goes back to a point in time when the frontiers of sub-Saharan Africa's first liberated country were fixed not only through flagship independence, but also by means of development aid. As a consequence, Ghana's national boundaries were actually conflated with those of the Volta Lake, which was the principal outcome of the river basin development scheme heralded as the primary tool of emancipation from (neo)colonialism. Realising the world's largest manmade lake also resulted in the forced relocation of 80,000 riverside dwellers to 52 model townships. These were projected to become modern settlements for the newly forged Ghanaians, who were in turn expected to leave behind ethnic distinctions and subsistence livelihoods.

While the lake was imagined as a connector, the opposite is true today. Differential movement across and around the lake becomes evident when focusing on one of the several model townships and the journeys from and towards it: the crossings of itinerant traders, produce sellers, local assemblers, roadside vendors, seasonal workers, and summer job seekers display complex mobility patterns which typify the necessity and opportunity of multi-sited co-existences. And while the lake incessantly thwarts the movement of goods and people, it nonetheless becomes a preferential channel for spreading water-borne diseases.

Viviana d'Auria based on Kwamina & Benneh (1971: 20); Chambers (1970: 50); Dickson (1969: 237); Nagels & Aucha Gomez (2011: 9), conflated borders in post-colonial Ghana: basin, nation, region, wards.

STATION

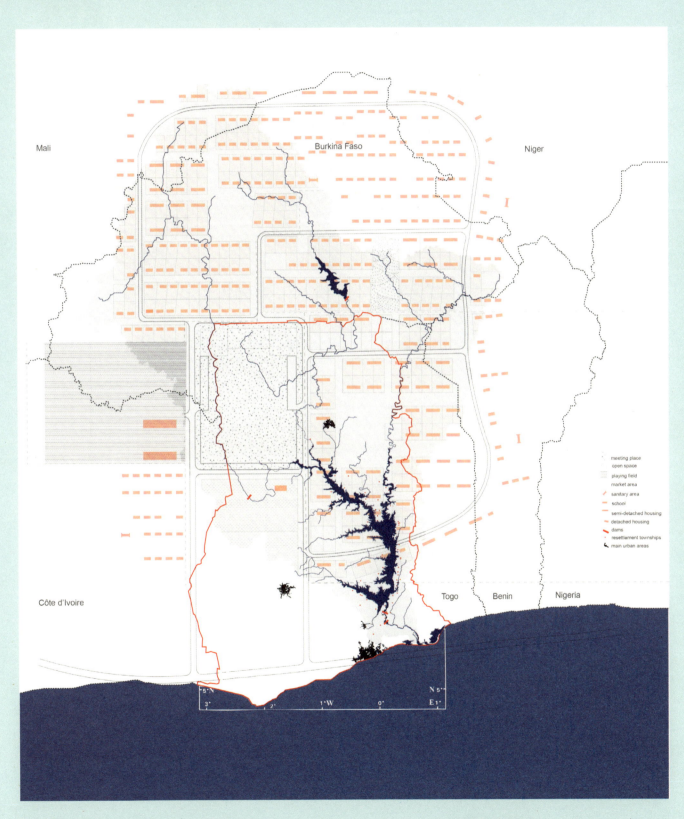

ACROSS BORDERS—*Station*

309

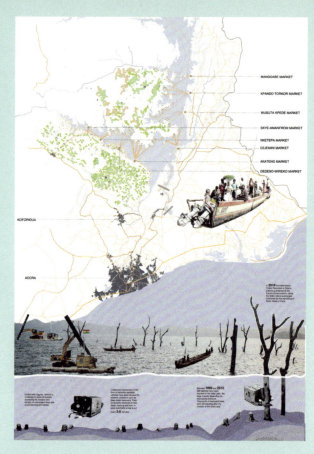

Viviana d'Auria based on Laura Nagels and Enrique Aucha Gomez (2011), *How Many Boat-stump Collisions Occur in the Volta Lake on a Yearly Basis?*, 2021

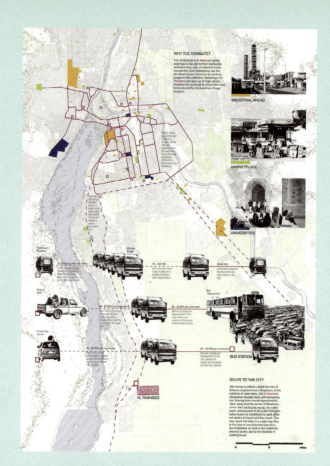

Khalda Imad Mubarak El Jack, *How Long Does it Take to Reach Khartoum's City Centre From the Periphery?*, 2021

Claire Bosmans, *Who Has the Right to Temporary Occupation in Brussels' North Quarter?*, 2021

Moreover, its shoreline has been offset as yet another prescriptive line, a buffer zone within which crucial activities for water-based communities, like drawdown agriculture, are controlled.

A comparable intricacy is found in contemporary Sudan and the three settlements that constitute the urban assemblage of Khartoum at the confluence of the White and Blue Nile. For decades, Sudan's capital city has exemplified the complexity of urbanisation–desertification interactions, with the former negatively impacting the latter, and vice versa. Although the country no longer leads world rankings on active internal displacement, the number of people who have been relocated by conflict remains significant and poses vital questions on what it may mean to reside within Khartoum's ever-shifting urban edge. This frontier is under constant interrogation because most IDPs dwell in so-called irregular settlements, and, though not assigned to a bounded site under a humanitarian regime, reverse migration remains the dominant official prospect to which they are subjected. Meanwhile, Khartoum's margins show how behaviours that transcend the binary oppositions that constitute widespread ethnic, linguistic, and religious antagonisms combine and are adapted through local practices.

Khartoum is also the city that gives its name to one of the EU member states' significant actions to externalise border control as part of its hard-line migration policy, especially in the aftermath of the 2015 'refugee crisis'. While externalisation means distance-creation between the locus of decision-making and the locus of surveillance, this does not mean that the politics of asylum are far removed from the everyday spatiality of Brussels, Europe's de facto capital city. Rather, the contrary seems to be true, as Maximilien Park illustrates. It is in this important public space that spontaneous camps, citizen-led mobilisations, and a multitude of individual journeys have converged and made demands for both movement and place. Nonetheless, the political possibilities of such practices and their enduring engagement with the urban remain under threat. While the spaces of solidarity stay precarious and mobile in themselves, the Maximilian Park is under redesign. The River Senne's trace, vaulted before the Park would see the light, is to be returned to Brussels. What and who will be displaced by its newly flowing waters is yet an open question.

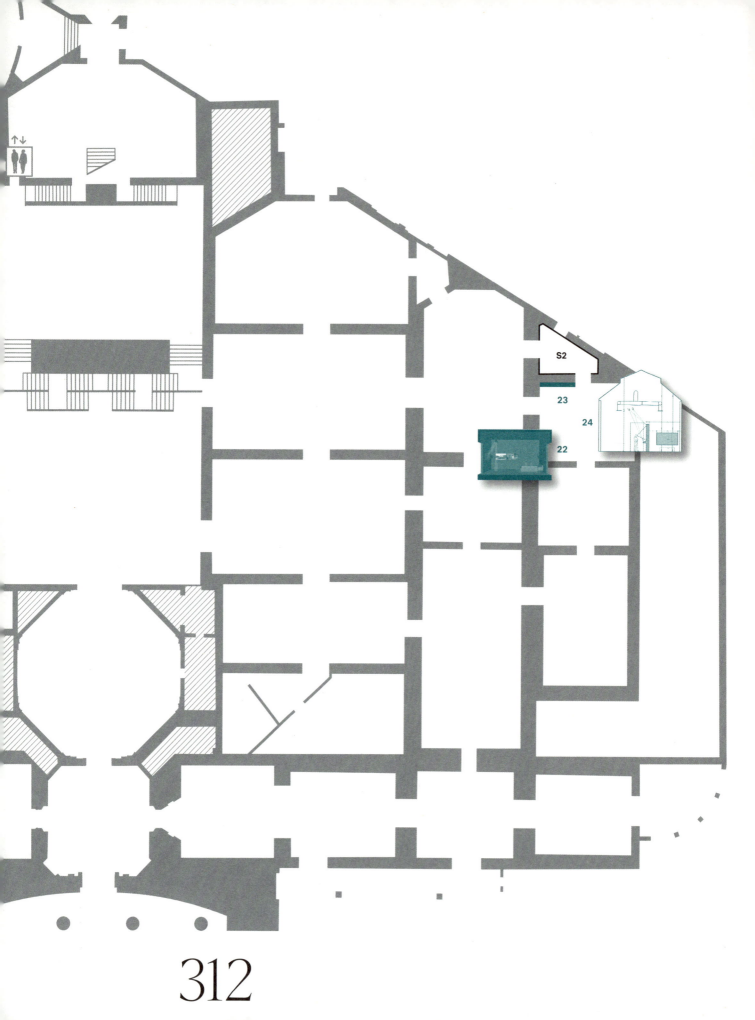

SEEKING REFUGE

ACROSS BORDERS

22 Decolonizing Architecture Art Residency (Alessandro Petti; Sandi Hilal)
315

23 Wissam Chaaya
317

24 Forensic Oceanography (Charles Heller; Lorenzo Pezzani)
319

S2 **STATION**: Justinien Tribillon, The Barlett School of Planning
320

We are all refugees seeking safe havens elsewhere. This spreading uprootedness has compelled architects to rethink the values of placemaking and cultural specificity usually attributed to architecture. The extreme cases of refugee camps represented in this room ask such difficult questions such as: What is heritage when those who claim it are no longer there? How is it possible to generate permanent architecture out of temporary materials? How does the act of building re-establish connectedness to a place? How can architecture express uprootedness in a dignified way?

All images: DAAR, Dheisheh Refugee Camp, *Stateless Heritage*.
Dheisheh Refugee Camp World Heritage Nomination, 2021

Stateless Heritage: Dheisheh Refugee Camp World Heritage Nomination, 2021

Sandi Hilal and Alessandro Petti of DAAR (Decolonizing Architecture Art Research) in collaboration with Luca Capuano

Audio-video (2), 8' loop, book, dimensions variable

Do refugee camps have a history? Is the camp just a site of misery or does it produce values that need to be acknowledged and protected? What would happen to the camp if the Dheisheh refugee camp were recognised as a UNESCO World Heritage site? And how should the notion of heritage change in order to acknowledge the camp's condition?

These are some of the questions at the basis of the idea of nominating Dheisheh Refugee Camp and the 44 villages from which its inhabitants come as a UNESCO World Heritage site.

The discussion about the implications of the nomination that this project prompted involved camp organisations and individuals, politicians, conservation experts, activists, governmental and non-governmental representatives, and proximate residents. The participants in these debates were ambivalent because, on the one hand, it was feared that the recognition would change the status quo and threaten to undermine the legally recognised right of return. On the other hand, requesting acknowledgement that refugee history was part of the heritage of humanity would thereby bring the right of return back to the centre of the political discussion.

From the very beginning, the nomination raised a series of contradictions and impossibilities. The World Heritage Convention states that 'Universal Values [...] transcend the interests of individual States Parties', yet only nation–states who have signed the World Heritage World Convention have the right to nominate.

Who has the right to nominate in the case of the Palestinian Refugee Camps – extraterritorial spaces carved out from state sovereignties? The states within which camps are located? The State of Palestine? The Palestinian Liberation Organisation? Popular committees within the refugee camps themselves? The Stateless Nation, with a population of more than 60 million?

Stateless Heritage is an attempt to understand and practice refugeeness beyond humanitarianism. It is not enough to rethink the refugee camp as a political space. We must understand refugees as beings in exile and exile as a current political practice capable of challenging the status quo. Recognising the heritage of a culture of exile is the perspective from which social, spatial, and political structures can be imagined and experienced beyond the idea of the nation–state.

Wissam Chaaya, *At the Cemeteries, Playscapes of Exile* 2019–2020. Children playing in cemeteries at the Al Baddawi Palestinian refugee camp, in Tripoli, Lebanon

Wissam Chaaya, *Pre-School Activities, Playscapes of Exile* 2019-2020. Children from the Syrian refugee camp in Jubb Jannine, Beqaa, Lebanon, waiting for the school bus to go to afternoon classes

Playscapes of Exile, 2019–2020

*Wissam Chaaya
(Lebanese, b.1977)*

Colour-printed photographs on Chromalux aluminium boards (9), 90 × 60 cm

They are hunted for their beliefs. They are persecuted for their national and social belonging. They are judged for their political views. They are displaced while fleeing war.

Placed in sprawling camps with little to no access to vital services, refugees in Lebanon do not have the right to live as normal citizens: They fear persecution should they be sent back to their countries of origin.

Palestinians have held the status of refugees in different countries around the world following the 1948 and 1967 Arab–Israeli wars. In Lebanon, they are scattered around the country in twelve camps where the Lebanese government has no legal power. Ghettoed and limited in space to one square kilometre per camp, a growing population has built vertically to accommodate its need for space. Moreover, public space has become scarce and public activities have become insignificant.

Syrian refugee camps are relatively new. They started emerging with the onset of the Syrian war in 2011, and consist of temporary, informal settlements rather than built structures. Indeed, Syrian refugees have erected tents on empty plots of terrain, rented, or squatted. They have rarely used abandoned structures as shelters. As a result, their camps reflect more visibly the emergency of settlement. Therefore, public spaces in these camps are seen as non-vital and as a consequence the quality of everyday life is degraded.

With time, unused space around camps has become useful in a way. Inhabitants have often transformed it because of their need for space. All sorts of activities take place spontaneously in improvised spaces around camps. The refugees use them in an unorganised, as-needed sort of way.

Refugee children are no strangers to this either – they are on the frontline of the quest for space. They are in a permanent search for grounds to play on. Their liveliness brings life to unused spaces and transforms them temporarily into playgrounds, fulfilling their needs far from home. These are the *Playscapes of Exile*.

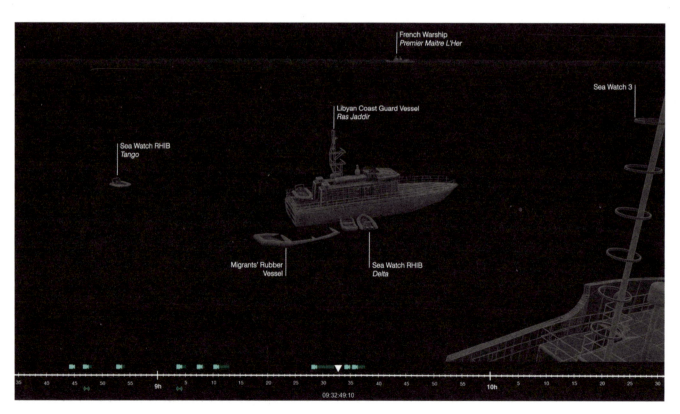

All images: Film still, *Mare Clausum – The Sea Watch vs Libyan Coast Guard Case*, 2018.
Video, 28'

Aesthetic Borders: Of Violence and (in)Visibility at Sea, 2011-ONGOING

Charles Heller (Swiss, b.1981) and Lorenzo Pezzani (Italian, b.1982) of Forensic Oceanography (UK, est.2011), in collaboration with Forensic Architecture (UK, est.2010)

Mixed media installation (2 video projections and archival materials), 650 × 350 cm

In this installation, Forensic Oceanography (FO) uses two of its recent investigations to interrogate the complex and ambivalent relation between border violence and aesthetics: it asks how particular conditions of (dis)appearance, (in)audibility, and (in)visibility have emerged at the maritime frontiers of Europe.

Since 2011, FO has investigated the militarised border regime in the Mediterranean, analysing the conditions that have led to the death of thousands of migrants over the last 30 years. By combining human testimonies with traces left across the digital sensorium of the sea (radars, satellite imagery, vessel tracking systems, and so on), FO has attempted to challenge the boundaries of what can be seen and heard within this area so as to contest the violence of borders.

The two investigations presented here, *The Crime of Rescue* and *Mare Clausum*, engage with the momentous shift that occurred in the Mediterranean in 2015, when non-governmental organisations started to conduct search and rescue operations in reaction to the persisting death of migrants and state authorities' inaction. While the critical presence of NGOs has invaluably enhanced the ability to monitor border violence at sea, it has also brought new dilemmas to the fore. As the investigations reveal, the sudden flooding of images they have generated has been used not only to demand accountability for that violence, but also to criminalise and discredit their own work. Moreover, revealing border violence can have ambivalent effects, such as reproducing racialised imaginaries of black and brown bodies upon which the very closure of EU borders is predicated.

By critically analysing the shifting aesthetic regime operating at the Mediterranean frontier, the installation seeks to confront and unravel some of these ethical and political dilemmas, dwelling on the challenges of representing violence.

Welcome to Borderland, 2021

Justinien Tribillon (French, b.1989) in collaboration with Cécile Trémolières (French, b.1989), Offshore Studio (Switzerland, est.2016) and Misia Forlen (French, b.1989).

Mixed-media installation including spoken texts, sound, and prints (postcards)

There are accepted rituals, conventions, abstractions humans collectively choose to acknowledge and, therefore, to enforce. Some of them are imposed on us; others we embrace. We are sometimes conscious of them, often not. Imaginary lines are examples of such conventions: from a benign looking one like the Prime Meridian in Greenwich, London, to more violent and expressive ones such as militarily enforced national borders. None of these lines has any ontological value: they exist because we decide they exist, because we find them meaningful, because they convey an imaginary.

Developing a critical understanding of the socially produced fabric(s) that structures the way we live together enables us to better understand the space we share. What are the terms and conditions of our spatial contract? Some of these frameworks are laced with hatred and oppression, others with political utopia, scientific discourse, cultural prejudice, fundamental fears, and/or deep-rooted social forms such as the idea of *community* or the *other*. They may also act asymmetrically: one's formality may be a life-threatening obstacle to another.

Political borders are such spaces of ritual and convention.

The actual *borderline* is one that a Westphalian political system, enmeshed with the idea of feudal property, has designed and enforces through various architectures and rituals – the checkpoints, lines painted on the ground, the signs 'Welcome to…' or 'You're now leaving…' the military outfits, the checking of IDs, and the required submission to the enquiry of an employee of the state, soldiers, or militiamen.

Yet borders are not limited to the immediate physical spaces and rituals that incarnate them – they expand, they branch out, they have deep ramifications. The idea of cultural and political borders structures many of the mundane actions and artefacts of our everyday lives. Borders are more than the lines that exist in space to delimit what is 'in' or 'out'.

The idea of borders is one that transcends geographic space to create a complex planetary architecture. Borders shape space and are shaped by it. They are more than the imaginary lines confined to the edge of a national territory. Borders – the symbols and meanings they carry, the

Justinien Tribillon, Welcome to Borderland – #1, 2020

STATION

Justinien Tribillon, *Welcome to Borderland – #4*, 2020

'architecture of force' they embody – are transversal. The fluidity of our modern interconnected shared global space exists in constant conflict and renegotiation with nations and their ultimate incarnation: the borders surrounding them.

We live in a planetary borderland – a 'space of flows', where sprawling networks of communication are connecting people while more fences and militarised walls are always being erected to forbid trespassing. We live in a globally integrated economy, feeding and fed by segregated socio-spatial archipelagos.

Welcome to Borderland explores the reality of border away from the geographical lines that define it via the prism of *plants*. A critical take on botany, identity, and space enables us to explore a tension, a nexus of architectures, social constructions, imaginaries, objects, and discourses. Plants are *invasive, wild, indigenous, naturalised.* Plants have IDs, and they follow rules. Yet, more often than not they flout them: they crack the walls. In all plants and their behaviours, we find traces of the borders away from the border, the contradictions of flows and fences.

Welcome to borderland.

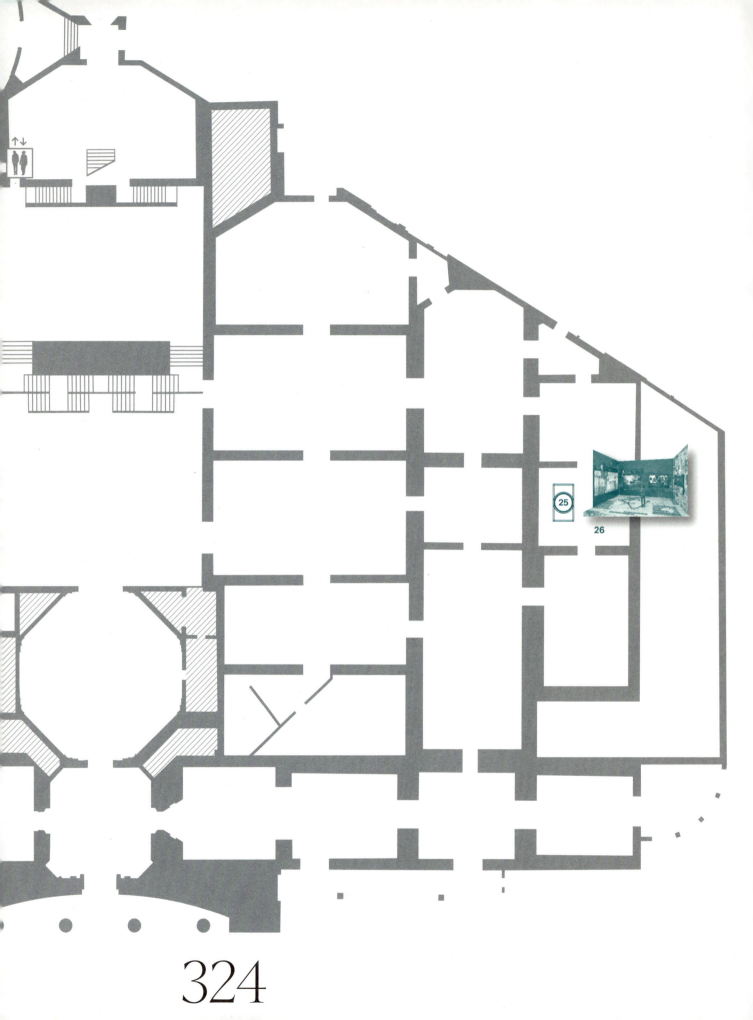

RE-SOURCING RESOURCES

ACROSS BORDERS

25   Chair of Günther Vogt
       ETH Zurich
       327

26   Olalekan Jeyifous and
       Mpho Matsipa
       329

Our resources are at once being depleted and mismanaged. They are also unevenly distributed among nations and communities. Whether water or energy, these vital supports of our daily lives need to be distributed and shared differently and more efficiently across borders. Their scarcity is also inspiring new habits of consumption and behaviour. The projects in this room take a closer look at the networks of resource distribution and imagine how they might be recast more effectively across natural and urban landscapes.

Chair of Günther Vogt, ETH Zurich, *The Alps as Ecological Island in the Middle of the European Continent*, 2019. Projection

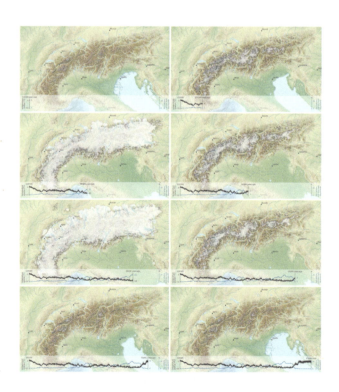

Julien Seguinot, *Advance and Retreat of the Alpine Glaciers During the Last Glacial Cycle*, 2018. Video stills

Common Water: The Alps, 2020

The Alps have always been integrated into the economic and social developments of the European continent, albeit in a usually delayed and milder form. With industrialisation came the distinction between intensively- and extensively-used landscapes. Climate change further fuels these developments.

When considering water as a central resource of the Alpine landscape, the consequences of rises in temperature become clear. The rapidly progressing melting of the glaciers and the declining significance of the snow are a 'liquefaction of the water balance' – that is, storing snow and ice becomes less important, and precipitations influence the hydrological conditions more powerfully. As a result, the Alps can no longer completely fulfil their function as Europe's water tower, particularly in summer. They will, however, continue to be of outstanding importance in the Central European water supply.

This installation proposes a new reading of the Alpine landscape as an 'ecological island' at the centre of the continent, integrating various disciplines such as art, natural sciences, engineering, and landscape architecture. Seen in a European framework unprecedented features arise: a resource space for (immaculate quality) water and energy, a hotspot of biodiversity, a tourist destination with pleasant climatic conditions, a cultural space free of the stress of dense populations, and a unique landscape.

New relationships between inner-Alpine and outer-Alpine Europe are founded on collaboration. As with the early agricultural communities in the Alpine region, the exchange will have to be based on a jointly negotiated and sustainable use. This will enable us to deal responsibly with the resource of the Alpine landscape, resisting traditional images and ideas and, instead, creating new images and meanings.

Günther Vogt (Liechtensteiner, b.1957) at the Department of Architecture at ETZ Zurich (Switzerland, est.1855) and Amalia Bonsack (Swiss, b.1991), Thomas Kissling (Swiss, b.1980), Andreas Klein (German, b.1987), Max Leiß (German, b.1982), Roland Charles Shaw (British, b.1984), and Sarem Sunderland (Swiss/British, b.1990) at ETH Zurich, in collaboration with Julian Charrière (Swiss, b.1987) of Studio Julian Charrière Berlin (Germany), Alessandro Tellini (Swiss, b.1984) of Raplab D-Arch at ETH Zurich, and Rolf Weingartner (Swiss, b.1954) at the University of Bern (Switzerland, est.1834) and ecosfera gmbh (Switzerland)

Physical model of the Alps, 650 × 350 cm, screen-project film essay, printed photographs, dimensions variable

Olalekan Jeyifous, *Petrotopia*

Olalekan Jeyifous, *Goddess of the Black Atlantic*

Liquid Geographies, Liquid Borders, 2021

Liquid Geographies, Liquid Borders explores the aural and visual landscape of the lagoon as a spatial metaphor for complex, slippery exchanges that seek to delineate ownership, but also gestures towards a terrain of blending, branching, and stratification of aquatic ecologies. One of the key questions the installation explores is the materiality of larger systems of power mediated by oil – and the spectralisation of those who refuse to remain structurally illegible, or legible – within that frame.

Such topographies escape proper or fixed physical demarcations, even while being constituted by the vectors of extraction, unbridled capitalist expansion, and recalibrations of territory, identity, and rule.

This fluid imaginary space that connects the Niger delta to other waterways emerges at the interface of aquatic ecologies and multiple figurations of Yemoja – the Yoruba goddess of the sea. Taking crude oil-spills as a point of departure, the installation connects oil-fuelled trade and degradation with the lived spatialities of these polymorphic landscapes. Yemoja presents a lens to introduce not only oral histories and culture to the discourse on oil, but also an eco-feminist, and deeply rooted critique of oil culture.

Olalekan Jeyifous (American, b.1977) and Mpho Matsipa (South African, b.1977) in collaboration with Wale Lawal (Nigerian, b.1992) and Dani Kyengo O'Neill (Kenyan/ South African, b.1993)

Digital printing on vinyl (wall), 1835 × 420 cm; Digital printing on vinyl (floor); Lightbox display (4), 92 × 122 cm each; Soundscape, Experimental video

As one Planet

EXHIBITION GIARDINI

A decade ago, Isabelle Stengers argued that the only politics is cosmopolitics. Globalisation and its consequences, such as climate change and pandemics, have prompted some cosmopolitical action, but humans have some distance to go to shape effective politics at the planetary scale.

Architects have risen to the challenge of climate change primarily by incorporating more responsible technologies in their buildings. But architects possess representational tools that allow them to project, like no other field, the impact of such changes on the totality of the planet. Architects have reimagined the impact of new technologies on the planet's future since at least the nineteenth century with expansive projects like Cerda's linear city and until the 1970s with more corrective approaches like Ekistics and Superstudio. Somehow, however, this imaginative work has waned. More than ever, such a collective imagination is necessary to understand better how globalisation and its risks are shaping our world. Can architects help us project the future of the planet as one living environment where we live together and protect it?

Architects in this section, along with other experts – ecologists, geo-engineers, global economists, sociologists – exercise their skills at imagining the spatial future of the planet.

FUTURE ASSEMBLY, 2020

COLLECTIVE EXHIBITION WITHIN THE EXHIBITION

Caroline A. Jones (American, b.1954), Hadeel Ibrahim (British/Sudanese, b.1983), Kumi Naidoo (South African, b.1965), Mariana Mazzucato (Italian/American, b.1968), Mary Robinson (Irish, b.1944), Olafur Eliasson (Danish/Icelandic, b.1967), Paola Antonelli (Italian, b.1963), and Sebastian Behmann (German, b.1969)

Dear Biennale Participants,

You have been brought together by Hashim Sarkis for the 17th International Architecture Exhibition of La Biennale. This year's selection of architects, designers, and artists is the most diverse ever, presenting a unique opportunity to come together to reflect on the question: What might a multilateral assembly of the future look like? This letter is our invitation to you all as participants to contribute to a project dedicated to this question and titled *Future Assembly*.

When the United Nations (UN), the paradigm for a multilateral assembly of the twentieth century, was founded in 1945, it was in response to political, social, economic, and humanitarian crises; its charter, consequently, is based on human-centric principles. Today, the future of the UN lies in an equally radical response to the urgent planetary crisis that faces us. This future, we believe, must become more inclusive, extending to all our planet's inhabitants and beyond – it must be more-than-human. The *Future Assembly* we envisage consists not only of humans but also of animals and plants, the ephemeral traces and voices of multiple species, and of the air, the water, the trees, the soil. How do we, as spatial practitioners, imagine giving standing to these voices in a vision for our shared future?

We begin by inviting each of you to choose a stakeholder that you believe should be represented in the *Future Assembly*. We invite you to design a seat in this assembly to give voice to the ephemeral and more-than-human players in your local environment. This can take the form of your choice, free of our current technical and social limitations.

We sincerely hope that you accept this invitation to imagine together – in collaboration rather than competition – a positive vision of the future of our world, based on creativity, sustainability, and inclusion.

Yours,
Caroline A. Jones, Hadeel Ibrahim, Kumi Naidoo, Mariana Mazzucato, Mary Robinson, Olafur Eliasson, Paola Antonelli, Sebastian Behmann

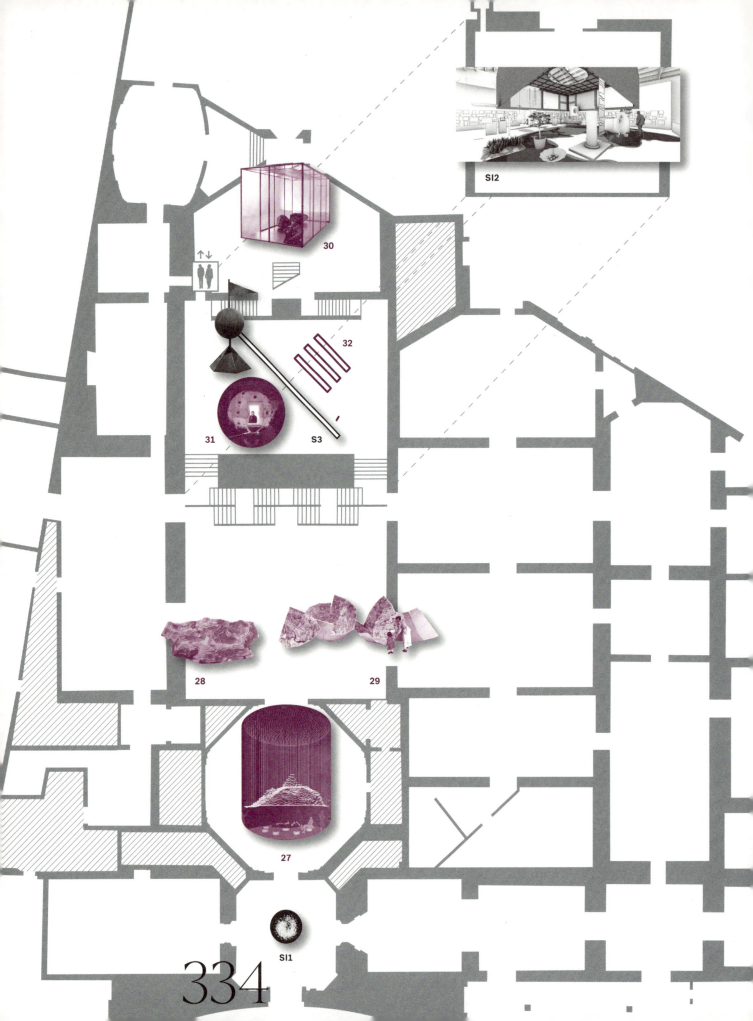

MAKING WORLDS

AS ONE PLANET

27 Cave_bureau (Karanja Kabage; Stella Mutegi)
339

28 TVK (Pierre Alain Trévelo; Antoine Viger-Kohler)
341

29 Plan B Architecture & Urbanism (Joyce Hsiang; Bimal Mendis)
343

30 Christina Agapakis, Alexandra Daisy Ginsberg & Sissel Tolaas
345

31 Daniel López-Pérez; Reiser + Umemoto; Princeton University School of Architecture
347

32 S.E.L; Verena Paravel; Lucien Castaing-Taylor
349

SI1 **FRONTISPIECE**: Michal Rovner
337

SI2 **COLLECTIVE EXHIBITION WITHIN THE EXHIBITION**: Future Assembly
333

S3 **STATION**: Architectural Worlds (Hashim Sarkis; Roi Salgueiro Barrio; Gabriel Kozlowski)
350

Globalisation has left us with much to be desired. No longer patiently waiting for cosmopolitics to rise to the occasion, the architectural imaginary is projecting better worlds: the world as a vital unity, as one megacity; the world where nature and infrastructure are intertwined; the world that recovers its biodiversity and natural history; the world that offers up mineral and ephemeral elements to our consciousness and our lives; the world where we give formal expression to the hidden systems that need to be protected and nurtured.

All images: Michal Rovner, *Culture-C1*, 2021. Video projection

FRONTISPIECE

CULTURE-C1, 2021

Michal Rovner (Israeli, b.1957)

Video projection, dimensions variable

Data Zone, exhibited in 2003 at the Biennale Arte, is a series of culture plates (petri dishes) in which tiny human figures move in different patterns of order and disorder. The work offers the visitor the viewpoint of a scientist observing the object of their research, magnifying its smallest details, while at the same time, offering a distant, 'objective', cold, scientific look at a group of humans, the human species.

The culture plates are becoming newly relevant these days. We are all critically affected by the Covid-19 pandemic, experiencing instability and uncertainty, following the data, charts, and graphs. We are all researching and being researched. The work from 2003 generated various questions, and among them one that recurred again and again: Who are these people? Is it us or is it them?

How will we live together? Some of the starkest images of these days of pandemic are of empty public spaces. This imagery evokes existential anxiety and an implicit threat to social structures, a dread that provokes in us the need to rethink contemporary social and cultural structures.

The pandemic, against the background of the global climate crisis, emphasises that we are all part of one human weave, with a common humanity, responsible for our collective fate on this earth. Alongside inspiring gestures of responsibility, help, compassion, and solidarity, we are also exposed to carelessness, indifference, economic and social segregation, and inequality, all of which together lead us to the question: How can we live together?

Like others that preceded it, this project starts with reality, filming real people in real places, so the human particles in the artist's work are concrete people moving through situations. It could be them; it could be us. How can we do the best for us, for them, for all?

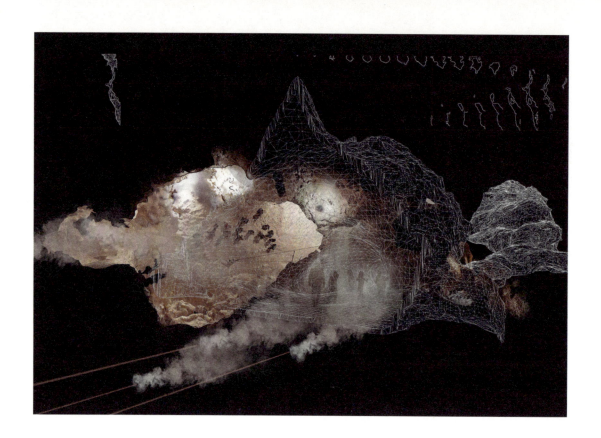

All images: Cave_bureau et al., *The Anthropocene Museum: Exhibit 3.0 Obsidian Rain*, 2017

The Anthropocene Museum: Exhibit 3.0 Obsidian Rain, 2017

Kabage Karanja (Kenyan, b.1979) and Stella Mutegi (Kenyan, b.1979) of Cave_bureau (Kenya, est.2014), in collaboration with Densu Moseti (Kenyan, b.1986)

Reproduction of a section of the Mbai cave (1:1): obsidian stone (1700), c. 10 × 5 × 5 cm each, and rope, supported by a timber and steel structure; Table: steel, obsidian, dimensions variable; Bronze and cement cast models, leather artefacts, dimensions variable; Tree stump stools (7), d. 45 cm

Experiencing caves that geologically date back millions of years is a celebration of the rich architectural heritage of cave inhabitation by early and more recent ancestors across the planet. Often, histories and theories of architecture inadequately frame this history, just as one reflects on the origin of one's first experiences of inside and out, light wells and echoes, among other aspects of our collective prehistoric consciousness.

The *Anthropocene Museum* revisits this genesis albeit with more sophisticated tools to grow a repository of architectural and geological records as written, drawn, and built elements. A kind of reverse architecture is employed, using 3D laser scanning technology to extract traditional architectural information of the caves. This information is then etched on leather maps, scaled in bronze models, narrated in short stories, and transposed to different locations. This project has been realised by convening with diverse indigenous communities in these various sites to address complex environmental and cultural challenges facing inhabitants of the African continent and the planet.

Obsidian Rain, at the 17th International Architecture Exhibition, is a transposed section of the Mbai cave in Kenya, which was inhabited in the middle of the twentieth century by anti-colonial freedom fighters who used it as a commune chamber to plan their resistance. The installation consists of a collection of obsidian stone hanging from the ceiling with sisal rope. Beneath it is a table to host discussions about the environment and the state of the architectural discipline in Kenya, the African continent, and beyond, among other relevant topics. The *Anthropocene Museum* here is not confined to the often-innocuous activities of a conventional museum building or its politics that often provide little freedom to overtly challenge the status quo of the prevailing times. It is a (re)construction of sorts of this age-old institution and the practice of architecture itself within the African context, while still in our own way contributing to the global consciousness and discourse surrounding the new geological age we live in – the Anthropocene.

All images: TVK et al., *The Earth is an Architecture*, 2015–2020

The Earth is an Architecture, 2015–2020

The constant and exponential increase of the world's population has always caused a profound change in ancestral terrestrial conditions. After being flat, the earth became a sphere, and today the Earth is architecture. This does not mean that architecture replaces the earth, but rather that the two are now inextricably linked by a common destiny. Inspired by contemporary ideas regarding the entanglement between nature and culture – the plan-relief model – *The Earth is an Architecture* is the representation of a situated manifesto of the Earth. It reinterprets the concept of infrastructure as a mediation between humanity and the Earth.

Much more than functional technical objects, infrastructures are things, both human and terrestrial, both programmes and sites. Beyond roads, networks, buildings, equipment, ports, canals, and dikes, these infrastructures allow societies to inhabit the planet collectively. The domain of architecture extends beyond buildings to the earthly infrastructure represented in the installation. Infrastructure connects humans to the Earth, and, thus, makes the world.

This 8 × 4 m plan-relief model represents a new theory of architecture and the Earth's infrastructure. It offers a new vision of the gigantic accumulation of infrastructural fragments. The fictional geography of this rectangular Earth enables one to decipher the fundamental conditions of infrastructure. Each major entity corresponds to an earthly element (the air, the sea, the ground, the living, energy) and tells the story of the associated infrastructures (lines, surfaces, volumes, pieces, metamorphoses). Together they form an intercontinental epic that traces the history of earthly infrastructure and open new horizons for architectural fictions.

Pierre Alain Trévelo (French, b.1973) and Antoine Viger-Kohler (French, b.1973) of TVK (France, est.2003) in collaboration with David Malaud (French, b.1988), Mathieu Mercuriali (French, b.1977), Océane Ragoucy (French, b.1983), Sarah Sauton (French, b.1980), Antoine Bertaudière (French, b.1987), Alexandre Bullier (French, b.1981), David Enon (French, b.1984), Victor Francisco (French, b.1972), Amaury Haumont (French, b.1989), Michael Loconte (American, b.1994), Stela Moceanu (Romanian, b.1991), Jihana Nassif (Brazilian, b.1988), and with the support of Fanny Maurel (French, b.1995), Maider Papandinas (French, Greek, Spanish, b.1997) and Mathilde Pichot (French, b.1993)

Physical plan-relief model, mixed media, 800 × 400 × 100 cm

Plan B Architecture & Urbanism, *The World Turned Inside Out*, 2021

The World Turned Inside Out, 2021

Joyce Hsiang (American, b.1977) and Bimal Mendis (Zimbabwean, b.1976) of Plan B Architecture & Urbanism (USA, est.2008)

Physical model: 86 milled convex foam panels mounted onto a wooden substructure with inset drawing panels. 1000 × 600 × 400 cm

The world is perforated by uncharted territory whose mysteries upend our claim to omniscience. *The World Turned Inside Out* cracks open the world, the one we think we know. It delineates a global project of *unknowing*. A modern reawakening of geographical mythologies of the unknown might conjure a new relationship between humans and the earth. The result is not the erasure of knowns but the revealing of other possibilities located somewhere between reality and speculation.

As a species, we have transformed the entire earth into the City of Seven Billion. To navigate and search this city, humans have set out a magnificent inscription of highways, railroads, shipping lanes, submarine cables, vaporous contrails, and orbital paths. It encompasses and overwhelms the planet. Esteemed as a sum of objective knowledge, this city is the result of a riotous collective that exalts ravenous exploration for the sake of profit. Centuries of aggressive curiosity that sought to shrink the unknown have produced the world we inhabit today. A wilful inversion of that posture will bring forth a new world – one replete with enchanted forests, *aqua incognita*, and free-roaming dragons and monsters.

The World Turned Inside Out calls for an unexploring of the earth. It mobilises practices of redacting, rewilding, and otherwise unclaiming the known. These can give way to phantom geographies and the wisdom of uncertainty. The time has come for a mandate of abandonment and forgetting, an epoch of great deceleration. Let's scour the world to engineer emptiness and celebrate omissions.

If one turns the world inside out, what will be unearthed?

Christina Agapakis of Ginkgo Bioworks taking tissue samples from a dried specimen of *Hibiscadelphus wilderianus* Rock at the Harvard University Herbarium, 2018

Christina Agapakis, Alexandra Daisy Ginsberg, and Sissel Tolaas, with support from Ginkgo Bioworks and IFF, Installation view of *Resurrecting the Sublime* at Biennale Internationale Design Saint-Étienne, 2019

Resurrecting the Sublime, 2019

Could we ever again smell flowers driven to extinction by humans?

Resurrecting the Sublime allows us a glimpse of an extinct flower, lost to colonial activity. The vitrine is filled with the smell of the *Hibiscadelphus wilderianus* Rock (*Maui hau kuahiwi* in Hawaiian), a flowering tree once indigenous to ancient lava fields on the southern slopes of Mount Haleakalā, Maui, Hawaii, before colonial cattle ranching decimated its habitat. The last tree was found dying in 1912.

Agapakis took tissue from a pressed flower stored in Harvard University's herbarium. The scientists at Ginkgo analysed DNA from this specimen, predicting gene sequences that might encode for fragrance-producing enzymes. Those DNA sequences were synthesised (printed) and tested in yeast, resulting in a list of smell molecules that the plant may have produced. Tolaas reconstructed the flowers' smell, starting with the list of detected molecules, by using identical or similar smell molecules in addition to other chemical compounds. However, while this process can predict what type of smells the flowers may have produced, the amounts, like the flower, are lost. Ginsberg has designed an installation in which fragments of the flower's smell are mixed. On display are various smell molecule combinations: there is no 'exact' smell. The lost landscape is reduced to its geology and the flower's smell; the human connects the two as they become the specimen on view.

Resurrecting the smell of extinct flowers so that humans may again experience something we destroyed is awesome and perhaps terrifying; it evokes the sublime. But this is not 'de-extinction'. Rather, biotechnology, smell, and digitally reconstructed landscapes reveal the complex interplay of species and places that no longer exist. *Resurrecting the Sublime* asks us to contemplate our actions and potentially change them for the future.

The project is a collaboration between Christina Agapakis (American, b.1984), Alexandra Daisy Ginsberg (British/South African, b.1982), and Sissel Tolaas (Norwegian, b.1965), with support from Ginkgo Bioworks (USA, est.2008) and IFF (USA, est.1889)

Glass vitrine, smells, smell technology, lava boulders, ambient sound, video animation, 500 × 250 × 280 cm

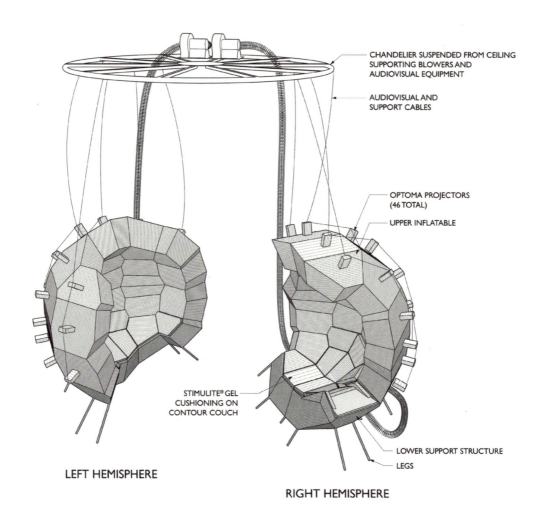

Reiser + Umemoto, RUR Architecture, Daniel López-Pérez et al., *Geoscope 2: Worlds*, 2021. *Geoscope 2* (modified)

Reiser + Umemoto, RUR Architecture, Daniel López-Pérez et al., *Geoscope 2: Worlds*, 2021. *Geoscope 2* with dashed line indicating separation into two hemispheres

Reiser + Umemoto, RUR Architecture, Daniel López-Pérez et al., *Geoscope 2: Worlds*, 2021. Interior view

Geoscope 2: Worlds, 2021

Geoscope 2 is an immersive, inflatable, multimedia split sphere occupied by the public. Starting with the legacy of R. Buckminster Fuller (1895–1983), whose planetary thinking aimed to measure physical experience into an ever-expanding pattern of relationships, *Geoscope 2* joins a century-long exploration of the world as an architectural project. It is a capsule and cockpit from which to experience six decades of architectural thinking at a planetary scale.

If Fuller's original *Geoscope* project aimed for a more comprehensive understanding of one's relationship to the world, *Geoscope 2* similarly challenges its occupants to gain an expanded planetary understanding, but now through contemporary means. A celebration of the publication of the book *R. Buckminster Fuller: Pattern-Thinking* (Lars Müller Publishers, 2020), expands the themes of geometry, structure, words, and patents in order to confront contemporary questions of environmental, social, and political justice in search of more equitable visions of the planetary scale. Presenting the work of architecture students, theorists, and practitioners, *Geoscope 2* offers a kaleidoscope of contemporary thoughts and visions at the planetary scale – from the widest reaches of the discipline – and responds to the current tsunami of upheavals within our global society and the natural world.

Fuller described himself as an 'engineer, inventor, mathematician, architect, cartographer, philosopher, poet, cosmogonist, comprehensive designer, and choreographer'; and the *Geoscope* as akin to the 'World looking at itself'. *Geoscope 2* similarly weaves physical, social, and political experience into an ever-expanding pattern of relationships and attempts to coordinate these into a conceptual network of words and concepts that can nurture and develop the basis of our thinking.

Daniel López-Pérez (Spanish, b.1973) and Jesse Reiser (American, b.1958) and Nanako Umemoto (Japanese) of Princeton University (USA, est.1746) in collaboration with Julian Harake (American, b.1991) and Katherine Leung (Hongkonger, b.1992) of Reiser + Umemoto, RUR Architecture (USA, est.1986), Lukas Fitze (Swiss, b.1968), and Jan Pistor (Swiss) of iart (Switzerland, est.2001), Pablo Kobayashi (Mexican, b.1976) of Unidad de Protocolos (Mexico, est.2010), Lars Muller (Norwegian, b.1955) of Lars Muller Publishers (Switzerland, est.1983), and Kira McDonald (American) of Princeton University

Inflatable, faceted, fabric hemispheres sitting on steel, fabric, polycarbonate, and Stimulite® bases, with 46 suspended Optoma short-throw projectors, 350 × 600 × 380 cm

S.E.L., *(How) Will We Live (Together)?*, 2021. Portraits of (from left to right) Emanuele Coccia, philosopher, Kwame Anthrony Appiah, philosopher, Richard Sennett, sociologist, Saskia Sassen, sociologist, Stephen Greenblatt, literary theorist, Vincent Brown, historian

(How) Will We Live (Together)?, 2020–2021

Verena Paravel (French, b.1971) and Lucien Castaing-Taylor (British / Australian / American, b.1966) of Harvard University Sensory Ethnography Laboratory (S.E.L) (USA / France, est.2007)

This project consists of an architectural audiovisual installation that directly addresses the theme of the Biennale, *How will we live together?*

It features voices from a diversity of fields, including architecture, philosophy, history, politics, literature, economics, anthropology, and cultural theory, as well as visual and performance art. Leading intellectuals, activists, and artists address the current ecological and political crises afflicting the world and imagine ways we might live and die together, whether more peacefully or more violently, both among ourselves, and also with other species.

An edited transcript of this film will be featured in a volume of two books produced separately from this exhibition catalogue.

Audiovisual installation, dimensions variable

Architectural Worlds, 2021

Hashim Sarkis, Roi Salgueiro Barrio, Gabriel Kozlowski

Print on white rigid ACM, 1800 cm; Original fragment of Aldo Rossi's *Teatro del mondo*; Metal

This research station aims to situate the projects included in the *As One Planet* section of the 17th International Architecture Exhibition 2021 within a historic lineage of architectural approaches to the world scale, one that has shaped the ways in which we live and think about our present.

The installation presents architecture as a planetary practice by showing the diversity of projects and designers elaborating processes of global structuring and intervening in them. It reveals how, from twentieth-century modernity on, such engagement with the world scale both accompanied the consolidation of globalisation, and generated alternative visions of an integrated planet. The research thus highlights how the capacity of design to visualise the impact of technological, social, and spatial advancements before they actually take place allows architects to test possible transformations of the earth well before they are realised in practice.

The projects showcased correspond to architectural modernity, and thus to a period when the international style quickly settled into a shorthand for what a cosmopolitan aesthetics of architecture could be. Yet the purpose of the research station is to show that modernity's attention to the world scale was not limited to the definition of a single formal language that could be implemented at the architectural scale. Modern architects were also trying to spatialise the cosmopolitan ideal ahead of its realisation in politics through plans for the whole earth, geopolitical proposals, analyses of continental processes, and interventions in them.

By unfolding the many scenarios that architecture developed in order to address the world scale, *Architectural Worlds* seeks to disentangle the conception of globes from the imposition of the global. Countering the many times in which the discipline has entertained totalising visions of the globe, architects have also imagined multiple ways to conceive of a common planet while acknowledging and fostering its internal singularities. Additionally, the projects show how ideating world systems does not depend on conceiving of and implementing a single global spatial logic or on operating at vast transcontinental scales. The world can be addressed by means that range from designing a building typology to conceiving of new methods of cartographic projection, from defining wearable devices to developing urban models, from constructing ephemeral interventions

STATION

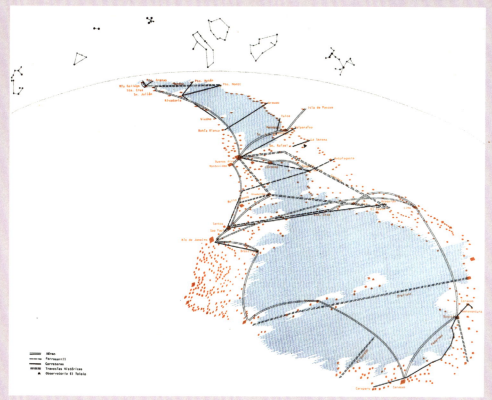

Alberto Cruz, Godofredo Iommi, et al., *Amereida: South America's inland seas*, 1970

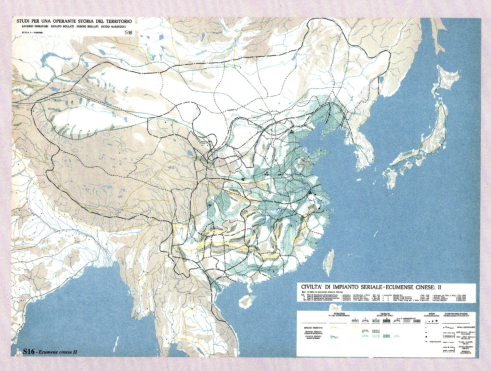

Saverio Muratori, *Civilisation of Serial Structure: Chinese Ecumene*, c. 1967

Juan Navarro Baldeweg, *Proposal for the Increasing of Ecological Experiences. Transferring Ecosystems*, 1972

Zaha Hadid, *The World (89 Degrees)*, 1983

Sergio Bernardes, *Universal Free Trade Points. The World in the Cybernetic Era*, 1965

to producing visual narratives. These strategies show how, in reflecting upon the world, architecture ultimately reflects upon its own mechanisms of world making.

The station presents a range of works spanning from 1892 to 2000. They are authored by architects Patrick Geddes, Bruno Taut, Rudolf Steiger with Wilhelm Hess and Georg Schmitt, Richard Buckminster Fuller, Alison and Peter Smithson, Le Corbusier with Oscar Niemeyer and Wallace K. Harrison, Ivan Leonidov, Constant Nieuwenhuis, Jacqueline Tyrwhitt, Noboru Kawazoe and Kiyonori Kikutake, Constantinos Doxiadis, Yona Friedman, Vittorio Gregotti, Takis Zenetos, Sergio Bernardes, Alberto Gruz and Godofredo Iommi, Saverio Muratori, ArchiZoom, Juan Navarro Baldeweg, Superstudio, Rem Koolhaas and Madelon Vriesendorp, Zaha Hadid, Aldo Rossi, Franco Purini and Laura Thermes, and Luc Deleu.

We detect in the work of these architects a constant interrogation of the ultimate possibilities, roles, and limits of architecture and urbanism vis-à-vis society. Merging spatial, political, and ecological configurations, the genealogy of architectural projects at the world scale they conceived gains a new relevance today, when we are revising our discipline in response to urgent global concerns, from human-induced climate change and worldwide urbanisation to the need for new forms of cosmopolitics.

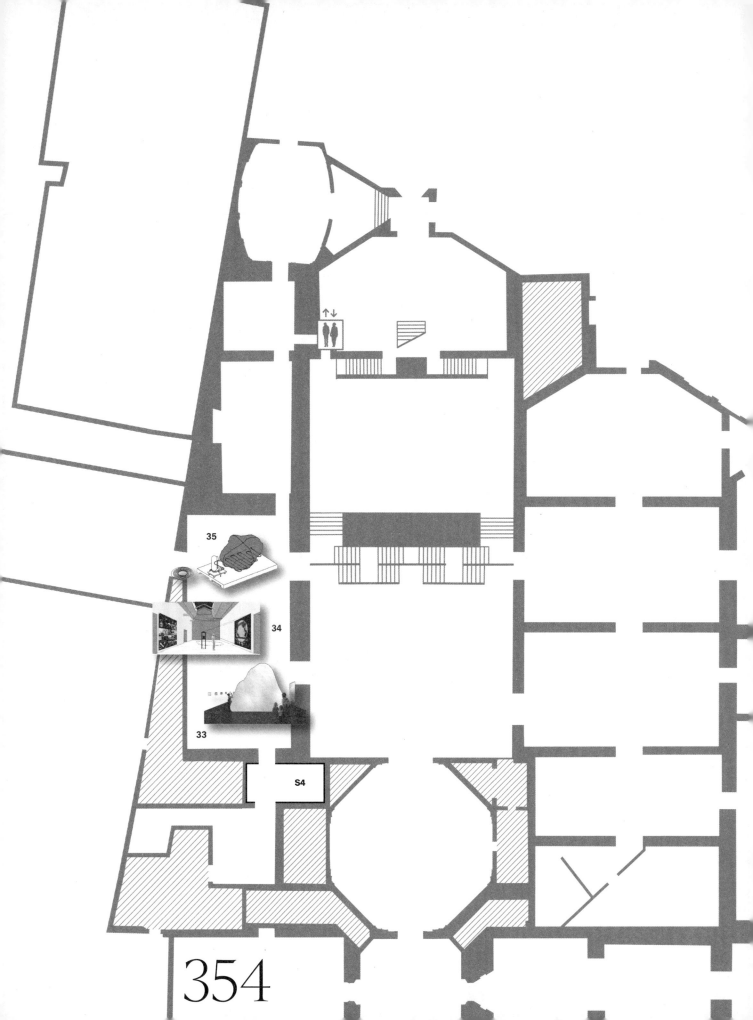

354

DESIGNING FOR CLIMATE CHANGE

AS ONE PLANET

33 Kei Kaihoh Architects
357

34 DESIGN EARTH
(Rania Ghosn;
El Hadi Jazairy)
359

35 OOZE and Marjetica Potrč
Eva Pfannes; Sylvain
Hartenberg; Marjetica Potrč
361

S4 **STATION**: Sheila Kennedy;
Janelle K Knox-Hayes; Miho
Mazereeuw, MIT Urban
Risk Lab; James Wescoat,
MIT Aga Khan Program for
Islamic Architecture at
MIT Venice Lab
362

The challenges of climate change are heightening architecture's responsibility regarding issues that affect its projects. The projects in this room foreground the technological tools that architecture has at hand to redress climate change, from geoengineering with its pros and cons, to local technologies that might be amplified to help mitigate climate change.

Kei Kaihoh Architects, *Melting Landscape*, 2021. Installation view

Kei Kaihoh Architects, *Yukimuro*, 2020. Outdoor Yukimuro covered with wood chips

Melting Landscape, 2021

Kei Kaihoh (Japanese, b.1982) of Kei Kaihoh Architects (Japan, est.2010) in collaboration with Giulia Chiatante (Italian, b.1991) and Kentaro Hayashi (Japanese, b.1994)

Snow, insulation, wooden structure, 500 × 650 × 450 cm, LED screens 12.9", prints panel 200 × 120 cm

What if there could be a way to change people's perception of snow? What if snow were seen as a free natural resource?

Since ancient times, ice and snow have been stored during the winter season to be used in summer. This worldwide practice was replaced by modern refrigeration technologies in the 1950s. In recent years, however, as a result of increasing energy cost and growing consciousness for more sustainable practices, there has been a renewed interest in the traditional technique of storing snow, and new technologies are being developed to generate energy from snow.

Melting Landscape is an installation of a modern version of 'Yukimuro', a traditional snow storage method used to preserve food on the mountains of Japan. In its original setting, the use of snow is connected to a delicate system. Heavily affected by climate change, land consumption, financial crisis, urbanisation, pollution, and unsustainable uses of limited natural resources, the small village of Yasuzuka bases its entire economy on a Yukimuro. The collected snow is used for a number of activities, such as the air-conditioning of public buildings, agriculture, food production, and the textile industry.

The installation represents research on new ways of using snow and new technologies to apply to it. This study wants to set the bases for the design of the future of these ephemeral landscapes. The use of storage methods, from valleys in small villages to empty plots and gardens of dense cities, can generate clean energy and bring attention to this disappearing resource. A new typology of architecture can branch out, one that works together with natural phenomena.

DESIGN EARTH, *Dust Cloud, The Planet After Geoengineering*, 2020

The Planet After Geoengineering, 2020

Rania Ghosn (Lebanese, b.1977) and El Hadi Jazairy (Algerian, b.1970) of DESIGN EARTH (USA, est.2010)

Digital printing on fabric (25), 70 × 70 × 2 cm each;

single channel video

The term 'geoengineering' refers to technologies that counteract the effects of anthropogenic climate change by deliberately intervening in Earth systems. The climate science community remains divided on whether the planet should be using geoengineering at all. Set in between the widening political visions on the future of the warming planet and the increasing instrumentalisation of supposedly neutral technical solutions, this work draws on speculative fiction to bring the abstract worlds of climate models into public debate and to interrogate humanity's responsibility to the Earth.

In five geostories, *The Planet After Geoengineering* makes climate engineering and its controversies visible and public in a speculative planetary section that cuts from the deep underground to the surface, atmosphere, and into outer space. Each geostory – *Petrified Carbon*, *Arctic Albedo*, *Sky River*, *Sulfur Storm*, and *Dust Cloud* – portrays the Earth following the deployment of a specific technique and situates such promissory visions within a genealogy of climate-control projects ranging from nineteenth-century rainmaking machines to Cold War military plans.

These cautionary tales for the Anthropocene unsettle geopolitics to present a new politics of the Earth that brings forth questions regarding which lifeforms are in need of being safeguarded, from what threat, by which actors and means, to which ends, and at which costs. The premise of this work is that the architectural project, as a narrative speculative practice, can galvanise such an essential shift toward public communication that explains the climate crisis as it anticipates other possible worlds.

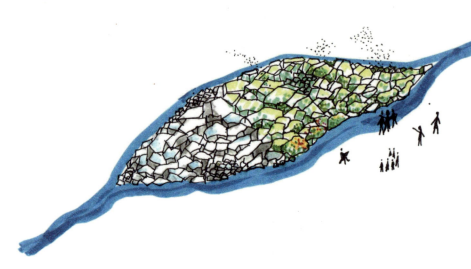

OOZE architects, Marjetica Potrč, *Future Island in Venice: The Time of Stone*, 2017–2117.
Future Island dual warm and cold environment, a view into the planet's future

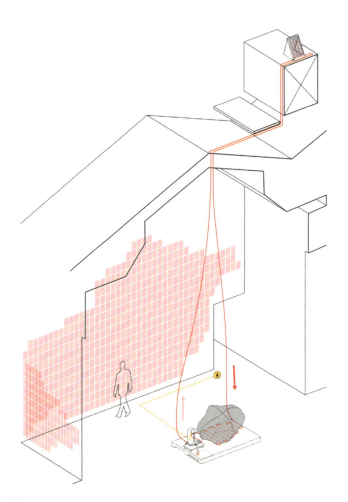

OOZE architects, Marjetica Potrč, *Future Island in Venice: The Time of Stone*,
2017–2117. Installation in the Giardini pavilion

Future Island in Venice: The Time of Stone, 2017–2117

Eva Pfannes (German, b.1970) and Sylvain Hartenberg (French, b.1968) of OOZE architects (The Netherlands, est.2003) and Marjetica Potrč (Slovenian, b.1953) in collaboration with Jesse Honsa (American, b.1985)

The rock, a heated prototype: Drilled rock granite, 135 × 180 × 105 cm, pump station, 55 × 37 × 75 cm, heated flexible insulated pipe system, 5000 cm, solar collector, 75 × 40 × 20 cm, wooden pallet, 150 × 250 × 14.5 cm; 600 colour-printed A4 sheet mosaic

Future Island is an experimental project that captures in miniature, through architecture, the planet's response to climate change. More than just a preliminary tool for measuring adaptive behaviours, the project uses simulation to create a shared imaginary of our possible future. Originally, this was a public art project and will be constructed as part of the main landscape at the new Albano Campus of Stockholm University.

Future Island is an island of stones, a pioneer landscape that will evolve over the next 100 years. It is a micro-ecosystem, a biotope of plants and animals, that is constantly adapting to slowly changing conditions. The island is divided into two zones along the latitude of 59°21'20.32"N: a warm zone in the north and a cold zone in the south. The warm zone is a landscape of heated rocks and soil, up to 5°C warmer than its surroundings. The rocks are heated by solar panels mounted on the surrounding buildings. This creates a perpetually future environment that corresponds to current global warming predictions. The landscape undergoes conditions similar to those of flora and fauna on the front lines of climate change.

Future Island in Venice consists of two parts:

1. The experience: One of the stones from *Future Island*, an original prototype of a heated rock, has been transported from Sweden to Venice and installed in the exhibition. It is heated by a solar collector installed on the roof of the Central Pavilion in the Giardini.

2. The wall: Architectural and process drawings explore past and future stories of adaptation, questioning and contemplating the obstinate tendency of our global society and architecture to focus on mitigating climate change in order to preserve an artificial way of life, rather than adapting to it.

Moving Together: A Gradient of Design Strategies for Voluntary Community Relocation, 2019–ONGOING

In the next three decades, 150 million people are projected to relocate due to environmental hazards and climate change. Living together increasingly means moving together. The world witnesses escalating processes of desperate migration, forced displacement, and failed resettlement. These processes of environmental migration are commonly unplanned, uncompensated, unfair, and reactive.

This installation asks: How can communities move together – peacefully, justly, and productively – and how can planning and design help fulfil these aims? The *Moving Together* station presents case studies of collaborative design with communities that face environmental hazards and climate change – from the coastal margins of Puerto Rico and Louisiana to high Pamir Mountain villages in Tajikistan. These communities, and countless others, seek to move together.

The deltaic settlement of Isle de Jean Charles in the Mississippi River delta faces coastal erosion, subsidence, saltwater intrusion, flooding, sea level rise, and tropical storm surges. The village is made up of a Native American tribe who made the decision to relocate as a community, and they have been planning for the better part of two decades. Despite receiving a large federal grant and finding a suitable plot of land, differences of values and priorities with the state agency in charge of their relocation have hindered the project. Collaborative research with the tribe seeks to understand this divergence of aims and identify creative ways forward.

Coastal cities on the island of Puerto Rico face increasing exposure to earthquakes, hurricanes, and sea level rise. The ENLACE corporation represents a coalition of eight largely informal communities along the Martín Peña Channel in San Juan, Puerto Rico, who experience increasing flood risk. Through the creation of a Community Land Trust, the agency is working to help relocate residents from flood-prone areas along the channel's edge to new resilient housing, while converting the lacustrine zone into a flood-buffering public park. The project illustrates how grassroots activism can link with formal government policies to

Sheila Kennedy (American, b.1959), Janelle Knox-Hayes (American, b.1983), Miho Mazereeuw (Japanese/Dutch, b.1974), and James Wescoat (American, b.1952) at MIT Venice Lab (USA, est.2019)

Digitally printed drawings, diagrams, and photographs, wood and metal tools, topographic milled model, projections, 500 × 300 cm

STATION

Map shows global locations and comparative impacts of earthquakes, climate change-driven floods, storms, and pandemic events that have caused significant human relocation, displacement, and migration

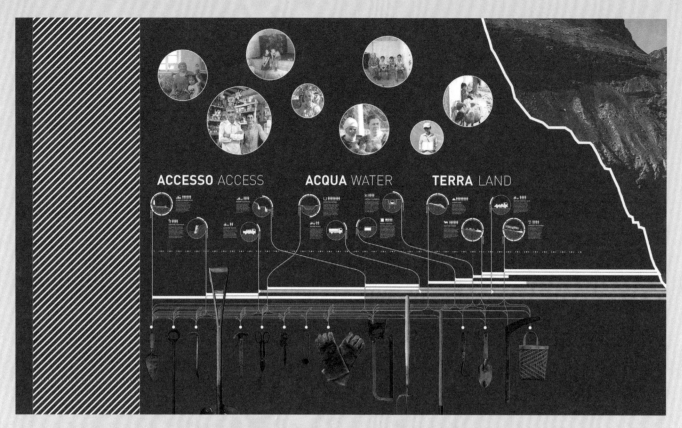

This design shows how a village community in the Bartang Valley of Tajikistan can use their own tools and knowledge in phased tasks that prepare them to implement the voluntary relocation of their community to a high plateau

This view shows the high plateau

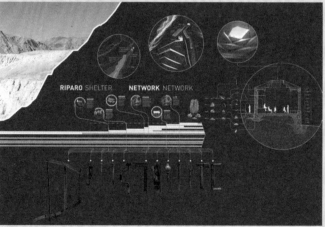

This design shows how a village community in the Bartang Valley of Tajikistan can use their own tools, knowledge, and local materials to construct community buildings to implement the voluntary relocation of their community to a high plateau

STATION

protect socially and spatially marginalised communities.

Highland villages in the Pamir Mountains face extreme geophysical hazards ranging from earthquakes to avalanches, landslides, mudflows, rockfall, flooding, and glacial lake outburst floods – all of them within a changing climate that alters snow and ice hydrology on which villages depend. Though an estimated 12% of the world's people live in mountain areas, mountain communities have not received proportionate research or design attention. This detailed case study of a tight-knit village in the Pamir Mountains explores a 'gradient' of voluntary relocation steps, with support from the Aga Khan Agency for Habitat.

In each case study, and myriad others, living together involves creative new ways and means of moving together. In contrast to the binary choice of moving or not moving, this research station explores the gradient of design alternatives for relocation design and implementation. This gradient ranges from emergency evacuation to seasonal and inter-annual mobility to full-scale stages of relocation. In each case, *Moving Together* encompasses:

- Supporting community consensus building and governance;
- Reflecting community values in planning and design;
- Ensuring safe access and egress;
- Linking landscape and livelihood strategies;
- Leveraging natural forces in the design of water infrastructures and balanced water budgets;
- Using local skills and materials in the design of new community buildings and spaces.

Moving Together demonstrates how simple common tools and assets – a footpath, a truck, a set of tools, a test garden, and a pop-up workshop – can be specific to local needs and conditions *and* replicable for global communities. This research station opens up an important discussion on how voluntary community relocation design can *move* from planning to implementation.

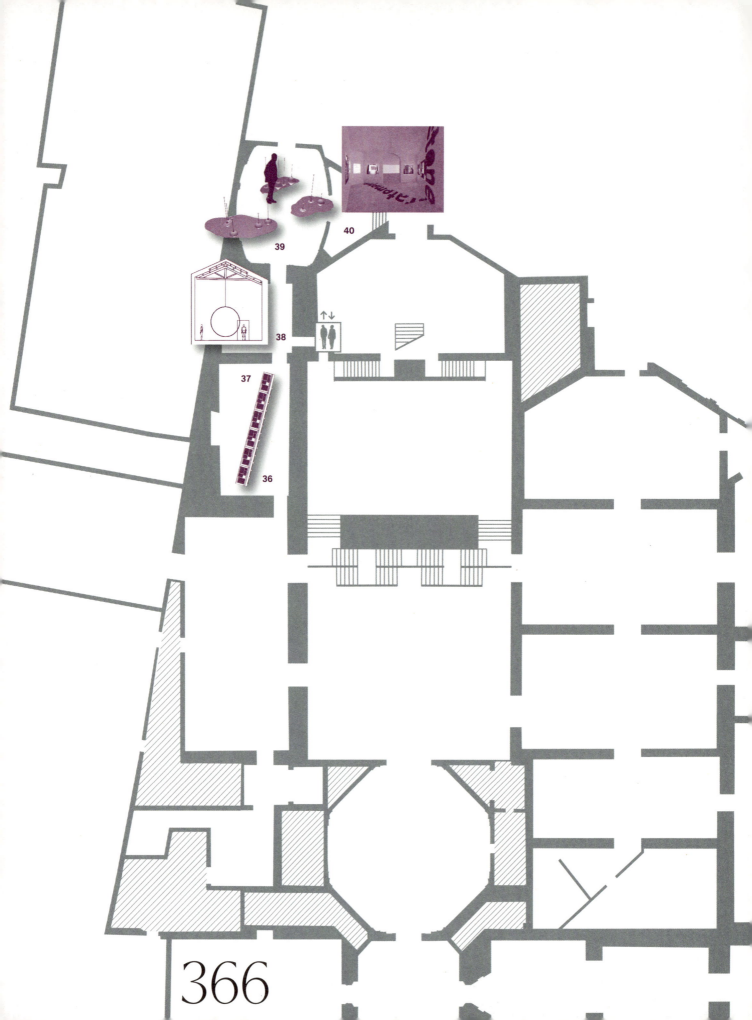

NETWORKING SPACE

AS ONE PLANET

36 Weitzman School of Design (Richard Weller)
369

37 Urban Theory Lab (UTL) Department of Architecture, ETH Zürich; Neil Brenner; Christian Schmid
371

38 spbr arquitetos (Angelo Bucci)
373

39 Bethany Rigby
375

40 Mabe Bethônico
377

The networks we have developed to connect the planet together are asphyxiating it. The projects in this sequence of four rooms aspire to disentangle the impact of such networks like our satellite system and to reimagine more viable ones. They extend the physical networks into virtual networks and into outer space. They also propose vital, ecological continuities. They reconnect cities with productive hinterlands and with outer space. They also help us better see and imagine the wondrous singularity of our planet from an imaginary Archimedean point. Our future lies in the stars. We have known this for millennia but now we design our own stars and send them out to look after us.

Richard Weller, Shannon Rafferty, Lucy Whitacre, Tone Chu, Misako Murata, *World Park*, Walking trials and landscape restoration from Australia to Morocco

Richard Weller, Claire Hoch, *Not the Blue Marble*, an image of the Earth showing protected areas

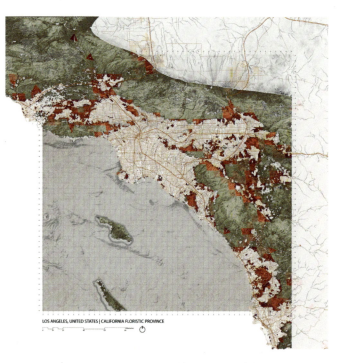

Richard Weller, Zuzanna Drozdz, Nanxi Dong, *Hotspot City: Los Angeles*, showing where urban growth and biodiversity are in conflict

What We Can't Live Without (at 3 scales), 2015–2020

Richard Weller (Australian, b.1963) of The University of Pennsylvania Stuart Weitzman School of Design (USA, est.1890)

The Hotspot Cities Project: digital printing, physical models, wood, chicken bones, 605 × 149 cm; *The World Park*: digital printing, physical model, acrylic, wood, 267.4 × 491.3 cm; *Not the Blue Marble*: physical model, wood, urethane, projection, 158 × 120 cm

Humans can't live without biodiversity, and yet we are actively perpetrating the sixth extinction. Biodiversity is not just about saving pandas; it is a proxy for healthy ecosystems, and it cuts across local, regional, and global scales of reference, reflected consecutively in the three research projects and artworks of this installation.

Hotspot Cities refers to the largest and fastest growing cities in the world's most biodiverse regions. Each city is represented by a map showing, in red, where its forecast 2050 growth is occurring in direct conflict with endangered species and remnant habitat. Between maps is a wooden panel etched with the names of the species this urban growth threatens and a trophy specimen of *gallus gallus domesticus* (chicken).

The World Park calls for the creation of three contiguous tracts of ecologically restored land from Alaska to Patagonia, from Australia to Morocco, and from Namibia to Turkey. Its territory is determined by maximising and connecting land within biodiversity hotspots where unique species are threatened with extinction. The catalysts for the amalgamation of its territory are walking trails, whose locations are determined by connecting existing protected areas. Its aim is not only to encourage people to *walk* the world but to *work* it by participating in restoring the lands between the existing protected areas. Restoring means creating a continuous habitat on a planetary scale, so biodiversity can migrate and adjust to the life-threatening pressures of climate change.

Not the Blue Marble is a view through a replica of the 1969 Apollo 11 hatch to a simulation of a depleted Earth. Instead of the door of the 'Eagle' through which the Astronauts stepped onto the Moon, the Apollo (control module) hatch is that through which the astronauts passed on their return to Earth.

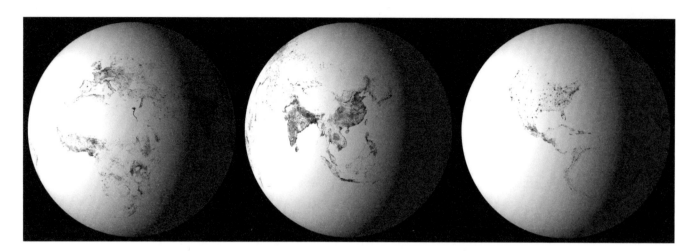

Nikos Katsikis / Urban Theory Lab, the global distribution of population in the early twenty-first century, 2020

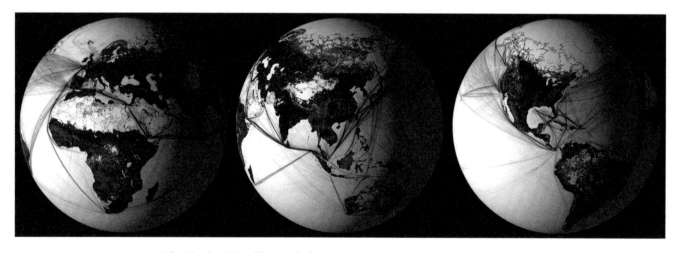

Nikos Katsikis/Urban Theory Lab, the 'used area' of the planet in the early twenty-first century. Cities constitute only a miniscule percentage of the planet's operationalised landscapes, which are mostly devoted to primary commodity production (cultivation, grazing, forestry), resource extraction, logistics, and waste disposal, 2020

Worlds of Planetary Urbanisation, 2020

Novel patterns of urbanisation are crystallising not only through the expansion of metropolitan regions, but in agrarian and extractive hinterlands, in zones of apparent wilderness and even in the oceans. Urbanisation has become planetary.

Worlds of Planetary Urbanisation proposes a radical rethinking of our understanding of the contemporary urban world. The perception that humans now live in an urban age because most of the world's population lives in cities is misleading: metropolitan agglomerations occupy no more than 3% of the earth's surface, but they are linked to wide-ranging planetary transformations. The interdependencies between urban areas and the metabolism of planetary life lie at the heart of contemporary urbanisation. This project explores such interdependencies – between agglomerations and hinterlands, political-economic and bio-geophysical processes, and local, national, and global scales – in order to stimulate reflection on living together under conditions of planetary urbanisation.

One stream of the installation explores how different conceptions of the urban yield divergent visualisations, and ultimately disparate visions, of an urbanising world. It juxtaposes city-centric representations with ones that connect the world's urban regions to the broader operational landscapes that support the metabolism of urbanisation. A second stream explores six territories of extended urbanisation, from the Peloponnese, the Amazon, and the US Cornbelt to the North Sea, the Pearl River Delta, West Bengal, and West Africa. These investigations illuminate the variegated patterns and pathways that are weaving a planetary fabric of urbanisation.

The installation highlights the urgency of formulating new theoretical and cartographic perspectives on urbanisation, fuelled by the goal of envisioning better urban worlds.

Neil Brenner (American, b.1969), Mariano Gomez-Luque (Argentine, b.1982), Daniel Ibañez (Spanish, b.1981) and Nikos Katsikis (Greek, b.1982) of the Urban Theory Lab-GSD at Harvard University (USA) and Christian Schmid (Swiss, b.1958), Milica Topalovic (Yugoslav, b.1971), AbdouMaliq Simone (American, b. 1952), Philippe Rekacewicz (French, b.1960), Rodrigo Castriota (Brazilian, b.1989), Nancy Couling (New Zealander, b.1961), Alice Hertzog-Fraser (British, b.1988), Metaxia Markaki (Greek, b.1987), and Kit Ping Wong (Chinese, b.1977) of Future Cities Laboratory Singapore and ETH Zurich (Switzerland, est.1855)

3D printed physical models (9), d. 30 cm, printed boards (9), 70 × 70 cm each; printed hand drawn maps and diagrams (18), various dimensions, screens (6), 30 × 20 cm

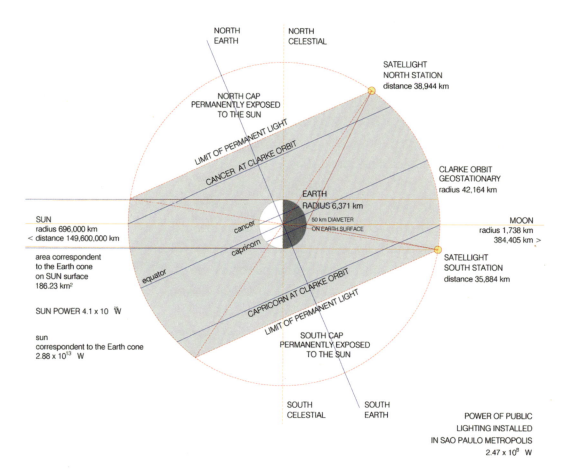

Angelo Bucci, *Satellights*, 2017

Satellights: Orbiting the Thin Layer of Human Life, 2017

Angelo Bucci (Brazilian, b.1963) of spbr arquitetos (Brazil, est.2003)

A perfect, stainless-steel circle built in the middle room represents the thin layer of human life on Earth. Its thickness is based on the inhabitable realm of the planet, a shallow zone given by the topographical difference of 5,098 metres between the highest and the lowest human settlements. Against the diameter of the Earth, at a scale of 1:5,000,000, the surface that humans occupy is only 1 mm thick. This fine and fragile line is the field we can live in, the evidence of a project under construction for thousands of years, the very confirmation of modernity.

Mirroring the planet's surface at 37,786 km above sea level, another line, the so-called Clark Orbit, maintains any object in its orbit aligned to any fixed location on Earth. It is in this zone that this project imagines the possibility of geostationary 'satellights', artificial sources of light powerful enough to light entire cities.

Taking São Paulo as a case-study, a pair of satellights of 250 megawatts orbiting on Clark, would bring light to 21 million people, replacing millions of light bulbs, thousands of kilometres of cables, and hundreds of thousands of light poles.

Stainless steel ring, d. 340 cm, light fixtures (2), video animation, dimensions variable

All images: Bethany Rigby, *Mining the Skies*, 2020. Apollo 14 Lunar Samples

Mining the Skies, 2020

*Bethany Rigby
(British, b.1995)*

Mineral and geological matter, acrylic, steel, MDF, 190 × 150 × 130 cm

For millennia, humankind has extracted natural resources from the terrestrial surface in order to build tools, homes, infrastructures, and cities. As space missions progress towards prolonged interplanetary exploration coupled with the depletion of Earth's reserves, the extraction of natural resources is no longer exclusive to Earth.

Extraterrestrial resource extraction is being considered as a way to sustain these endeavours; nations and corporations are attracted to the expanding frontier of asteroid, lunar, and planetary mining prospects to fulfil increasing needs. Commercial prospects face considerable challenges before they can be feasible, yet their financial and material potential is undeniably accelerating new, explorative missions and scientific understanding of extraterrestrial geology. The aptly named NASA rover Perseverance, launched during the Covid-19 pandemic in July 2020, is tasked with the sole purpose of travelling to Mars to collect rock and soil samples, where ancient other-worldly life may reside.

This work examines three different strands of extraterrestrial resource uses. First, the mining of resources to bring back for use on Earth, such as rare metals; second, ISRU (In Situ Resource Utilisation) research and development where materials are extracted in space and processed for use on location; and third, for planetary science research missions where we seek to recover samples in order to discover new truths of our universe. Each of these has differing values and challenges, all contributing to the evolving discourse surrounding extraterrestrial commodification and sovereignty legislation. Encoded within the work are the feasibility and value of each resource, the Outer Space and Moon Treaties (1967 and 1979), and the US Space Act (2015). Untangling these complexities forces us to confront the shortcomings of our mining practices on Earth, consider our global geological dependencies, and strive for a wiser use of resources.

Mabe Bethônico, *StoneStatements Editions, A Vocabulary of Proximity*, 2020.
Book cover by Elaine Ramos

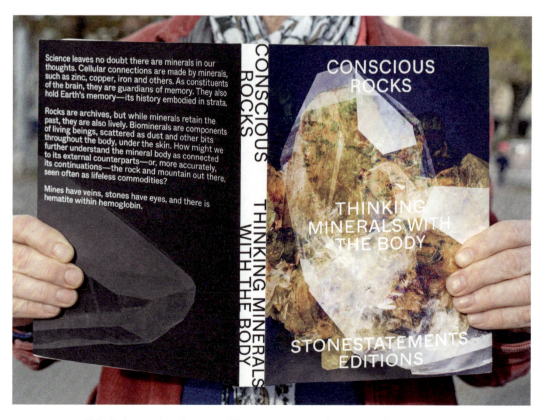

Mabe Bethônico, *StoneStatements Editions, Conscious Rocks*, 2020. Book cover by NASK

StoneStatements Editions, 2021

StoneStatement Editions sees stones and rocks as components of Earth's life, belonging to an overall living system despite the fact that they may seem lifeless and extractable. The work takes the form of an editorial concept that acts like a *geomediator* and consists of the announcement of five book titles. These are all imagined, wished for, and suggested volumes, carrying relevant questions about humans' relationships to stones to be further elaborated and debated. The announcements are photographs of book covers and posters and displays.

This project proposes giving new meaning to stones and rocks, whether gravel or mountains, thereby transforming humans' view of them as lifeless objects of extraction without agency. The not so fictive *StoneStatements Editions* aims to solicit a debate, encouraging ideas that problematise our relationship as humans to stones and minerals at large, and allow these problematic relationships to emerge to the public and become visible. In epistemological terms, the project considers discursive constructions and language used by contemporary theorists who expose the necessity and urgency of considering mineral entities beyond the usual pair of binary oppositions of life and non-life. Part of the work includes identifying theoretical sources, creating a space to expand and share a debate which engages the question of how we can relate differently to minerals.

Although the initial aim of the project is to offer questions directly about the books' covers, the title–statements outline potential inquiries that can lead to collective writing, whether as extended introductions, tables of contents, summaries, critiques, and occasional images, etc. Moreover, the installation is supplemented by a concurrent platform, in order to convey collaborations. A first collective publication will be available at www.mabebethonico.online.

Mabe Bethônico (Brazilian, b.1966) in collaboration with Elaine Ramos (Brazilian, b.1974), Enrique Fontanilles (Spanish, b.1951), Gilles Eduar (Brazilian, b.1958), Gisa Bustamante (Brazilian, b.1963), Hannah Stewart (English, b.1992), Jônio Bethônico (Brazilian, b.1973), NASK (Switzerland, since 2012) by Nadja Zimmermann (Swiss, b.1980) and Skander Najar (Swiss, b.1973), Rodrigo Martins (Brazilian, b.1986)

Photographs, 175 × 135 cm each, projection, poster, e-book, Instagram campaign (#stonestatementseditions)

EXTERIOR INTERVENTIONS

Aristide Antonas, *The Corridor House, Vol d'oiseau*, 2021

Patrick Berger, *The Bird's Pavilion*, model, 2004

Grancey-le-Château, A World at the Edge, 2019

In search of a symbiosis between humans and animals.

It seems that animal wildness has earned its place in today's built environment. Animals may be perceived as collaborators for humans, no longer exotic, but sharing territories instead. As part of the Fondation de France New Patrons programme, the architectural project of an ethological site located within the town of Grancey-Le-Château in Burgundy, France, is a space for researching, producing, and experimenting new ways of being and living inside a complex environment where humans, animals, and vegetation live together. Animal life is at the core of this architectural process. Specifically, how can a human–animal relationship be created that would escape the principles of consumption and segmentation that have long governed most interspecies relations?

Le Consortium has invited Patrick Berger, Aristide Antonas, and Junya Ishigami to submit architectural proposals based on relationships between humans and animals, viewed from different perspectives. The study of animal behaviours and the way one can draw lessons from them is the foundation for Patrick Berger's project; his architectural contributions *The Bird's Pavilion* and *The Den For The Living* are dedicated to animals. Junya Ishigami has conceived a 'scattered' house/village that allows for true porosity between humans, animals, and vegetation. As for *The Corridor House* imagined by Aristide Antonas, it is directly inspired by animal architecture. The horizontal part of the house is conceived as an ant gallery that is half buried on the site, whereas the vertical part recalls a bird nest in a tree.

Franck Gautherot (French, b.1953), Seungduk Kim (Korean, b.1954), Catherine Bonnotte (French, b.1955), Géraldine Minet (French, b.1980) of Le Consortium - Land (France, est.2019) in collaboration with Patrick Berger (French, b.1947), Aristide Antonas (Greek, b.1963), and Junya Ishigami (Japanese, b.1974)

The Bird's Pavilion: steel, wood, tree branches, 900 × 1400 × 780 cm; *Grancey, a film*: LED panels, metal, electronic devices, computer, steel, concrete blocks, 200 × 432 × 20 cm (screen)

EXTERIOR INTERVENTIONS

Matilde Cassani, Ignacio G. Galán, and Iván L. Munuera, *Your Restroom is a Battleground*, 2021. Interior of the bathrooms at the Giardini della Biennale, Venice

Matilde Cassani, Ignacio G. Galán, and Iván L. Munuera, *Your Restroom is a Battleground*, 2021. Advertising banner for the bathrooms at the Giardini della Biennale, Venice

Your Restroom is a Battleground, 2021

Matilde Cassani (Italian, b.1980), Ignacio G. Galán (Spanish, b.1982), and Iván L. Munuera (Spanish, b.1980) in collaboration with Leonardo Gatti (Italian, b.1991), Pablo Saiz del Rio (Spanish, b.1993), and Paula Vilaplana de Miguel (Spanish, b.1985)

Restroom interventions, various materials and dimensions

Restrooms and toilets are often described as neutral facilities or mere utilitarian infrastructures catering to the universal needs of individuals, when in fact they are contested spaces that are shaped by and in turn shape the ways bodies and communities come together. Toilets are architectures where gender, religion, race, ability, hygiene, health, environmental concerns, and the economy are defined culturally and articulated materially. In the last few years, the climate crisis, the Covid-19 pandemic, and growing tensions derived from population displacements have made these entanglements more evident. Toilets are not an isolated design problem but rather symptoms of larger disputes that can be mediated through architectural tools. They are political architectures; they are battlegrounds.

This project presents the issues and conflicts raised by these facilities through an intervention in the public toilets of the Giardini grounds at La Biennale. *Your Restroom is a Battleground* particularly reflects on the aesthetic and technical role that tiling has played in sustaining modern and contemporary ideas of hygiene in the architecture of the toilet. Intervening in this key architectural material, the project unveils how hygiene has most times operated through the creation of increasingly isolating and discriminating practices (with the expulsion of waste to increasingly further spaces, the separation of genders, the eradication of ecosystemic relations, the normalisation of activities, the division of tasks). Countering this tendency, the new tiling defined for this intervention conveys the conflicts and limitations of these hygienic practices in the pursuit of a more inclusive world within the facility.

This intervention localises in Venice the toilet battles presented in the research station installed in the Arsenale by operating at 1:1 scale. The two components of the project relate to each other through the logic of medical research: 'from bench to bedside' – from abstractions in the laboratory to the specificities of lived experience. The intervention in the facilities allows visitors to experience and confront the toilet as a key space in which to explore how we live together and to rehearse new forms of coexistence. Toilets are spaces of segregation, yet they can also become spaces of freedom.

How will we play together?

FORTE MARGHERA

How we play together as children prepares us for the challenge of coexistence. The grounds of Forte Marghera feature a 'Children's Biennale' consisting of several projects under the subtheme of How will we play together?, bringing the Biennale out to the citizens of the mainland and to children in the larger recreational grounds of the old fort. Here the 17th International Architecture Exhibition presents five strategies to expand bodily experience, rehearse domestic spaces, reinvent communal rules of games, elevate transgressive play, and reintroduce natural phenomena into the space of play.

1   SKULL studio +
    MOLOARCHITEKTI
    (Matej Hajek; Tereza Kucerova)
    387

2   HHF Architects
    (Tilo Herlach; Simon Hartmann;
    Simon Frommenwiler)
    389

3   Sean Ahlquist — Lab for
    Sociomaterial Architectures at the
    University of Michigan
    391

4   AWILDC — AWP London
    (Alessandra Cianchetta)
    393

5   Ifat Finkelman
    & Deborah Pinto Fdeda
    395

FORTE MARGHERA—*How will we play together?*

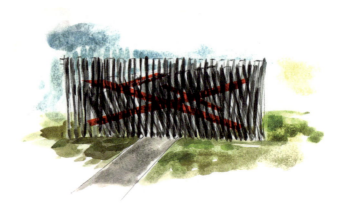

SKULL studio + Moloarchitekti, *Off Fence*, 2020. Sketch

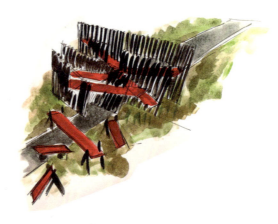

SKULL studio + Moloarchitekti, *Off Fence*, 2020. Sketch

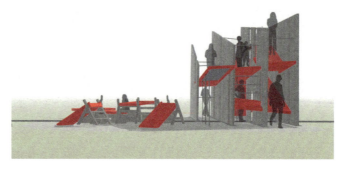

SKULL studio + Moloarchitekti, *Off Fence*, 2020. Side view

Off Fence, 2020

Matěj Hájek (Czech, b.1982) of SKULL studio (Czech Republic, est.2020) and Tereza Kučerová (Czech, b.1982) of MOLO architects (Czech Republic, est.2008)

Steel, painted plywood, wooden laths, 950 × 350 × 400 cm

A fence, a wall, an enclosure. We have all been children, playing with excitement, caught in the game, and suddenly there is a gate. It is locked. Game over. Peering through, there is an old wall and, behind it, the unknown, a secret garden, a place for lions where only the fearless dare go. For the brave, a new adventure begins.

In this installation, visitors are confronted with an obstacle on the path leading them to it. They must deal with it if they wish to continue. They may give up, or they can choose to go around it, or they could walk through the obstacle. Either way, their decision, their reaction to this impediment, becomes symbolic.

A fence separates, but it is also a symbol of separation. Throughout history, walls have separated society physically, geographically, and socially. In response to this Biennale's theme, the installation asks: What is it that separates us? What pushes us away from the state that we strive for?

The *Off Fence* installation confronts the separation phenomenon as it playfully blocks access along a path with a barrier. It transforms this obstacle into an *impulse of change.* The objective is to initiate transformation within a playful context as one symbolically embraces the physicality of a problem.

The freedom to enter the fence, to be drawn in further, to play the game and fearlessly dissolve the obstacle. The path is blocked, but the way is free. It only takes encouragement and mutual courage to overcome that which separates people.

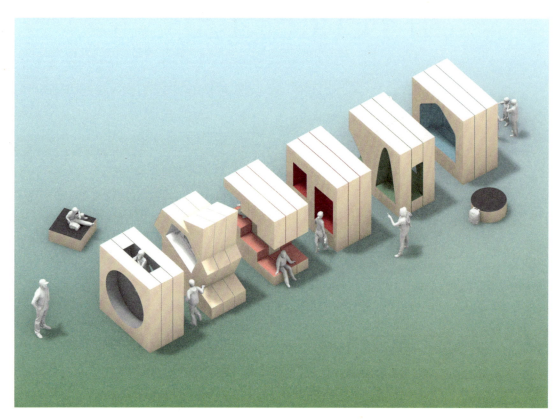

HHF architects, *The Playful Eight*, 2021

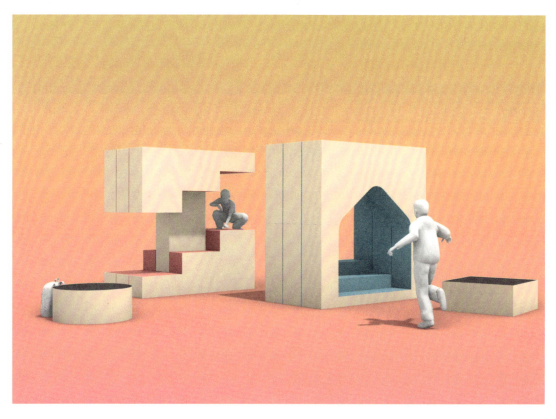

HHF architects, *The Playful Eight*, 2021

The Playful Eight, 2021

The extended period of imposed isolation made clear that togetherness is not a choice but a condition that exists and that needs to receive attention. There are more and less intuitive parts to that togetherness, but one ought to consider it a global fact and a significant design topic.

Children's playgrounds are one of the most joyful subjects in the history of architecture. Unfortunately, the task of designing them has been increasingly taken out of the hands of architects. It is not a coincidence that playgrounds resemble more and more a naive and rather scary model of human society based on a new localism promoting an idea of perimeter control to keep out all that is feared. This project wants to reclaim the subject of playground design for architects – not only for children but also for adults, as an alternative offer to playgrounds, which are defined by planning regulations, as unsolicited elements offering the possibility to escape control, productivity, and commerce.

In the installation in Venice, each wooden element captures the central spatial quality of one of HFF Architects' earlier projects and makes it tangible on a smaller scale. *The Playful Eight* is a statement against this new localism, and the objects are conceived as part of an international flow. It is not an attempt to denounce and dismantle existing global networks, but rather an attempt to knit new, kinder, and more meaningful networks, networks that could, we hope, remain long enough to become part of the next generation's intuitive togetherness.

The entire process of making this installation involves and is centred around children, from the collective experience of producing it in Switzerland to its intended use on Biennale grounds, as well as giving it to a refugee camp playground in its life after the Biennale.

Tilo Herlach (Swiss, b.1972), Simon Hartmann (Swiss, b.1974), and Simon Frommenwiler (Swiss, b.1972) of HHF Architects (Switzerland, est.2003) in collaboration with Mariana Santana (Portuguese, b.1988), Margherita Borroni (Italian, b.1990), Felix Booz (German, b.1995), Vincent Witt (German, b.1995), Sebastian Koelliker (Swiss, b.1990)

Wood, 225 × 117 × 225 cm (6), 100 × 100 × 40cm (2)

Sean Ahlquist, Lab for Sociomaterial Architectures, University of Michigan, *Social Equilibria*, 2021. Rendering of sensorial playscape installation

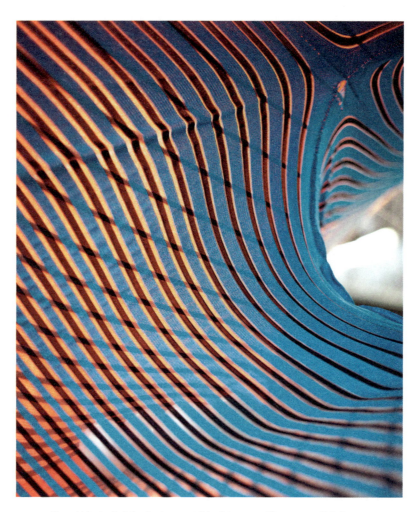

Sean Ahlquist, Lab for Sociomaterial Architectures, University of Michigan, *Social Equilibria*, 2021. CNC knitted multi-material textiles, fabricated with polyester, nylon, and thermoplastic elastomer fibres

Social Equilibria, 2021

Inclusion, central to this Biennale, often trains the architect's focus solely on *access*. Adherence to such policy ensures the physical and technological means necessary for marginalised and underrepresented communities to attain resources and opportunities. While valuable, access alone breeds social hierarchies and speaks little to support the creative imagination inherent in communities often forced to adapt to ill-fitting societal circumstances. The provisions for access themselves express distinctions between the 'preferred' norm and the 'vulnerable' diverse. Feminist scholar Sara Ahmed best illustrates this form of inclusion: 'to be welcomed is to be positioned as the one who is not at home'.

Public spaces are commonly lined with cultural and material cues that strongly imply a social etiquette. Shared knowledge of environment's societal implications arises through common paths of education, social activity, and civic interaction. Yet, by its very nature, an underrepresented community, defined by combinations of exceptional physical, behavioural, neurological, and cultural make-up, will have grown up through alternative means. The physical and social cues of our built environment often cannot withstand interpretations born of contrasting experiences. As a result, distinctions between the normative and the diverse are exacerbated and environment's exclusionary effects magnified.

To *play together* means creating architecture with a capacity to reveal the unknown bounds of social, physical, and cognitive diversity. The *Social Equilibria* installation seeks to discover equity amidst the agency to activate and characterize space. One orchestrates one's 'fitted-ness' amidst the social function of play. Textiles become media that entice discovery for the qualities of tactility. Sensorial abilities – to perceive, motivate, and act upon a malleable architecture – become inherently social as they resonate from the textile landscape, moment by moment. Architecture becomes a live canvas for communication, rather than the consequence of a doctrine of preconceived expectations.

Sean Ahlquist (American, b.1972) of the Lab for Sociomaterial Architectures at the University of Michigan (USA, est.2012), in collaboration with Evgueni Filipov (Bulgarian/American, b.1988), and Maria Redoutey (American, b.1996), John Hilla (American, b.1989), Yi-Chin Lee (Taiwanese, b.1991), Tracey Weisman (American, b.1992), Ruxin Xie (Chinese, b.1995), and Yingying Zeng (Chinese, b.1985)

CNC knitted textiles (with polyester and thermoplastic elastomer fibres), glass-fibre reinforced polymer rods, polycarbonate, and high-density foam, 475 × 475 × 275 cm

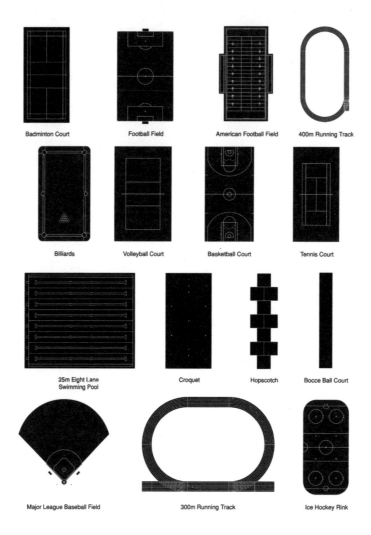

AWP/AWILDC, *Field of Lines series Atlas of Games*, 2021

AWP/AWILDC, *Field of Lines series #01*, 2021

AWP/AWILDC, *Field of Lines series #02*, 2021

Field of Lines, 2021

This project started by looking into sports games and playfields from ancient Mesopotamia to Egypt and ancient Britain under the Roman Empire – hopscotch, senet, croquet, running, sprinting, Chinese cuju, and other ball games. It draws a collection of such fields and games by overlapping them, oversizing or under-sizing, and sometimes scaling some of them; fragmenting them to create a new field of games and plays. Rules to be yet invented.

In the Venice installation, the field is flat, lines in polished reflective steel are materialised on the ground. Space holder sculptures in steel and concrete by artist Sonia Leimer are located within the field. Such sculptures are urban space fragments isolated in an abstract context; they are potential indicators of pauses, actions, construction sites, and shifting productive geographies. Manufactured as assemblages of urban remnants such as asphalt, metal, and plastic, they denote an interruption in the spatial continuum of the metropolis. They allude to spaces that are occupied for the moment and that are not accessible. These objects function on a collective unconscious that defines the everyday use of urban ground. Like a chessboard of urban phenomena of power and control, they set the stage for a reflection on urban space and its changes, as well as a reflection on its purpose as a place of emotional investment, of possible political militancy, and of flânerie.

In times characterised by unprecedented displacements, permanent crises of both environmental and political natures, and also by a shift toward post-globalisation, the question of how we may imagine a new possible space for provisional communities becomes more pertinent. Especially when for many people change is the only constant and the very notion of belonging – to a country, to a geographic area, to a community, to a defined gender – is so fluid. How may we negotiate new rules? Bruno Bettelheim noted in his article 'The Importance of Play' that 'A child, as well as an adult, needs plenty of what in German is called *Spielraum* [...] "free scope, plenty of room" [...] to experiment with things and ideas at [their] leisure, or, to put it colloquially, to toy with ideas'.

Alessandra Cianchetta (Italian, b.1971) of AWILDC /AWP (US/UK, est.2008) in collaboration with Stephanie Marie Bigelow (American, b.1992), Marco Kuo (Canadian, b.1995), Sonia Leimer (Italian, b.1977), Florian Gauss (German), Thorsten Helbig (German) of Knippers Helbig Advanced Engineering (Germany/USA, est.2001) and Tadzio Armengaud-Cianchetta (Italian/French, b.2009)

Field: stainless steel, mirror polished, steel, steel pins, c. 1300 × 600 cm; Space holder sculptures: stainless steel, acrylic colour, concrete, d. 57 × 70 cm

All images: Deborah Pinto Fdeda, Ifat Finkelman, Stav Dror; *level -313.9*, 2021

level-313.9, 2021

Deborah Pinto Fdeda (French, b.1978) and Ifat Finkelman (Israeli, b.1972) in collaboration with Stav Dror (Israeli, b.1988)

Painted steel,
90/1076/460 cm;
90/50/45 cm

In response to the question *How will we live together?*, this playscape is testing equilibrium – a state of balance between actions and forces, between human and nature, between human and human – through acts of communication and collaboration.

This project seeks to produce a new reference plane raised above the existing ground to a new ground zero. A simple structure, which gives the concept of a chair a unique interpretation, is placed in a selected node.

It is based on a new standard, not the industry standard of a seat at a height of 45 centimetres, which uses the ground of the built environment as reference point, but rather the 350 centimetres height that refer to landscape (elevation line -313.9). The act of sitting takes place within the new datum of the adjacent canopies.

Research has already shown that beneath every forest and wood there is a complex underground web of roots, fungi, and bacteria that connects trees and plants to one another. This subterranean social network, which is nearly 500 million years old, has become known as the 'wood wide web'.

With respect to this underground network, the programme of the playground is defined by experiencing the surroundings from a new point of view combining both humans and trees, and from the collective effort of getting back to a new equilibrium.

Embodied Action

Three Collaborations between Biennale Danza and Biennale Architettura

WAYNE MCGREGOR
Director of the Dance Department
of La Biennale di Venezia

In this bespoke collaboration with the Biennale Architettura, the Biennale Danza will present a trio of *physical* works bursting with inspirational life beyond the stage. In this series, artists working in the mediums and intersections of body, dance, technology, film, science AR and AI will share their installations in site-specific environments to be experienced durationally by audiences.

The three works, although distinct and surprising in their individual expansions of body as space and space as body, all speak to the central question of *How will we live together?* How will we live together; interact, dialogue, share, and connect – communication is the heart of our experience, our most basic human need. The dynamic interplay between our motivations, what we want to express and exchange, how effectively we do that, and how we 'read' and respond to the impulses of others is a communication that sits primarily through and with the body. Today, our understanding of our bodies and the bodies of others is exploding in multiple dimensions, blurring with its once external environments, and augmented in a myriad of startling and perception-altering ways. We are learning how to communicate anew – and so too is dance, an art form where embodied action and physical empathy speak beyond borders and often to universal truths.

Additionally, in a special intervention created for the *Among Diverse Beings* section, six young dance artists from Biennale College Danza will create choreographic responses on location in the Arsenale. Inspired by the concepts and provocations presented in the architectural spaces, the choreographers will develop their ideas in intimate dialogue with their chosen site. Each solo can be caught during the making process itself or viewed in a uniquely crafted guided dance + architecture tour.

NOT ONCE.
Based on a monologue written by Jan Fabre, *NOT ONCE.* unveils – through eleven imaginary rooms of a photographic exhibition – the platonic relationship between the subject and a female photographer who, for years, has manipulated his body and reworked it into different entities.

    The multimedia work is conceived for film and explores the relations between an artist, their work and life, their public, and ultimately, the balance between giving and taking – between dependence and independence.

NOT ONCE.
70', 2021

World Premiere

Conceived, written and directed by
Jan Fabre

Performed by
Mikhail Baryshnikov

Film directed by
Jan Fabre and Phil Griffin

Music and sound design
Stef Kamil Carlens

Dramaturgy
Miet Martens

2nd unit director and Editor
Giulio Boato

Post production and grading
Tom Aston

Voice recordings
Lorenzo Danesin

Foley
Stef Kamil Carlens
and Lorenzo Danesin

Mastering voice and music
Gilles Martin

A project by
Angelos (Antwerp),
Jan Fabre/Troubleyn
(Antwerp), Baryshnikov
Productions (New York)

Executive Producer
EdM Productions

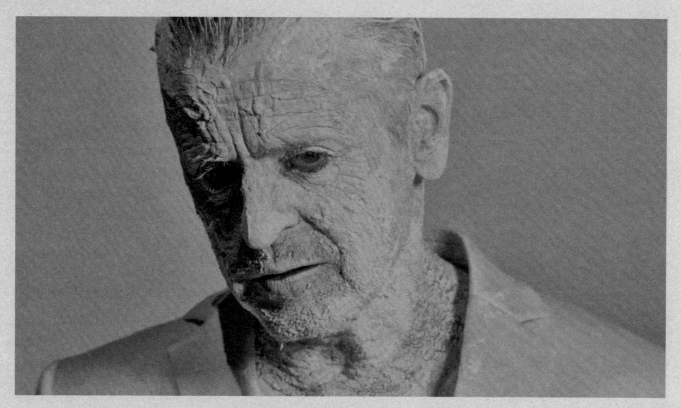
NOT ONCE.

Future Self

Future Self
Future Self studies human movement, what it can reveal about identity and the relationship we have with our own image. The installation captures movement in light, creating a three-dimensional 'living' sculpture from the composite gestures of those who surround it. Viewers are bound together – in the moment – as an ethereal, illuminated presence.

 Future Self is a performative light installation by Random International. The installation is presented in a unique collaboration and extensively explored, as a contemporary dance work choreographed by Wayne McGregor with an original score, by Max Richter.

 Two Company Wayne McGregor dance artists, Jacob O'Connell and Rebecca Basset Graham, intently communicate, with each other and with their own reflections, through light as well as through the body. Throughout the performance, music, artwork, and the human form are unified into one immediate and emotional experience.

Future Self
10'

Italian Premiere

Installation
Random International

Choreography
Wayne McGregor

Performed by
Company Wayne McGregor:
Jacob O'Connell and
Rebecca Basset Graham

Original music
Max Richter

Costume design
Moritz Junge
originally designed for
The Production Far

Commissioned and supported by
Mac, Berlin and Random International

Future Self Was first presented by Random International and Company Wayne McGregor at Made Gallery, Berlin on 27 April 2012

TOM

Set in the hinterland between the civilised world and the wilderness, *TOM* tells the story of one man's journey to rediscover who he really is. Will he find the answers he needs, or is the real *TOM* lost forever?

TOM is a meditative exploration of memory and reality, exploring narrative using the hip-hop language of b-boying, bringing it together with cutting-edge technologies including animation, projection mapping, sound design, and film installation. Playing with negative space and the projection of the work to create a depth of field, *TOM* is a unique and innovative dance for camera installation. *TOM* has been hand-crafted in fine detail – from handmade 3D models to using 360 photogrammetry techniques, chroma-key capture of dance, and digital animation.

TOM
60', 2020

European Premiere

Created by
Wilkie Branson

Cast
Wilkie Branson
Eben Hayward

Dramaturg
Adam Peck

Compose
Benji Bower

Projection artist
Barret Hodgson

Sound designer
Mat Clark

Costume designer
Cristiano Casimiro

Production manager
Andrew Hammond

Producer
Luisa Hinchliff

Commissioned and co-produced by Sadler's Wells. Co-Produced by Pavilion Dance South West. Research and development supported by Sadler's Wells New Wave Associate Programme and Lakeside Arts Centre, Nottingham. With additional support from the Film + TV Charity, Unicorn Theatre, Theatre Bristol and Capture Reality

Supported using public funding by the National Lottery through the Arts Council England

TOM

CREDITS

The projects in the Exhibition have been realized with the additional support of

Among Diverse Beings - Arsenale

ANI LIU
p. 43

Princeton Arts Fellowship

AZRA AKSAMIJA
p. 45

Austrian Federal Chancellery
Styrian State Government
Rubelli Venezia

ALLAN WEXLER STUDIO
p. 49

Parsons School of Design, School of Constructed Environments
Ronald Feldman Gallery

STATION CASSANI, GALAN, MUNUERA, SANDERS
p. 50

Elise Jaffe + Jeffrey Brown
Barnard College (Columbia University)
Princeton University School of Architecture
Yale University School of Architecture
Spanish Government – Ministry of Transport, Mobility and Urban Agenda, and Acción Cultural Española (AC/E)

STATION GISSEN, STAGER, ZARMAKOUPI
p. 54

The New School University
Johns Hopkins University
The Center for Hellenic Studies, Harvard University
Humanities + Urbanism + Design Initiative, University of Pennsylvania
Powered by Onassis Scholars' Association

REFIK ANADOL STUDIO and GÖKHAN S. HOTAMIŞLIGIL
p. 61

Siemens
NVIDIA
Epson USA
Epic Games
ARUP London
AiBuild
SAHA Association
Sabri Ülker Foundation

STUDIO OSSIDIANA
p. 63

Stimuleringsfonds creatieve industrie
Het Nieuwe Instituut / Jaap Bakema Study Centre
Jan Van Eyck Academy

LUCY MCRAE
p. 65

SCI_Arc and Creative Victoria

PARSONS & CHARLESWORTH
p. 67

Consort Display Group
British Council
The Graham Foundation

MAEID
p. 69

Bundeskanzleramt Wien / Federal Chancellery Republic of Austria
ABB
Universität für angewandte Kunst Wien
Stadt Graz, Land Steiermark
Leopold-Franzens-Universität Innsbruck – Institut für experimentelle Architektur and Department of Microbiology

STUDIO LIBERTINY
p. 73

Lakeside Collection
Het Stimuleringsfonds Creatieve Industrie

PHILIP BEESLEY & LIVING ARCHITECTURE SYSTEMS GROUP / UNIVERSITY OF WATERLOO SCHOOL OF ARCHITECTURE
p. 75

4DSOUND
Acrylite™
Atelier Iris van Herpen
Canada Council for the Arts
Christie Digital Systems
Embassy of Canada to Italy
EnTimeMent
Gaslight Events Company
Gorbet Design
HIP Developments
Immortal Productions
MITACS
Pierre Lassonde Family Foundation
Rock Paper Robot
Salvador Breed
Social Sciences and Humanities Research Council (SSHRC)
Stimuleringsfonds
Toronto Arts Council
TU Delft
Voltera
Warren + Nick,
Waterloo Architecture Cambridge
Wicked Pixels
Conservatorio di Musica di Vicenza 'Arrigo Pedrollo'

As New Households - Arsenale

OPAFORM ARCHITECTS
p. 81

Det norske Utenriksdepartementet v/Kulturseksjonen, Kathrine Lund
Svenska Kulturfonden
Bergen kommune, Internasjonal kunst- og kulturutvikling
Voss Bygdesag
Solberg Sag
Hillesvåg Ullvarefabrikk
Gudbrandsdalens Uldvarefabrik
Dansk Filt
Bergen Bil og Båt
May Hvistendahl
Rolf Olsen Eiendomsselskap v/ Andreas Grimelund
Sørværet Villsau v/Hilde Buer

LEOPOLD BANCHINI ARCHITECTS
p. 83

Swiss Arts Council ProHelvetia
Holcim Foundation for Sustainable Construction

SUPERFLUX
p. 87

This project has received funding from the European Union's Horizon 2020 research and innovation programme under grant agreement No 870759
British Council

AW-ARCH
p. 89

PRODEMA, Spain
RT London, USA

LEONMARCIAL ARQUITECTOS
p. 93

Rafael Osterling
Arquitecma Peru
Thermia Barcelona
Illusione

ECOLOGIC STUDIO
p. 95

University of Innsbruck
Swarovski
Ecoduna
A secret donor has supported the project educational

STATION JARZOMBEK AND PRAKASH
p. 102

Andrew W. Mellon Foundation

ROJO / FERNANDEZ-SHAW, ARQUITECTOS
p. 99

Spanish Government – Ministry of Transport, Mobility and Urban Agenda, and Acción Cultural Española (AC/E)
FINSA Financiera Maderera Santiago de Compostela, Galicia, Spain
Runnymede College La Moraleja, Madrid, Spain
CERÁMICA CUMMELLA Granollers, Barcelona, Spain
IRPEN Materiales Plásticos y de la Construcción Alcalá de Henares, Madrid, Spain

THE OPEN WORKSHOP
p. 101

California College of the Arts Architecture Division
CCA Urban Works Agency with the San Francisco Planning Department
The University of New Mexico, School of Architecture + Planning
Canada Council for the Arts
George F. Jewett III
Kimberly & Simon Blattner and Stephen Engblom & Lance Relicke

NADAAA
p. 107

Elise Jaffe + Jeffrey Brown

ACHIM MENGES / ICD UNIVERSITY OF STUTTGART AND JAN KNIPPERS / ITKE UNIVERSITY OF STUTTGART
p. 109

University of Stuttgart
Cluster of Excellence IntCDC, EXC 2120
Ministry of Science, Research and the Arts, Baden-Wuerttemberg
GETTYLAB
Teijin Carbon Europe GmbH
Bipaled s.r.l. with Elisabetta Cane
Trimble Solutions Germany GmbH

GRAMAZIO KOHLER ARCHITECTS / NCCR DFAB
p. 111

Empa Swiss Federal Laboratories for Materials Science and Technology
Institute of Technology in Architecture, ETH Zurich
Holcim Foundation for Sustainable Construction
Department of Architecture, ETH Zurich
Swiss Arts Council Pro Helvetia
Sika Schweiz AG
Sika Services AG
seele cover GmbH

FERNANDA CANALES
p. 115

Welt desarrolladora

AIRES MATEUS
p. 117

Tintas Robbialac

ALISON BROOKS ARCHITECTS
p. 119

British Council

LIN ARCHITECTS URBANISTS
p. 121

GEWOBA Bremen

FARSHID MOUSSAVI ARCHITECTURE
p. 125

Les Nouveaux Constructeurs

LINA GHOTMEH — ARCHITECTURE
p. 129

Peter & Nathalie Hrechdakian
Rony Zibara
Marwan El Khoury
Mohamad Arayssi
Taymour Arayssi
S2T ingénierie
Ariss Lumière Group Sal
Sultan Metals

SSD
p. 131

Wonik Group
Blue Sky Investments

STATION ABALOS+SENTKIEWICZ AS+
p. 132

GSD / Harvard Graduate School of Design
ETSAM / UPM
Spanish Government – Ministry of Transport, Mobility and Urban Agenda, and Acción Cultural Española (AC/E)

STATION KOCKELKORN AND SCHINDLER
p. 136

gta Institute
Department of Architecture (D-ARCH)
Ernst Göhner Stiftung
Swiss Arts Council Pro Helvetia
Allgemeine Baugenossenschaft Zürich (ABZ)
Wohnbaugenossenschaften

Schweiz (WBG)

STATION AMES, BAIRD-ZARS, FRAMPTON
p. 140

The IDC Foundation
Columbia GSAPP

As Emerging Communities - Arsenale

COHABITATION STRATEGIES
p. 147

School of Design Strategies, Parsons School of Design, The New School
Lanificio Bigagli for providing the sustainable felt

STORIA NA LUGAR
p. 151

Acqua Minerale San Benedetto S.p.A., Italy
Ministry of Culture and Creative Industries of the Republic of Cabo Verde
Order of Architects of Cabo Verde (OAC)
Embassy of Cabo Verde in Rome, Italy
Chromatech Europe, B.V., Netherlands

ARQUITECTURA EXPANDIDA
p. 153

Colombian Ministry of Culture
Bogotás Secretariat for Culture
Design Museum of London
Spanish Embassy's Cultural Council
Ateliers Medicis
Mao Jihong Arts Foundation
Centre Pompidou
Spanish Government – Ministry of Transport, Mobility and Urban Agenda, and Acción Cultural Española (AC/E)

LACOL
p. 155

Institut Ramon Llull - Catalan Language and Culture
Barcelona City Hall (Ajuntament de Barcelona)
Spanish Government – Ministry of Transport, Mobility and Urban Agenda, and Acción Cultural Española (AC/E)

ENLACE ARQUITECTURA
p. 157

Venezuela Affairs Unit - United States
Venancio González

RAUMLABORBERLIN
p. 159

Installation in collaboration with Kulturprojekte Berlin
Institut für Auslandsbeziehungen - ifa

PRÁCTICA
p. 161

Spanish Government – Ministry of Transport, Mobility and Urban Agenda, and Acción Cultural Española (AC/E)
Jung Ibérica
iGuzzini
Urbidermis
Diasen

STATION SEGAL, WILLIAMS
p. 162

Mosiac.us
Future Urban Collectives Lab, MIT
Civic Data Design Lab, MIT

STUDIO L A
p. 199

Het Stimuleringsfonds Creatieve Industrie
Van Eesteren-Fluck & Van Lohuizen

Stichting
Embassy and Consulate General of the Kingdom of the Netherlands

ARISTIDE ANTONAS
p. 169
ETH Zürich
D-ARCH
Hochschule für Künste Bremen, Department Kunst und Design
Kent University, Law Department, Centre for Interdisciplinary Spatial Studies
Gwaertler Foundation
Matadero Madrid

EFFEKT
p. 171

RealDania
Statens Kunstfond
Dreyers Fond

ATELIER MASŌMĪ
p. 173

The Rolex Foundation
Boyd & Ogiers
The Prince Claus Awards Foundation

MANUEL HERZ ARCHITECTS AND IWAN BAAN
p. 175

Swiss Arts Council Pro Helvetia

EMBT MIRALLES TAGLIABUE
p. 181

Institut Ramon Llull - Catalan Language and Culture
Spanish Government – Ministry of Transport, Mobility and Urban Agenda, and Acción Cultural Española (AC/E)

RONAN & ERWAN BOUROULLEC
p. 183

Samsung
Atelier blam

SEAN LALLY
p. 189

University of Illinois at Chicago Award for Creative Activity
Graham Foundation for Advanced Studies in the Fine Arts

BASE STUDIO
p. 191

Chilean Ministry of Culture, Arts and Heritage

OMA
p. 193

Matadero Madrid Centre for Contemporary Creation
Carl Zeiss Meditec AG
GROHE

DOXIADIS+
p. 195

OLIAROS SA
Consolidated Contractors Company
Agriturismo Casetta
Anonymous
Outset Contemporary Art Fund (Greece)

BISÀ , DE MONCHAUX , MOLL— VENICE
p. 201

Valmarana Memorial Fund
ACTV Spa

FREGOLENT - MALANOTTE RIZZOLI—VENICE
p. 235

Research Programme Venezia2021, with the contribution of the Provveditorato for the Public Works of Veneto, Trentino Alto Adige and Friuli Venezia Giulia, provided through the concessionary of State Consorzio Venezia Nuova and coordinated by CORILA

ANGÉLIL, BLÜMKE, HEBEL, RODENHOUSE, KIFLE WOLDEYESSUS — ADDIS ABABA
p. 209

Swiss Arts Council Pro Helvetia

TALESNIK, LEPIK — SÃO PAULO
p. 211

Architekturmuseum der Technische Universität München
Förderverein des Architekturmuseums der Technischen Universität München e.V.
Fakultät für Architektur an der Technischen Universität München

AKSAMIJA, PHILIPPOU — AZRAQ CAMP
p. 213

MIT supporters:
CAST - International Exhibition and Performance Grant
J-WEL Grant in Education Innovation
LCAU - Leventhal Center for Advanced Urbanism
MISTI Program for the Arab World
MITx
MIT School of Architecture and Planning
Transmedia Storytelling Initiative
UROP - Undergraduate Research Opportunities Program

Other supporters
The Aga Khan Museum Toronto
The Art Prize of the City of Graz
The Graham Foundation
Kunsthaus Graz
Margarete Schütte-Lihotzky project grant by the Austrian Federal Chancellery
Sharjah Museum of Islamic

Civilization
In-kind and institutional support by:
CARE Jordan
MIT program in Art, Culture and Technology
Norwegian Refugee Council, Jordan
School of Architecture and Built Environment at the German-Jordanian University

MEHROTRA, KUMAR BISWAS — INDIA
p. 215

The Lakshmi Mittal and Family South Asia Institute
The Architecture Foundation India
Harvard Graduate School of Design

FREM, DOUAIHY — BEIRUT
p. 217

ArD | Department of Architecture and Design, American University of Beirut (AUB)
MSFEA | Maroun Semaan Faculty of Engineering and Architecture, AUB

EL DAHDAH, METCALF, HEYMAN, BURGI — RIO DE JANEIRO
p. 219

Getty Foundation (Los Angeles, USA)
Rice University (Houston, USA): Moody Center for the Arts
Center for Research Computing's Spatial Studies Lab
Humanities Research Center
Instituto Moreira Salles (Rio de Janeiro, Brazil)
Axis Maps (Madison, USA)

RAMKU — PRISHTINA
p. 221

Kosovo Ministry of Culture, Youth and Sports
The President of the Republic of Kosovo

Prishtina Municipality
Ministero della Cultura, dei Giovani e dello Sport - Kosovo

AKAWI, EBER, KALLIPOLITI, KOGOD, VANABLE — NEW YORK
p. 225

The Irwin S. Chanin School of Architecture of The Cooper Union
IDC Foundation

ELEMENTAL
p. 229

Arauco

Thanks to
Asociación Comunal de Comunidades Mapuche de Loncoche, Mario Mila, Elba Matuz, Fidel Curallanca, Luis Hueraman, Charles Kimber, Sebastián Donoso, Verónica Figueroa, Víctor Caniullan, Leonel Lienlaf, Pablo Huaiquilao, Mauricio Leiva, David Gutiérrez, Katherine Coppelli, Juan Anzieta, Rene Sandoval, Jorge Retamal, Cristián Durán, Eugenio Marcos, Rodrigo Araya, Flavia Berger y Roberto Reveco

VOGT LANDSCAPE ARCHITECTS
p. 231

ARBOR, Excellence in growing, Belgium
ACO AG, Schweiz
Holcim Foundation for Sustainable Construction
Swiss Arts Council Pro Helvetia

IGNEOUS TECTONICS
p. 235

MIT International Science and Technology Initiative _MISTI
Center for the Art Science and Technology at MIT_CAST
Council for the Arts at MIT_

CAMIT
Cuellar Stone Company
Ministerio de las Culturas, las Artes y el Patrimonio_ Gobierno de Chile
Filantropía Cortés Solari
Fundación Meri
Spanish Government – Ministry of Transport, Mobility and Urban Agenda, and Acción Cultural Española (AC/E)

NADAAA
p. 237

Means Method Mission
Canducci Group
Elise Jaffe + Jeffrey Brown
Payanini srl

SAHEL ALHIARY ARCHITECTS
p. 239

Raghida Ghandour
The Khalid Shomant Foundation

PERFORMANCE ADAM KAASA
p. 247

School of Architecture, Royal College of Art

Across Borders

DAN MAJKA & GARY SETZER
p. 259

University of Arizona College of Fine Arts Fund for Excellence, The Morgan and Salomon Professional Development Endowment at the University of Arizona School of Art, The Faculty Professional Development Grant at the University of Arizona School of Art, and the Nature Conservancy.

AEROCENE FOUNDATION
initiated by TOMÁS SARACENO
p. 261

Institut für Auslandsbeziehungen - ifa

GFA
p. 263

Alastair Swayn Foundation
University of Technology Sydney
Spanish Government – Ministry of Transport, Mobility and Urban Agenda, and Acción Cultural Española (AC/E)

MONSOON ASSEMBLAGES
and OFFICE OF EXPERIMENTS
p. 265

European Research Council
University of Westminster

JOHN PALMESINO and ANN-SOFI RÖNNSKOG TERRITORIAL AGENCY
p. 267

TBA21–Academy,
Svenska kulturfonden
Swiss Arts Council Pro Helvetia

PINAR YOLDAS
p. 269

SAHA Association

GIUDITTA VENDRAME
p. 271

Creative Industries Fund NL

SELF-ASSEMBLY LAB
p. 273

Invena
Department of Architecture, MIT
School of Architecture + Planning, MIT
International Design Center, MIT
National Geographic

SOMATIC COLLABORATIVE
p. 275

University of Virginia

ACASA GRINGO CARDIA
DESIGN
p. 277

Queen Mary University of London
Sandhini Poddar and William
Sargent.
UK Research and Innovation
(UKRI)
Arts Council England.

LA MINGA
p. 279

OPSYS Inc.
Facultad de Arquitectura, Diseño y
Artes de la Universidad Católica del
Ecuador
Facultad de Arquitectura
Universidad de las Américas Quito
Facultad de Arquitectura
Universidad Internacional SEK

ATELIER MARKO BRAJOVIC
p. 281

Vento Leste

UNLESS
p. 283

D-Air Lab
Graham Foundation for Advanced
Studies in the Fine Arts
Lavazza Group

LATERAL OFFICE and ARCTIC
DESIGN GROUP
p. 285

University of Toronto Daniels
Faculty of Architecture Landscape
and Design
University of Waterloo, Social
Science and Humanities Research
Council of Canada University of

Virginia School of Architecture,
Jefferson Trust, Anchorage Museum

DOGMA
p. 289

Vlaanderen, Kunsten en Cultureel
Erfgoed, Departement Cultuur,
Jeugd en Media

RURAL URBAN FRAMEWORK
p. 291

Design Trust (an Initiative of
the Hong Kong Ambassadors of
Design)

PAULA NASCIMENTO
p. 295

FAS - For Arts Sake

SMOUT ALLEN
p. 297

The Bartlett School of
Architecture, University College
London
British Council

ARCHITEKT CHRISTOPH
LECHNER & PARTNERS
p. 299

Josef PRÖDL Tischlerei GmbH

FOUNDATION FOR
ACHIEVING SEAMLESS
TERRITORY (FAST)
p. 305

Foundation for Achieving Seamless
Territory
Creative Industries Fund, The
Netherlands

AAU ANASTAS
p. 307

Zina Jardaneh
Rana Sadiq

DECOLONIZING
ARCHITECTURE ART
RESIDENCY
p. 315

Iaspis, the Swedish Arts Grants
Committee International
Programme for Visual Artists Van
Abbemuseum
Jameel Arts Centre in Dubai
the Royal Institute of Art,
Stockholm

FORENSIC OCEANOGRAPHY
p. 319

Borderline Europe
the Economic and Social Research
Council
Goldsmiths, University of London
the House of World Cultures
the Republic and Canton of Geneva
the Swiss National Science
Foundation
Transmediale
the WatchTheMed platform
Swiss Arts Council Pro Helvetia

STATION JUSTINIEN
TRIBILLON
p. 321

The Bartlett Faculty of the Built
Environment, University College
London
Migrant Journal

CHAIR OF GÜNTHER VOGT
ETH ZÜRICH
p. 327

Department of Architecture
(D-ARCH), ETH Zurich
(Switzerland)
Network City and Landscape (NSL)
Swiss Arts Council Pro Helvetia
Holcim Foundation for Sustainable
Construction

OLALEKAN JEYIFOUS and
MPHO MATSIPA
p. 329

University of the Witwatersrand
The Richard and Mary L Gray Center
for Arts, University of Chicago

As One Planet

SPECIAL PROJECT
STUDIO OTHER SPACES
p. 333

Ege Carpets
Flexmirror

CAVE_BUREAU
p. 339

Pacific Africa Group
FUN - Future Urban Narrative

PLAN B ARCHITECTURE &
URBANISM
p. 343

Yale School of Architecture
Elise Jaffe + Jeffrey Brown
Franke Program in Science and the
Humanities at Yale

CHRISTINA AGAPAKIS,
ALEXANDRA DAISY
GINSBERG & SISSEL TOLAAS
p. 345

The vitrine is co-produced by
MU Eindhoven
THERME ART PROGRAM
Office for Contemporary Art
Norway (OCA)

DANIEL LÓPEZ-PÉREZ, REISER
+ UMEMOTO
p. 347

Monica Ponce de Leon, Dean and
Professor of Architectural Design,
Princeton University School of

CREDITS

Architecture
Noelle Norton, Dean of the College of Arts and Sciences, Department of Art, Architecture, and Art History, College of Arts and Sciences, University of San Diego
Supracor, Inc.
Spanish Government – Ministry of Transport, Mobility and Urban Agenda, and Acción Cultural Española (AC/E)

STATION ARCHITECTURAL WORLDS
p. 350

MIT School of Architecture: Planning

DESIGN EARTH
p. 359

Massachusetts Institute of Technology Center for Art, Science & Technology
University of Michigan Taubman College of Architecture and Urban Planning

OOZE AND MARJETICA POTRČ
p. 361

Statens Konstrad (Public Art Agency of Sweden, founded in 1937), Lotta Mossum
Akademiska Hus (Public developer, founded in 1993), Tomas Persen
Svenska Bostäder (Public housing developer, founded on 1944)
Stimuleringsfonds (Creative industries fund NL)

STATION KENNEDY, KNOX-HAYES MAZEREEUW, WESCOAT
p. 362

Aga Khan Program for Islamic Architecture at MIT
Aga Khan Agency for Habitat
Norman B. Leventhal Center for Advanced Urbanism

URBAN THEORY LAB (UTL) / DEPARTMENT OF ARCHITECTURE, ETH ZÜRICH
p. 371

Formlabs (Somerville, Massachusetts)
Swiss Arts Council Pro Helvetia

BETHANY RIGBY
p. 375
Many thanks to the Freelands Foundation for providing financial support to the Artist, during the pandemic
British Council

MABE BETÔNICO
p. 377

ESAAA [École Supérieure d'Art Annecy Alpes]
Subventionné par la Ville de Genève

LE CONSORTIUM – LAND
p. 379

Fondation de France
Consortium Unlimited, Fonds de dotation

MATILDE CASSANI, IGNACIO G. GALÁN, IVAN L. MUNUERA
p. 381

Elise Jaffe + Jeffrey Brown, Barnard College (Columbia University)
Princeton University School of Architecture
Spanish Government – Ministry of Transport, Mobility and Urban Agenda, and Acción Cultural Española (AC/E)

Forte Marghera - How will we play together?

SKULL STUDIO + MOLOARCHITEKTI
p. 387

PSN
BAYO.S THE GROUNDSCROO
SFS Group CZ
Česká centra
BoysPlayNice
LINKA

HHF ARCHITECTS
p. 389

Swiss Arts Council Pro Helvetia

SEAN AHLQUIST - LAB FOR SOCIOMATERIAL ARCHITECTURES AT THE UNIVERSITY OF MICHIGAN
p. 391

the University of Michigan's Taubman College of Architecture and Urban Planning, and Department of Civil and Environmental Engineering.
Quantum Materials, LLC provided material support through the donation of specialized thermoplastic monofilament yarns

AWILDC-AWP LONDON
p. 393

Rick Owens corporation

IFAT FINKELMAN & DEBORAH PINTO FDEDA
p.395

Fahd Hariri
Global Creation

PRODUCTION CREDITS

Credits closed on April 16

Among Diverse Beings - Arsenale

p. 41
Art accent studio artists: Segun Obadiya, Rilwan Yusuf, Alli Raheem Owolabi, Chinonso Amarikwa. Ade Shokunbi, PWDC studio; Denrele Sonariwo- Rele Gallery; Fidelis Odogwu and the universal studios Igomu team; Yinka Akingbade and GNO studio teamNana Sonoiki- Artpatheon; Remi Adegbite; Abu Momogima

p. 43
Research team: Andrea Li, Michelle Lim, Ryan Thorpe, John Ahloy, Jenny Zhang
Maternity Menswear: Technical collaborator Philip Sawyer

p. 45
Concept, design and prototyping: Azra Akšamija
Pattern development, prototyping and fabrication of vests: Azra Akšamija, Sophia Giordano, Lillian P.H. Kology
Fabrication of glass helmets: Berengo Studio, Venice (glass mold blowing), Kailin Jones (research and laser cutting)
Prototyping and fabrication of coveralls: Azra Akšamija, Lillian P.H. Kology
Material: Rubelli Venezia

p. 47
Glove prototypes: manufactured by ILC Dover, Courtesy Bill Ayrey
Exhibit fabrication: with Davis Griffith

p. 50
Research and design: Matilde Cassani, Ignacio G. Galán, Iván L. Munuera, Joel Sanders
Research and design Collaboration: Seb Choe, Leonardo Gatti, Vanessa Gonzalez, Marco Li, and Maria Chiara Pastore
Graphic design and Multimedia Production: Paula Vilaplana de Miguel
Model design and Production: Pablo Saiz del Rio

p. 54
Project management and fabrication: Alessandro Borgomainerio
Project design assistant and fabrication: SeungHyuk "Avo" Choe
Actor: Christopher Tester
Filmmaker: Dragana Latinovic
ASL Interpreter: Pilar Marsh
Advisor: Georgina Kleege
Translations: Schreiber Translation, Incorporated

p. 61
Refik Anadol Studio: Alex Morozov, Arda Mavi, Brian Chung, Carrie Ha, Christian Burke, Daniel Lee, Efsun Erkilic, Heyji Yang, Ho Man Leung, Kerim Karaoglu, Nicholas Boss, Nidhi Parsana, Pelin Kivrak, Raman K. Mustafa, Refik Anadol, Rishabh Chakrabarty, Tobias Heinemann
In Collaboration with: Taylor Kuhn, Ty Wishard, Sergio Becerra

p. 63
Production: Studio Ossidiana, Tomaello BV, Luigi d'Oro Studio
Thanks to: Dirk van den Heuvel, Ahmet Topbas, Hicham Khalidi, Huib Haye van der Werf, Peter del Tredici, Adèle Naudé Santos, Rafi Segal, Mario Covini, Giulio Tomaello, Creative Industries Fund NL

p. 65
Concept & Prototyping: Lucy McRae
Creative Producer: Alice Parker
Fabricator: Steven Joyner, Machine Histories
Senior Designer: Tina Joyner
Soft stuff: Lucy McRae

p. 67
Lead Artists: Jessica Charlesworth and Tim Parsons
Graphic Identity: Michael Savona
Digital Media: Hour Studio

p. 69
Magic Queen is a project by: MAEID
Concept, design and fabrication: Tiziano Derme, Daniela Mitterberger
Team: Alex Karaivanov, Noor Khadher, Andrea Cancian, Bahar Al Bahar, Edurne Morales Zuniga, Rodrigo Perez Hernandez, Andreea Bunica
Visual Interface: Andrea Reni
AI/sound: Martin Gasser and Lukas Lauermann, Francesco D'Abbraccio, Luca Pagan

p. 71
Created by: The Living, David Benjamin, Lindsey Wikstrom, Ray Wang, Jim Stoddart, Lorenzo Villaggi, John Locke, Damon Lau, Dale Zhao, with FactoryNYC and Columbia GSAPP

p. 75
Artistic project: Philip Beesley
Curatorial project: Sascha Hastings
Project Lead/design Director: Timothy Boll
Film and CGI: Warren Du Preez and Nick Thornton Jones
Spatial Sound Technology: 4DSOUND
Composer: Salvador Breed
Behaviour Director: Matt Gorbet
Engineering Director: Michael Lancaster
LASG Interactive Systems Lead: Rob Gorbet
LASG Theory Lead: Sarah Bonnemaison
Operations Director: Ellie Hayden
Grants Director: Salvador Miranda
Film/CGI Producer: Campbell Beaton

PBSI Studio:
Gwynne Allenford, Bria Cole, Filipe Costa, Kevan Cress, Jochem Esser, Mark Francis, Dimah Ghazal, Ilana Hadad, Lisa Jiang, Angie Kwon, Glenn Lu, Mike Matyszczuk, Nikola Miloradovic, Farhan Monower, Anne Paxton, Ashley Peebles, Stephen Ru, Nathan Shakura, Muhammad Tahir Pervaiz, Mackenzie Van Dam, Bianca Weeko Martin, Meghan Won, Karen Zwart Hielema

As New Households - Arsenale

p. 81
OPA FORM: Marina Bauer & Espen Folgerø
Team members: Turid Skåden, Tord Træen, Nikolina Søgnen, Tzuchien Chang

p. 83
Team: Román Alonso Gómez, Mariangela Beccoi, Roxana Cucu,
Production: DiSé

p. 85
Principal Architect 1: Kabage Karanja (cave_bureau):
Principal Architect 2: Stella Mutegi (cave_bureau)
Artist / Designer: Osborne Macharia (K63.Studio):
Contractor: Ogeto Nyamwaya (Aando Custom Works):

p. 87
Gareth Huw Lewis, Classic Watercraft
Ed Lewis, Leanne Fischler, Matt Edgson, Nicola Ferrao, Miranda King,Wild and King

p. 89
Design and prototyping, models, drawings: AW-ARCH
HOUSE Modular building fabrication: PRODEMA
PLUS modular furniture fabrication: RT London

p. 91
Meng Fanhao

p. 93
Architects: Alexia León, Lucho Marcial
Project team: Alex Cuadra (construction coordinator), Gustavo Reyna (visuals), Arturo Pereda y Marisol Michilot (models)
Construction Management: Fernando Flores/ Arquitecma Peru
Structural engineer: Carlos Casabonne/ GCAQ Ingenieros
Photography: Lucho Marcial

p. 95
Project: ecoLogicStudio (Claudia Pasquero, Marco Poletto) with Synthetic Landscape Lab at Innsbruck University, Urban Morphogenesis Lab at The Bartlett UCL.
Design Team: Claudia Pasquero, Marco Poletto with Eirini Tsomokou, Claudia Handler, Oscar Villarreal, Korbinian Enzinger, Terezia Greskova
Partners for Glass 3D printing and project relocation: Swaroski, Destination Wattens
Structural engineering: YIP engineering
Structural prototyping: GV Filtri
Biological medium: Ecoduna

p. 97
Concept design: Atelier RITA
Video and interview records: David Boureau;
Le Pavé: Sasminimum;
Metal structure: Pro Tech System;
Audio arrangement: People Are Sound

p. 99
Rojo/Fernandez-Shaw arquitectos

p. 101
Design Team: Neeraj Bhatia, Cesar Lopez, Andrew Bertics, Hannah Jane Kim, Shawn Komlos, Katharina Sauermann
Research Team: Neeraj Bhatia, Antje Steinmuller, Donna Mena, Duy Nguyen, Ireny Abrahim, Vishnu Balunsat, Sayer Al Sayer, Bella Mang, Alma Davila, Clare Hacko, Zhongwei Wang, Zizheng Wu

p. 102
AUL Contributors
Artistic project and installation design: Paul Montie
Students Angela Loescher-Montal, Olivier Faber, Thaddeus Lee, Kailin Jones, Sacha Moreau, Natasha Hirt, Ana Arenas, Arditha Auriyane, Melika Konjicanin, Ardalan SadeghiKivi, Sanjana Lahiri (Cooper Union)

Research Assistant: Angie Door

A House Deconstructed In memory of Aditya and Henry
GAHTC Contributors
GAHTC Project Management: Eliana AbuHamdi Murchie, PhD
Digital Developer: 100Danish

p. 107
Christian Borger
Phoebe Cox
Harry Lowd
Alexandru Vilcu

p. 109
Robotically fabricated lightweight composite structure: Material Culture – Maison Fibre
ICD Institute for Computational Design and Construction, IntCDC - University of Stuttgart, Achim Menges

Niccolo Dambrosio, Rebeca Duque, Fabian Kannenberg, Katja Rinderspacher, Christoph Schlopschnat, Christoph Zechmeister

ITKE Institute of Building Structures and Structural Design, IntCDC - University of Stuttgart, Jan Knippers

Nikolas Früh, Marta Gil Pérez, Riccardo La Magna

Student Assistance: Vanessa Costalonga Martins, Sacha Cutajar, Christo van der Hoven

FibR, Stuttgart: Moritz Dörstelmann, Ondrej Kyjanek, Philipp Essers, Philipp Gülke with support of: Erik Zanetti, Elpiza Kolo, Prateek Bajpai, Jamiel Abubaker, Konstantinos Doumanis, Julian Fial, Sergio Maggiulli

Project Support: University of Stuttgart; Cluster of Excellence IntCDC, EXC 2120/1 – 390831618; Ministry of Science, Research and the Arts, Baden-Württemberg; GETTYLAB; Teijin Carbon

Europe; Bipaled with Elisabetta Cane; Trimble Solutions Germany

p. 111
Installation
Scenography: Sarah Schneider, Hannes Mayer of Gramazio Kohler Research, ETH Zürich
Photography: Roman Keller, Zürich
Videos: Marc Schwarz & Marcel Schwarz
Local Support: Tommaso Rava + Rebiennale

Project NEST
Architecture: Gramazio Kohler Architects
Collaborators: Philipp Hübner, Claudia Kuhn, Sarah Schneider (project lead), Basile Diem, Julian Gatterer, Matthias Helmreich, Kathrin Hiebler, Marco Jacomella, Panagiota Michailidou, Marion Ott, Sebastian Pajakowski, Poltak Pandjaitan, Jürgen Pauger, Henning Proske, Christian Schwarzwimmer, Miriam Zehnder
Client: Empa - Swiss Federal Laboratories for Materials Science and Technology
Client tradurrei committenza

Planning team
Structural Engineer: Schwartz Consulting
Construction Management: FFBK Architekten
Building physics and HVAC planner: Raumanzug
Electrical engineering and building automation: Mosimann+Partner
Lighting design: Sommerlatte+Sommerlatte
Fire protection planner: Makiol+Wiederkehr
Facade engineering: Mebatech
Signaletics: iart

Consultants
Fire protection: Mario Fontana
HVAC and building technology: Urs Rieder
Legal Advisor: Christoph Fritsche

Project DFAB House:
Research: tradurrei Chair (cattedra di) con "docente di"
Matthias Kohler, Gramazio Kohler Research, ETH Zurich; Fabio Gramazio, Gramazio Kohler Research, ETH Zurich; Benjamin Dillenburger, Digital Building Technologies Group, ETH Zurich; Jonas Buchli, Agile & Dexterous Robotics Lab, ETH Zurich; Robert Flatt, Chair of Physical Chemistry of Building Materials, ETH Zurich: Joseph Schwartz, Chair of Structural Design, ETH Zurich; Walter Kaufmann, Chair of Structural Engineering - Concrete Structures and Bridge Design, ETH Zurich; Guillaume Habert, Chair of Sustainable Construction, ETH Zurich
Architecture
Concept: Matthias Kohler, Konrad Graser
Design and project management: Konrad Graser (Lead), Marco Baur, Sarah Schneider
Contributors: Arash Adel, Aleksandra Anna Apolinarska, Benjamin Dillenburger, Kathrin Dörfler, Rena Giesecke, Fabio Gramazio, Norman Hack, Matthias Helmreich, Andrej Jipa, Matthias Kohler, Ena Lloret-Fritschi, Dr. Mania Aghaei Meibodi, Fabio Scotto, Demetris Shammas, Andreas Thoma

Structural design
Concept: Joseph Schwartz
Project engineer: Marco Bahr
Contributors: Jaime Mata Falcón, Walter Kaufmann, Daniel Rönz, Thomas Wehrle

Client: Empa - Swiss Federal Laboratories for Materials Science and Technology

Planning team
Architecture: NCCR Digital Fabrication
General planner: ERNE AG Holzbau
Structural engineering: Schwartz Consulting
Building physics: BAKUS Bauphysik & Akustik GmbH
Electrical engineering: Elektro

Siegrist
HVAC/Sprinkler planner: Häusler Ingenieure
Building technology: Schibli Gebäudetechnik
Lighting design: Sommerlatte & Sommerlatte

NCCR DFAB General management and communications
Managing director: Russell Loveridge
Finances: Blanca Hren
Communications: Dr. Linda Seward, Tanja Coray, Giulia Adagazza, Orkun Kasap

p. 115
Fernanda Canales and Aarón Jassiel

p. 119
Alison Brooks, Ceri Edmunds, Liam Denhamer, Antonio Callejon, Juliana Rocha, Base Models

p. 121
Production: Luna Catteeuw, Germain Chan, Elif Civici, Ömer Demir, Jonathan Gamers, Finn Geipel, Aleksandre Iashvili, John Klepel, Maja Lešnik, Andrea Mologni, Timo Panzer, Sören Wernitz

p. 125
Farshid Moussavi Architecture
Team: Farshid Moussavi, Guillaume Choplain, Marco Ciancarella, Yotam Ben-Hur
Film: Tapio Snellman
Project: Farshid Moussavi Architecture
Project Director: Farshid Moussavi
Project Team: Guillaume Choplain, Marco Ciancarella, Philippe Dufour-Feronce, Sebastian Gey, Álvaro Fernández García, Giulio Pellizzon, Walee Phiriyaphongsak, Ahmadreza Schricker, Emory Smith, Azizah Sulor, Joann Tang
Associate Architect: Richez Associés
Structural Engineering: Werner Sobek Structure
Building Services: Berim, Ginko Ingenierie
Cost/QS: Prima Ingenierie

p. 127
Nicolas Laisné Architectes, Guy Limone Volume Agencement ,C²CI Ingénierie, Thomas de La Taille, Le Sommer Environnement, Habx, Colonies
Displayed projects: Arbre Blanc, Nicolas Laisné Architectes, Sou Fujimoto Architects, Oxo Architectes & Dimitri Roussel / ANIS, Nicolas Laisné Architectes & DREAM / Woodwork, Nicolas Laisné Architectes & DREAM

p. 129
Lina Ghotmeh — Architecture: Lina Ghotmeh, Mark Abdel-Shaheeb, François Adelis,
India Alarcon Rojas, Donald Au, Malek Pierre Arif, Anna Bukowy, Anna Checchi,
Alessandro Colli, Caterina Cicognani, Ambra Chiesa, Selma Feriani, Theïa Flynn,
Stephanie Ganahl, Michela Garau, Arthur Gaudenz, Luca Houllemare, Konstanty KosmaMikołajczak, Lucas Macabéo, Silvia Maciel, Federico Mannino, Léa Markatsch, JohannaMattsson, Sovanna Mauve, Alice Mohan, Seyed Mahan Mousavi, Enrique Orts Costa, Pauline Parizot, Sara Saur, Laura Tiron, Roberto Triveli, Paul Youenn, Hussam Zbeeb.
Modelab: Marco Galofaro and Ilaria Benassi
Printed photography and footage in model featuring Artists: Ali Cherri, Gilbert Hage,
Gregory Bouchakjian, Nadim Asfar, Ieva Saudergaité, Ghassan Salhab
Large Screen film and drone filming: Drone film by Chloé Domat, Wissam Charaf
Large screen Photography: Iwan Baan

p. 131
SsD, architect: Jinhee Park, Sohun Kang, Eunjin Shin, Sarah Short, Yoon Cha, Youjin Jaegal, Gyuha Lee
Arup, structure engineering consultant: Rory McGowan, Connor McGrath

p. 132
Research director: Iñaki Ábalos
Coordinators: Sofía Blanco Santos, Armida Fernández and José de Andrés Moncayo
Students from: Open Studio 'Subjects, Forms and Performances of the Contemporary Hybrid' (GSD / Harvard University. Fall 2016); Ud. Ábalos / Máster Habilitante 'How to Live Together? Nuevo Palacio Atemporal' (ETSAM / UPM. Fall 2019 – Spring 2020)

p. 136
Monobloque with Clara Neumann Rebekka Hirschberg, Kristin Sasama

p. 140
Hyun Hye Bae, Maria E Perez Benavides, Jenna Marie Kimmel Davis, Lanier Hagerty, Joseph, Weil Huennekens, Jin Hong Kim, Yousu Jang, Jiazhen Lin, Adela Locsin, Genevieve Mateyko, Kate McNamara, Zeineb Sellami, Michael Snidal, Ericka Song, Angela Sun

As Emerging Communities - Arsenale

p. 149
Installation Design: Sheng-Feng Lin
Film Director: Ming-Liang Tsai
Curatorial Project: Chun-Hsiung Wang
Project Coordination: Nancy Lin
Administration: Wen-Jui Chang
Schedule Records: Yao-Ting Wu
Visual Design: Atelier Or
Cinematography/Film Editor: Jhong-Yuan Chang
Production: Claude Wang (Homegreen Films)

Production:
Project Executive: Jia Rong Tsai (Atelier Or), Chun-Wei Cheng (Atelier Or)
Component Manufacturer: Cheng-Hung Chen (Kung Far Iron Works)
Lighting: Ching-Yu Lin (CosmoC Design)

p. 151
Production (Italy):
Architect: Alessandro Zorzetto, *Drawings*: Gaudino Tavares Cardoso Júnior, Eudes Silveira, Vasco Garcia

p. 153
Arquitectura Expandida with the communities and neighborhoods of: San Vicente, La Cecilia, Ciudad de Cali, Potosí and Parques de Bogotá, in Bogotá (CO); Shiyan Village, in Sichuan (CN) and Clichy Sous Bois, in Paris (FR). In association with the community based organizations and of the civil society: Corporación Promotora Cívico Cultural Zuro Riente, Colectivo Territorios-Luchas, Escuela de Cine Comunitaria Ojo al Sancocho, La Francia Skateboarding, la Vereda Films, Monstruación and Golpe de Barrio. In Collaboration with Latura Studio (Juan David Marulanda López), in the production of physical models and outreach material.

p. 155
Lacol; La Borda
Photography: Álvaro Valdecantos
Model: BUIT Taller

p. 159
Elisa Silva, Sergio Dos Santos, María Virginia Millán, Sofía Paz, Carol Arellano, Verónica González, Jaeson Montilla, Gabriela Álvarez, Emily Yánez, Valeria De Jongh

Integration Process Caracas: organized by Enlace Foundation, Ciudad Laboratorio, Fundación Bigott, Hacienda La Trinidad PC, Alcaldía Baruta, Laboratorio Ciudadano, Ensayo Colectivo, Tradición 360, Gabriel Nass and Ambar Armas and the community of La Palomera.
Ciudad Laboratorio: Cheo Carvajal, Gerardo Zavarce, Diana Chollett, Fundación Bigott, Hacienda La Trinidad Parque Cultural, Alcaldía Baruta,Taller Verde, Gabriel Nass, Ambar Armas, Laboratorio

Ciudadano Noviolencia Activa, Dora Peña, María Fernanda Abzueta, Rogmy Armas, Ensayo Colectivo, Tradición 360, Harold Palacios, Marialejandra Orozco, Sara Medina
Consultant on plant biology: Enrique Blanco

p. 159
Installation in collaboration with Kulturprojekte Berlin. The production by members of the collective. Markus Bader and Florian Stirnemann, together with Claire Mothais Anna Foerster-Baldenius, Enrica Daniele coordinated the presence. Graphic work by Roman Karrer

p. 161
PRÁCTICA Team: Jaime Daroca, José Mayoral, José Ramón Sierra, Amanda Castellano, José Manuel Arteaga, Sebastián Correa
Physical model: Métrica Mínima
Video production: Pedro Arnanz
Video mapping: Ignacio González

p. 162
Open Collectives Installation Design: Rafi Segal A+U (Lead), Alina Nazmeeva
Open Collectives Digital Platform: Civic Data Design Lab - Sarah Williams (Lead), Ashley Louie, Dylan Halprin, Prabhakar Kafle, Alina Nazmeeva, Angela Wang
Open Collectives Film: Directed and Edited by Marisa Morán Jahn, Music by John Eric Steiner
Research Team: Kelly Leilani Main, David Birge, Sarah Rege, Ana Paula Arenas, Adiel Alexis Benitez, Matt Bradford, Jonathon Brearley, Laura Cadena, Sydney Cinalli, Max Drake, Nisha E. Devasia, Darla Earl, Emelie A. Eldracher, Livia Foldes, Gabriela Romero Garibay, Charvi Gopal, Fiel Guhit, Dylan Halpern, Samuel H. Ihns, Effie Jia, Mengfu Kuo, Sheng-Hung Lee, Clare Liu, John Liu, Lesley Onstott, John Rao, Viviana Rivera, Carol-Anne Rodrigues, Vaidehi Supatkar, Evellyn Tan, Yegor Vlasenko, Marisa Waddle, Su Yang, Olivia J. Yao

p. 169
Antonas Office, Project Team: Aristide Antonas, Katerina Koutsogianni, Dimo Axiotis, Asimina Koutsogianni, Christina Ehrmann, Christopher Gruber, Tamino Kuny
In collaboration with: Elina Axioti, Mona Mahall and Asli Serbest (m-a-u-s-e-r, and Hochschule für Künste Bremen), Thanos Zartaloudis (Centre for Interdisciplinary Spatial Studies, Law Department in Kent University)

p. 173
Design Team: Mariam Kamara, Raymond Oloo, Mariama Kah
Artisans Team: Alhassane Bayi and the Tuareg Sculptors Collective

p. 175
Xenia Vytuleva-Herz, Matthias Persson, Edouard Detaille, Allegra Itsoga, Jonas Popp, Alexis Schulman

p. 181
Design Team: Elena Nedelcu, Nazaret Busto Rodríguez, Julia de Ory Mallavia, Arturo Mc Clean, Daniel Hernán García, Youssef Shabo
Models Makers: Gabriele Rotelli, Darragh Casey

p. 183
Conception © Ronan et Erwan Bouroullec
Production © Atelier blam

p. 185
SOM: Colin Koop, AIA; Daniel Inocente, LEED AP; Georgi Petrov, PE, AIA, LEED; Preetam Biswas, PE, LEED; Christoph Timm, AIA; Saul Hayutin, AIA; Stanley King, PE; Catharine Pyenson, AIA; Lu Lu; Yike Qin, AIA; Edwin O'Brien; David Amdie; Leathen Hanlon; Luke Leung, PE, LEED Fellow; Jesse Beacom; Alice Guarisco; Michael Cascio, PE; Tony Zhang, AIA; NCARB; Donald Marmen; Marzia Sedino; Michael Filar; Alexander Smillie; Sheya Finkelstein; Nathan Bluestone; Ryan Flores; David Vanderhoff; Grace Hsu

ESA: Johann-Dietrich Wörner; Claudie Haigneré; Isabelle Duvaux-Bechon; Dr. Advenit Makaya; David Binns; Brigitte Lamaze; Piero Messina; Hanna Lakk; Marlies Arnhof; Ina Cheibas; and the ESA Concurrent Design Facility (CDF) Team

MIT: Jeffrey A. Hoffman, Valentina Sumini

Playdead:
Managing Director: Pamela Nelson,
Creative Director: Kevin McCrae,
Producer: Tita Ortega, *Art Director:* Timo Noack, *Lead Designer:* Ross Sneddon, *Senior Designer:* Daniel Harper,
3D Artist Craig Simmers, Elis Ekdahl; *VFX Generalist* Olaf Blomerus; Music & Sound Design, BXFTYS

RJ Models
Founder/Director: Ray Cheung, *Partner:* Jeff Lam, *PA to Partner:* Summer Zhao, *Senior Project Manager:* Hong Hui

Translation: Camilla Pieretti

p. 187
Michael Maltzan, Jen Lathrop, Genevieve Pepin, Paul Stoelting, Khoa Vu, Tim Williams, Iwan Baan (Photographs)

p. 189
Game Development: Louis Lettry - Fruits of Yggdrasil Sàrl *Interactive Design Consultant*: Adetokunbo Ayoade, *Lighting Fabrication*: Radiant Architectural Lighting, *Lighting Consultant*: Lux Populi

p. 191
Architecture: BASE studio; Bárbara Barreda + Felipe Sepúlveda
Collaborators: Miguel Reyna, Matías Ramírez, Pamela Cortez, Catalina Ellena, Ignacio Salinas, Rodrigo del Campo, Francisca Feliú, Macarena Alvarado
Engineering: Arup; Ed Clark, Chris Clarke
Digital Consultant: PO_LLC; Kensuke Hotta, Jiang Lai, Aqil Cheddadi, Akito

p. 195
doxiadis+ - Landscape Architects, Architects:
Architect: Marina Antsakli
Principal: Thomas Doxiadis
Architect, Landscape Architect: Despoina Gkirti,
Architect, Landscape Architect: Dionysia Liveri,
Architect, Landscape Architect: Angeliki Mathioudaki
Architect, Landscape Architect: Ioanna Potiriadi
Architect: Alexandra Souvatzi
Collaborators
Mycologist, Scientific Collaborator: Zacharoula Gonou-Zagou
Installation Interpretation Consultant: Julia Pitts
Lighting Designer: Alkestie Skarlatou
Sound Design, Composer, mixing: Peter Aslanidis
Sound, mixing: Kostas Linoxylakis
Sound, assistance, sourcing: Lars Ohlendorf
Structural Engineer: Helliniki Meletitiki
Photographer: Cathy Cunliffe
Mycologist, Mushroom Supplier: Lefteris Laxouvaris
Designer, Manufacturer: Manos Vordonarakis

p. 199
Specialist in architectural concrete, terrazzo concrete and natural stone: Tomaello,
Photos: Marco Cappelletti

p. 201
Steel fabrication Bacciolo Gelsomino e Figli

p. 203
Comune di Cavallino-Treporti,

Comune di Chioggia, Comune di Venezia, Massachusetts Institute of Technology, Regione del Veneto Università Iuav di Venezia

p. 207
Special thanks to the nonprofits in each location, who helped to make this work possible: Dawar Kitchen, Ruwwad; Círculo de Amigos Treffpunkt, Universidad de Guadalajara; and Chicoco Cinema

With(in) was also made possible by the following people: MIT City Science Team: Markus Elk ElKatsha, Leticia Izquierdo, Cristina Panzarini, Suleiman Alhadidi, Ariel Noyman, and Jason Nawyn
Head of Nonprofits and Institutions: Ana Bonaldo, Michael Uwemedimo – Chicoco Cinema, Port Harcourt; Edith Sauer - Círculo de Amigos Treffpunkt, Guadalajara; Mayra Gamboa - University of Guadalajara; Nada Al Shazly - Dawar Kitchen, Cairo.
Film crews: Ashley Fell and Charles de Graaf (Guadalajara, Mexico); Menna El-Azzamy, Sarah Riad (Cairo, Egypt); and: Ana Bonaldo, Michael Uwemedimo, Gloria Dandison, Grace Timi, Imanny Cleverstone, Prince Peter, Promise Sunday, Tammy Dasetima, Tekena Fubara (Port Harcourt, Nigeria)
Video Editing: Lucas Seixas, Pedro Ribeiro (Brasilia, Brazil).
Music: Holger Prang (Hamburg, Germany)

p. 209
ETH Zurich, KIT Karlsruhe, EiABC Addis Ababa / Marc Angélil, Katharina Blümke, Dirk Hebel, Jenny Rodenhouse, Bisrat Kifle Woldeyessus, Willy Abraham, Nikolai Babunovic, Emmanuel Bekele Fulea, Uta Bogenrieder, Sascha Delz, Sarah Graham, Andreas Heil, Felix Heisel, Ben Hooker, Philipp Jager, Anita Knipper, Ephrem Mersha Wolde, Manfred Neubig, Manuel Rausch, Bernd Seeland, Cary Siress, Marta H. Wisniewska, Elena Boerman, Luca Diefenbacher, Georg Heil, Sebastian Kreiter, Selin Onay, Rouven Ruppert, Philipp Schmider, Julius Schwarz, Sonja Steenhoff, Clemens Urban

p. 211
Installation organized and supported by Architekturmuseum of the TUM
Curatorial Project: Daniel Talesnik
Museum Director: Andres Lepik
Assistants: Joao Bittar Fiammenghi, Marcello Della Giustina, Pia Nurnberger, Anna List, Mariana Lourenco, Anna-Maria Meister
Graphic Design: Kathryn Gillmore
Architectural Design: Mariana Vilela
Munich Construction Team: Andreas Bohmann, Thomas Lohmaier
Preservationist: Anton Heine
Plans: Guilherme Pianca, Gabriel Sepe und Team
Illustrations: Danilo Zamboni
Interviews and Film: Pedro Kok
Interviewees: Marta Moreira, Renato Cymbalista, and Alexandre Delijaicov
Editing: John Wriedt, Dawn Michelle d'Atri, and Camila Schaulsohn
Translations: Daria Ricci
With contemporary photographs by Ciro Miguel

p. 213
Research PI and Artistic Project: Azra Aksamija
Installation Concept: Azra Aksamija, Lillian P. H. Kology, Zeid Madi, Dietmar Offenhuber, Melina Philippou.

T-Serai Tent
Tent concept and design: Azra Akšamija
Research team: Azra Akšamija, Natalie Bellefleur, Lillian P. H. Kology, Jonathan Kongoletos, Daniella Maamari, Melina Philippou
Prototype development and fabrication: Azra Akšamija, Natalie Bellefleur, Lillian P. H. Kology
Fabrication assistance: Lyza Baum, Joseph Burnhoe, Graham Yaeger
T-Serai Workshop at the American University of Sharjah produced in collaboration with Alya Alzaabi, Rebecca Beamer, Isabela Marchi Tavares De Melo
T-Serai Workshops in Al Za'atari Refugee Camp in Jordan conducted in collaboration with the Norwegian Refugee Council
Creators of T-Serai tapestries from Azra Aksamija's MIT course "Foundations in the Arts, Design, and Spatial Practices," (Spring 2019): Zidane Abubakar, Lisbeth Acevedo Ogando, Erika Anderson, Alexander Boccon-Gibod, Landon Buckland, Jierui Fang, Alejandro Gonzalez-Placito, Alice Ho, Effie Jia, Seo Yeon Kwak, Daniel Landez, Christopher Larry, Yi Yang, Annie Zhang, with the support of Cherie Miot Abbanat, Jaya Eyzaguirre, Yaara Yacoby
Syrian participants of T-Serai Workshop in Al Za'atari (Fall 2019): Lames Ajaber, Amal Alali, Yusra Alalo, Emarat Aldokhi, Haneen Alhenawi, Asma Almahasneh, Qosoon Almatar, Asma Aljaber, Khaldeja Alkhalef, Yusra Aloa, Khazna Alramleh, Khlood Alramleh, Nada Alsalem, Nisreen Alzayed, Mervat Asad, Misaa Arajeb, Fatma Alqadi, Marwa Nsyrat, with the support of Azra Akšamija and Melina Philippou

Reverse Urbanization Almanachs
Research leads: Azra Aksamija, Melina Philippou, Zeid Madi, Raafat Majzoub, Muteeb Awad Al Hamdan
Syrian designers at the Azraq camp: Ali Fawaz, Abu Al Ajnabi, Abu Mohammad Al Homsani, Amer Yassin Abu Haitham, Mohammed Khaled Marzouqi, Majid Al Kan'an, Farez Jamel Vousel
Syrian authors of poems and stories at the Azraq Camp: Heba Al Saleh, Nagham Al Saleh, Nour Ghassan, Samer Al-Naser, Hana'a Ahmed, Kifah Akeel, Hussein Al-Abdallah, Hasan Al-Abdallah, Hatem Al-Balkhy, Wa'el Al-Faraj, Nagham Alsalha, Heba Caleh, Mohammed Al-Hamedy, Ahma Al-Hassan, Jar Al-Naby Abazaid, Yassin Al-Yassin, Mustafa Hamadah, Jameel Homede, Abdulkarim Ihsan, Ahmad Khalaf, Rawan Maher Hossin, Mohammed Mizail, Jameel Mousli, Mohammed Shaban
Photographic survey of inventions at the Azraq camp: Zeid Madi, Nabil Sayfayn and Al Azraq Journal Team members: Hussain Al-Abdullah, Yassin Al-Yassin, Mohammad Al-Qo'airy, Mohammad Al-Mez'al
2D & 3D representation of inventions by MIT students and alumni: Noora Aljabi, Andrea Baena, Catherine Anabella Lie, Khan Nguyen, Melina Philippou, Michelle Xie, Stella Zhujing Zhang, Calvin Zhong, Ziyuan Zhu
Advisors in Amman - German-Jordanian University: Rejan Ashour, Mohammad Yaghan.
Banners design: Azra Aksamija, Natalie Bellefleur, Jaya A. Eyzaguirre, Stratton Koffman, Lillian Kology, Zeid Madi, Mary Mavrohanna, Dietmar Offenhuber, Melina Philippou, Calvin Zhong.
Denim laser-burn fabrication: Azra Aksamija, Stratton Koffman, Lillian Kology, Cameron Silva
Poem: Hana'a Ahmed, Muteeb Awad Al-Hamdan, Azra Aksamija, Omar Dahmous, Omar Darwish, Raed Suleiman
Collaboration diagram: Dietmar Offenhuber

p. 215
Isabel Oyuela-Bonzani, Maria Letizia Garzoli, Lamia Almuhanna, Juan David Grisales, Cole P. Skaggs, Angela Sniezynski, Sanjiv Shah, Prathmesh D. K., Meena Hewitt, Ela Singhal, Dan F. Borelli, R. S. Iyer of Associated Press Photo

Installation: Design consultant Dan Borelli

p. 217
platau: Sandra Frem, Boulos Douaihy

American University of Beirut (AUB): Carla Aramouny, Rana Haddad, Nicolas Fayad
Contributors: Nayla Al Ak, Ahmad Nouraldeen, Joanne Hayek, Joanne Harik (Rice University)

Production Team: Yara Abdallah, Nour Abdel Baki, Salameh Abla, Rabih Arasoghli, Yasmine Atoui, Ghinwa Azzi, Michelle Azzi, Nour Balshi, Mia Baraka, Taha Barazy, Lama Barhoumi, Christina Battikha, Mariana Boughaba, Joseph Chalhoub, Annabelle Chebat, Dina Chehab, Araz Demerdjian, Gina Ghaoui, Souraya Hammoud, Yara Haidar, Joanna Howayek, Ismail Hutet, Lynne Khater, Tara Kanj, Karen Madi, Thea Maria Maroun, Carmen Matta, Careen Matta, Nathalie Mounzer, Mohammad Nahle, Rayanne Njeim, Yasmine Saad, Clara Saade, Lama Salameh, Tala Salman, Hala Stouhi, Lea Tabaja, Sarah Tannir, Nicol Yamin, Hussein Zaarour, Maya Ziade

Featured Projects:
si trova spesso Studio co-taught by possiamo mettere un "insegnamento congiunto di"?

PIIIISSSST, 2018
Rana Haddad, Pascal Hachem

In Between, AUB. 2016
Students: Mira Al Jawahiry, Luzan Al Munayer, Mia Baraka, Ibrahim Kombarji, Shada Mustafa
Studio co-taught by: Rana Haddad and Joanne Hayek

Corniche Extended, AUB. 2012
Students: Jalal Makarem, Farah Harake, Marianne Safi, Mustafa Chehab, Rami Saab
Studio co-taught by Rana Haddad, Carole Levesque, Sandra Richani
Crates' Play, 2018
Students: Mohamad Chami, Tala Salman, Taha Barazy, Andrea Chaanine

Moving Monument, 2018
Students: Amina Kassem, Sari El Kantari, Elie Geha, Tamara Salloum

Let's Park, 2018
Students: Nicolas Abou Haidar, Soraya Hammoud, Nicol Yamin, Lina Akkaoui, Carl Yammine
6.5 m Beach Cart, 2018
Students: Nicolas Abou Haidar, Soraya Hammoud, Nicol Yamin, Lina Akkaoui, Carl Yammine
Studio co-taught by Rana Haddad and Pascal Hachem, AUB

"Stop Pushing Us Away", AUB. 2019
Student: Abdo Kanachat
Studio co-taught by Rana Haddad and Pascal Hachem

1 Acte / 2 Pieces, 2001
Rana Haddad and Pierre Hage-Boutros in collaboration with the Atelier de Recherche, ALBA

Radio Silence, 2016
Rana Haddad and Joanne Hayek

Basket Ball Net, AUB. 2018
Students: Mohamad Chami, Tala Salman, Taha Barazy, Andrea Chaanine
Studio co-taught by Rana Haddad and Pascal Hachem

Air Rights, AUB. 2012
Students: Youssef Ibrahim, Jana Aridi, Loulwa Achkar, Thea Hallak, Micheline Nahra.
Studio co-taught by Rana Haddad, Carole Levesque, Sandra Richani

[In]Contemplation, AUB. 2019
Students: Abdo Khanachat Yara Kamali, Lina Badda, Ralph Karam, Jamie Lau, Sama Beydoun
Studio co-taught by Rana Haddad and Pascal Hachem

Nature's Calling, AUB. 2012.
Students: Tracey Eid, Lamia Dabaghi, Hala Tawil, Mira Moussa, Sara Batal
Studio co-taught by Rana Haddad, Carole Levesque, Sandra Richani

Video and Photo Credits: Ali Chehade, Wissam Chaaya, Louay Kabalan, Joanne Hayek, Rana Haddad

Acknowledgments: Archives and Special Collection Department, Jafet Library - American University of Beirut, Sursock Museum Library and Archive, Arab Image Foundation, Beirut Urban Lab, Emerge Beirut, Antoine Atallah, Rawan Bazergi, Michael and May Davie, Fadi Ghazzaoui, Balsam Madi, Camille Tarazi, Serge Yazigi

p. 219
Project Manager: Martim Passos, Instituto Moreira Salles

Team: Bruno Sousa, Uilvim Ettore, Ualas Barreto Rohrer, Bruno Buccalon, Lisa Spiro - Rice University (Houston, USA), Ben Sheesley, Andy Woodruff - Axis Maps (Madison, USA) Cíntia Mechler, Maiara Pitanga - Instituto Moreira Salles (Rio de Janeiro, Brazil)

Partners: Naylor Vilas Boas - Universidade Federal do Rio de Janeiro (Rio de Janeiro, Brazil) Asla Medeiros e Sá, Paulo Cezar P. Carvalho - Fundação Getulio Vargas (Rio de Janeiro, Brazil) Aruan Braga, Lino Teixeira - Observatório de Favelas (Rio de Janeiro, Brazil) Ana Luiza de Abreu, Ana Luiza Nobre, Antônio Firmino, Fernando Ermiro, Michel Silva, Luiz Carlos Toledo - Memória Rocinha (Rio de Janeiro, Brazil), Jens Ingensand, Stéphane Lecorney, Nicolas Blanc, Loïc Fürhoff, Timothée Produit - Haute École d'Ingénierie et de Gestion du Canton de Vaud (Yverdon-les-Bains, Switzerland)

On-Site Production: David Heyman - Axis Maps (Madison, USA), Bruno Buccalon, Rice University (Houston, USA)

p. 223
Research and theoretical framework: Merve Bedir and Sampson Wong

Drawings: chongsuen, Monique Wong, Nicole Lau, Jennifer Yip, Merve Bedir
Videos (use of mobile applications): Sampson Wong.

The first iteration of Unsettled Urbanism was produced for the *12 Cautionary Urban Tales* exhibition in Matadero, Madrid, with generous facilitation by the exhibition's curator Ethel Baraona Pohl

p. 225
Research Collaborators: Austin Wade Smith, Pamela Cabrera Pardo, Eduardo Rega, Ziad Jamaleddine, Xiaoxiao Zhao, Niki Kourti

Student Team: Sally Chen, Yingxiao Chen, Nienying Lin, Jamie Lindsey, Austin McInnis, Roni Schanin, Doosung Shin, Qicheng Wu

p. 227
Construction Management: Ceren Özşahin, Zeynep Tümertekin – Studio Mada
Architectural Assistants: Ali Gürer, Erman Soyman
Structure: Ahmet Demir, Kimia Jozaghi
Video Production: VERfilm
Assistant Director: Ozan Yoleri
Cinematography: Ahmet Aslan Mahmut
Sound Recording: Alper Çağan Arslan
Editing: Enes Tural
Sound Mix: Ahmet Burak Gürbüz
Communication Management: Selin Süter – Artı Communication
Graphic Design: Emre Çıkınoğlu
Models: Murat Küçük – K Atölye

p. 229
Construction Team: Luigi d'Oro and Flaminio Bovino
Executive Production: Arguzia
Video Production: Vicente Fernández

p. 233
Principal: William O'Brien Jr.
Project Managers: Adam Murfield,

John David Todd
Designers: Grace McEniry, Justin Gallagher
Collaborators: Akane Moriyama, Quarra Stone Company

p. 235
Design: Cristina Parreño Alonso & Sergio Araya Goldberg.
Fabrication: Cristina Parreño Alonso & Sergio Araya Goldberg with Cuellar Stone Company
Installation Concept and Design: Cristina Parreño Alonso & Sergio Araya Goldberg.
Videos and Samples on Basalt CO_2 sequestration: Pĕc Lab and Carb Fix

Video CarbonToRock sneak peek.
Concept: Cristina Parreño Alonso and Sergio Araya Goldberg;
Assistant editor: Ruth Blair Moyers

Models and Drawings on Basalt Cycle and Carbon Cycle
Concept: Cristina Parreño Alonso and Sergio Araya Goldberg.
Contributors from Sergio and Cristina's studio "Igneous Tectonics: CarbonToRock" class (Spring 2020): Tayloe Boes, Daniel Griffin, Melika Konjicanin, Florence Ma, Ana McIntosh, Jitske Swagemakers, Carolyn Tam and Lynced Torres.

p. 237
project coordinators: Alexandru Vilcu, Eric Cheung

p. 239
Design team: Wissam Al Shareef, Nojoud Ashour, Tahrid-Alina Al Smairat, Qusai Sayed Ahmad

p. 241
Commissioned by: Vuslat Foundation
Chairwoman of Vuslat Foundation: Vuslat Doğan Sabancı
Artist: Giuseppe Penone
Curator at Large of Vuslat Foundation: Chus Martinez
Artistic Director: Merve Yeşilada Çağlar
Project Assistant: Umutcan Özen
Studio Giuseppe Penone: Ruggero Penone and Federica Grosso
Project Management, Engineering & Artwork Set-Up: DH Office and OTTART
Graphic Design: Meiré und Meiré
Communication and PR: Scott & Co.
Editor: Emine Etili

Across Borders

p. 259
Data visualization would not have been possible without Brad McRae's (1966–2017) assistance and pioneering work applying electrical circuit theory to ecological connectivity models.

Data adapted from
Dati adattati da: Lawler, J.J., A.S. Ruesch, J.D. Olden, and B.H. McRae. 2013. Projected climate-driven faunal movement routes. Ecology Letters 16: 1014-2022.
Video Production Assistants: Angie Zielinski, Carlton Bradford, Aaron Coleman, Kareem-Anthony Ferreira, Sam Heard, Marisa Lewon, India Raven Moffett, Jared Robison, Marina Shaltout, Bella Maria Varela.

p. 261
Museo Aero Solar (est. 2007): This is an ongoing collective project initiated by artist Tomás Saraceno through conversations with Alberto Pesavento

Museo Aero Solar Reconquista/Arte (2018) has been made possible by Aerocene Foundation International, especially Aerocene Argentina, participants within Criminal Unit No. 48 of the Buenos Aires Penitentiary Service, The Bella Flor Recycling Cooperative, the National University of San Martín and the community of CUSAM. With Joaquin Ezcurra, Carlos Almeida, Ernesto "Lalo" Paret, Camila Almeida, Nehuen Serpa Manuel Gómez, Lorena Fiorence, Gabriela Longo, Fernando Orecchio, Maria Paula Company, Daniel Pagnota, Laura Gómez Pescuma, Walter Dantes, Rocío García, Carla Guerra, Nora Rodríguez with Daiana Recalde, Griselda Taborda, Silvia Sánchez, Alcira Sánchez, Marcos Perearnau, María Laura Compañía, Juan Perea Pons, Chaparro Acosta, Pablo Sánchez, Arce Rolón, Iván Coronel, Diego Armóa, Jonatan Martínez Gómez, Brian Matínez, Alejandro Vertoti, Gayoso Martínez, Leonel Malinovsky, Guillermo Martínez, Ángel Silva, Damián Vallejos, Luis Varas, Víctor Vivas Molina, Acevedo Gómez, Silvana Ortiz Casco, Macarena Sosa, Rodrigo Altamirano; and many many more...

Exhibited with footage from Museo Aero Solar and Aerocene community members around the world.

Aerocene Backpack, 2016 - ongoing
Developed by the Aerocene Foundation and community.
The Aerocene Backpack is licensed under the open source Creative Commons CC BY-SA 4.0 license.

Tomás Saraceno
Aerocene, launches at White Sands, NM United States, 2016
Video by Frederik Jacobi and Anthony Langdon.
The launches in White Sands and the symposium "Space without Rockets", initiated by Tomás Saraceno, were organized together with curators Rob La Frenais and Kerry Doyle for the exhibition "Territory of the Imagination" at the Rubin Center for the Visual Arts. The sculpture D-0 AEC Aerocene is made possible due to the generous support of Christian Just Linde.
Courtesy the Artist and Aerocene Foundation.
© Studio Tomás Saraceno

Tomás Saraceno with Maximiliano Laina
Pacha, 2020
Part of the film series *Fly with Aerocene Pacha* produced by Tomás Saraceno.
With Gabriela Sorbi, Alejandro Ortigueira, Adriano Salgado, Fernando Ribero, Camille Valenzuela, Olivia Laina, Martín Torres Manzur, Agustín Kazah, Mariana Cayón, Javier Hick, Santiago Mourino, Nubia Campos Ribeira, Ivanna Hryc
Interviewed: Virginia Vilte, Aurora Nélida Liquin, Olga Beatriz Liquin, Ana María Chuichuy, Amelie Victoria Chuichuy, Luciana Fernanda Chuichuy, Leandro Facundo Galian, Clemente Flores, Rubén Fernando Galian, Nestor Alberto, Idefonso Córdoba, Andrés René Castillo, Lilia Alancay, Eulalio Loreto; Musicians: Saraí Arjona, Rafael Arjona.
The Fly with Aerocene *Pacha* film series was produced by the Aerocene Foundation and Studio Tomás Saraceno. Supported by Connect, BTS, curated by DaeHyung Lee First exhibited at CCK, curated by Veronica Fiorito
Courtesy the Artist and Aerocene Foundation © Studio Tomás Saraceno

p. 263
Production Team: Copy Nature Office (Ed Cook and Umi Graham), Ellie Skinner and Harrison Stockdale

p. 265
Design: Monsoon Assemblages
Sensory Environment:
Electronics and Control Systems: Erik Kearney
Sound Composition: by Bill Thompson of Office of Experiments using audio and visual data by Monsoon Assemblages
Columns: Monsoon Assemblages with Fabrication Lab, University of Westminster, Jed Baron and James Merchant and SKB Sails
Print: Monsoon Assemblages

p. 267
Concept, Design: John Palmesino, Ann-Sofi Rönnskog
Design Development: Eva Ibañez Fuertes, Sahir Patel
Bathymetric data of the Venice Lagoon: ISMAR–CNR
Bathymetric data: GEBCO gridded bathymetric dataset, MGDS Marine Geoscience Data System
Lidar data: USGS, AHN Actueel Hoogtebestand Nederland, UK National LIDAR Programme
Satellite data: ESA European Space Agency, Copernicus Sentinel Program, Landsat program
Satellite data analysis: Territorial Agency
Visualisations: Territorial Agency
CTBTO hydro-acoustic and infrasonic data analysis: Sahir Patel
Installation coordination: DH Office
Installation technical execution: Mattia Biadene, Philipp Krummel, OTT ART

Sensible Zone is a spin-off from the Territorial Agency research project Oceans in Transformation, by TBA21—Academy. Oceans in Transformation is exhibited in Ocean Space, Church of San Lorenzo, Venice 22.3-29.8.2021.

p. 273
Self-Assembly Lab, MIT
Principals: Schendy Kernizan, Jared Laucks, Skylar Tibbits
Self-Assembly Lab Team: Alice Song, Jeremy Bilotti, Nitzan Zilberman, Heather Nelson, Maya Koneval, Yuxuan Lei, Violetta Jusiega, Emile C. Theriault-Shay, Amelia Wong, Nicole Teichner, Olivia Yao, Stephen Colar, Jacqueline Chen, Björn Sparrman
Invena: Sarah Dole, Hassan Maniku, Ali Amir, Ibrahim Maniku, Mommo Maniku, Fahad Shiham
Tencate: Albert Lim Lum Kong, Muhammad Abdullah Bin Ahmad, Tan Jun Yuen, Tom Stephens, Siew Kok Hau
Research Collaborators: Taylor Perron - MIT, James Bramante – MIT, Andrew Ashton - Woods Hole Oceanographic Institute
SASe Construction: Saudulla Ahmed, Abdulla Sawad, Athif

p. 275
The preview video also features the track Fragile Data by the composer Blear Moon, which is available for use, royalty free through creative commons.

p. 277
OCA RED has been produced by the Kuikuro People in partnership with ACASAGRINGOCARDIA and People's Palace Projects (Queen Mary University of London)

Curatorial project Takumã Kuikuro, Gringo Cardia, Paul Heritage
Artistic project: ACASAGRINGOCARDIA
Production: Thiago Jesus, Jackson Tinoco, Corinne Mazzoli
Video Installation: Takumã Kuikuro and Kuikuro Cinema Collective, Glauber Vianna
Sound: Nathaniel Mann, Takumã Kuikuro

p. 279
Creative Team: Alejandra Pinto, Patricia Yallico, Alexander Arroyo, Hernan L. Bianchi Benguria, Natalia Dueñas, Tiffany Kaewen Dang

We would like to acknowledge that this project is conceived on lands of the Kechwa Peoples of Quito, whose struggles for self-determination are rooted in the appropriation of their lands by the Spanish Conquistador Sebastian de Benalcazar in 1534. At the origins of the histories of appropriation is the exploration and the extraction of quinine from the Cinchona tree that is the underlying premise for European colonization based on the extraction of Quinine that has persisted until today for over 390 years. This Indigenous struggle emerges from ongoing territorial dispossession, violence against women, and dehumanization of the Saraguro, Palta, Tsachila, Chachi, Epera, Awa, Kechwa, Shuar, Achuar, Shiwiar, Cofan, Siona, Secoya, Zapara, Andoa, Waorani Peoples, within and beyond the settler colonial boundaries of the nation state of Ecuador.

p. 281
Institution, clients and partners: Architectural Association Visiting School Amazon (AAVSA)
Program: Architectural Association School of Architecture

Mamori Community Floating Library
Institutions: Goethe Institut and Prince Claus Fund

Creative Laboratory of the Amazon (LCA)
Initiative by: Amazonia 4.0

Ceremonial House
Donation for: Ashaninka indigenous people

Mirante Madada
Client: Mirante do Gavião - Amazon Lodges

Riverside education
Institution: Fundação Almerinda Malaquias

Science Museum of the Amazon (MuCA)
Institution: MuCA

Native Village
Client: Aldeia Global

Araquém Alcântara expedition
Client: Vento Leste

Production:
Atelier Marko Brajovic team
Creative Director: Marko Brajovic
Project Director: Bruno Bezerra
Project Designer: Guilherme Giantini
Content production: May Shinzato
Graphic design: Barbara Helena Morais
Biomimicry consultancy: Alessandra Araujo
Material system consultancy: Nacho Marti

p. 283
Giulia Foscari / UNLESS
UNLESS team: Eleonora Cappuccio, Sonja Draskovic, Giulia Foscari (founder and director), Giulio Marchetti, Antonella Mariani, Ines Molinari, Olimpia Presutti, Sabrina Syed, Olympia Simopoulou, Lloyd Sukgyo Lee, Federica Sofia Zambeletti (Antarctic Resolution project manager).

250 times per second:
Artwork: Arcangelo Sassolino, developed in collaboration UNLESS.
Scientific data: David Vaughan (British Antarctic Survey).
Production: Maurizio Munari, Ermene Spagnolo, Diego Chilò.

Call for Action:
Research, Curation and Production: Giulia Foscari / UNLESS
Antarctic Atlas: Polar Lab (directors: Francesco Bandarin, Sol Camacho, Juan Du, Giulia Foscari, Arturo Lyon, Florencia Rodriguez).
Expert Contributors: Doaa Abdel-Motaal (World Trade Organisation), Conrad Anker (Mountaineer), Carlo Barbante (University Ca' Foscari), James N. Barnes (Antarctic and Southern Ocean Coalition), Thomas, Barningham (British Antarctic Survey), Carlo Baroni (University of Pisa), Susan Barr (International Council on Monuments and Sites), Elisa Bergami (University of Siena), Marcelo Bernal (ARQZE Ltd), Anne-Marie Brady (University of Canterbury), Ralf Brauner (Jade University of Applied Sciences), Cassandra M. Brooks (University of Colorado Boulder), Shaun T. Brooks (University of Tasmania), Hugh Broughton (Hugh Broughton Architects), Bert Bücking (bof Architekten),

David Burrows (Environmental Systems Research Institute), Sanjay Chaturverdi (South Asian University), Swhadheet Chaturvedi (Architectural Association School of Architecture), Christy Collis (Queensland University of Technology), Peter Convey (British Antarctic Survey), Geoff Cooper (United Kingdom Antarctic Heritage Trust), Gabriele Coppi (University of Pennsylvania), Ilaria Corsi (University of Siena), Lino Dainese (Dainese and D-Air Lab), Klaus Dodds (Royal Holloway, University of London), Julian Dowdeswell (Scott Polar Research Institute, Cambridge University), Chris Drury (Artist), Juan Du (The University of Hong Kong), Graeme Eagles (Alfred Wegener Institute for Polar and Marine Research), Tess Egan (Australian Antarctic Division), Alexey A. Ekaykin (Arctic and Antarctic Research Institute), Fausto Ferraccioli (British Antarctic Survey), Joe Ferraro (Ferraro Choi and Associates), James Rodger Fleming (Boston University), Adrian Fox (British Antarctic Survey), William L. Fox (Nevada Museum of Art), Bob Frame (University of Canterbury), Peter T. Fretwell (British Antarctic Survey), Lutz Frisch (Artist), Jacopo Gabrielli (National Research Council), Hartwig Gernandt (Alfred Wegener Institute for Polar and Marine Research), Andrew J. Gerrard (New Jersey Institute of Technology), Neil Gilbert (Constantia Consulting), El Glasberg (New York University), Karsten Gohl (Alfred Wegener Institute for Polar and Marine Research), Francis Halzen (University of Wisconsin–Madison), Kael Hansen (Wisconsin IceCube, Particle Astrophysics Center), Teasel Muir-Harmony (National Air and Space Museum, Smithsonian Institution), Ursula Harris (Australian Antarctic Data Centre), Judith Hauck (Alfred Wegener Institute for Polar and Marine Research), Robert Headland (Scott Polar Research Institute, Cambridge University), Beth Healey (European Space Agency), Alan D. Hemmings (University of Canterbury), Alfred Hiatt (Queen Mary University of London), Gretchen Hoffman (University of California, Santa Barbara), Adrian Howkins (University of Bristol), Kevin A. Hughes (British Antarctic Survey), Andrew T. Hynous (National Aeronautics and Space Administration), Julia Jabour (University of Tasmania), Stéphanie Jenouvrier (Woods Hole Oceanographic Institution), Solan Jensen (Quark Expeditions), Kevin Johnson (University of California, Santa Barbara), Andrea Kavanaugh (The Pew Charitable Trusts), Daniel Kiss (Architectural Association School of Architecture), Georg Kleinschmidt (Alfred Wegener Institute for Polar and Marine Research), Alexander, Klepikov (Arctic and Antarctic Research Institute), Peter Landschützer (Max Planck Institute for Meteorology), Louis John Lanzerotti (New Jersey Institute of Technology), Elizabeth Leane (University of Tasmania), Sang-Lem Lee (Space Group), Inti Ligabue (Giancarlo Ligabue Foundation), Daniela Liggett (University of Canterbury), Bryan Lintott (Scott Polar Research Institute, Cambridge University), Vladimir Lipenkov (Arctic and Antarctic Research Institute), Cornelia Lüdecke (University of Hamburg), James Masden (Wisconsin IceCube Particle Astrophysics Center), Craig McCormack (University of Western Australia), Tony McGlory (Ramboll), Hans-Jürgen Meyer (Alfred Wegener Institute for Polar and Marine Research), Joseph Micallef (Military.com), Christel Misund-Domaas (University of Tromsø), Nicholas de Monchaux (Massachusetts Institute of Technology), Chiara Montanari (Antarctic Expedition Leader), Michael Morrison (Purcell), John Nelson (Environmental Systems Research Institute), Camilla Nichol (United Kingdom Antarctic Heritage Trust), Miranda Nieboer (University of Tasmania), Dirk Notz (Max Planck Institute for Meteorology), Shaun O'Boyle (Photographer), Madeleine O'Keefe (IceCube Neutrino Observatory), Lucy + Jorge Orta (Artists), Lawrence A. Palinkas (University of Southern California), Scott Parazynski (National Aeronautics and Space Administration), Carolina Passos (RADDAR), Michael Pearson (International Council on Monuments and Sites, International Polar Heritage Committee), Francesco Pellegrino (National Agency for New Technologies, Energy and Sustainable Economic Development), Rick Petersen (OZ Architecture, Inc.), Katherina Petrou (University of Technology Sydney), Andrea Piñones (Austral University of Chile), Jean-Yves Pirlot (Council of European Geodetic Surveyors), Ceisha Poirot (Antarctica New Zealand), Jean de Pomereu (Photographer), Alexander Ponomarev (Artist, Antarctic Biennale), Brian Rauch (Washington University in St. Louis), Ron Roberts (Kingston University), Donald R. Rothwell (Australian National University College of Law), Juan Francisco Salazar (Western Sydney University), Jean-Baptiste Sallée (French National Centre for Scientific Research), Sir Philippe Samyn (Philippe Samyn and Partners), Bojan Šavrič (Environmental Systems Research Institute), Mirko Schienert (Dresden University of Technology), Didier Schmitt (European Space Agency), Thomas Schramm (Ramboll), Daniel Schubert (Alfred Wegener Institute for Polar and Marine Research), Karen Nadine Scott (University of Canterbury), Cara Seitchek (American University), Maria Ximena Senatore (International Council on Monuments and Sites), Jonathan Shanklin (British Antarctic Survey), Yuri Shibaev (Arctic and Antarctic Research Institute), Santiago Sierra (Artist), Tim Stephens (University of Sydney), Pavel Grigorievich Talalay (Jilin University), Paul Taylor (ARQZE Ltd.), Steve Theno (United States Antarctic Program), Paul Thur (United States Antarctic Program), Philip Trathan (British Antarctic Survey), Francisco Valdivia (Federico Santa María Technical University), David Vaughan (British Antarctic Survey), Emerson Vidigal (Estudio 41), Priscilla Wehi (University of Otago), Claudio Willams (Amancio Williams ʳ Archive), Gary Wilson (Department of Marine Science, University of Otago), Juliet Wong (University of California, Santa Barbara), Gillian Wratt (Independent Consultant), Angela Wright (Colour Affects).
Infographics: UNLESS and POMO.
Book design: UNLESS and Lars Müller Publishers (Lars Müller, Martina Mullis, Maya Ruegg).

SNOW GOGGLES. Tools of resistance:
On loan by the Scott Polar Research Institute.

THE ANTARCTIC SUIT. The first architectural envelope:
D-Air Lab, Dainese: Lino Dainese (founder), Luigi Ronco, Vittorio Cafaggi, Alberto Piovesan, Michele Villani, Giulia Fabbro, Irina Potryasilova, Marco Manuzzi, Nicola Parise; developed in collaboration with UNLESS.

Exhibition Assembly: Altrofragile - Lupo Gavioli, Francesco Rovaldi.

p. 285
Lateral Office + Arctic Design Group: Anthony Averbeck, Leena Cho, Benjamin DiNapoli, Vincent Chuang, Cam Fullmer, Matthew Jull, Jane Lee, Tyler Mauri, Julia Nakanishi, Kearon Roy Taylor,

Lola Sheppard, Zihao Wei, Mason White.

p. 289
Pier Vittorio Aureli and Martino Tattara with Celeste Tellarini, Anna Panourgia, Antonio Paolillo, Mariapaola Michelotto, Yi Ming Wu, Theodor Reinhardt, Perla Gísladóttir, and Rachel Rouzaud.

p. 291
Authors: Joshua Bolchover and John Lin, Rural Urban Framework
Project Lead: Chiara Oggioni

p. 293
EPISODE 1
Prototypes of the transition
Soil and Labour: a Vision for the Grand Genève
2018-2021 Habitat Research Center, EPFL with the students of the Design Studios BA 5-6, MA 1-2, SAR-IA (in the frame of the *Prospective Visions for Great Geneva - The Eco-Century Prohect*', Fondation Braillard Architectes, Geneva
HRC: Paola Viganò (HRC director, LAB-U), Vincent Kaufmann (HRC-LASUR), Alexandre Buttler (HRC-ECOS), Luca Pattaroni (HRC-LASUR), Corentin Fivet (HRC-SXL) with Roberto Sega (HRC e.b., LAB-U, coordinator of the team), Martina Barcelloni Corte (HRC executive board coordinator), Qinyi Zhang (HRC e.b., LAB-U), Tommaso Pietropolli (LAB-U, co-coordinator of the team)
External experts: Pascal Boivin (inTNE-HEPIA, HES-SO Genève), Olivier Crevoisier (Université de Neuchâtel), Walter R. Stahel (Product-Life Institute), Jonathan Normand (B Lab Switzerland), Isabel Claus, Marie Velardi
With: Fazaneh Bahrami (Université de Groningen), Chiara Cavalieri (Université Catholique de Louvain), Thomas Guillaume, Shin A. Koseki (HRC e.b.), Delphine Rime (Université de Bern), Matthew Skjonsberg (HRC e.b.), Marine Durand (LAB-U), Sylvie Nguyen (LAB-U), Eloy Llevat Soy (Politecnico di Torino), Irène Desmarais
Client: Fondation Braillard Architectes, Genève

EPISODE 2
Brest 2050 city landscape in transition.
Vision and Strategies
Studio018-021PaolaViganò (ongoing)
Paola Viganò, Alessia Calò, Morvan Rabin, Pietro Manaresi, Mathilde Meurice, Bertrand Plewinski, Etienne Schillers, Laure Thierrée
With: Idea Consult, Egis, Scopic, Guam Conseil
Client: Brest Métropole

Utopia for our time.
'War on Poverty'.
Towards a Research on Appalachia
2017 University of Virginia
Paola Viganò (Thomas Jefferson Visiting Professor), with Anthony Averbeck, Lecturer UVA, Roberto Sega, Visiting Ph.D. EPFL and the students of UVA: Batul Abbas, Joshua Aronson, Joseph Brookover, Luke Harris, Laurence Holland, Jennifer Hsiaw, Elizabeth Kulesza, Lemara Miftakhova, Shannon Ruhl, Christian Storch, Xiang Zhao, Bonnie Kate Walker

Amphibia.
Water Coexistences
2018-2021 EMU – European Master in Urbanism, IUAV
Teaching Staff: Paola Viganò, Alvise Pagnacco, Irene Guida, Riccardo Avella. Students: Flore Guichot, Francesco Lombardi, Nathan Fredrick (EMU), Martina Princivalle (MA) and with the contribution of BA students (teaching staff: Paola Viganò, Anna Livia Friel, Alessio Tamiazzo)
EPISODE 3
Design a Horizontal Metropolis
Brussels 2040: A Metropolitan Vision.
The Horizontal Metropolis
Studio010-012 Secchi-Viganò
Bernardo Secchi, Paola Viganò, Myron Devolder, Emmanuel Giannotti, Michele Girelli, Chunxiao Liang, Carlo Pisano, Ana Rafful, Veronica Saddi, Wim Wambecq, Qinyi Zhang
With: Creat- Centre d'Études en Aménagement du Territoire, Egis Mobilité, TU München (Department of Building Climatology and Building Services) and Ingenieurbüro Hausladen GMBH, Karbon', IDEA Consult
Client: Brussels Capital Region

Antwerp Park Spoor Noord.
A central place for villages and metropolis on a dismissed railway site
Studio03-08 Secchi-Viganò
Bernardo Secchi, Paola Viganò, Elisa Alfier, Kaat Boon, Andrea Carlesso, Giovanni De Roia, Umberta Dufour, Lorenzo Fabian, Tommaso Fait, Steven Geeraert, Anna Moro, Christian Nitti, Günter Pusch, Uberto degli Uberti, Kasumi Yoshida, Giambattista Zaccariotto
With: Pieter Kromwijk, Rob Cuyvers, Iris Consulting, Frans Steffens, Dirk Jaspaert
Client: Antwerp Municipality
Photos: Teresa Cos

Mechelen Three Squares.
A system of public spaces
Studio00-012 Secchi-Viganò
Bernardo Secchi, Paola Viganò, Kaat Boon, Matteo D'Ambros, Giovanni De Roia, Umberta Dufour, Lorenzo Fabian, Steven Geeraert, Rita Miglietta, Pieter Ochelen, Günter Pusch, Uberto degli Uberti, Wim Wambecq, Kasumi Yoshida, Giambattista Zaccariotto
With: N.V. Giluco, D+A consult nv
Client: Mechelen Municipality

Antwerp Theatre Square.
'Spazio s-misurato'
Studio05-10 Secchi-Viganò
Bernardo Secchi, Paola Viganò, Steven Geeraert, Emmanuel Giannotti, Günter Pusch, Uberto degli Uberti, Kasumi Yoshida
With: Dirk Jaspaert and Marc de Kooning (BAS), Dries Beys (ARA)
Client: Antwerp Municipality
Photos: Teresa Cos, Tom Cortoos

De Hoge Rielen educational center masterplan and projects.
Sharing a forest, living together
Studio 02-014 Secchi-Viganò; Studio015-018 PaolaViganò
Bernardo Secchi, Paola Viganò, Umberta Dufour, Lorenzo Fabian, Tommaso Fait, Steven Geeraert, Emmanuel Giannotti, Griet Lambrechts, Tullia Lombardo, Stefano Peluso, Günter Pusch, Pieter Thibaut, Uberto degli Uberti, Guillaume Vanneste, Wim Wambecq, Maarten Wauters, Kasumi Yoshida, Giambattista Zaccariotto, Qinyi Zhang
With: Dirk Jaspaert and Marc de Kooning (BAS), Dries Beys (ARA)
Client: Flemish Government, AFM
Photos: Frederik Buyckx

Kortrijk Cemetery.
A place in the landscape
Studio96-00 Secchi-Viganò
Bernardo Secchi, Paola Viganò, Giovanna Comana, Greta Giunta, Nardo Goffi, Giorgio Manzoni, Barbara Martino, Annacarla Secchi, Tom van Mighiem
With: Ann Cnockaert, Phlippe Cnockaert, Griet Robyn, Paul Vandeputte
Artist: Paul Van Rafaelghem («The table»)
Client: Kortrijk Municipality
Photos: Syb'l S.- Pictures, Carine Demeter

Tournai Station Square and the "Rue Royale".
A public space for a city in transition
Studio018-021PaolaViganò (on going)
Paola Viganò, Etienne Schillers, Qinyi Zhang, Uberto degli Uberti, Pietro Manaresi, Mathilde Meurice
With: SWECO, Yellow Window, Aliwen, D2S international, AG licht, EnergyConsulting
Client: Tournai Municipality, SNCB, SPW, TEC

Regatta Village and Park.
Public spaces and a park along the

Galgenweel
Studio07-014 Secchi-Viganò,
Studio015-021Paola Viganò
(ongoing)
Bernardo Secchi, Paola Viganò,
Simona Bodria, Uberto degli Uberti,
Jordi De Vlam, Myron Devolder,
Maarten Wauters; Steven Geeraert,
Stefano Peluso, Gunther Pusch,
Ana Rafful, Kasumi Yoshida,
Guillarme Vanneste; Qinyi Zhang,
Matthias Lamberts
With: ARA (park), SWECO (village public space)
Client: Vooruitzicht SA, City of Antwerp

Peterbos, Anderlecht - Brussels Capital Region, public space masterplan and projects.
Living in the Park, Inhabiting the City
Studio019-021PaolaViganò
(ongoing)
Paola Viganò, Bertrand Plewinski, Pietro Manaresi, Mathilde Meurice, Stefano Gariglio, Eugénie Laharotte
With: vvv - Nicolas Willemet, Guillaume Vanneste, Mathieu Auquier
And with: ARA, Brat
Client: Anderlecht Municipality, Brussels Capital Region

OVK – Future scenarios for the core region of East Flanders.
Three worldviews on sustainable development
Studio018Paola Viganò
Paola Viganò, Kasumi Yoshida, Uberto degli Uberti, Etienne Schillers, Jordi De Vlam, Qinyi Zhang
With: Architecture Workroom Brussels
Client: IABR and Provincie Oost-Vlaanderen
Eurometropolis Lille-Tournai-Kortrijk, a vision for a dispersed metropolis.
The Blue Space
Studio015-018Paola Viganò
Paola Viganò, Michaël Stas, Etienne Schillers and Chiara Cavalieri (EPFL)
With the participation of: ENSAP Lille, EPFL Lausanne, IUAV Venice, UCL Tournai, Ugent
Client: Eurometropolis Lille-Tournai-Kortrijk

Rethinking Wallonia: three images. Val de Sambre development plan. New life-cycles
Studio017-018PaolaViganò
Paola Viganò, Alessia Calò, Bertrand Plewinski, Morvan Rabin
With: Idea Consult
Client: Sambreville Municipalitiy

Rethinking Wallonia: three images. La Louvière 2050, a vision for the transition
Studio018-021PaolaViganò
(ongoing)
Paola Viganò, Alessia Calò, Achille Pelletier, Klara Sladeckova
With: Idea Consult, ICEDD
Client: La Louvière Municipality

Rethinking Wallonia: three images. Herstal, Liège, site requalification of ACEC former industrial area. Green Life
Studio017-018Paola Viganò
Paola Viganò, Alessia Calò, Bertrand Plewinski, Morvan Rabin
With: Idea Consult, SWECO, Rsk Benelux sprl, Origin Architecture & Engineering
Client: Herstal Municipality, SPI

EPISODE 3 Video Credits: Maarten Verstraete, editor

EPISODE 4
Towards an urbanism of the living soil
ZAC de la Courrouze, Rennes and Saint-Jacques-de-la-Lande.
Living in the city, inhabiting a park
Studio 03-014 Secchi-Viganò,
Studio015-021PaolaViganò
(ongoing)
Bernardo Secchi, Paola Viganò, Simona Bodria, Alessia Calò, Andrea Carlesso, Dao Ming Chang, Irene Cogliano, Giovanna Comana, Marine Durand, Stefania Dussin, Tommaso Fait, Carla Greco, Stella Armeli Iapichino, Griet Lambrechts, Adrien Lefèvre, Carlo Neidhart, Christian Nitti, Alvise Pagnacco, Tommaso Pietropolli, Larisa Rudko, Ani Tafilica, Alessio Tamiazzo, Uberto degli Uberti, Silvia Urbano, Kasumi Yoshida
With: Charles Dard, Amco
And with: Pierre Bazin-Aubépine, Gwenael Desnos
Client: Rennes Métropole
Photos: Fabrizio Stipari

Progetto Flaminio, Rome. Masterplan.
The city is a renewable resource
Studio015-021PaolaViganò
(ongoing)
Paola Viganò, Uberto degli Uberti, Kasumi Yoshida, Alessio Tamiazzo;
Concorso: Paola Viganò, Simona Bodria, Uberto degli Uberti, Laura-May Dessagne, Kasumi Yoshida, Alessio Tamiazzo *with* Rina Consulting

EPISODE 4 Video Credits:
Maarten Verstraete, *editor*

If not specified otherwise and for all other credits: StudioPaolaViganò

p. 295
Concept: Paula Nascimento + Jaime Mesquita
Architectural Design: Jaime Mesquita (Oba Architects)
Technical Drawings / Collaborators: Dedaldina de Paula, Raquel Santos, Luzineide da Silva, Ricardo Neves, Robilson Tombela, Egídio da Fonseca, Mirian Vanda
Film Directed by: Kiluanji Kia Henda
Image and Graphics: Iris Buccholz Chocolate
Photography: Ngoi Salucombo, Claudio Chocolate
Texts: Paula Nascimento, Jaime Mesquita
Technical Advice: Raul Betti (Dumbo Design Studio)
Production in Venice: Raul Betti (Dumbo Design Studio)
Production in Luanda: Oba Architects

p. 297
Design and Production Assistant: Vanessa Lafoy
Research Assistants: Doug John Miller, Matei Alexandru

p. 299
Principal: Christoph Lechner
Studio: Architekt Christoph Lechner & Partners, Vienna
Exhibition Design Collaborators: Georg Wizany, Reto Schindler
Curatorial Project: Kevin Moore, Trevor Smith
Contributions Content, Research, Design: Alfred Berger (Berger + Parkkinnen), Raoul Bukor (Lindle & Bukor), Tony Collins, Bernhard Hachleitner, Eva Guttmann, Gmeiner Haferl ZT GmBH, Thomas Haunschmid, Hardy Hanappi, Roman Horak, Flora Lechner mit Sebastian Scholz, Matthias Marschik, Rudolf Müllner, Erich Prödl, August Sarnitz, Wolfgang Thaler
Institutions: Qatar Olympic and Sports Museum, University of Vienna, Institute of Sport Sciences, Park Books, Zürich

p. 308
ACTLD, Damien Lemaitre

p. 315
Nomination Dossier Prepared by DAAR: Alessandro Petti and Sandi Hilal with Ishaq Al Barbary, Elsa Koehler, Husam Abusalem, Sandy Rishmawi, Mark Romei, *in consultation with*: Campus in Camps, Dheisheh Camp Popular Committee, Finiq Cultural Center, Ibdaa Cultural Center, Riwaq Center for Architectural Conservation, Centre for Cultural Heritage Preservation in Bethlehem.

p. 319
Forensic Oceanography is a project of Charles Heller and Lorenzo Pezzani initiated within the Forensic Architecture agency at Goldsmiths, University of London

Video Screenings
Forensic Oceanography and

Forensic Architecture, *The Crime of Rescue—The Iuventa Case* (2018, 33').
Project Team Forensic Oceanography: Charles Heller, Lorenzo Pezzani, Rossana Padaletti, Richard Limeburner
Project Team Forensic Architecture: Nathan Su, Christina Varvia, Eyal Weizman, Grace Quah
Produced with the Support of: Borderline Europe, the WatchTheMed platform and Transmediale

Forensic Oceanography and Forensic Architecture, *Mare Clausum—The Sea Watch vs Libyan Coast Guard Case* (2018, 28').
Project Team Forensic Oceanography: Charles Heller, Lorenzo Pezzani, Rossana Padaletti
Project Team Forensic Architecture: Stefan Laxness, Stefanos Levidis, Grace Quah, Nathan Su, Samaneh Moafi, Christina Varvia, Eyal Weizman
Produced with the Support of: the WatchTheMed platform, the Swiss National Science Foundation, the Republic and Canton of Geneva

ARCHIVE
Forensic Oceanography, *Mare Clausum: Italy and the EU's undeclared operation to stem migration across the Mediterranean* (2018).

Forensic Oceanography, *Interview with a survivor of the Sea Watch vs Libyan Coast Guard Case* (2019, 28').
Project Team: Charles Heller, Lorenzo Pezzani, Violeta Y. Mayoral, Laure Vermeersch

Forensic Oceanography, *Blaming the Rescuers: Criminalising Solidarity, (Re)enforcing Deterrence* (2017).

Forensic Oceanography, *Interview with Iuventa rescuer Laura Martin* (2019, 13').
Project Team: Charles Heller, Lorenzo Pezzani, Laure Vermeersch

p. 320
Curatorial Project: Justinien Tribillon
Scenography: Cécile Trémolières with additional architectural wisdom from Misia Forlen
Visual Design: Offshore Studio (Isabel Seiffert and Christoph Miler).

p. 327
© Chair of Günther Vogt, Department of Architecture (D-ARCH), ETH Zurich (Switzerland)

p. 329
Art and Installation Design: Olalekan Jeyifous
Research and Writing: Mpho Matsipa, Wale Lawal
Soundscape: Dani Kyengo O'Neill

As One Planet

p. 333
WeExhibit

p. 339
Cave_bureau, Kabage Karanja, Stella Mutegi, and Densu Moseti

p. 341
TVK
Model Making: The Consortium Team

p. 343
Joyce Hsiang and Bimal Mendis with Robert Cannavino
Research and Design: Gustav Nielsen, Diana Smiljkovic with Claire Gorman, Rachel LeFevre, Page Comeaux *assisted by*: Bobby Chun, Josh Greene, Claire Hicks, Max Ouellette-Howitz, Ingrid Pelletier, Noah Sannes, Rhea Schmid, Christine Song, Maya Sorabjee, Paul Wu, Christina Zhang
Fabrication: Jack Rusk with Adare Brown, Christopher Cambio and Tyler Krebs
Cosmic Map in Consultation with: Priyamvada Natarajan

p. 345
Ginkgo Bioworks: Christina Agapakis, Natsai Audrey Chieza, Grace Chuang, Jason Kakoyiannis, Jason Kelly, Scott Marr, Krishna Patel, Kit McDonnell, Christian Ridley, Dayal Saran, Atsede Siba, Dawn Thompson, Jue Wang.
Alexandra Daisy Ginsberg: Alexandra Daisy Ginsberg, Cecilie Gravesen, Johanna Just, Ness Lafoy, Ioana Man, Ana Maria Nicolaescu, Stacie Woolsey, Nicholas Zembashi.
Sissel Tolaas: Smell Re_searchLab Berlin, Kathrin Pohlmann
Production Management: Kathrin Pohlmann
Paleogenomics: Joshua Kapp, Beth Shapiro, Paleogenomics Lab, University of California, Santa Cruz
DNA Synthesis: Twist Bioscience
Documentary Editing: Inferstudio
Sound Design: Sam Conran
Thanks to: Michaela Schmull, Harvard University Herbaria

p. 347
Curatorial Design: Daniel López-Pérez, University of San Diego, Jesse Reiser, Princeton University School of Architecture
Geoscope 2 Design: Jesse Reiser, Nanako Umemoto, Reiser + Umemoto, RUR Architecture
RUR Architecture Team: Julian Harake, Katherine Leung
Inflatable Design: Pablo Kobayashi / Unidad de Protocolos
UdP Fabrication Team: Lucía Aumann, Ernesto Falabella, Emilio Robles, Pablo Kobayashi
Experience Design: Jan Pistor and Lukas Fitze, iart
Graphic Design: Lars Müller, Esther Butterworth / Lars Müller Publishers
Logistics Coordinator: Kira McDonald
Fabrication: Grey Wartinger, Bill Tansley, Princeton University School of Architecture Staff

p. 349
Produced in S.E.L

p. 357
Snow Engineering: Yoshiomi Ito

Video: Tomoko Mikanagi
Graphic Designer: Yoshihisa Tanaka
Construction: Slowbuilding
Research: Guglielmina Adele Diolaiuti, Stefano Pierpaolo Marcello Trasatti, Dipartimento di Scienze e Politiche Ambientali at the Università degli Studi di Milano

p. 359
Rania Ghosn + El Hadi Jazairy, Ayusha Ariana, Reid Fellenbaum, Monica Hutton, Kelly Koh, Meng-Fu Kuo, Anhong Li, Joude Mabsout, Avery Nguyen, Michael Stradley, Jane (Jia) Weng

Animation Music: Christine Southworth & Evan Ziporyn; ©2021 Airplane Ears Music (ASCAP)
Narration: Evan Ziporyn

p. 361
Design Team: OOZE (Eva Pfannes, Sylvain Hartenberg), Marjetica Potrč *in collaboration with*: Jesse Honsa
Coordination and Communication Support: Lotta Mossum / Staten Konstrad
Heated Rock Prototype Engineering and Production: Tomas Persen / Akademiskahus
Heated Rock Prototype Engineering Control: Mikael Nygren / Tyrens
Installation: La Biennale di venezia production team

p. 369
Richard Weller, Tatum Hands, Claire Hoch, Chieh Huang, Tone Chu, Zuzanna Drozdz, Nanxi Dong, Misako Murata, Emily Bunker, Rob Levinthal, Shannon Rafferty, Lucy Whitacre, Lujian Zhang, Francesca Garzilli, Allison Nkwocha, Oliver Atwood, Madeleine Ghillany-Lehar, Alice Bell, Elliot Bullen, Dennis Pierattini

p. 362
Research and Design Team: Nick Allen, Chris Cassidy, Charlotte Isabel D'Acierno, Alessandra Fabbri, Kira Intrator, Osamu

Kumasaka, Clarence Yi-Hsien Lee, Joude El-Mabsout, Camila Ostolaza, Larisa Ovalles, Jitske Swagemakers, Dorothy Tang, Ben Widger, Jaehun Woo, Zhicheng Xu, and Elizabeth Yarina
Collaborating Organizations: ENLACE (Puerto Rico), Isle de Jean Charles Native American Tribe (Louisiana), Aga Khan Agency for Habitat (Tajikistan), Aga Khan Program for Islamic Architecture (MIT), Kennedy & Violich Architecture, Norman B. Leventhal Center for Advanced Urbanism (MIT), and Urban Risk Lab (MIT).

p. 371
Neil Brenner, Christian Schmid, Milica Topalovic, AbdouMaliq Simone, Rodrigo Castriota, Nancy Couling, Mariano Gomez-Luque, Alice Hertzog-Fraser, Daniel Ibañez, Nikos Katsikis, Metaxia Markaki, Philippe Rekacewicz, Kit Ping Wong

p. 373
Exhibition Design: spbr *in collaboration with*: Ciro Miguel, Felipe Barradas, Lucas Roca
Video Animation: Jenny Rodenhouse based on Angelo Bucci's drawings for the exhibition *Terrestrial Tales: 100+ Takes on Earth*, curated by: Marc Angélil et al., ETH Zurich, 2019
Production: Marco Ballarin
Model Structural Engineer: Andrea Pedrazzini
Model Fabrication: Claudio Moreno, Andrea Pedrazzini

p. 375
Production Credit: Joseph Thompson
Mineral Sample Loans: European Space Agency Exploration Sample Analogue Collection, Asteroid Mining Corporation
Additional Research Development Credit: Dayl Martin, European Space Agency, Melissa Roth, Vince Roux, Off Planet Research, Mitch Hunter Scullion, Joel Burkin, Asteroid Mining Corporation,
Laszlo Kestay, USGS, Kevin Cannon, University of Central Florida, John Pernet-Fisher, University of Manchester
With Many Thanks to: Andrew Weatherhead, Martin Conreen, Goldsmiths University of London

p. 377
Artist: Mabe Bethônico
Collaborators: Elaine Ramos, Enrique Fontanilles, Gilles Eduar, Hannah Stewart, Gisa Bustamante, Jônio Bethônico, NASK, Rodrigo Martins, Victor Galvão
With Thanks to: Camille Garnier, Emilie-Cerise Pelloux, Emily Eliza Scott, Flavia Peluzzo, Gaël Paradis, Galeria Celma Albuquerque, Júlio Landmann, Galeria Marilia Razuk, Joerg Bader, Júlio Landmann, Lara Bethônico, Philippe Thaize, Sonia Pérez, Stéphane Sauzedde, Tomás Bethônico and all collaborators

p. 379
The Birds' Pavilion
Consortium-Land: Kevin Baudrot, Félix Gautherot, Damien Pasteur, Christina Vryakou, 3 Mat, Saint-Broing-les-Moines, Aña-Cūa, Grancey-le-Château, Axionys, Magny-les-Hameaux
Film: Grancey, a film (2021)
Executive Production: Anna Sanders Films
Installation: Shenzhen Multimedia, St Genis Laval

Forte Marghera - How will we play together?

p. 387
DOBY constep, BAYO.S THE GROUNDSCROO, JJ-konstrukt, Taros Nova

p. 393
The *Social Equilibria* installation was developed by a multidisciplinary team of faculty, students, and researchers in architecture and civil engineering and with input from kinesiology and behavioral science.
Lead Investigators: Sean Ahlquist,
Evgueni Filipov,
Researchers: John Hilla, Tracey Weisman, Yingying Zeng
Students: Yi-Chin Lee, Maria Redoutey, and Ruxin Xie
With Special Thanks to: Mick Kennedy, Larken Marra, John Shaw

p. 393
Faroldi
Installation Team: Francesco Bruno, Giorgia Del Tedesco, Nicola Alessio Persic, Greta Zancopè (coordinator)

p. 395
Production: Niccolò Salvato, Marco Altan- TECHWOOD Venezia
Structural Engineer: Giovanni Zivelonghi
Structural Consultant: Amnon Medad

BIOGRAPHIES

Among Diverse Beings - Arsenale

PEJU ALATISE
p. 41

Peju Alatise (b. 1975) is an artist, architect, and writer. She is fellow at the National Museum of African Art – Smithsonian Institution. Alatise received formal training as an architect at Ladoke Akintola University in Oyo State, Nigeria.

ANI LIU
p. 43

Ani Liu is a research-based artist whose work examines the reciprocal relationships between technology and its influence on human subjectivity, culture, and identity. Her studio is in New York City.

AZRA AKSAMIJA
p. 45

Azra Akšamija, PhD, is an artist and architectural historian. She is an Associate Professor in the MIT Program in Art, Culture, and Technology and directs the MIT Future Heritage Lab.

The MIT Future Heritage Lab (FHL) is an art and research lab working on creative responses to conflict and crisis through performative preservation and co-creation with affected communities.

MODEM
p. 47

Kathryn Moll and Nicholas de Monchaux collaborate as modem, combining their experience in software, architecture, urban design, and digital fabrication. Nicholas de Monchaux is Professor and Head of Architecture at MIT. He is the author of *Spacesuit: Fashioning Apollo* (MIT Press, 2011) and *Local Code: 3,659 Proposals about Data, Design, and the Nature of Cities* (Princeton Architectural Press, 2016). Kathryn Moll is an architect, with a decade of experience leading the design and construction of net-positive energy buildings and award-winning, adaptive-reuse projects in California. Together, they use architectural tools to transform objects, environments, and urban situations, strengthening and improving connections between buildings, cities, and ecologies.

ALLAN WEXLER STUDIO
p. 49

Allan Wexler is an architect in an artist's body. His studio is a laboratory. His works mediate the gap between fine and applied art using the mediums of sculpture, architecture, drawing, and photography. His work investigates simple things: how to walk through walls, people dining together, our first marks on the primal landscape as builders. He re-evaluates basic assumptions about the human relationship to the built and natural environments. Wexler is represented by Ronald Feldman. He teaches at Parsons School of Design in New York City. He is a recipient of a 2016 Guggenheim Fellowships and a 2004 Rome Prize Fellowship.

STATION CASSANI, GALAN, MUNUERA, SANDERS
p. 50

Matilde Cassani operates on the border between architecture, installation, and event design. Her practice deals with the spatial implications of cultural pluralism in the contemporary Western city. Ignacio G. Galán is an architect and historian whose work focuses on architecture's relation to nationalism, colonialism, migration, diversity, and access. He is Assistant Professor at Barnard College, Columbia University.

Iván L. Munuera is a New York-based scholar, critic, and curator working at the intersection of culture, technology, politics, and bodily practices in the modern period and on the global stage.

Joel Sanders directs the New York-based architecture studio JSA, and MIXdesign, an inclusive design lab and consultancy. He is Professor in Practice at the Yale School of Architecture.

STATION GISSEN, STAGER, ZARMAKOUPI
p. 54

David Gissen works at the intersection of architecture, history, and experimental design. He is Professor of Architecture and Urban History at the Parsons School of Design, New School University.

Jennifer Stager is an art historian and writer based at Johns Hopkins University in Baltimore, Maryland. Her areas of focus include theories of colour and materiality, feminisms, multilingualism and cultural exchange, ancient Greek and Roman medicine, and classical receptions.

Mantha Zarmakoupi, an architectural historian and classical archaeologist, is the Morris Russell and Josephine Chidsey Williams Assistant Professor in Roman Architecture at the University of Pennsylvania. Her research addresses the broader social, economic, and cultural conditions underpinning the production of Greek and Roman art, architecture, and urbanism.

REFIK ANADOL STUDIO
p. 61

Refik Anadol (b. 1985, Istanbul, Turkey) is a media artist and director. He currently resides in Los Angeles, California, where he owns and operates Refik Anadol Studio. Anadol is also a lecturer and researcher for UCLA's Department of Design Media Arts from which he obtained his Master of Fine Arts.

STUDIO OSSIDIANA
p. 63

Studio Ossidiana is a practice based in Rotterdam that works at the intersection of architecture, visual arts, and design, and is led by Alessandra Covini and Giovanni Bellotti.

Alessandra Covini holds a MArch from TuDelft (NL) and is the winner of the Dutch Prix de Rome Architecture 2018.

Giovanni Bellotti holds a postgraduate degree from MIT, and a MArch from IUAV, Università degli studi di Venezia.

LUCY MCRAE
p. 65

Lucy McRae is a science fiction artist and body architect with a finely tuned ability to imagine other ways of being and, crucially, other possibilities for the human body, which sees her speculate on how it might evolve. She considers how human biology might be augmented by a mixture of physical design, modification of genes and emotions – technology transforming the body and ethics. Her prophetic aesthetic is flung far from archetypal tropes, boldly staring down the status quo – creating nostalgia for a future that is about to happen.

PARSONS & CHARLESWORTH
p. 67

Tim Parsons is a product designer, writer, and educator. He is Associate Professor in Designed Objects at the School of the Art Institute of Chicago.

Jessica Charlesworth is an artist, designer, and educator. She is co-founder of the London-based arts salon Alterfutures and she lectures at The School of the Art Institute of Chicago.
Working across a variety of media, Parsons & Charlesworth create objects, exhibits, texts, and images that encourage reflection upon the current and future state of our designed culture.

MAEID
p. 69

AEID Büro für Architektur und transmediale Kunst
MAEID (Daniela Mitterberger, Tiziano Derme) is an interdisciplinary practice based in Vienna, interested in the relationship between human, space, and performativity. The work of MAEID is a continuous act of hybridisation between different agents – Local: Remote, Physical: Virtual, Natural: Synthetic.

Daniela Mitterberger is an architect, researcher, and director of MAEID. Currently, she is leading a research project at the University of Applied Arts in Vienna, and she is a PhD candidate at the ETH Zürich, Gramazio Kohler Research, focusing on intuition in digital design and robotic fabrication.

Tiziano Derme is an Architect and Media Artist and director of MAEID. Currently he is Assistant Professor and PhD Fellow at the University of Innsbruck and a lead researcher at the University of Applied Arts in Vienna. His research focuses on biofabrication, robotics, and material performativity.

THE LIVING
p. 71

The Living is a design studio and an experiment in living architecture. David Benjamin is Founding Principal of The Living and Associate Professor at Columbia University GSAPP.

STUDIO LIBERTINY
p. 73

Tomáš Libertíny was born in Slovakia, the son of an architect and a historian. He studied at the Technical University Košice in Slovakia focusing on engineering and design and was awarded the Open Society Institute Scholarship to study painting and sculpture at The University of Washington in Seattle. He continued his studies at the Academy of Fine Arts and Design in Bratislava in painting and conceptual design. After winning the prestigious Huygens Scholarship, he received his MFA from The Design Academy, Eindhoven.

PHILIP BEESLEY & LIVING ARCHITECTURE SYSTEMS GROUP / UNIVERSITY OF WATERLOO SCHOOL 4DSOUND
p. 75

Philip Beesley is an artist and architect in the field of responsive architecture. He is a professor at the University of Waterloo and represented Canada at La Biennale in 2010.

As New Households - Arsenale

OPAFORM ARCHITECTS
p. 81

Marina Bauer is an architect and theorist. Her work is concerned with rethinking both the role of architecture and the architect as a practitioner. She holds a BA in art history and an MA from Bergen School of Architecture. She has founded two architectural studios.

Espen Folgerø is an architect and educator. After working as a cabinet maker and studying literature, he received his MA (with Distinction) from Bergen School of Architecture (BAS) in 2007. He is an architect at OPAFORM and professor at BAS where he continuously leads design and build projects.

LEOPOLD BANCHINI ARCHITECTS
p. 83

Leopold Banchini Architects is a multidisciplinary research team exploring the frontiers of space shaping. Deliberately ignoring borders and embracing globality, it aims to expend the traditional definitions of project-making using DIY culture and eclecticism as means of emancipation.

Lukas Feireiss is a Berlin-based international curator, artist, and writer known for his role in the discussion and mediation of art, design, and architecture in both theory and practice beyond disciplinary boundaries.

Dylan Perrenoud is a Swiss-based photographer. He teaches at the Vevey School of Photography and develops his own artistic practice, exhibiting in various galleries and institutions in Switzerland and abroad. He is particularly interested in architecture and the relation of mankind with its environment.

Lloyd Kahn is the founding editor-in-chief of Shelter Publications, Inc., and is the former Shelter editor of the *Whole Earth Catalog*. He is also an author, photographer, and pioneer of green architecture movements.

K63.STUDIO
p. 85

K63.Studio: Founded in 2013 by Osborne Macharia, K63.Studio is a boutique photography and visual arts studio exploring Afrofuturism. Their projects repurpose postcolonial African narratives by integrating historical elements and present reality and the future aspirations of people of African descent.

Cave_bureau: Cave_bureau is a Nairobi-based studio of architects and designers charting explorations into architecture and urbanism in/as nature. Their work addresses the anthropological and geological context of the African city as a means to confront the challenges of our contemporary rural and urban lives.

SUPERFLUX
p. 87

Anab Jain is a designer, filmmaker, co-founder of experiential futures studio Superflux, and Professor, Design Investigations at the University of Applied Arts, Vienna. Her work can be viewed at www.superflux.in.
Jon Ardern is an artist, technologist, cofounder of

experiential futures studio Superflux, and leads the Studio's projects around climate change. His work can be viewed at www.superflux.in.

Superflux is an art and design studio imagining plural futures at the intersections of climate crisis, technology, and more-than-human politics, founded by Anab Jain and Jon Ardern.

AW-ARCH
p. 89

Alex Anmahian is a founding partner of AW–ARCH, a research driven interdisciplinary design practice located in Cambridge, Massachusetts. Alex received a MArch from Harvard University's Graduate School of Design and a BA from the University of Florida.

LINE+ STUDIO
p. 91

Meng Fanhao, cofounder & chief architect of line+ studio, devotes himself to the creative practice in both urban and rural areas and promotes design to create value with diversified strategies.

LEONMARCIAL ARQUITECTOS
p. 93

Alexia León + Lucho Marcial: leonmarcial arquitectos

Alexia León (1970) and Lucho Marcial (1962) set up leonmarcial arquitectos studio in 2011 in Lima, Perú. León studied architecture at Ricardo Palma University and opened her studio leondelima in 2006. She taught as visiting professor at the Graduate School of Design at Harvard University (2007) and was nominated for the Mies van der Rohe Prize for Latin American Architecture (2000) with Casa Mori at age 28, the Marcus Prize (2009), MCHAP (2014) with Casa Vertical, and the BSI-Swis Architectural Award (2016). Marcial received his BArch from Columbia University, NYC, in 1985 and his MArch from Harvard University, Cambridge Massachusetts, in 1989. After his studies, he worked with Rafael Moneo in Barcelona on large mixed-use urban projects where he founded Lucho Marcial Arquitectos (1999) working on independent projects. Both have given seminars, lectures, and workshops in Peru and abroad. The studio's built work rethinks the relationship between society, structure materiality, and landscape at different territorial scales. The National Museum of Peru (MUNA), a public competition from 2014, is their last completed work (2020), and was built in the Pachacamac archaeological site.

ECOLOGIC STUDIO
p. 95

Claudia Pasquero is cofounder and director of ecoLogicStudio ltd, Professor of Synthetic Landscapes at the University of Innsbruck, Director of the Urban Morphogenesis Lab at The Bartlett UCL. Her research focuses on bio-computation in architecture and urban design.

Dr Marco Poletto is an architect, educator, and innovator based in London. He is co-founder and Director of the architectural practice ecoLogicStudio and the design innovation venture PhotoSynthetica, focused on developing architectural solutions to fight climate change.

ATELIER RITA
p. 97

Atelier RITA is an Architectural studio founded by Valentine Guichardaz-Versini in 2016 in Paris. The firm won the Équerre d'argent catégorie Première Œuvre Prize in 2017 for the Emergency Shelter for Refugees and Roma Community in Ivry-sur-Seine. David Boureau is a Franco-Dutch independent architectural photographer and has been working for international architects based in Paris for 25 years. Since 2008, he has been working with other media, including video and installation. His is a multi-faceted approach, that concentrates on related social architecture, public space, and the urban mutability process.

Sasminimum was founded in 2017. From waste to resource, their project *Le Pavé* proposes a sustainable and sensible material made from plastic waste to meet their architectural vision and offer aesthetic and eco-friendly buildings.

ROJO / FERNÁNDEZ-SHAW, ARQUITECTOS
p. 99

Rojo/Fernández-Shaw, arquitectos is an architecture office based in Madrid, Spain, founded as a partnership between the architects María Begoña Fernández-Shaw and Luis Rojo in 1994. The firm has oriented its practice to the design and construction of public works, architectural competitions, and academic research.

Begoña Fernández-Shaw obtained a degree in architecture from the Escuela Técnica Superior de Arquitectura de Madrid in 1987 and a MArch from Cornell University, Ithaca, NY. In 2001, she was appointed Adjunct Secretary to EUROPAN/Spain.

Luis Rojo de Castro graduated from the Escuela Técnica Superior de Arquitectura de Madrid in 1987, where has been teaching architecture design since 1992. He obtained a MArch from Harvard University and a PhD in Architecture Design from the Polytechnic University of Madrid. He is currently an associate professor of architecture at the ETSAM, UPM.

Franco Gilardi obtained a degree in architecture from the Universidad de Buenos Aires in 2017 and recently completed a MArch in Design at the Universidad de Navarra in 2019.

Luis Moreda obtained a degree in architecture from the Escuela de Arquitectura de Toledo, Universidad de Castilla-La Mancha, in 2016 and completed a MArch at the ETSAM UPM in 2019.

THE OPEN WORKSHOP
p. 101

THE OPEN WORKSHOP is a design–research practice examining the relationship between territory, politics, and form. It is led by Neeraj Bhatia, an architect and urban designer, originally from Toronto, Canada.

STATION JARZOMBEK AND PRAKASH
p. 103

Jarzombek works on a wide range of topics, both historical and theoretical. He is one of the country's leading advocates for global history and has published several books and articles on the topic, including the groundbreaking textbook *A Global History of Architecture* (Wiley Press, 2006), co-authored with Vikramāditya Prakash and illustrated by the renowned Francis D. K. Ching.

Prakash is an architect, architectural historian, and theorist. He is Professor of Architecture at the University of Washington and received his BArch from Chandigarh College of Architecture, India, and his MA and PhD in History of Architecture and Urbanism from Cornell University. Vikram works on issues of modernism, postcoloniality, global history, and fashion and architecture.

NADAAA
p. 107

For his contributions to architecture as an art, Nader Tehrani is the recipient of the American Academy of Arts and Letters' 2020 Arnold W. Brunner Memorial Prize. Nader Tehrani is Founding Principal of NADAAA. He is also Dean of the Irwin S. Chanin School of Architecture at The Cooper Union.
Arthur Chang, AIA is a Principal of NADAAA and head of NADLAB, the practice's material research arm. Chang has led internationally recognised projects including the Melbourne School of Design, Rhode Island School of Design's North Hall, and the Beaver Country Day School's Research + Design Center.

ACHIM MENGES / ICD UNIVERSITY OF STUTTGART AND JAN KNIPPERS / ITKE UNIVERSITY OF STUTTGART
p. 109

Achim Menges is a registered architect in Frankfurt and full professor at the University of Stuttgart, where he is the founding director of the Institute for Computational Design and Construction (ICD) and the director of the Cluster of Excellence Integrative Computational Design and Construction for Architecture (IntCDC).

Jan Knippers is the founder of Jan Knippers Ingenieure and full professor at the University of Stuttgart, where he is the director of the Institute for Building Structures and Structural Design and the deputy director of the Cluster of Excellence Integrative Computational Design and Construction for Architecture (IntCDC).

GRAMAZIO KOHLER ARCHITECTS / NCCR DFAB
p. 111

Fabio Gramazio and Matthias Kohler are architects with multidisciplinary interests ranging from computational design and robotic fabrication to material innovation. In 2000, they founded the award-winning architecture practice Gramazio Kohler Architects. They are both full professors at ETH Zurich and lead Gramazio Kohler Research, a pioneering group of researchers at the forefront of digital fabrication. They initiated the world's first architectural robotic laboratory at ETH Zurich, creating a new research field merging advanced architectural design and additive fabrication processes through the customised use of industrial robots.

NCCR DFAB was initiated in 2014 and aims to revolutionise architecture through the seamless combination of digital technologies and physical building processes: multidisciplinary academic research to develop ground-breaking technologies.

FERNANDA CANALES
p. 115

Fernanda Canales holds a PhD from ETSAM, Madrid. She has been awarded the Emerging Voices Award from The Architectural League of New York and is author of three books: *Shared Structures, Private Space* (Actar 2020); *Vivienda Colectiva en México* (Gustavo Gili, 2017); and *Architecture in Mexico 1900–2010* (Arquine, 2013).

AIRES MATEUS
p. 117

Francisco Aires Mateus (Lisbon, 1964) and Manuel Aires Mateus (Lisbon, 1963) studied Architecture at FA/UTL in Lisbon. After collaborating for several years with architect Gonçalo Byrne, they founded the AIRES MATEUS firm in Lisbon in 1988. Professors at Accademia di Architettura in Mendrisio since 2001 and at Universidade Autonoma in Lisbon since 1998, they participate as lecturers in numerous design seminars at various universities.
Their projects, ranging from single-family homes to urban infrastructures and including public buildings and ephemeral installations, are part of the contemporary international architectural debate and have been built in several countries.

ALISON BROOKS ARCHITECTS
p. 119

Alison Brooks is one of the UK's leading architects. Born and educated in Canada, she moved to London in 1988 and founded Alison Brooks Architects in 1996. Her design philosophy fuses history, community, and locality to produce architecture with clear civic purpose, encompassing urban design, housing, higher education, and the arts. A Visiting Professor at ETSAM, she also lectures internationally.

LIN ARCHITECTS URBANISTS
p. 121

LIN is a European agency for architecture and urbanism and is based in Berlin. LIN develops singular architectural projects as well as urban and landscape projects. Flexibility, open programming, and the reduction of resource consumption are recurring themes.

BAAG
p. 123

Buenos Aires Arquitectura Grupal (BAAG) is an architecture office in Argentina founded by Griselda Balian, Gabriel Monteleone, and Gastón Noriega, dedicated to carrying out works, projects, installations, and architectural competitions, among other things. It aims to generate a contribution to the discipline by understanding architecture as a product of practice and a situated thought. BAAG's approach proposes innovation, research, putting into practice, thinking.

FARSHID MOUSSAVI ARCHITECTURE
p. 125

Farshid Moussavi OBE RA is an internationally acclaimed architect and Professor in Practice of Architecture at the Harvard University Graduate School of Design. She previously cofounded Foreign Office Architects (FOA).

Tapio Snellman is a London-based filmmaker engaged predominantly in architectural and urban subjects.

His work includes immersive film installations, documentaries, experimental 3D animation, and site-specific film projections for museums, theatre, dance, and opera.

LAISNÉ
p. 127

Founded in 2005 and based in the Paris region, nicolas laisné architectes share their vision of an open architecture – open to the sensitive world, to new horizons, to the diversity of talents.

Guy Limone lives and works in Angoulême, France. He transforms sociological statistics into rich-in-colour visual statements in the form of small plastic figurines that recreate our society in miniature and provoke philosophical contemplation.

LINA GHOTMEH — ARCHITECTURE
p. 129

Lina Ghotmeh – Architecture is an international, award winning, multidisciplinary practice based in Paris. It was founded by French Lebanese architect Lina Ghotmeh. With its team of 25 professionals, the studio develops research-driven and environmentally engaged architecture. As an 'Archaeology of the Future' – a design methodology Ghotmeh devised – each creation is a projection of the past into a meaningful future. See www.linaghotmeh.com.

Our greatest gratitude to the partnership and contribution of: Peter & Nathalie Hrechdakian

Modelab Marco Galofaro and Ilaria Benassi

Printed artworks in Model featuring artists: Ali Cherri, Gilbert Hage, Gregory Bouchakjian, Nadim Asfar, Ieva Saudergaité, Ghassan Salhab

Large Screen film: *Drone* by Chloé Domat, Wissam Charaf

SSD
p. 131

Jinhee Park is a founding principal at the award-winning New York- and Seoul-based architecture firm SsD, which approaches design as a convergent, interdisciplinary, and sustainable venture. Since 2015, Jinhee Park has served as Adjunct Professor at Columbia University Graduate School of Planning and Preservation and previously taught as a Design Critic in Architecture at the Harvard GSD, as Morgenstern Chair Professor at the Illinois Institute of Technology.

ABALOS+SENTKIEWICZ AS+
p. 132

Iñaki Ábalos has a PhD in Architecture, has been Chair Professor of Architectural Design at the ETSAM since 2002, and is Visiting Critic at Harvard GSD. He was Kenzo Tange Professor (2009), Design Critic in Architecture (2010–2012), and Chair of the Department of Architecture at Harvard University Graduate School of Design (2012–2016). He has also obtained a Master of Science from CAUP Tongji University, Shanghai (2015), and a RIBA Fellowship (2009).

STATION KOCKELKORN AND SCHINDLER
p. 136

Anne Kockelkorn is an architectural historian focusing on the intersections between design, territorial politics, and processes of subjectivation. Since 2021, she has been assistant professor for dwelling at the TU Delft. Susanne Schindler is an architect and historian focused on the intersections of design, policy, and finance in housing, with a special focus on post-war developments in the United States. Since 2019, she has directed the MAS GTA ETH in Zurich.

STATION AMES, BAIRD-ZARS, FRAMPTON
p. 140

The GSAPP Housing Lab gathers leaders across planning, design, and development to innovate for action at the intersection of housing and climate change. Through interdisciplinary partnerships in research, pedagogy, and practice, the lab deploys methods that aim to shift the rules of existing systems of housing toward resilience, inclusion, and access.

Daisy Ames is an Adjunct Assistant Professor at Columbia University's GSAPP, where she teaches architecture studios and also serves as the architecture faculty of the GSAPP Housing Lab. Ames is the founding principal of Studio Ames, an architectural design studio based in New York City. She holds a BA from Brown University and MArch I from Yale School of Architecture.

Adam Snow Frampton, AIA, is the Principal of Only If, a New York City-based design practice for architecture and urbanism that he founded in 2013. He also teaches at Columbia University GSAPP and co-authored *Cities Without Ground: A Hong Kong Guidebook* (2012). He previously worked for seven years as an Associate at OMA and holds a MArch from Princeton University.

Bernadette Baird-Zars is the IDC fellow at the GSAPP Housing Lab and a PhD candidate in urban planning at Columbia University. As a partner at Alarife Urban Associates, she leads projects on land use and housing innovation. Recent publications include *Zoning: A Guide for 21st-Century Planning* (Routledge, 2020) and articles on planning practices in *JPER* (2018) and *MELG* (2019).

As Emerging Communities - Arsenale

COHABITATION STRATEGIES
p. 147

Cohabitation Strategies (CohStra) is a non-profit organisation for socio-spatial research, design, and development. It was founded in the city of Rotterdam, right after the 2008 financial crash, by Lucia Babina, Emiliano Gandolfi, Gabriela Rendón, and Miguel Robles-Durán. CohStra brings transdisciplinary methodologies to a comprehensive understanding of the agents affecting urban areas and provides working frameworks to communities to generate sustainable transformations. This is undertaken through active engagement with a range of locally embedded actors in governments, non-profit organisations, and civic groups as well as activists, artists, and researchers who coalesce around the desire for social, spatial, and environmental justice.

FIELDOFFICE ARCHITECTS
p. 149

Sheng-Yuan Huang was born in Taipei. He holds a BA from Tunghai University and an MA from Yale. Huang established his practice in Yilan in 1994, which has, since 2005, evolved into a group practice known as Fieldoffice. Huang has lectured and exhibited widely in Asia, the US, and Europe. He has been teaching at the Christian Chuang Yuan University since 1994.

Sheng-Feng Lin is an Associate Professor at Shih Chien University and the founder of Atelier Or. He received his MArch from Cranbrook Academy of Art. In 2018, as the recipient of the Outstanding Award in Taiwan Landscape Architecture Award, and Honourable Mention for the Taiwan Architecture Award, Lin is recognised for his cross-disciplinary works in architecture, landscape, and exhibition design.

Born in Malaysia, Ming-Liang Tsai premiered his *Rebels of the Neon God* at the 1992 Berlinale. His awards include the Golden Lion Award at the Venice Film Festival, the Jury Award at Berlin, and 5 FRIPESCI Awards. Tsai is a promoter of the Art Museum as Cinema concept. *Face* was the first film ever included in the Louvre's *Le Louvre s'offre aux cinéastes*.

STORIA NA LUGAR
p. 151

Patti Anahory is an architect, architectural critic, and independent curator. She holds a MArch degree from Princeton University and a BArch from the Boston Architectural College. Her work focuses on interrogating the presupposed relationships of place and belonging to identity, memory, and gender. She explores the politics of identity from an African island perspective – as a fugitive edge and radical margin characterised by spatial-temporal currents that offer complex readings of the conceptual and historical continuities and ruptures constituent of African worlds.

César Schofield Cardoso is a photographer, filmmaker, and web developer. His work uses installation, video, and the language of the Web, both in physical locations and in the online space. He has been working in collaboration with artists, architects, and others seeking a dialogue about common citizenship in the Global South.

ARQUITECTURA EXPANDIDA
p. 153

Arquitectura Expandida – AXP is a multidisciplinary collective based in Bogotá; engaged since 2010 in the physical and social self-construction of collective infrastructure for cultural autonomy in peripheral urban areas.

LACOL
p. 155

Lacol is a cooperative of 14 architects based in Sants (Barcelona). They work as architects to transform society, using architecture as a tool to intervene critically.

ENLACE ARQUITECTURA
p. 157

Enlace Arquitectura and Enlace Foundation are established in Caracas, Venezuela. Work focuses on urban and rural projects addressing territorial inequality and promoting greater social inclusion. The studio was founded by Elisa Silva, visiting professor at Princeton University and the University of Toronto, associate professor at Florida International University, recipient of the Rome Prize, Wheelwright Fellowship from Harvard University, Graham Foundation Grant, Lucas Artist Fellowship, and author of several publications.

Integration Process Caracas is a recent, year-long cultural and educational initiative sponsored by the United States Venezuela Affairs Unit that creates opportunities for people to question the stigmas associated with barrio communities and acknowledge them as part of the city through walks, events, art, and celebrations. It is organised by Enlace Arquitectura, Ciudad Laboratorio, Fundación Bigott, Hacienda La Trinidad PC, Alcaldía Baruta, Laboratorio Ciudadano, Ensayo Colectivo, Tradición 360, Gabriel Nass and Ambar Armas, and the community of La Palomera.

RAUMLABORBERLIN
p. 159

raumlabor (est. 1999) is a collaborative practice of around 20–30 practitioners with a core of nine long-term members whose works sit at the intersections of architecture, urbanism, public art, and activism, often proposing playful, temporary, or speculative urban prototypes aimed at transforming the city, our collective imaginaries, and our (different) ways of doing in society.

PRACTICA
p. 161

Jaime Daroca (Spanish, b. 1986) is an architect and academic based in Madrid. He holds a MArch from Harvard Graduate School of Design and a BA and MArch from ETSAS.

José Mayoral (Spanish, b. 1985) is an architect and academic. He holds a MArch from Harvard Graduate School of Design and is currently a PhD candidate at Universidad Católica de Chile and Università Iuav di Venezia.

José Ramón Sierra (Spanish, b. 1989) is an architect and academic based in Madrid. He holds a MArch with Distinction from Harvard Graduate School of Design and a BA and MArch from ETSAM.

STATION SEGAL, WILLIAMS
p. 162

Sarah Williams is Associate Professor of Technology and Urban Planning at MIT, where she also directs the Civic Data Design Lab and chairs the new undergraduate program in Urban Science. Williams combines her training in computation and design to create communication strategies that expose urban policy issues to broad audiences. Her design work has been widely exhibited including at the Guggenheim, the Museum of Modern Art, and the Cooper Hewitt Museum in New York City. Williams has won numerous awards including being named one of the Top 25 Leading Thinkers in Urban Planning and Technology and Game Changer by *Metropolis Magazine*.
civicdatadesignlab.mit.edu

Rafi Segal is an architect and Associate Professor of Architecture and Urbanism at MIT. His work involves design and research at the architectural, urban, and regional scale, currently focused on how emerging notions of collectivity can impact the design of buildings and cities. Segal has exhibited his work at Storefront for Art and Architecture; KunstWerk, Berlin; Witte de With, Rotterdam; Venice La Biennale International Architecture Exhibition; Museum of Modern Art; and the Hong Kong/Shenzhen Urbanism Biennale. He holds a PhD from Princeton University and a MSc and BArch from Technion, Israel Institute of Technology.
www.rafisegal.com
Of Ecuadorian and Chinese

descent, Marisa Morán Jahn is an artist, filmmaker, and creative technologist whose work redistributes power. Since 2012, she has collaborated with the National Domestic Workers Alliance on *CareForce*, a public art and film project that amplifies the voices of America's fastest growing workforce, caregivers. Jahn has presented work at Obama's White House, the United Nations, New Museum, and Creative Time among others. She has received awards from Creative Capital, Tribeca Film Institute, Rockefeller Foundation, and Open Society Foundation. She is a Lecturer at MIT and has taught at The New School and Columbia University.
www.marisajahn.com

Greg Lindsay is the director of applied research at the NewCities Foundation and director of strategy at its mobility offshoot, CoMotion. His writing and research on the future of cities, work, and organisations has been published in *The New York Times, Harvard Business Review, Time, Wired, Fast Company, The New Republic*, and many other publications. His work has been displayed internationally in venues such as The Museum of Modern Art in New York as well as the Venice La Biennale International Architecture Exhibition, among others. He was guest curator of the 2018 and 2019 editions of the reSITE festival in Prague.
www.greglindsay.org

ARISTIDE ANTONAS
ETH Zürich, D-ARCH
p. 169

The work of Aristide Antonas includes writing, design, installations, filmmaking, building, and photography, all operated under an interest for literature and philosophy. His work is published and exhibited worldwide.

EFFEKT
p. 171

EFFEKT was founded in 2007 under the creative direction of Sinus Lynge and Tue Foged. The office upholds a distinguished international track record of architecture and planning projects across a broad spectrum of building typologies. It has established a reputation for devising sustainable solutions with high social value, that benefit the environment, society, user, and the economy.

ATELIER MASŌMĪ
p. 173

Mariam Kamara is a Nigerien architect and Principal of atelier masōmī. Her work uses design to strengthen communities, while maintaining a dialog among architecture, people, and the environment. Her projects have earned numerous accolades, including the 2018 Global Silver LafargeHolcim Award. She is a 2019 Prince Claus Award Laureate and Sir David Adjaye's protégé in the 2018-2019 Rolex Mentor Protégé Initiative.

MANUEL HERZ ARCHITECTS AND IWAN BAAN
p. 175

Manuel Herz is an architect based in Basel and a professor at the University of Basel. His office is engaged in projects of multiple scales and programmes across Europe, Asia, and Africa.

Iwan Baan is a Dutch photographer who is known for images that narrate the life and interactions that occur within architecture. He works with many of the foremost architects around the world.

Nicholas Fox Weber runs the Josef and Anni Albers Foundation, writes books and essays, and spearheads a non-profit organisation he founded to assist with medical care and education in Senegal.

Magueye Ba is a medical doctor educated in Dakar and living in eastern Senegal where he has established several rural clinics. He is also the general contractor for the Tambacounda Hospital.

Therese Aida Ndiaye is a medical doctor and director of the regional hospital of Tambacounda in eastern Senegal. She was previously the head of department at the Grand-Yoff hospital of Dakar.

DESVIGNE
p. 177

Michel Desvigne is a landscape architect internationally renowned for his rigorous and contemporary designs and for the originality and relevance of his research work. He has developed projects in more than 25 countries, where his work helps in highlighting the landscapes and rendering them visible, understanding the mechanisms at work by giving them form, and acting upon these mechanisms in order to transform the landscapes and imbue them with meaning.

TUMO
p. 179

TUMO is a global network of learning centres at the intersection of technology and design. Over 20,000 teenagers currently study free-of-charge at TUMO centres in Europe, Asia, and the Middle East.

EMBT MIRALLES TAGLIABUE
p. 181

Benedetta Tagliabue is a well-known architect whose works can be found throughout the world. Along with Enric Miralles, she founded the studio Miralles Tagliabue EMBT in 1991, with offices in Barcelona, Shanghai, and Paris. She is the director of the Enric Miralles Foundation and jury member at some of the most prestigious international awards, including the Pritzker Prize and the Princess of Asturias Award.

RONAN & ERWAN BOUROULLEC
p. 183

Ronan Bouroullec and Erwan Bouroullec, French designers born in Quimper (Brittany) in 1971 and 1976 respectively, have been working together since 1999. From industrial design to craft work, from large production runs to research, from the object to public space, Ronan and Erwan Bouroullec's creations span multiple fields of expression and have gradually entered our daily lives.

SKIDMORE, OWINGS & MERRILL
p. 185

SOM is a collective of architects, designers, engineers, and planners who have created some of the world's most transformative and sustainable buildings and vibrant public spaces. Working at all scales, from a strategic regional plan to a single piece of furniture, SOM designs anticipate change in the way we live and work in communities around the world. ESA's mission is to shape the development of Europe's space capability and ensure that investment in space continues to deliver benefits to the citizens of Europe and the world.

MICHAEL MALTZAN ARCHITECTURE
p. 187

Michael Maltzan, b.1959, received a Master of Architecture degree from Harvard University's Graduate School of Design and holds both a Bachelor of Fine Arts and a Bachelor of Architecture from the Rhode Island School of Design. He founded Michael Maltzan Architecture in 1995 and is a recipient of the American Academy of Arts and Letters Architecture Award and is the 2016 AIA Los Angeles Gold Medal Honoree.

SEAN LALLY
p. 189

Sean Lally is an architect based in Lausanne, Switzerland. Lally is the author of *The Air from Other Planets: A Brief History of Architecture to Come* (Lars Müller Publishers). Lally is the host of the *Night White Skies* podcast and is associate professor of architecture at the University of Illinois at Chicago.

BASE
p. 191

BASE studio is a design–research practice focused on exploring non-conventional geometrical, material, and spatial formulations through a systemic-thinking approach; combining the potential of digital design tools with low-tech analogue processes.

OMA
p. 193

Reinier de Graaf (1964, Schiedam) is a Dutch architect and writer. He is a partner in the Office for Metropolitan Architecture (OMA), where he leads projects in Europe, Russia, and the Middle East. Reinier is the co-founder of OMA's think tank AMO and Sir Arthur Marshall Visiting Professor of Urban Design at the Department of Architecture of the University of Cambridge. He is the author of Four Walls and a Roof: The Complex Nature of a Simple Profession, named best book of 2017 by both the Financial Times and The Guardian.

DOXIADIS+ OLIAROS SA
p. 195

doxiadis+ is a pioneering team of experts creating landscapes and architecture with a deep respect for people and nature. Since 1999, the Athens-based practice has been designing for symbiosis.

STUDIO LA
p. 199

Studio L A is an architecture studio founded by architects Lorien Beijaert and Arna Mačkić. For L A, the practice of architecture is a device through which societal issues, phenomena, and narratives can be investigated and placed in transformed perspectives.

Baukje Trenning is a designer, researcher, and educator whose practice is aimed at the design and research of architectural materials and surfaces.

BISÀ, DE MONCHAUX, MOLL
p. 201

Bisà associati is an architectural practice founded in 2012 by Sandro Bisà and Silvia Lupi. The studio distinguishes itself by its intensely imaginative yet logical approach to the built environment at every scale of intervention: completed projects range from individual buildings to urban infrastructure. Besides his professional activity, Sandro Bisà has been conducting a continued investigation on the greater Venetian Lagoon as an urban space by promoting and curating a number of structured investigations and academic programmes, among others with the European Commission, TUDelft, UC Berkeley, and, more recently, as visiting critic of the Venice programme of the School of Architecture at the University of Virginia.

Kathryn Moll and Nicholas de Monchaux collaborate as modem, combining their experience in software, architecture, urban design, and digital fabrication. Nicholas de Monchaux is Professor and Head of Architecture at MIT. He is the author of *Spacesuit: Fashioning Apollo* (MIT Press, 2011) and *Local Code: 3,659 Proposals about Data, Design, and the Nature of Cities* (Princeton Architectural Press, 2016). Kathryn Moll is an architect, with a decade of experience leading the design and construction of net-positive energy buildings and award-winning, adaptive-reuse projects in California. Together, they use architectural tools to transform objects, environments, and urban situations, strengthening and improving connections among buildings, cities, and ecologies.

Catalogtree is a multidisciplinary design studio based in Arnhem (NL). It was founded in 2001 by Daniel Gross and Joris Maltha who met at Werkplaats Typografie. Nina Bender was part of the studio from 2011 until 2020. The studio works continuously on commissioned and self-initiated projects. Experimental toolmaking, programming, typography, and the visualisation of quantitative data are part of their daily routine. Daniel Gross and Joris Maltha teach at ArtEZ University of the Arts in Arnhem (NL). The work of Catalogtree is in the collection of the Cooper Hewitt, Smithsonian Museum of Design, and the Museum für Gestaltung Zürich.

William Sherman is the Mario di Valmarana Professor of Architecture and Director of the Venice Program in the School of Architecture at the University of Virginia. As a practicing architect and educator, his work examines dynamic cultural and environmental processes in architectural design, ranging in scale from human physiology to global energy flows. His work explores the intersection of these processes with the cultural frameworks that inform the design of buildings and cities.

FREGOLENT - MALANOTTE RIZZOLI
p. 203

Laura Fregolent, architect, is Full Professor of Urban Planning at the University Iuav of Venice. Her research focuses on urban sprawl and interactions w\ith policy and planning tools; urban transformations and social dynamics; the relationship between processes of growth; and morphological and socioeconomic transformations. In the last several years, her research case study has concentrated on the city of Venice. http://www.iuav.it/AteneoI/docenti/pianificaz/docenti-st/Laura-Freg/index.htm

Paola Malanotte-Rizzoli joined the Massachusetts Institute of Technology in 1981. She is Professor of Physical

Oceanography and Climate. She is the author or co-author of 147 scientific refereed publications in international journals and of 14 refereed books. She has worked since the early 1970s on the problems affecting Venice and its lagoon.
https://eapsweb.mit.edu/people/rizzoli

LARSON, ADVINCULA – NIGERIA
p. 207

Kent Larson directs the City Science group at the MIT Media Lab. His research focuses on developing urban interventions that enable more entrepreneurial, liveable, and resilient communities. To that end, his projects include advanced simulation and augmented reality for urban design, transformable micro-housing for millennials, mobility-on-demand systems that create alternatives to private automobiles, and Urban Living Lab deployments via a connected network of international collaborators.
Gabriela Bilá Advincula is a graduate researcher, architect, multimedia designer, and artist. She explores the contemporary city as raw material, combining new media and tangible interfaces to reimagine our future. She has completed past exhibitions including *Teleport City* and *New Guide to Brasilia* in addition to a City Science collaboration at the Cooper Hewitt Museum.

Luis Alonso is a research scientist and the principal Investigator of the City Science Lab @Andorra. He has a PhD in architecture and coordinates several projects in the City Science Network. His research focus includes urban indicators, big data analysis, urban planning, architectural robotics, building design and construction, smart materials, energy simulation, building efficiency, sustainability, and other emerging technologies.

Maitane Iruretagoyena is a technical associate and researcher working on several projects on new technologies to create innovative places where people live and work. Iruretagoyena studied Building Engineering and Technical Architecture and has an MA in Sustainable Construction and Energy Efficiency at the University of the Basque Country in San Sebastian, Spain.

Guadalupe Babio is a graduate researcher with a high-level understanding of emerging technologies. Her research is focused on bridging the interface between urban planning, architecture, and new technologies to improve the quality of life in cities. Guadalupe graduated from the School of Architecture of Madrid, ETSAM, including student exchanges at Tongji University in China and Technion University in Israel.
Thomas Sanchez Lengeling is a research scientist, artist, and engineer interested in creating experiences that will allow people to change their perspective by blending perceptual experiences with digital information. His research is at the intersection between science, art, and technology. He works in mobility, artificial intelligence, wearable technology, immersive experiences, music, and educational outreach.

Holger Prang is a research associate in the City Science Lab at HafenCity University in Hamburg, Germany. He is part of the CityScope team involved in the development of data-driven negotiation themes and knowledge management to support participation and collaboration throughout disciplines. His PhD studies focus on semantic data analytics and knowledge-mapping in spatial and social phenomena.

Nicolas Ayoub is a product designer and strategist. Previously, he was a visiting researcher in the City Science group at MIT. Nicolas has an MA in Design and Technology from Harvard University. He works at the nexus of society, technology, and design and has worked with design studios and startups in Europe, Asia, and the United States.

Margaret Church is responsible for research coordination, events, and workshops at the MIT Media Lab. She also helps with communications and proposals for the City Science Network, a group of international cities striving to create more liveable and equitable communities. She co-organises the annual City Science Summit with collaborators from the home institutions.

ANGÉLIL, BLÜMKE, HEBEL, RODENHOUSE, KIFLE WOLDEYESSUS — ADDIS ABAB
p. 209

Marc Angélil
Marc Angélil is a practicing architect at agps architecture, with ateliers in Los Angeles and Zurich. He holds the 2021 Kenzo Tange Visiting Professorship at Harvard University and is professor emeritus at ETH Zurich, conducting research on socio-spatial developments of metropolitan regions worldwide. His most recent publication, *Mirroring Effects: Tales of Territory*, was written in collaboration with Cary Siress.

Katharina Blümke
Katharina Blümke is an architect and teaching assistant in Professor Dirk Hebel's Sustainable Construction programme at the Karlsruhe Institute of Technology, Germany. She is also working on an innovative roof extension, which will be made using a circular construction method and will contain neither adhesives nor other composite materials.

Dirk Hebel
Dirk E. Hebel is Professor of Sustainable Construction at the Karlsruhe Institute of Technology, Germany. He was the founding director of the Ethiopian Institute of Architecture, Building Construction and City Development in Addis Ababa, Ethiopia. His most recent publication, *Addis Ababa: A Manifesto on African Progress*, written in collaboration with Felix Heisel, Marta Wisniewska, and Sophie Nash, examines the deficits and potentials of accelerated urbanisation processes.
Jenny Rodenhouse
Jenny Rodenhouse is a media artist and designer. She is Assistant Professor of Interaction Design and Director of the Immersion Lab at the Art Center College of Design. Prior to this, she was a research fellow at Media Design Practices (Art Center) and at Microsoft Research conducting research on social media and community networks.

Bisrat Kifle Woldeyessus
Bisrat Kifle is an architect and researcher at the Ethiopian Institute of Architecture, Building Construction and City Development (EiABC) at Addis Ababa University. Currently, he is the Project Director of Meskel Square to City Hall Project in Addis Ababa. He has been teaching at ETH Zurich at the chair of Marc Angélil in 2008/09. In 2011, he co-initiated the *spaces* movie series and co-edited *Lessons of Informality* with Felix Heisel (2017).

TALESNIK, LEPIK — SÃO PAULO
p. 211

Daniel Talesnik is Assistant Professor of the History of Architecture and Curatorial Practice and Curator at the Architekturmuseum der TUM. He is a trained architect from the Universidad Católica de Chile and was awarded a PhD in History and Theory of Architecture by Columbia University. He specializes in modern and contemporary architecture and urbanism, with a particular focus on architectural pedagogy and relationships between architecture and political ideologies.

Andres Lepik is Professor of the History of Architecture and Curatorial Practice and Director of the Architekturmuseum der TUM. He has been a Curator at Neue Nationalgalerie, Berlin, and the Architecture and Design Department at The Museum of Modern Art, New York, presenting the exhibition *Small Scale, Big Change, New Architectures of Social Engagement* (2010).

Mariana Vilela is an architect from the University of São Paulo. As an intern in the City of São Paulo Building Department, she participated in the development of Unified Educational Centres (CEUs). She has collaborated with several architectural offices such as André Vainer, participating on the refurbishment of the Museum of Modern Art – MAM Bahia, and Herzog & de Meuron, developing Arena do Morro sports hall in Natal. She currently has her own practice and also collaborates with other architects.

Kathryn Gillmore is a graphic designer from Pontificia Universidad Católica de Chile and has an MA in new media from the ENSCI – Les Ateliers in Paris. With more than 15 years' experience, she leads her design studio in collaboration with other design teams, editors, and architects, developing projects mainly related to signage, editorial design, information design, and visual identity. She has worked as a teacher at several design schools and currently teaches at the Universidad San Sebastián, overseeing the architecture school's visual identity, including the art direction and design of *Materia Arquitectura* magazine.

Ciro Miguel is an architect, visual artist, and photographer. He is an architect from the University of São Paulo and holds an MA from Columbia. He has worked as an assistant professor in architectural design at ETH Zurich since 2013, collaborating with the departmental chair, Marc Angélil, since 2014. He has worked at Angelo Bucci/ SPBR arquitetos and Bernard Tschumi Architects in New York. He participated in various exhibitions in both Brazil and Europe, including the two last editions of the Venice International Architecture Biennale. He was one of the curators of the 12th International Architecture Biennale of São Paulo *Todo dia/Everyday.*

Pedro Kok engages with photography and videography of architecture and urban structures. He is an architect from the University of São Paulo and holds an MA in Fine Arts from the Hogeschool voor de Kunsten, Utrecht. He has collaborated with architects and curators on exhibitions and archives. His work has been exhibited at the Centre Georges Pompidou, MAXXI, La Biennale di Venezia, La Triennale di Milano, and MAM São Paulo.

Danilo Zamboni (daniloz) is an architect from the University of São Paulo and an illustrator. He has worked at Isay Weinfeld's Architect office since doing hand drawings for his presentations. He also does illustrations for newspapers and magazines and collaborates with artists and other architects.

Guilherme Pianca is an architect and MA graduate from the University of São Paulo. He has collaborated with several architecture offices in São Paulo and is the director of Pianca Arquitetura. Some of his published projects are the renovation of the ground floor of IAB-SP, in partnership with Gabriel Kogan; the exhibition design and drawings for the exhibition *Paulo Mendes da Rocha: Le Regard* (Geneva, 2018), in partnership with Sabiá Arquitetos.

Gabriel Sepe is an architect from the University of São Paulo. He has collaborated with several architecture offices in São Paulo. He also develops architectural research, and his work has been presented at the 12th International Biennial of Architecture in São Paulo (2019) and at the Le Corbusier International Congress, *50 Years Later,* in Valencia (2015).

AKSAMIJA, PHILIPPOU — AZRAQ CAMP
p. 213

Azra Akšamija, PhD is an artist and architectural historian, director of the MIT Future Heritage Lab and Associate Professor at MIT's Art, Culture, and Technology Program. Her work explores how social life is affected by cultural bias and by the deterioration and destruction of cultural infrastructures within the context of conflict, migration, and displacement.
Natalie Bellefleur is an architect and designer based in Cambridge, Massachusetts. She is Lead Design Consultant at the MIT Future Heritage Lab and designer at Perkins + Will, Boston. In addition, she is a cofounder of SomeThingsWeMade, which explores the future of craft through the marriage of machine automation and the hand made.
Stratton Coffman is an artist and architect based in Cambridge, Massachusetts. Coffman works with scores, props, performance sets, videos, and texts to examine overlooked spatial histories of the subject. They are half of the research initiative Proof of Concept with Isadora Dannin and Research Associate at the MIT Future Heritage Lab.
Jaya A. Eyzaguirre is an MIT alumna and former design researcher at MIT's Future Heritage Lab. Currently based in Chicago, her independent work focuses on endemic approaches to resiliency and how architecture and design is adapted and transformed by its users.
Lillian P. H. Kology is an artist based in Boston, Massachusetts. In addition to her studio practice, she is Assistant Professor of Sculpture at Montserrat College of Art in Beverly, Massachusetts, and Lead Artistic Researcher at the MIT Future Heritage Lab.
Catherine Lie is an interdisciplinary artist and designer from Indonesia. Her work critically engages time and temporality to unfold the everyday entanglement of the materials she investigates. She recently received her MArch from MIT with her thesis 'Sourdough Architecture' and has practiced in New York, Indonesia, Chile, Puerto Rico, Jordan, and Berlin.
Zeid Madi is an architect and urban researcher based in Amman, Jordan. His work focuses on patterns and networks of formal and informal settlements via critical cartography, GIS, and spatial data analysis. He directs the Cluster Labs in Amman, Jordan.
Raafat Majzoub positions his work

at an intersection between politics, intimacy, and futurecasting – exploring fiction as a tool for individual and collective agency and an arena to construct new worlds. He is the founding director of The Khan: The Arab Association for Prototyping Cultural Practices, and Lecturer in the Architecture and Design Department at the American University of Beirut.

Mary Mavrohanna is an architectural designer based in Cyprus with a degree in Interior Architecture. In addition to her first degree, she is currently studying Architecture at the University of Cyprus.

Dietmar Offenhuber, PhD, is a media artist and urban planner based in Cambridge, Massachusetts. He is Associate Professor at Northeastern University in the Departments of Art + Design and Public Policy, where he directs the graduate programme in Information Design and Visualisation. He currently holds visiting appointments at Princeton and Harvard University.

Melina Philipppou is an urban designer and researcher. Her work explores the agency of spatial practices in the context of forced displacement. She is the Program Director of the Future Heritage Lab at the School of Architecture and Planning at MIT and a Teaching Fellow at the University of Cyprus. She is the design research lead of work presented in the installation.

Calvin Zhong is a multidisciplinary designer based in Brooklyn, New York. His current work examines issues of media, representation, and technology in architecture. He is currently pursuing a MArch degree at MIT.

MEHROTRA, KUMAR BISWAS — INDIA
p. 215

Rahul Mehrotra is a practising architect, urban designer, and educator. He works in Mumbai and Boston and teaches at Harvard University's Graduate School of Design where he is professor of urban design and planning. His practice, RMA Architects (founded 1990), has executed a range of projects, mainly in India. Mehrotra has written, co-authored, and edited a vast repertoire of books on Mumbai, its urban history, historic buildings, public spaces, and planning processes.

Sourav Kumar Biswas is a landscape planner and spatial analyst with design and planning experience in Afghanistan, China, India, and the US. He is the Practice Area Lead for Urban and Landscape Planning at Geoadaptive in Boston. He has written books on urban informality, nature-based solutions, and co-authored a forthcoming book on India's emergent urbanisation patterns.

FREM, DOUEIHY — BEIRUT
p. 217

Sandra Frem is a lecturer at the American University of Beirut and Lebanese American University, and co-founder of platau | platform for architecture and urbanism. Working between academic research and practice, her work probes the overlays of architecture, landscape, and practices of the urban environment to open up speculations on their interdependence. She holds a SMArchS in Urbanism from MIT and a DES in Architecture from the Lebanese University.

Boulos Douaihy is an architect, geographer, activist, and lecturer at the Lebanese American University. He is the main founder of platau | platform for architecture and urbanism, a design research practice dedicated to expanding the agency of architecture at multiple scales, from material to territory. He holds a DES in Architecture from the Lebanese University and an MA in Environment et Aménagement du Territoire from the Université St Joseph.

Carla Aramouny is an architect and assistant professor at the American University of Beirut, Department of Architecture and Design, where she is founder and director of ArD TechLab, a digital fabrication unit. Her work and research reflect on the intersections of architecture and the expanded environment. She holds a MArch from the University of Pennsylvania, and a BArch from the Lebanese American University.

Nicolas Fayad is a Beirut-based architect who completed his BArch at the American University of Beirut before earning a MArch with distinction from the Harvard University Graduate School of Design. He is a founding partner at East Architecture Studio, a collective practice committed to architectural design and experimental research. Fayad is a senior lecturer at the American University of Beirut and a visiting lecturer at MIT.

Rana Haddad, an AA graduate, acquired the title of activist as she practiced architecture and design in post-war Beirut. Starting 1997, her research workshop was set up with the aim of questioning the ability of objects and places to become means of political expression in Beirut. In 2013, she co-founded 200Grs. She is currently an assistant professor at the American University of Beirut where she founded BePublic Lab.

EL DAHDAH, METCALF, HEYMAN, BURGI — RIO DE JANEIRO
p. 219

Farès el-Dahdah is Professor of Humanities and Director of the Humanities Research Center at Rice University. El-Dahdah's research focuses on developing geodatabases that describe cities and sites over time, as they existed and as they have come to be imagined, and with Alida Metcalf and Axis Maps he has developed the cartographic platform *imagineRio*.

Alida C. Metcalf is Harris Masterson Jr Professor of History at Rice University in Houston, Texas. Metcalf is the author of *The Return of Hans Staden: A Go-between in the Atlantic World* (2012) with Eve M. Duffy and *Mapping an Atlantic World circa 1500* (2020). With Farès el-Dahdah and Axis Maps, she has developed the cartographic platform *imagineRio*.

David Heyman is an interactive cartographer and managing director of Axis Maps, a cartographic design studio specialising in bringing the traditions of cartography to interactive media. With partners Andy Woodruff and Ben Sheesley, Axis Maps designs and builds interactive maps and data visualisations that communicate geographic phenomena for clients in diverse fields ranging from spatial history to healthcare to the environment.

Sergio Burgi heads the photography department of the Moreira Salles Institute in Rio de Janeiro, Brazil's leading institution dedicated to the conservation and preservation of photographic collections. Burgi recently curated the exhibition *Marc Ferrez – Território e Imagem* (2019).

RAMKU — PRISHTINA
p. 221

Bekim Ramku, architect and urbanist, is the founding director of the Kosovo Architecture Foundation (est. 2012) and the Kosovo Architecture Festival; he manages his Prishtina-based practice OUD+Architects. Ramku served as a technical reviewer and coordinator to the Aga Khan Award for Architecture, 2016 and 2019 cycles. He was educated at the University of Prishtina, the AA School of Architecture, and MIT.

Nol Binakaj, architect, serves as the deputy director of the Kosovo Architecture Foundation, the Kosovo Architecture Festival, CHwB-Kosovo; he is also a practising architect with OUD+Architects. He was educated at the University of Prishtina and MIT.

MERVE BEDIR, SAMPSON WONG, HONG KONG
p. 223

Merve Bedir and Sampson Wong are Hong Kong-based practitioners whose interests intersect at urbanism. Merve Bedir is an architect, focusing on design as a research-based, collective, trans-scalar, and ultra-disciplinary act. She is an adjunct assistant professor at Hong Kong University's Faculty of Architecture. Sampson Wong is an academic, artist, and independent curator working on the topics of contemporary urbanism, space and geography, art and the public, cultural resistance and hope. He is responsible for the upkeep and maintenance of the Umbrella Movement Visual Archive, and he is a member of the Add Oil Team.

AKAWI, EBER, KALLIPOLITI, KOGOD, VANABLE — NEW YORK
p. 225

Nora Akawi is Assistant Professor of Architecture at The Cooper Union. Previously, Nora taught at Columbia University, where she was Director of Studio-X Amman. She coedited *Architecture and Representation: The Arab City* (2016). Selected exhibitions include *Friday Sermon* (2018 Architecture Biennale in Venice), and *This Land's Unknown* (Biennale d'Architecture d'Orléans 2019).

Hayley Eber is an architect and educator. She is currently Assistant Dean at The Cooper Union and the Principal of Studio Eber, an award-winning New York-based practice for architecture and design. She has taught at Princeton University and Columbia University GSAPP, and her work has been published in *Domus*, *Praxis*, *DETAIL*, and *Pidgin*, amongst others.

Lydia Kallipoliti, PhD, is an architect, engineer, theorist, curator, and educator with degrees from Princeton University and MIT. She is currently Assistant Professor at The Cooper Union. Previously, she has taught at Rensselaer Polytechnic Institute where she directed the MS Program, Syracuse University, and Columbia University. Her work has been exhibited internationally, including at the Oslo Triennale, the London Design Museum, the Disseny Hub Barcelona, the Istanbul Biennial, the Shenzen Biennale, and the Storefront for Art and Architecture. She is the author of the awarded book *The Architecture of Closed Worlds* (Lars Muller, 2018).

Lauren Kogod is an architect and architectural historian with essays published in *Assemblage*, *A+U*, *Quaderns*, *AD Monograph: Enric Miralles*, *Harvard Design Magazine*, *Grey Room*, and *Architecture and Capitalism: 1845 to the Present* (edited by Peggy Deamer, Routledge, 2014). She has taught at The Cooper Union, Yale University, and Barnard/Columbia College, among other schools.

Ife Vanable is an architect, theorist, and historian who holds degrees in architecture from Cornell and Princeton. Ife is founder and leader of i/van/able, Visiting Professor at the Irwin S. Chanin School of Architecture of The Cooper Union, and a PhD candidate in architectural history and theory at Columbia University GSAPP.

HAN TUMERTEKIN
p. 227

Han Tümertekin is a practicing architect based in Istanbul and Strasbourg, exploring the relationship between daily life and design in his practice and lectures. He is the recipient of many awards including an Aga Khan Award.

Ayfer Bartu Candan is an Associate Professor of Social Anthropology in the Sociology Department at Bogazici University, Istanbul. Her research interests include urban inequality and segregation, political ecology, and social and cultural theory.

Mert Kaya is a filmmaker and video artist based in Istanbul. Academically trained in social sciences, he focuses on memory, urban questions, and social movements in his works. He has produced films in Turkey and Brazil.

Tuna Ortaylı Kazıcı is a project manager based in Istanbul. She has worked in various international culture and arts projects, including artist residencies and the Turkish pavilion at La Biennale di Venezia.

Sena Özfiliz is an architect, lecturer, and visual documenter based in Istanbul. His process-based practice focuses mainly on daily routines of architectural spaces, urban transformation, and sports landscapes.

Hayriye Sözen is a practicing architect, lecturer, and founder of HS Architects and is based in Istanbul. She works on both historical and contemporary projects. Her latest works have been nominated for various awards.

Hakan Tüzün Şengün has a PhD in architecture, is a lecturer and studio instructor at the ITU Faculty of Architecture and a cofounder of PARCH, an architecture and landscape design practice based in Istanbul.

Ahmet Topbaş is a structural engineer who studied in Turkey and the USA, with 25 years of experience in acclaimed projects. Founder of ATTEC, he is a creative and RnD-oriented designer of special structures and a lecturer at prestigious universities.

Zeynep Tümertekin is an architect and lecturer who specialises in exhibition design. She studied in London CSM and is based in Istanbul. She is the cofounder of architecture and design office Studio Mada.

ELEMENTAL
p. 229

ELEMENTAL is a Do Tank founded in 2001, led by Pritzker Prize 2016 Alejandro Aravena and partners Gonzalo Arteaga, Juan Cerda, Victor Oddó, and Diego Torres. ELEMENTAL's work stands out for engaging in projects that range from housing to public space, from objects to buildings, covering a wide spectrum of interests. Its unbiased approach to a given question enables the office to enter fields it has not explored before, generating an original contribution to people's quality of life.

VOGT LANDSCAPE ARCHITECTS
p. 231

Günther Vogt epitomises the vigorous process of exchange between practice, theory, and other disciplines, with the Case Studio functioning as an interface between them. Over the years, various collaborative partnerships have developed with artists and specialists from other disciplines, and he has earned the Günther Vogt's Chair at ETH Zurich. His awards include the Prix Meret Oppenheim and an honorary doctorate from the University of Liechtenstein.

Violeta Burckhardt studied architecture at UNAM in Mexico City and Urban Design at TU Berlin and Tongji University in Shanghai. She currently works for Vogt Landscape Architects as Project Manager in Case Studio, where she designs projects geared towards research and practice. She has curated and developed several exhibitions as a member of Vogt Landscape, such as *Environment[al]* in SCI Arc and *First the Forests* in Harvard GSD.

Simon Kroll studied landscape architecture at the University of Hanover from 2005 to 2010. He has been part of Vogt Landscape Architects in Zurich since October 2010. Kroll has worked as project manager since 2012 and has a wide range of professional experience and a deep understanding of complex performance requirements. As Head of the Case Studio VOGT, he has been part of the management team since 2017.

WOJR
p. 233

WOJR is an organisation of designers based in Cambridge, Massachusetts. We consider architecture to be a form of cultural production. Our work extends across the globe and engages the realms of art, architecture, and urbanism.

IGNEOUS TECTONICS
p. 235

Igneous Tectonics is a research practice that addresses pressing cultural conflicts and environmental opportunities by engaging local materials through advanced technology, where stone, wood, glass, or metal but also climate, history, geology, scientific research, and indigenous knowledge are among the materials of the architectural project.

Cristina Parreño Alonso is an architect, designer, and educator at the Massachusetts Institute of Technology where her research on Transtectonics explores cultural, contextual, and environmental implications of expanded temporal sensibilities in architectural material practice. Her *tectonic translations* – material transfers across mediums, temporal scales, the human, and the more-than-human – embody narratives that are told in the form of essays, exhibitions, and through architectural projects and installations.

Sergio Araya Goldberg, is an architect, researcher, and educator at the University Adolfo Ibañez (UAI) where he is the director of the design lab. He has a doctorate in Architecture and Computation from MIT, where he is currently visiting scientist. He develops his research on architecture, digital fabrication, and materials at the Center for Architecture and Materials of the UAI. He has been lecturer at the Faculty of Architecture, Design, and Urban Studies of the Pontifical Catholic University and professor at the Faculty of Architecture, Art, and Design of the Diego Portales University.

NADAAA
p. 237

For his contributions to architecture as an art, Nader Tehrani is the recipient of the 2020 Arnold W. Brunner Memorial Prize from the American Academy of Arts and Letters, to which he was also elected as a member in 2021, the highest form of recognition of artistic merit in the United States. Nader Tehrani is Founding Principal of NADAAA, a practice dedicated to the advancement of design innovation, interdisciplinary collaboration, and an intensive dialogue with the construction industry. Tehrani is also Dean of the Irwin S. Chanin School of Architecture at The Cooper Union. His work has been recognised with notable international awards in architecture.

Arthur Chang, AIA, is a Principal of NADAAA and head of NADLAB, the practice's material research arm. Chang has led internationally recognised projects including the Melbourne School of Design, Rhode Island School of Design's North Hall, and the Beaver Country Day School's Research + Design Center.

SAHEL ALHIARY ARCHITECTS
p. 239

Sahel Alhiyari is the owner and principal architect at Sahel Alhiyari Architects. A multidisciplinary design studio established in 1998 in Amman, Jordan.
www.sahelalhiyari.com

VUSLAT FOUNDATION
p. 241

Vuslat Foundation is a global initiative established in 2020 with the intent of creating a movement that will make generous listening to oneself, to others and to nature the new norm of human connectedness. Founded by Vuslat Doğan Sabancı, the foundation denotes not her name but honours the perennial concept of *vuslat*, which refers to both the journey and the blissful experience of reuniting with ourselves and with others.
Established in Switzerland with offices in Istanbul and London, Vuslat Foundation works with artists, storytellers, changemakers, and thought leaders. By implementing global programmes reaching diverse constituencies, Vuslat Foundation is committed to placing generous listening at the very core of human connection by 2030, in parallel with the UN SDGs. Through partnerships with academia, the Foundation develops knowledge, research, methodologies, and tools on generous listening; cultivates generous listening in the ecosystems of youth and children; partners with civil society to offer the practices of generous listening in their work; and engages with artists and storytellers to inspire and build awareness on generous listening.

Across Borders

DAN MAJKA & GARY SETZER
p. 259

Dan Majka works at the crossroads of conservation science, data visualisation, and technology for the global environmental non-profit The Nature Conservancy. Trained as a landscape ecologist, Majka has built tools for designing wildlife corridors, measuring conservation return on investment, and calculating marine ecosystem benefits. He is currently building tools to map natural climate solutions for mitigating climate change.

Gary Setzer's transdisciplinary practice probes the language/meaning divide while incorporating performance art, video art, electronic music, installation, sculpture, and photography. Setzer has toured his performance art extensively, and his works have been included in solo and group exhibitions internationally. He currently lives and works in Tucson, Arizona, where he is a professor of Art at the University of Arizona.

AEROCENE FOUNDATION
initiated by TOMÁS SARACENO
p. 261

The Aerocene Foundation (est. 2015), founded by artist Tomás Saraceno, is a non-profit organisation with the Aerocene community at its core. Devoted to community building, scientific research, artistic experience, and education, Aerocene is active in 126 cities across 43 different countries. Collaborators and supporters include EAPS, CAST at MIT, CNES, FabCity, CCK Argentina, Public Lab, the Goethe Institute, and many more.
For more info visit aerocene.org or download the Aerocene app.

GFA
p. 263

Urtzi Grau is an architect, director of the Master of Architecture and Master of Research at the University of Technology Sydney (UTS) and founding partner of the office GFA and Fake Industries.

Guillermo Fernández-Abascal is an architect, lecturer at UTS, and founding partner of the offices GFA and GFA2. Based in Sydney, Australia, and Santander, Spain, his recent work destabilises the dichotomy of research vs buildings and includes diagrams, stories, exhibitions, films, prototypes, housing, and public buildings across the globe.

MONSOON ASSEMBLAGES and OFFICE OF EXPERIMENTS
p. 265

Monsoon Assemblages is a research project funded by the European Research Council (ERC) under the European Union's Horizon 2020 research and innovation programme (Grant Agreement No. 679873).

Lindsay Bremner is an architect and scholar and principal investigator of the research project Monsoon Assemblages at the University of Westminster in London.

Beth Cullen is an anthropologist and postdoctoral research fellow with Monsoon Assemblages. Her work explores more-than-human worlds using ethnographic and participatory visual and spatial research methods.

John Cook is an architect and research associate of Monsoon Assemblages. He is also co-tutor of the MArch design studio DS18, at the University of Westminster, London.

Office of Experiments is an independent research network founded by artist Neal White to support interdisciplinary research projects. Projects, installations, and experiments are developed across disciplines, through fieldwork, acting on new bodies of knowledge from a variety of cultural social, technological, institutional, and environmental contexts.

Neal White is an artist, researcher, and founder of Office of Experiments.

Eric Kearney has a qualification in electronic engineering from Limerick Regional Technology College. He develops advanced custom-made electronic systems with artists and designers. He has been working with artist Neal White since 1996.

Bill Thompson is a sound artist and composer who has worked primarily with live electronics, sound installation, and performance for the past twenty years. He has been working with Office of Experiment since 2019.

JOHN PALMESINO AND ANN-SOFI RÖNNSKOG
p. 267

Territorial Agency is an independent organisation established by architects and urbanists John Palmesino and Ann-Sofi Rönnskog. Territorial Agency combines contemporary architecture, art, spatial analysis, remote sensing, advocacy, and action to promote comprehensive territorial transformations. Their work focuses on the integration of science, architecture, and art in the challenges posed by climate change. www.territorialagency.com

PINAR YOLDAS
p. 269

Pinar Yoldas is an infradisciplinary architect/artist/researcher. Her work develops within biological sciences through architectural installations, kinetic sculpture, sound, video, and drawing with a focus on eco-nihilism, the Anthropocene, and feminist technoscience. Dr Yoldas has exhibited her work internationally and is a Guggenheim fellow, a Macdowell fellow, and FEAT award recipient. She holds a BArch, MA, MS from top institutions in Turkey, an MFA from UCLA, and a PhD from Duke University in USA.

Merve Akdoğan is an interdisciplinary designer and architect who works in the field of architectural design, representation, computational design, and fabrication. As a student, she participated in several international workshops and competitions. Since her graduation in 2018, she has worked on several professional architectural projects. Merve is currently a speculative designer and the studio manager in Yoldas Studio Lab. When away from her desk, she runs a private tattoo practice.

Ege Doğan is an artist and a graduate student currently enrolled in the M. Arch programme, Middle East Technical University. His main areas of interest are architectural representation and computational design. His contribution to *Hollow Ocean* is in the area of design and fabrication through algorithmic modelling tools. He is also part of the *Hollow Ocean* VR team. Offscreen, Doğan likes oil painting and multimedia work.

Uzay Doğan is an artist and studies architecture. He is currently enrolled in the M. Arch programme, Middle East Technical University, where he also received his BA degree in Architecture. His main interests are architectural/spatial representation, architectural archives, and computational design. Besides architecture, he is passionate about painting and sculpture.

We would also like to thank Nan Renner and the Department of Visual Arts UCSD.

GIUDITTA VENDRAME
p. 271

Giuditta Vendrame is an Italian artist, designer, and researcher based in the Netherlands. She works at the intersections between design, art practice, and legal systems, focusing on personhood, space, and mobility.

SELF-ASSEMBLY LAB
p. 273

Schendy Kernizan is a Haitian-American Architectural Designer with a professional degree in Architecture from Philadelphia University. Schendy is currently a Research Scientist and Director at the Self-Assembly Lab in the Department of Architecture, MIT. Jared Laucks is a trained designer and fabrication specialist. He is currently a Research Scientist and Director at the Self-Assembly Lab in the Department of Architecture, MIT.

Skylar Tibbits is the founder of the Self-Assembly Lab at the MIT, and Associate Professor of Design Research in the Department of Architecture.

SOMATIC COLLABORATIVE
p. 275

Somatic Collaborative is a NYC based design practice, which focuses on speculative approaches to architecture, landscape, and urbanism. Somatic uses the architectural commission, design competitions, and diverse forms of applied research as conduits that facilitate an inventive construction of space.

Felipe Correa is a founder and managing partner of Somatic Collaborative. Through Somatic Collaborative, Correa has directed a wide range of applied research and design projects across multiple contexts in the Americas, Asia, and Europe.

Anthony Acciavatti is a founding partner of Somatic Collaborative. Trained as an architect, historian, and geographer, Acciavatti has worked in North America, Asia, and Europe.

Devin Dobrowolski is Director of Applied Research Projects at Somatic. He is a trained architect and landscape architect, and his work encompasses cartographic research, material supply chains, and advanced fabrication techniques.

ACASA GRINGO CARDIA DESIGN
p. 277

Takumã Kuikuro is an internationally recognised filmmaker and president of AIKAX. He grew up and lives in the Ipatse village in the Upper Xingu Indigenous Territory in Mato Grosso State, Brazil.

AIKAX (Upper Xingu Kuikuro People Indigenous Association) was founded in 2002 to support the documentation and preservation of the cultural heritage of the peoples of the Xingu.

Gringo Cardia is a designer, architect, scenographer, and museum and exhibition curator. He is the founder of the social youth project Spectaculu School of Art and Technology in Rio.

ACASAGRINGOCARDIA Design Studio is a team of architects, scenographers, musicians, editors, animators, designers, and iconographic researchers based in Rio de Janeiro and led by Gringo Cardia and his sister Gringa Cardia.

Paul Heritage is Professor of Drama and Performance at Queen Mary University of London. For three decades he has been creating award-winning cultural projects addressing human rights issues in Brazil and the UK.

People's Palace Projects is an East London-based independent arts charity that advances the practice and understanding of art for social justice and a subsidiary of Queen Mary University of London.

LA MINGA
p. 279

Pablo Escudero is an Ecuadorian architect, urbanist, and farmer from Angochahua, traditional territories of the Kechwa People. He is founder of La Minga, a collective action group focused on territorial conflicts in Ecuador.

Alejandra Pinto, screen writer, architect, and actor, works as a cultural promoter for artistic endeavours for the elimination of violence against women.

Patricia Yallico, filmmaker, screen writer, producer, and activist. Founder of ACAPANA Cine, a collective that works for the empowerment and dissemination of audiovisual work from Indigenous, Afro-Ecuadorian, and Montubios People from Ecuador.

Ghazal Jafari is a designer of Persian and Azeri descent and Assistant Professor of Landscape Architecture at the University of Virginia, traditional lands of the Monacan Nation.

Hernán Bianchi-Benguria is a planner, architect, and PhD candidate in Geography at the University of Toronto, traditional lands of the Huron-Wendat, the Seneca, and the Mississaugas of the Credit River, covered by Treaty 13.

Tiffany Kaewen Dang is a landscape architect and current PhD candidate in Geography at the University of Cambridge, UK, originally from Edmonton, Treaty 6 territory on the traditional lands and meeting place of the Cree, Blackfeet, Métis, Nakoda Sioux, Haudenosaunee, Dene, Anishnaabe, Inuit, and other nations.

Alexander Arroyo is an environmental designer and current PhD candidate in Geography at the University of California, Berkeley, territory of Huichin, the ancestral and unceded land of the Chochenyo Ohlone People.

Pierre Bélanger is a settler designer, originally from Montréal and Ottawa, now in Boston, lands of the Massachusett Peoples, traditional territory of the Wampanoag and Nipmuc Nations (Treaty of Casco 1698–03, Treaty of Portsmouth 1713, Treaty of Boston 1725)

Together, they are founding board members of OPEN SYSTEMS/Landscape Infrastructure Lab™, an organising sponsor of the Ecuadorian exhibition. Operating under the moniker and portmanteau OPSYS®, they are a design-based non-profit research organization of builders, educators, and farmers, dedicated to opening systemic knowledge related to complex socioecological challenges and geopolitical conflicts – at the intersection of land, water, environmental justice, spatial inequality, climate change, community self-determination, and sovereignty. Focused on transformative change, the main activities of the organization involve counter-cartography and retroactive mapping, independent publications, pedagogical media, open access initiatives, public exhibitions, and demonstration projects.

ATELIER MARKO BRAJOVIC
p. 281

Atelier Marko Brajovic is an international, award-winning, transdisciplinary, creative team based in São Paulo, Brazil. Composed of architects, designers, and biologists, this professional practice develops projects in architecture, exhibitions, education, and creative direction.

UNLESS
p. 283

Giulia Foscari is an architect, researcher, and writer practising in Europe, Asia, and the Americas. She is the founder of UNA, an architecture studio focused on cultural projects, and founder of its alter-ego UNLESS, a not-for-profit agency for change devoted to interdisciplinary research on extreme environments.
Giulia has taught at Hong Kong University and at the Architectural Association, where she ran a Diploma Unit and founded the Polar Lab. She is the author of *Elements of Venice* and editor of *Antarctic Resolution* (Lars Müller Publishers). Giulia has contributed to multiple editions of the Venice Architecture Biennale.

LATERAL OFFICE and ARCTIC DESIGN GROUP
p. 285

Leena Cho is Assistant Professor in Landscape Architecture at the University of Virginia and a founding director of Arctic Design Group and design practice Kutonotuk. Her research focuses on material agencies of the arctic environment in landscape design and field-based scientific practices that produce landscapes in the arctic. She is co-author of *Mediating Environments* (AR+D, 2019).

Matthew Jull is Associate Professor in Architecture at the University of Virginia and a founding director of Arctic Design Group and design practice Kutonotuk. A former theoretical geophysicist and architect at OMA, Rotterdam, Jull's research explores the potentials of architecture and urban design within the frame of extreme climates. He is co-author of *Mediating Environments* (AR+D, 2019).

Lola Sheppard is Professor at the University of Waterloo and a founding partner of Lateral Office. Her work explores new roles for architecture and infrastructure in rural and remote communities. Sheppard has run design studios in Nunavut, Northwest Territories, and Nunavik, Canada, and in Greenland. She is co-author of *Many Norths: Spatial Practice in a Polar Territory* (Actar, 2017).

Mason White is Professor at the University of Toronto and a founding partner of Lateral Office. His work explores the intersection of architecture, geography, and the environment. White has worked extensively with Indigenous partners across Canada, exploring architecture's capacity for cultural empowerment. He is co-author of *Many Norths: Spatial Practice in a Polar Territory* (Actar, 2017).

DOGMA
p. 289

Dogma was founded in 2002 by Pier Vittorio Aureli and Martino Tattara and is based in Brussels. In the last few years, Dogma has been working on a research-by-design trajectory that focuses on domestic space and its potential for transformation.

RURAL URBAN FRAMEWORK
p. 291

Rural Urban Framework (RUF) is the research and design collaborative between Joshua Bolchover and John Lin. The objective of their work is to engage in the process of rural-to-urban transformation of China and Mongolia through built projects, research, exhibitions, and writing. RUF operates as a non-for-profit and collaborates with NGOs, development agencies, local government bureaux, and charities. The work is conducted within the Faculty of Architecture at The University of Hong Kong.

STUDIO PAOLA VIGANÒ
p. 293

Paola Viganò, professor in Urbanism and Urban Design at EPFL and IUAV, founded Studio with Bernardo Secchi in 1990 and StudioPaolaViganò in 2015. Her awards include the Grand Prix de l'Urbanisme (2013), the Flemish Award for Architecture (2017), and the Golden Medal of Architecture. She has exhibited at the Milan Triennale (2018), Doctor Honoris Causa, Université Catholique de Louvain, and in the frame of *Utopias for our Times*, 2016.

PAULA NASCIMENTO
p. 295

Paula Nascimento is an architect and curator based in Luanda. Her work is at intersection of architecture, contemporary art, and geopolitics.

Jaime Mesquita is an architect, designer, and educator, principal of Oba Architects. His interests range from the study of informality in the African cities to the use of technology and low-cost architecture.

Iris Buchholz Chocolate is an artist and designer who lives and works in Luanda. Much of her work dissects and brings into question notions of perception and memory, between the canon of history and collective memory archive.

Kiluanji Kia Henda is a conceptual artist who works with photography, film, performance, and sculpture. Using humour and irony, he interferes on subjects such as identity, politics, perceptions of post-coloniality, and modernism in Africa.

Ngoi Salucombo is a freelance photographer, art director, and cultural producer who lives between Luanda and Cape Town. Over the last ten years he has been capturing the urban transformations of cities as diverse as Namibe, Paris, Cape Town, and Luanda.

SMOUT ALLEN
p. 297

Laura Allen is Professor of Architecture and Augmented Landscapes at the Bartlett School, UCL, a director of the Landscape Architecture program, and Director of Smout Allen Design Research Practice (smoutallen.com).

Mark Smout is Professor of Architecture and Landscape Futures at the Bartlett School, UCL, a director of the Landscape Architecture program and Director of Smout Allen Design Research Practice (smoutallen.com).

Geoff Manaugh is a Los Angeles-based freelance writer, curator, educator, and author of the long-running website BLDGBLOG (bldgblog.com), exploring architectural conjecture, urban speculation, and landscape futures.

SPORT PLATFORM
p. 299

Christoph Lechner (b. 1966, Vienna, Austria) studied architecture at the Academy of Fine Arts in Vienna and Urban Design at the GSD, Harvard University. Having established an architectural studio in Vienna, he focuses on subsidised housing, condominiums, nursing homes, sport structures, urban design, and design. He has taught at Technical University Vienna, Technical University Graz, GSD, and OTH Regensburg. He has published essays on architecture and urban design.

Dr Kevin Moore is the Deputy Director of Curatorial Affairs, Qatar Olympic and Sports Museum. He has had a highly successful 35-year career in museums and academia. Moore established the National Football Museum for England in 2001 and was its CEO for 20 years. Under his leadership the National Football Museum attracted over 500,000 visitors a year. He has an international professional and academic reputation in museum studies, sports history, and sports museums and heritage. He has published extensively on aspects of museums, sport, and culture in academic and professional journals. Moore has also advised sports museums around the world.

Trevor Smith is owner and Managing Director of SPORTSMITH, a sport and physical activity consultancy that operates internationally in support of policy, programme, and processes to enable populations to embrace sport and physical activity. Prior to forming SPORTSMITH, Smith held a number of senior roles within the sport and leisure sectors, including local authorities, national UK charities, and an international elite performance centre. His field of experience covers community sport, health promotion, physical education development, active landscape design, coaching development, heritage, and culture. His clients and partners have included national governments and NGOs, Olympic legacy programmes, local education authorities, professional football associations and clubs, community sport and physical activity agencies, and individual schools and clubs.

FOUNDATION FOR ACHIEVING SEAMLESS TERRITORY (FAST)
p. 305

Yael Berda is an Israeli lawyer and holds a PhD from the Department of Sociology at Princeton University. Born in New York City and raised in West Jerusalem, Yael has been highly engaged in social justice activism and politics in Israel. She is an Academy Scholar at the Harvard Academy for International and Area Studies, the Weatherhead Center for International Affairs in Cambridge, MA.

Sandra Kassenaar is an independent graphic designer, living and working in Amsterdam. She graduated with an MA from the Werkplaats Typografie, Arnhem, in 2007 and since then has worked with artists, curators, writers, and architects, focusing mainly on printed matter. Her work has won a European Design Award, Best Book (Best Verzorgde Boeken), and the DAM Architectural Book Award.

Amir Qudaih is a farmer from Khuzza, who moved to Boston from the Gaza Strip, Palestine, in 2016. He is currently pursuing his BA in Engineering at UMass-Lowell. In 2014, he founded a non-profit organisation called Lifeline to Gaza. Before moving to the US, he worked with CNN and France2 as a local producer and translator. He gave talks about his journey from Gaza to Boston to pursue his education, which took him almost three years. Leaving Gaza was a lengthy, challenging, and painful journey that involved him jumping a 30-foot wall between the West Bank and Jerusalem to make it to an interview at the US embassy.

Malkit Shoshan is the founding director of the Foundation for Achieving Seamless Territory (FAST), an Amsterdam- and New York-based think-tank that develops projects and campaigns at the intersection of architecture, urban planning, and human rights. She is a researcher, award-winning author, designer, and Area Head of Art, Design, and the Public Domain MDes at Harvard GSD. Her socially and politically engaged work has been published and exhibited internationally.

AAU ANASTAS
p. 307

Born into a family of architects in Bethlehem, Elias and Yousef Anastas studied architecture in Paris and worked there until winning a competition to build a music conservatory in their hometown. After returning to Palestine in 2010, they expanded into furniture design and research projects celebrating local artisanal skills. They are partners at AAU ANASTAS and the founders of Local Industries, a community of bold artisans and designers dedicated to industrial furniture-making.

VIVIANA D'AURIA
p. 309

Viviana d'Auria is Associate Professor at the International Centre of Urbanisms, Department of Architecture, KU Leuven. Her research explores how the epistemological contribution of development aid to the discipline of urbanism has unfolded trans-locally. This comprises how cities are produced through migration and displacement as part of a more general concern with socio-ecological challenges to inclusion.

Claire Bosmans is a doctoral researcher at the OSA research group, International Centre of Urbanisms, Department of Architecture, KU Leuven. Her research focuses on residents' lived experience in post-war social housing estates in Brussels, experimentally combining architecture, urbanism, and ethnography through drawing and design. She is also an active member of the Action-Research Collective for Hospitality (ARCH).

Khalda Imad Mubarak El Jack is a doctoral researcher at the OSA research group, International Centre of Urbanisms, Department of Architecture, KU Leuven. Her research investigates active citizenship in Khartoum, using mapping as a main tool of inquiry. It further aims to reframe urban displacement by foregrounding lived experiences as entangled with the geographies of place and its transformations over time.

DECOLONIZING ARCHITECTURE ART RESIDENCY
p. 315

DAAR (Decolonizing Architecture Art Research) is an architectural collective that combines conceptual speculations and pragmatic spatial interventions, discourse, and collective learning. The artistic research of Sandi Hilal and Alessandro Petti is situated between politics, architecture, art, and pedagogy.
Luca Capuano is an artist and professional photographer who specialises in architectural photography.

WISSAM CHAAYA
p. 317

Wissam Chaaya is an architect, urban planner, and photographer. He holds a MArch and an MA in urban planning from the Fine Arts Institute at the Lebanese University. As well as participating in multiple workshops in urban planning, he has long-term experience in designing and executing diverse projects. He is also a practising architectural and street photographer.

FORENSIC OCEANOGRAPHY
p. 319

Charles Heller is a researcher and filmmaker whose work has long been focused on the politics of migration. In 2015, he completed a PhD in Research Architecture at Goldsmiths, University of London. He is currently research fellow at the Graduate Institute in Geneva.
Lorenzo Pezzani is an architect and researcher. In 2015, he completed a PhD in Research Architecture at Goldsmiths, University of London, where he is currently Lecturer and leads the MA studio in Forensic Architecture. His work deals with the spatial politics and visual cultures of migration, with a particular focus on the geography of the ocean.

Working together since 2011, Charles Heller and Lorenzo Pezzani co-founded the Forensic Oceanography project, which critically investigates the militarised border regime and the politics of migration in the Mediterranean. Their collaborative work has generated human rights reports, academic articles, and internationally exhibited videos.

CHAIR OF GÜNTHER VOGT ETH ZÜRICH
p. 327

Günther Vogt is owner and head of VOGT Landscape Architects with offices in Zürich, Berlin, London, and Paris. He epitomises the vigorous process of exchange between practice, theory, and other disciplines, with the Case Studio functioning as an interface among them. Over the years, various collaborative partnerships have developed with artists and specialists from other disciplines as well as with Günther Vogt's Chairmanship position at the ETH Zurich.

Amalia Bonsack studied architecture at the Swiss Federal Institute of Technology in Lausanne (EPFL) and in Zurich (ETH), from which she graduated in 2017. Since 2018, she has worked as a scientific assistant at the Chair of Professor Günther Vogt at the ETH Zurich. She is involved in research and teaching, with a focus on current transformation processes in European metropolitan landscapes.
Thomas Kissling studied architecture at the Swiss Federal Institute of Technology (ETH) Zurich. He has been working as a research associate since 2010 at the Chair of Professor Günther Vogt at the ETH Zurich, focusing on transformation processes in the Alpine landscape. Thomas Kissling is co-editor of *Landscape as a Cabinet of Curiosities* (2015) and *Mutation and Morphosis* (2020).

Andreas Klein studied architecture at the Swiss Federal Institute of Technology (ETH) Zurich, University of Stuttgart, and FADU Buenos Aires. After graduating in 2013, he worked in various architectural firms and travelled extensively. In 2016 he started as a research and teaching assistant at the Chair of Professor Günther Vogt at the ETH Zurich. In addition, he works on architectural projects at various scales and mainly in an Alpine context.

Max Leiß studied visual arts (sculpture) at AdBK Karlsruhe and ENSBA Paris and has received numerous awards for his international exhibition activities, such as the *junger westen* Art Prize 2017. Since 2016, he has been developing and teaching the annual Summer School Experimental Landscape Furniture at the Chair of Professor Günther Vogt at the ETH Zurich. He is preparing a publication on outdoor seating and promenadology.

Roland Charles Shaw read Sanskrit at Oxford and Munich (LMU) universities. In 2014 he completed a degree in architecture at the Architectural Association in London (AA Dipl). He has been an academic assistant at the Chair of Professor Günther Vogt at the ETH Zurich since 2015, where he is responsible for the elective course, Urban Food.

Sarem Sunderland studied architecture at the Swiss Federal Institute of Technology in Lausanne (EPFL) and landscape architecture at the Delft University of Technology (TU Delft), where he graduated *cum laude* in 2016. After practicing as a landscape architect in firms in Zurich and Winterthur, he joined the Chair of Professor Günther Vogt as a PhD fellow in 2019. His research examines the shaping of Alpine landscapes through hydroelectric infrastructures.

OLALEKAN JEYIFOUS and MPHO MATSIPA
p. 329

Olalekan Jeyifous is a Brooklyn-based visual artist/designer whose practice often re-imagines social spaces around issues relating to the relationship between architecture, community, and the environment. His work has been exhibited at venues such as the Studio Museum in Harlem, the MoMA, and the Guggenheim Bilbao.
Mpho Matsipa is an urban and architectural scholar and curator based at the University of the Witwatersrand, South Africa. Educated at the University of Cape Town and UC Berkeley, her research-driven curatorial practice aims to build transnational experimental research platforms and projects across Africa and the diaspora.

Wale Lawal is a Lagos-based writer and was recently named to the Quartz list of top African innovators. Educated at the University of Bath, the London School of Economics, and the University of Oxford, Wale is a senior researcher at Harvard Business School, and the founder and editor-in-chief of *The Republic*, a journal of Nigerian and African affairs.

JUSTINIEN TRIBILLON
p. 320

Justinien Tribillon (French, b. 1989) in collaboration with Cécile Trémolières (French, b. 1989), Offshore Studio (Switzerland, est. 2016) and Misia Forlen (French, b. 1989).

As One Planet

FUTURE ASSEMBLY
p. 332

Caroline A. Jones
Caroline A. Jones works at MIT where she teaches art history, runs the Transmedia Storytelling Initiative, and plans an exhibition to reveal us as *Symbionts* with the scrum of life.

Hadeel Ibrahim
Caroline A. Jones works at MIT where she teaches art history, runs the Transmedia Storytelling Initiative, and plans an exhibition to reveal us as *Symbionts* with the scrum of life.

Hadeel Ibrahim
Hadeel has worked on public policy issues across African development, global governance, and humanitarian financing with a particular focus on multilateral, cultural, and civil society institutions.

Mariana Mazzucato
Mariana Mazzucato is Professor of the Economics of Innovation and Public Value at University College London, where she is Founding Director of the Institute for Innovation and Public Purpose. She is author of *The Entrepreneurial State* and *The Value of Everything*.

Mary Robinson
Adjunct Professor for Climate Justice at Trinity College Dublin and Chair of The Elders. She served as President of Ireland from 1990 to 1997 and UN High Commissioner for Human Rights from 1997 to 2002.

Paola Antonelli
Antonelli's goal as Senior Curator of Architecture and Design at The Museum of Modern Art, as well as MoMA's founding Director of Research and Development, is to promote design's public understanding until its positive influence on the world is universally acknowledged. Her work investigates design's impact on everyday experience and possible futures, combining design, architecture, art, science, and technology.

MICHAL ROVNER
p. 337

Michal Rovner's work in video, photography, sculpture, and installation shifts between the poetic and the political, addressing issues of identity, dislocation, and the human condition. Her work has most notably been featured in a retrospective at the Whitney Museum, New York (2002), as well as the Israeli Pavilion at the Venice Art Biennale (2003), in a solo exhibition at the Louvre (2011), a permanent video-fresco at the Stazione Municipio, Naples (architects Alvaro Siza and Eduardo Souto de Moura) (2015), and a permanent installation at Canary Wharf station, London (architects Foster + Partners) (2015).

CAVE_BUREAU
p. 339

Cave_bureau is a Nairobi-based studio of architects and researchers founded by Kabage Karanja and Stella Mutegi. Their work charts geological explorations into architecture and urbanism within nature.

TVK
p. 341

TVK is an international architecture and urban design office created in 2003 by Pierre Alain Trévelo and Antoine Viger-Kohler. Based in Paris, TVK produces singular projects and research, at once both theoretical and built.

PLAN B ARCHITECTURE & URBANISM
p. 343

Joyce Hsiang and Bimal Mendis are the principals of Plan B Architecture & Urbanism, an award-winning research and design practice based in New Haven, USA. Their work explores urbanisation at the scale of the world. Joyce is the Director of Undergraduate Studies in Urbanism and an Assistant Professor at the Yale School of Architecture. She received her BA and MArch from Yale University and was born in Taiwan. Bimal is an Assistant Dean, Director of Undergraduate Studies in Architecture, and an Assistant Professor Adjunct at the Yale School of Architecture. He received his BA and MArch from Yale University and was born in Sri Lanka.

CHRISTINA AGAPAKIS, ALEXANDRA DAISY GINSBERG & SISSEL TOLAAS
p. 345

Alexandra Daisy Ginsberg is an artist examining our fraught relationship with nature and technology. Through artworks, writing, and curatorial projects, Daisy's work explores subjects as diverse as artificial intelligence, exobiology, synthetic biology, conservation, biodiversity, and evolution, as she investigates the human impulse to better the world.

Sissel Tolaas has been intensively working with, researching, and experimenting with the topic of smell, on both the micro and macro level, since 1990. Sissel is a pioneer and unique in her approach to smells and the process of smelling. She has developed a range of revolutionary projects worldwide with smells based upon her own knowledge: organic chemistry, linguistics, and visual art.

Christina Agapakis is a synthetic biologist, artist, and writer involved in the synthetic biology community for over a decade. She is Creative Director of Ginkgo Bioworks, a synthetic biology company based in Boston.

DANIEL LÓPEZ-PÉREZ, REISER + UMEMOTO
p. 347

Daniel López-Pérez (Madrid, 1973) holds a PhD in the History and theory of architecture from Princeton University and is an associate professor and founding faculty member of the Architecture Program at the University of San Diego. López-Pérez is the author of *R. Buckminster Fuller: Pattern-Thinking* (Lars Müller Publishers, 2020) and editor of *Fuller in Mexico* (Arquine, 2015) and *R. Buckminster Fuller: World-Man* (Princeton University Press, 2013), which was named Design Book of the Year 2013 by *Architecture* magazine.

Reiser + Umemoto, RUR Architecture, is a New York-based, internationally recognised architecture firm operating at a wide range of scales and contexts. In 2010, the firm was awarded first prize for the Taipei Music Center and the Kaohsiung Port Terminal in Taiwan, both set to be completed in 2021. Central to the firm's ethos is the reciprocity between building theory and building buildings. The firm's *Atlas of Novel Tectonics* (2006) initiated new materialist approaches in architecture and quickly became a touchstone in the discipline. The firm's first comprehensive monograph, *Projects and Their Consequences*, was published in 2019.

Jesse Reiser (New York, 1958) is a registered architect in New York, principal of Reiser + Umemoto, RUR Architecture, and Professor of Architecture at Princeton University. He is a fellow of the American Academy in Rome in 1985, and has worked in the offices of John Hejduk and Aldo Rossi.

Nanako Umemoto (Kyoto) is a principal of Reiser + Umemoto, RUR Architecture. Nanako has taught at various schools in the US, Europe, and Asia – including Harvard University, the University of Pennsylvania, Columbia University, EPFL in Lausanne Switzerland, Hong Kong University, Kyoto University, and the Cooper Union – and has lectured extensively at various educational and cultural institutions throughout the United States, Europe, and Asia.

SENSORY ETHNOGRAPHY LABORATORY
p. 349

Verena Paravel and Lucien Castaing-Taylor collaborate as anthropologists and artists in the S.E.L., based in Cambridge, USA, at Harvard University, and in Paris, France. Their work conjugates art's negative capability with an ethnographic attachment to the flux of life and addresses the pressing ecological and political challenges of our day.

KEI KAIHOH
p. 357

Kei Kaihoh is a multidisciplinary architect based in Tokyo. His work ranges from artistic installations to urban planning, focusing on the blurred line between human beings and natural phenomena.

DESIGN EARTH
p. 359

DESIGN EARTH, led by Rania Ghosn and El Hadi Jazairy, deploys speculative geographic fiction to communicate concerns of climate change. They are authors of *Geostories: Another Architecture for the Environment* (2018, 2020) and *Geographies of Trash* (2015).

OOZE AND MARJETICA POTRČ
p. 361

OOZE architects work across scales, from regional urban (landscape) strategies to temporary art works, combining an elaborate understanding of natural, ecological processes and deep insights into the social-cultural behaviour of users of the built environment. The cyclic closed-loop processes found in nature are the foundation for each intervention and integrate the human scale within a comprehensive vision.

Marjetica Potrč is an artist and architect based in Ljubljana, Slovenia. Potrč's interdisciplinary practice includes on-site projects, research, architectural case studies, and series of drawings. Her work documents and interprets contemporary architectural practices and the ways people live together.

STATION KENNEDY, KNOX-HAYES MAZEREEUW, WESCOAT
p. 362

Sheila Kennedy is an American architect, innovator, and Professor of Architecture at MIT. She is a Principal of KVA Matx, an interdisciplinary design practice recognised for innovation in architecture, research on material cultures, and the design of resilient infrastructure for emerging public needs. Her work examines intersections between natural ecologies and hybrid 'high' and 'low' technologies in networked cities and rural global regions impacted by climate change.

Janelle Knox-Hayes is an Associate Professor and head of the Environmental Policy and Planning Group in the Department of Urban Studies and Planning at MIT. She directs the Resilient Communities Lab, a research team examining the interface of values and sustainability and weaving Traditional Ecological Knowledge (TEK) and Science, Technology, Engineering, Arts, Maths (STEAM) disciplines to assess risks, vulnerabilities, and strategies of adaptation in coastal regions.

Miho Mazereeuw is Associate Professor of Architecture and Urbanism at MIT. With the Urban Risk Lab at MIT, she engages in action research through fieldwork and workshops to focus on the needs of diverse cultures and contexts. The Lab aspires to proactively embed preparedness and reduce risk in a rapidly urbanizing world.

James Wescoat is an Aga Khan Professor Emeritus of Landscape Architecture and Geography at MIT. His research focuses on water systems from the site to river basin scales. His site-scale studies focused on gardens in India, Pakistan, and Tajikistan. His water resources research includes rural drinking water and river basin planning in South and Central Asia.

RICHARD WELLER
p. 369

Richard Weller is Professor and Chair of Landscape Architecture, Meyerson Chair of Urbanism, and Co-Executive Director of the McHarg Center at The University of Pennsylvania.

URBAN THEORY LAB (UTL) / DEPARTMENT OF ARCHITECTURE, ETH ZÜRICH
p. 371

Neil Brenner is Lucy Flower Professor of Urban Sociology at the University of Chicago. His most recent book is *New Urban Spaces: Urban Theory and the Scale Question* (Oxford University Press, 2019).

Christian Schmid is a geographer, sociologist, and urban researcher. He is Professor at the Department of Architecture, ETH Zürich. His scholarly work is on planetary urbanisation, comparative urban analysis, and theories of urbanisation and space.

Milica Topalović is Associate Professor of Architecture and Territorial Planning at the ETH Zürich Department of Architecture. Concerned with territories and urbanisation beyond the city, Topalović undertook a range of studies around the world in remote regions, resource hinterlands, and countrysides, in an effort to decentre and 'ecologise' architects' approaches to the city, the urban, and urbanisation.

AbdouMaliq Simone is Senior

Professorial Fellow at the Urban Institute, University of Sheffield, research associate at the Max Planck Institute for the Study of Religious and Ethnic Diversity, and Visiting Professor, African Centre for Cities, University of Cape Town. He works on the spatial composition in extended urban regions and the production of everyday life for urban majorities in the Global South.

Rodrigo Castriota is a PhD candidate at the Centre for Development and Regional Planning at the Federal University of Minas Gerais, Brazil. His research interests include extended urbanisation, extractivism, Amazonia, and decolonial theory.

Nancy Couling is Associate Professor, Bergen School of Architecture, and Senior Researcher at ETH Zürich with the FCL Global programme. She holds a BArch (hons) from Auckland University and a PhD from the EPFL. Her research focuses on the urbanisation of the sea.

Mariano Gomez-Luque is an architect and researcher. He holds a Doctor of Design degree from the Graduate School of Design, Harvard University, where he is currently a Postdoctoral Fellow.

Alice Hertzog is a social anthropologist whose work focuses on mobility, migration, and urban development. She has recently completed her PhD at the ETH Zürich, researching urban transformations along the Lagos–Abidjan corridor.

Daniel Ibañez is an architect and urbanist. He currently serves as Assistant Professor in the Department of Architecture, RISD, and as Co-director of the MA in Advanced Ecological Buildings and Biocities at IAAC,

Barcelona. His most recent book is *Wood Urbanism: From the Molecular to the Territorial* (Actar, 2019).

Nikos Katsikis is an urbanist working at the intersection of urbanisation theory, design, and geospatial analysis. He holds a Doctor of Design degree from the Graduate School of Design, Harvard University, and is currently Assistant Professor at the Urbanism Department, TU Delft.

Metaxia Markaki is an architect and researcher. She has taught territorial research and design at the ETH Zürich (Studio Basel and Architecture of Territory) and is pursuing a PhD on the Greek countryside. Her work intertwines territorial research and architecture and develops through design projects, teaching, and writing.

Philippe Rekacewicz is a French geographer, cartographer, and information designer. He is associate researcher, Department of Anthropology, University of Helsinki, and co-coordinator with Philippe Rivière of the website visionscarto.net, which is dedicated to radical and experimental cartography and geography.

Kit-Ping Wong holds a PhD in urban sociology at the ETH Zürich. At FCL Singapore, her research focuses on both urbanisation in a comparative perspective and extended urbanisation, in particular urban theory and politics in Hong Kong and the Pearl River Delta.

SPBR ARCHITECTS
p. 373

Angelo Bucci is an architect and educator. He is the founder and principal in charge of spbr architects, (est. 2003). Bucci has been a professor at FAU USP since 2001 and is currently a visiting professor at MIT. For over 25 years, he has split his time between professional and academic duties. These parallel activities define a special approach to his projects: professional demands are opportunities to research new possibilities.

BETHANY RIGBY
p. 375

Bethany Rigby is a designer based in London, exploring humankind's relationship to terrestrial and extraterrestrial surfaces.

MABE BETÔNICO
p. 377

Mabe Bethônico is a Brazilian artist living in Geneva, Switzerland, and working on issues related to memory and mineral extraction in Brazil, conveying debate over environmental destruction, economy, and labour within the extractive industries. She exhibits internationally and is member of the project World of Matter. She obtained her MA and PhD from the Royal College of Art, London, and is presently researcher in the Franco-Swiss project Effondrement des Alpes at the École Supérieure d'Art Annecy Alpes and teaches at Head–Genève.

Collaborators:
Elaine Ramos is a graphic designer and runs a design studio in São Paulo that is mostly focused on the cultural field. She is also a founding partner of the Brazilian publishing house Ubu.

Enrique Fontanilles is a multimedia artist who works with words and typography, performance, photography, and moving images. He founded and directed educational programmes at international art schools including schools in Basel, Cologne, and Geneva.

Gilles Eduar is a writer and illustrator who focuses on children's books. He has published in Brazil, France, and the USA, and has been translated into many languages. He publishes with Albin-Michel, Boyds Mills Press, Companhia das Letras, and WMF.

Gisa Bustamante has a graphic design studio and works in Brazil, Switzerland, the UK, and France. She develops visual identity projects, publications, and exhibition architecture using her own methodology for collaborations, in which reflexion and debate enhance the multidisciplinary character of design.

Hannah Stewart is a London-based sound artist and music producer. She holds a Music Masters in socially engaged art (Guildhall School of Music & Drama, 2019). She explores how sound can be used to sculpt environments, tell stories, and reimagine urban landscapes. Alongside her own music projects, she creates sound design and music for short films and animation.
Jônio Bethônico is a graphic designer and researcher on education and language, with a doctorate in education (UFMG, Brazil and Universidade do Minho, Portugal). He is visiting professor at UFMG, Brazil, working with future teachers to bring to students critical debate on issues of advertising and consumption.

Nadja Zimmermann and Skander Najar are a design duo working in Geneva, Switzerland, in the field of visual communication, design, and art direction. They run a studio – NASK – and their practice expands into teaching, consulting, publishing, and exhibitions.

Rodrigo Martins lives and works in Geneva, Switzerland, where he has his own architecture and design studio, working on projects in Europe and Brazil. He worked as intern at Oscar Niemeyer's Centro Administrativo de Minas Gerais in 2008 and collaborated on exhibition projects with the Brazilian office Vecci Lansky.

LE CONSORTIUM – LAND
p. 379

Patrick Berger obtained a PhD in town planning in 1977. In the 1990s, he won three architectural awards – for his School of Architecture in Rennes, the André Citroën Park, and the Bastille Viaduct. He was awarded the French national Grand Prix for architecture in 2004. With their *Canopy* project, he and Jacques Anziutti won the international contest to renovate the Forum des Halles in Paris. In addition to his work as an architect, Patrick Berger devotes his time to teaching and research, notably at Lausanne's École Polytechnique Fédérale.

Aristide Antonas holds a PhD in Philosophy from the University of Paris X. His art and architecture work have been featured in the Istanbul Design Biennial, Venice Biennale, São Paulo Biennale, Display Prague, and the New Museum. He won the ArchMarathon 2015 prize for his *Open Air Office*, and was nominated for the Iakov Chernikov Prize (2011) and for a Mies Van der Rohe Award (2009) for his *Amphitheatre House*. He is Professor of Architectural Design and Theory, director of the MA Program in Architectural Design at the University of Thessaly, Greece. He also serves as visiting professor at The Bartlett School of Architecture and at the Freie Universität in Berlin.

Junya Ishigami studied at Tokyo University of the Arts. He founded his studio Junya.Ishigami + associates and gained international recognition with the KAIT Workshop (2007). He received the Golden Lion for Best Project at La Biennale's 12th International Architecture Exhibition. His recent projects are the Botanical Farm Garden Art Biotop (2018), which won the Obel Award (2019); the Serpentine Pavilion (2019); and a University Multipurpose Plaza (2020).

MATILDE CASSANI, IGNACIO G. GALÁN, IVAN L. MUNUERA
p. 381

Matilde Cassani operates on the border between architecture, installation, and event design. Her practice deals with the spatial implications of cultural pluralism in the contemporary Western city.

Ignacio G. Galán is an architect and historian whose work focuses on architecture's relation to nationalism, colonialism, migration, diversity, and access. He is an assistant professor at Barnard College, Columbia University.

Iván L. Munuera is a New York-based scholar, critic, and curator working at the intersection of culture, technology, politics, and bodily practices in the modern period and on the global stage.

Forte Marghera - How will we play together?

SKULL STUDIO + MOLOARCHITEKTI
p. 387

Matěj Hájek is a sculptor and art activist. He explores the potential of connecting art and elements of play. Overstepping the borders of sculpture and architecture are significant features of his work.

Tereza Kučerová is an architect focusing on wooden structures ranging from homes, institutions, and cafés to interior design. She collaborates on grand playscape projects, mainly playgrounds for children.

BAYO.S THE GROUNDSCROO, www.bayo-s.com
JJ-konstrukt, www.jj-konstrukt.cz
Taros Nova, www.taros-nova.cz

HHF ARCHITECTS
p. 389

Tilo Herlach
Born 1972 | 1992–1998 studied at ETH Zurich and ETH Lausanne | 2003 founded HHF Architects | Since 2006 Member of the Board for Urban Planning and Architecture, SIA Basel | 2007 member of the Berlin Chamber of Architects | Since 2010 member of BSA | Since 2015 permanent member of the Berlin Chamber of Architects | Since 2018 Visiting Professor at Harvard GSD
Simon Hartmann
Born 1974 | 1994–2000 studied at ETH Lausanne, TU Berlin, and ETH Zurich | 2002–2007 Teaching Assistant, ETH Studio Basel | 2003 founded HHF Architects | 2009–2017 Professor at HEIA Fribourg | Since 2010 member of BSA | 2011 Guest Professor at UIBK Innsbruck | 2014 Visiting Professor at KIT Karlsruhe | 2018 Visiting Professor at Yale School of Architecture | Since 2018 Visiting Professor at Harvard GSD | Since 2019 Chair of *Bauplanung und Entwerfen* at KIT Karlsruhe

Simon Frommenwiler
Born 1972 | 1994–2000 studied at ETH Zurich | 2003 founded HHF Architects | 2005–2007 Teaching Assistant at ETH Lausanne | Since 2010 member of BSA | 2011 Guest Professor at HEIA Fribourg | 2011–2013 Visiting Professor at ENSA Strasbourg | 2013–2018 Associate Professor at ENSA Strasbourg | 2014 Lecturer at Boston MIT | Since 2016 Chairman of Bund Schweizer Architekten BSA Basel | Since 2018 Visiting Professor at Harvard GSD

LAB FOR SOCIOMATERIAL ARCHITECTURES AT THE UNIVERSITY OF MICHIGAN
p. 391

Sean Ahlquist is Associate Professor of Architecture at the University of Michigan, focusing on exploring the links between material, form, and human behaviour. The work studies the effects of agency – the individual or collective capacity to reshape the physical and social nature of environments – to better engage neurodiverse audiences in civic and educational spaces.

AWILDC-AWP
p. 393

Alessandra Cianchetta is an architect, urbanist, and founding partner of AWP UK/AWILDC, a practice based in London and New York (formerly in Paris). Her projects have been shown at and collected by museums and venues worldwide such as MAXXI in Rome, Cité de l'architecture e du patrimoine, The Museum of Modern Art in New York (MoMA), the Storefront for Architecture & Art and Architecture, the Design Museum in London, among others. Cianchetta currently teaches at Cornell University and has previously taught architecture and urban design at The Cooper Union, the University of Virginia, Columbia University, the Pratt Institute, ENSA Bordeaux, the University of Westminster, among others. Besides architecture, Cianchetta has modelled for haute couture brand Adeline Andre in Paris and acted in the forthcoming film directed by French director Michel Zumpf.

FINKELMAN + PINTO
p. 395

Ifat Finkelman and Deborah Pinto Fdeda are both Tel Aviv-based architects and senior lecturers at the Architecture Department at Bezalel Academy of Arts and Design, Jerusalem. Since 2010, they have been collaborating on cross-disciplinary projects of varying scales. They were co-curators of the Israeli Pavilion at the 16th International Architecture Exhibition in 2018, and editors of the book that accompanied it, *In Statu Quo: Structures of Negotiation* (Hatje Cantz, 2018).

Stav Dror is a Tel Aviv-based architect and a lecturer at the Architecture Department at Bezalel Academy of Arts and Design, Jerusalem. She was a member of the Israeli Pavilion team at the 16th International Architecture Exhibition in 2018 and a winner of the International Archiprix Award 2019. She currently lives in the US as a full scholarship graduate student at the Yale School of Architecture.

IMAGE CREDITS

Among Diverse Beings - Arsenale

p. 41
Courtesy Yinka akingbade

p. 43
Courtesy Ani Liu

p. 45
Photomontage by Azra Akšamija and Natalie Bellefleur, 2020. Courtesy Azra Akšamija. Photomontage by Azra Akšamija, 2020. Courtesy Azra Akšamija. Palazzo Ducale photo: Courtesy Andrew Balet, 2007. Source: Wikipedia CC. BY 3.0

p. 47
Courtesy modem

p. 49
All photos Allan Wexler courtesy Ronald Feldman Gallery, New York City

p. 50
Courtesy Geoff Livingston
Courtesy GroundUp
Courtesy UNICEF
Courtesy Shane Burcaw and Hannah Elizabeth
Courtesy of Pablo Saiz del Rio and the authors

p. 54
Courtesy Library of Congress, Digital Collections
Courtesy Mantha Zarmakoupi

p. 61
Courtesy Refik Anadol Studio

p. 63
Courtesy Studio Ossidiana © 2019
Courtesy Johannes Schwartz © 2019
Courtesy EH (Kyoungtae Kim) 2020

p. 65
Courtesy Ariel Fisher
Courtesy Lucy McRae

p. 67
All images courtesy Parsons & Charlesworth

p. 69
all images ©MAEID (Mitterberger, Derme)

p. 71
Courtesy The Living

p. 73
Photo Eric Zee
Photo Studio Libertiny

p. 75
Courtesy Philip Beesley Studio Inc./Living Architecture Systems Group

As New Households - Arsenale

p. 81
Courtesy Espen Folgerø
Courtesy Mir

p. 83
Photo Dylan Perrenoud

p. 85
Courtesy Osborne Macharia

p. 87
Courtesy Superflux and Sebastian Tiew

p. 89
Courtesy AW-ARCH

p. 91
©Yao Li
©Hu Dong

p. 93
leonmarcial arquitectos

p. 95
ecoLogicStudio. Renderings by Vyonix.
ecoLogicStudio. Photo by Naaro
ecoLogicStudio. Photo by Naaro

p. 97
Courtesy and © David Boureau; © urbamutability. All rights reserved

p. 99
Courtesy Rojo/Fernandez-Shaw arquitectos

p. 101
Courtesy Neeraj Bhatia & Antje Steinmuller
Courtesy The Open Workshop

p. 102
Courtesy PAUL MONTIE
Courtesy 100DANISH

p. 109
Courtesy ICD/ITKE University of Stuttgart

p. 111
Courtesy Roman Keller. Zürich

Living Apart Together

p. 115
Fernanda Canales

p. 117
Courtesy Aires Mateus

p. 119
Courtesy Alison Brooks Architects

p. 121
© Nikolai Wolff, Fotoetage

p. 123
Courtesy BAAG

p. 125
Photo Tapio Snellman

p. 127
courtesy of Ola Rindal
courtesy of Guy Limone
courtesy of nicolas laisné architectes
courtesy of nicolas laisné architectes
courtesy of nicolas laisné architectes
courtesy of nicolas laisné

p. 129
© Photo Joe Lahdou
© Photo Takuji Shimmura

Courtesy © Lina Ghotmeh—Architecture. Photography © Iwan Baan (riferito all'esposto?)
Project design: Lina Ghotmeh with Lina Ghotmeh—Architecture & Dorell.Ghotmeh.Tane

p. 131
Courtesy SsD

p. 132
DIGITAL IMAGE © 1996
DIGITAL IMAGE © 1926, The Museum of Modern Art (MoMA), New York /Scala, Florence
DIGITAL IMAGE Public domain
DIGITAL IMAGE © FLC/ADAGP

p. 136
Copyright Monobloque
Copyright Anna Derriks
Copyright Sasama
Copyright Rebekka Hirschberg
Copyright Anna Derriks

As Emerging Communities - Arsenale

p. 147
Courtesy Cohabitation Strategies

p. 149
Courtesy Fieldoffice Architects

p. 151
Photos by César Schofield Cardoso

p. 153
Courtesy Arquitectura Expandida – AXP

p. 155
Courtesy Lluc Miralles, Chopo/Col·legi d'Aparelladors and Lacol

p. 157
Courtesy of Enlace Arquitectura
Photography: Jaeson Montilla, Gabriel Nass
Image edition: Jaeson Montilla, Sergio Dos Santos, Gabriela Álvarez, Emily Yánez.

p. 159
©VictoriaTomaschko
©raumlaborberlin

p. 161
Courtesy PRÁCTICA.

p. 163
SRafi Segal A+U
Civic Data Design Lab, MIT Future Urban Collectives Lab
Marisa Morán Jahn with Rebeka Rodriquez
Rafi Segal A+U

p. 169
Courtesy Aristide Antonas

p. 171
Courtesy EFFEKT

p. 173
Courtesy atelier masōmī
© atelier masōmī

p. 175
© Iwan Baan, 2020

p. 177
Courtesy MDP Michel Desvigne Paysagiste

p. 179
© Forum des Images

p. 181
Miralles Tagliabue EMBT

p. 183
© Studio Bouroullec

p. 185
Courtesy SOM | Slashcube GmbH

p. 187
City of Los Angeles, Bureau of Engineering, Michael Maltzan Architecture, Inc. / HNTB Corporation
Iwan Baan

p. 191
Courtesy BASE studio

p. 193
Courtesy and © OMA

The images may not be passed to any third parties without further permission.
No part of the work may be reproduced or utilized in any form or by any means, electronic or mechanical, including photocopying, recording or by any information storage retrieval system, without permission in writing from OMA.

p. 195
Cathy Cunliffe
Zacharoula Gonou-Zagou

p. 199
Courtesy Studio L A

p. 201
Courtesy modem

p. 203
Luca Pilot (Laboratorio Fotografico – Università Iuav di Venezia)
RAI – Telegiornale del 4 Novembre 1966

p. 209
Katharina Blümke, Dirk Hebel and Bernd Seeland, KIT Karlsruhe

p. 211
Courtesy Ciro Miguel, Kathryn Gillmore, Danilo Zamboni, Pedro Kok, Guilherme Pianca, Gabriel Sepe

p. 213
Courtesy MIT Future Heritage Lab

p. 215
Courtesy Rahul Mehrotra and Sourav Biswas

p. 217
Wissam Chaaya

p. 219
Courtesy Instituto Moreira Salles and Rice University

p. 221
Ibai Rigby, 2018

p. 223
Merve Bedir and Monique Wong

p. 227
Photo Sena Özfiliz. 3d editing by Ali Gürer and Zeynep Tümertekin
Photo Sena Özfiliz. 3d editing by Ali Gürer

p. 229
"Un Malón". Atlas de la historia física y política de Chile by Claudio Gay. París: Imprenta de E. Thunot, 1854.
"Parlamento del presidente Ambrosio O'Higgins, Negrete 3 de marzo 1793". Atlas de la historia física y política de Chile by Claudio Gay. París: Imprenta de E. Thunot, 1854.

p. 231
© Vogt Landscape, © Wikipedia

p. 233
Courtesy WOJR

p. 235
Courtesy CarbFix
Courtesy Igneous Tectonics

p. 237
Courtesy NADAAA

p. 239
Courtesy Sahel Alhiyari Architects

p. 241
Copyright Archivio Penone

p. 247
Courtesy and © Linn Phyllis Seeger

Across Borders

p. 259
Courtesy Dan Majka & Gary Setzer

p. 261
Photo Studio Tomás Saraceno.
Courtesy Museo Aero Solar and Aerocene Foundation.
Licensed under CC BY-SA 4.0

p. 263
Hamish McIntosh

p. 265
Courtesy John Cook, Monsoon Assemblages

p. 267
Courtesy Territorial Agency

p. 269
Pinar Yoldas for Yoldaş StudioLab

p. 271
Courtesy the Artist

p. 273
Courtesy Self-Assembly Lab, MIT

p. 275
Courtesy Somatic Collaborative

p. 277
Courtesy AIKAX

p. 279
La Minga / OPSYS Media
Chez Levrault, Schoell et Cie, 1805.
Courtesy Biblioteca Nacional del Ecuador Eugenio Espejo

p. 281
Courtesy Marko Brajovic, Alessandra Araujo, Nacho Marti, AAVSA

p. 283
© 2020 NASA, Map data © 2020
© D-Air Lab

p. 285
LO+ADG. Courtesy Lateral Office and Arctic Design Group

p. 298
Courtesy Dogma

p. 291
Rural Urban Framework

p. 293
Studio Paola Viganò

p. 295
Courtesy Jaime Mesquita and Paula Nascimento

p. 297
Photo Smout Allen

p. 299
Courtesy Architekt Christoph Lechner & Partners ZT
Wikimedia Commons
Private collection, Courtesy Architekt Christoph Lechner & Partners ZT

p. 305
Image by FAST
Photo by Amir Qudaih

p. 307
Elias & Yousef Anastas of AAU ANASTAS

p. 308
Courtesy the Authors

p. 315
Photo Luca Capuano

p. 317
Courtesy Wissam Chaaya

p. 319
Courtesy Forensic Oceanography and Forensic Architecture

p. 320
Justinien Tribillon, 2020

p. 327
© Chair of Günther Vogt, ETH Zurich
© Julien Seguinot

p. 329
All images courtesy Olalekan Jeyifous

As One Planet

p. 333
Courtesy Studio Other Spaces

p. 337
Copyright Michal Rovner

p. 339
Courtesy Cave_bureau

p. 341
Courtesy TVK

p. 343
Plan B Architecture & Urbanism

p. 345
© Pierre Grasset
Photo Grace Chuang. Courtesy Harvard University Herbaria. © Ginkgo Bioworks, The Herbarium of the Arnold Arboretum of Harvard University

p. 347
Courtesy Reiser + Umemoto, RUR Architecture
Courtesy Reiser + Umemoto, RUR Architecture
Courtesy Princeton University School of Architecture

p. 350
Courtesy Juan Navarro Baldeweg.
Courtesy Kikah Bernardes.
Courtesy Archivo Histórico José Vial Armstrong, Escuela de Arquitectura y Diseño, Pontificia Unversidad Católica de Valparaiso.
Courtesy Biblioteca Civica d'Arte Luigi Poletti.
Courtesy Zaha Hadid Foundation.

p. 357
Courtesy Kei Kaihoh Architects and Yoshiomi Ito

p. 359
Courtesy DESIGN EARTH

p. 361
Courtesy Ooze architects

p. 362
Courtesy MIT/KVA Tajikistan Workshop 2019

p. 369
Richard Weller, Shannon Rafferty, Lucy Whitacre, Tone Chu, Misako Murata. Courtesy Richard Weller
Richard Weller, Claire Hoch.
Courtesy Richard Weller
Richard Weller, Zuzanna Drozdz, Nanxi Dong. Courtesy Richard Weller

p. 371
Based on data from: European Commission Joint Research Center, 2016, Global Human Settlement Layer, http://ghsl.jrc.ec.europa.eu/. Courtesy Urban Theory Lab
Based on data from: European Commission Joint Research Center, 2016, Global Human Settlement Layer; K.-H. Erb, V. Gaube, F. Krausmann, C. Plutzar, A. Bondeau and H. Haberl, 'A comprehensive global 5 min resolution land-use dataset for the year 2000 consistent with national census data," Journal of Land Use Science 2, 3 (2007): 191-224; Vector Map Level 0 (VMap0) dataset released by the National Imagery and Mapping Agency (NIMA), 1997. Courtesy Urban Theory Lab

p. 375
Bethany Rigby, NASA/JPL-Caltech/MSSS/ ID: PIA18092, NASA/JPL-Caltech/ University of Arizona/ ID: PIA23454
Bethany Rigby, NASA/ ID: S71-19489

p. 377
Courtesy the Artist

p. 381
Project Patrick Berger Architecte (assistant Edouard Ropars). Model: Thierry Martin and Michel Delarasse, 2002. Photo Gaston F. Bergeret & Cécile Septet
© Aristide Antonas

p. 381
Collage by Matilde Cassani and Leonardo Gatti.
Courtesy the Authors

Forte Marghera - How will we play together?

p. 387
Courtesy SKULL studio and MOLO architekti

p. 389
Courtesy HHF Architects

p. 391
Courtesy Sean Ahlquist

p. 393
Courtesy Alessandra Cianchetta / AWP (UK) ltd AWILDC llc

p. 395
Courtesy Deborah Pinto Fdeda, Ifat Finkelman, Stav Dror

p. 398
(c) Phil Griffin

p. 400
Photo Ravi Deepres

ACKNOWLEDGMENTS

Manuela Luca' Dazio
Reem Acra
Fwad Afzal
Aisha al Khater
Abdulla Yousuf Al Mulla
Hussa Sabah al-Salem al-Sabah
Al Mayassa Al Thani
Boston Society of Architects
Cecilia Alemani
Paola Antonelli
Alejandro Aravena
Archivo Histórico José Vial Armstrong: Pontificia Universidad Católica de Valparaiso
ASSET Production Studio, Anne-Sophie Springer
Arundhati Banerjee
Alberto Barbera
Carla Barbieri
Biblioteca Cívica d'Arte Luigi Poletti
Shpresa Binjaku
Malvina Binjaku
Melissa Budinic
Ricky Burdett
Peggy Cain
Inaqui Carnicero
Phil Clay
Martha Collins
Pierre d'Arenberg
Luc Deleu
Nicholas de Monchaux
Jean-Jacques Degroof
Sharon DeMarco
Valeria Rivera Deneke
Dineen Doucette
Lina El Achi
Fares El Dahdah
Diala Ezzeddine
Tania Ezzeddine
Marilys Ezzeddine
Gianni Forte
Nina Fialkow
Faber Futures, Natsai Audrei Chieza
Barbara Feldman
Floating Farm, Minke van Wingerden
Ken Goldsmith
Svafa Gronfeldt
Thomas Heatherwick
Victoria Hindley
Hosh Ibrahim
Mo Ibrahim
Rola Idris
Fady Jameel
Mohammed Jameel
Sahar Khraibani
Mitsunori Kikutake
Yuki Kikutake
Rem Koolhaas
Maria Kozlowski
Elizabeth Kozlowski
Scott Lawin
Leong Leong, Christopher and Dominic Leong
Alan Leventhal
Amanda Levete
Alain Levy
Joe Manok
Nicholas Marmor
Tod Machover
Wayne McGregor
Victor Menezes
Bethany Millard
Robert Millard
MIT School of Architecture + Planning
Jose Miguel Bejos
Khadija Mneimneh
Amina Mohammed
Doreen Morris
Ignacio Moreno
Marisa Moreira Salles
May Nasrallah
Maher Nasser
Juan Navarro Baldeweg
Adriana Navarro
John Ochsendorf
Samuel Omans
Gabriel Orozco
Carmen Parga Ures
Young Park
Payanini srl
Vladimir Payano
Cynthia Reed
Rafael Reif
Todd Reisz
Stefano Ricci
George Richards
Lucia Ronchetti
Michal Rovner
Vuslat Sabanci
Alvar Salgueiro Parga
Hayden Salter
Suha Samaha
Manuel F. Sanfuentes
Aida Sarkis
Dunia Sarkis
Ghassan Sarkis
Lorenza Savini
Martin Schmidt
Edward Schwarz
Makeela Searles
Talal Shair
Mutsuku Smith-Kikutaki
Alan Spoon
Kenneth Wang
Jad Tabet
Nader Tehrani
Ben Teresi
UN Studio, Ben van Berkel Caroline Mos
United Nations Department of Global Communications
Lawrence Vale
Melissa Vaughn
Marissa Volk
Wikihouse, Alastair Pavin
Jayashri Wyatt
Chris Zegras

LA BIENNALE DI VENEZIA

Since its inception, the International Architecture Exhibition has become the world's foremost forum for the field, bringing together the art form's greatest minds to debate, innovate and shape its future. Now, more than ever, Rolex celebrates the individuals and organisations that continue to bring out the best in the arts.

#Perpetual

OYSTER PERPETUAL DATEJUST 41

VENICE, ITALY
22 MAY TO 21 NOVEMBER 2021

17th International Architecture Exhibition
How will we live together?

La Biennale di Venezia
Editorial Activities and Web

Head
Flavia Fossa Margutti

Editorial Coordination
Maddalena Pietragnoli

Editorial Team
Francesca Dolzani
Giulia Gasparato
Lucia Toso

Graphic Design
Omnivore, Inc.

Editorial Realisation
Liberink srls, Padova
Coordination
Stefano Turon
Layout
Livio Cassese
Copy editing
Rosanna Alberti
Caterina Vettore

*Translations
and English language copy editing*
alphaville
traduzioni e servizi editoriali

Photolithography and Print
Graficart, Resana (TV)

by SIAE 2021
Juan Navarro Baldeweg
Giuseppe Penone
Michal Rovner
Cécile Septet

© La Biennale di Venezia 2021

All Rights Reserved under international copyright conventions. No part of this book may be reproduced or utilised in any form or by any means, electronic or mechanical, including photocopying, recording or any information storage and retrieval system, without permission in writing from the publisher.

Printed on

Paper made from cellulose from environmentally respectful, socially useful, and economically sustainable forests, production and supply chains, and other controlled sources

9788836648597
DISTRIBUTED BY SILVANA EDITORIALE

La Biennale di Venezia
First Edition May 2021